SARAH MELLAND   MARCUS AURELIUS

MEDITATIONS
& DATING

ISBN:
Paperback: 978-1-969137-22-8
Hardcover: 978-1-969137-23-5

Printed in the United States of America

First Edition

Table of Contents

INTRODUCTION
Marcus Aurelius, Stoicism, and Why We Need Him in Dating

Marcus Aurelius Antoninus was not just a Roman emperor. He was a philosopher, a warrior, a reluctant ruler, and perhaps most importantly, a man quietly trying to survive humanity without losing himself.

Born in A.D. 121 into a noble Roman family, Marcus Aurelius was shaped early by loss, discipline, and philosophical rigor. Trained in Stoicism from childhood, he was taught to live simply, think deeply, and resist the temptations of ego, excess, and emotional chaos. Long before he ruled an empire, he learned to rule himself.

Which, as anyone who has ever opened a dating app knows, is the real battle.

His private writings, now known as *Meditations*, were never intended for publication. They were not speeches, sermons, or attempts to impress anyone. They were personal notes, written to steady his own mind during war, political pressure, betrayal, grief, and the exhausting unpredictability of people. Marcus wrote not as a guru above the world, but as someone inside it, trying daily to respond with wisdom instead of reaction.

Two thousand years later, the battlefield looks different. Instead of invading tribes and imperial politics, we navigate ghosting, mixed signals, performative dating culture, algorithm-driven connection, and emotional ambiguity disguised as modern romance. But the underlying struggle remains exactly the same: how to remain grounded, clear, and self-directed in a world that constantly pulls us into distraction and emotional chaos.

Stoicism was never about suppressing emotion. It was about understanding what belongs to us and what does not. Marcus taught that our thoughts, reactions, and character are within our control, while other people's actions, opinions, and outcomes are not. This distinction becomes revolutionary when applied to dating.

Because dating, at its core, is an arena where people try to control what they cannot.

We try to predict attraction, manage perception, decode silence, or force outcomes that were never ours to command. Marcus Aurelius reminds us that peace does not come from controlling others but from mastering our own response to uncertainty.

1

Meditations & Dating exists because ancient wisdom translates shockingly well into modern relationship dynamics. Marcus was navigating betrayal, ego clashes, political alliances, loss, disappointment, and human inconsistency long before swipe culture existed. His reflections offer a framework for approaching relationships with clarity, dignity, and emotional sovereignty.

This book is not about becoming detached from love. It is about becoming rooted enough in yourself that love does not destabilize you.

Marcus Aurelius wrote to survive the weight of an empire. We read him today to survive the emotional noise of modern dating.

And perhaps, like him, to remember that the greatest victory is not finding the perfect partner, but becoming the person who remains steady, self-respecting, and whole regardless of who comes or goes.

THE FIRST BOOK
Who Made You Strong
(And Who Made You Tired)

I. YOU WERE TRAINED BEFORE YOU WERE TESTED

"Of my grandfather Verus I have learned to be gentle and meek, and to refrain from all anger and passion. From the fame and memory of him that begot me I have learned both shamefastness[1] and manlike behaviour. Of my mother I have learned to be religious, and bountiful; and to forbear, not only to do, but to intend any evil; to content myself with a spare diet, and to fly all such excess as is incidental to great wealth. Of my great-grandfather, both to frequent public schools and auditories, and to get me good and able teachers at home; and that I ought not to think much, if upon such occasions, I were at excessive charges."

What Marcus meant (core philosophy)

Marcus begins by acknowledging that character is not created in isolation. He credits the people who shaped him: a grandfather who modeled gentleness, a father who embodied dignity, a mother who demonstrated generosity and restraint, and teachers who invested in his education. The core Stoic idea here:

- Virtue is learned through observation.
- Identity is formed through example.
- Discipline and values are inherited through influence, not declared through ego.

He is grounding himself in gratitude, not nostalgia. This is not sentimentality. It is clarity about origin.

Dating translation (emotional/social meaning)

You did not walk into dating as a blank slate. You carry:

- emotional standards you absorbed growing up
- relationship patterns you watched
- boundaries you learned or never saw modeled
- beliefs about love, worth, loyalty, and conflict

Some women blame themselves for how they respond in relationships without realizing: you were trained long before you were triggered.

The question is not: "Why am I like this?"
The real question is: "Which lessons still serve me and which ones need to retire immediately?"

---

[1] Shamefastness is an archaic term denoting modesty, bashfulness, or a sense of propriety, rooted in a steadfast, humble character. Derived from Old English, it signifies being firmly established in modesty, not merely acting shy. It is frequently found in 17th-century texts, notably in 1 Timothy 2:9, distinguishing it from "shamefacedness," which implies sheepishness.

Dating becomes easier when you understand your emotional blueprint instead of judging it.

Savage takeaway
You didn't choose your original programming. But you absolutely choose whether you keep running outdated software.

Quiet power mantra
"I honor where I came from. I decide who I become."

II. DO NOT WORSHIP THE ARENA
"Of him that brought me up, not to be fondly addicted to either of the two great factions of the coursers in the circus, called Prasini, and Veneti: nor in the amphitheatre partially to favour any of the gladiators, or fencers, as either the Parmularii[2], or the Secutores[3]. Moreover, to endure labour; nor to need many things; when I have anything to do, to do it myself rather than by others; not to meddle with many businesses; and not easily to admit of any slander."

What Marcus meant (core philosophy)
Marcus describes being taught not to become emotionally entangled in public factions, rivalries, or spectacle. In his time, people divided themselves into obsessive loyalties over chariot teams or gladiators, attaching identity to sides and conflicts that ultimately had little to do with personal virtue. The deeper Stoic lesson is restraint from unnecessary emotional investment. He also highlights several principles of disciplined living:
- Endure effort without complaint.
- Need less, not more.
- Take responsibility for your own tasks.
- Avoid scattering your energy across too many pursuits.
- Do not accept gossip or slander easily.

This is the training of independence. Emotional sobriety. Refusal to be pulled into noise that does not elevate character.

Dating translation (what this means emotionally/socially)
Modern dating is full of arenas. Team narratives. Gender wars. Social media debates about who is right, who is wrong, who is the villain, who is the victim. Endless commentary that encourages people to pick sides instead of developing self-awareness. Emotional maturity in dating means refusing to perform loyalty to a narrative that disconnects you from your own judgment. You do not need to:
- adopt extreme positions about men or women

---

[2] Parmularii were Roman gladiators who fought with a small, typically round or square shield known as a *parmula*.
[3] The secutor (plural *secutores*), or "chaser," was a specialized, heavily armored Roman gladiator type designed to fight the *retiarius* (net-fighter). Emerging around 50 CE, they were armed with a *gladius* (sword) and a large *scutum* (shield), wearing a distinctive, smooth, egg-shaped helmet with small eyeholes to prevent injury from trident thrusts and entanglement.

- treat dating like a competitive sport
- participate in group outrage to feel validated

Independence also shows up in smaller ways. Doing your own emotional work instead of outsourcing it. Not juggling five situationships to avoid sitting with yourself. Not believing every rumor, interpretation, or assumption about someone without direct experience. Discipline in dating is often quiet. It looks like choosing clarity over chaos.

Savage takeaway
Not every fight deserves your emotional investment. Most of them are just loud distractions dressed as identity.

Quiet power mantra
"I do not belong to the crowd. I belong to my standards."

III. STOP CHASING ILLUSIONS

"Of Diognetus[4], not to busy myself about vain things, and not easily to believe those things, which are commonly spoken, by such as take upon them to work wonders, and by sorcerers, or prestidigitators, and impostors; concerning the power of charms, and their driving out of demons, or evil spirits; and the like. Not to keep quails for the game; nor to be mad after such things. Not to be offended with other men's liberty of speech, and to apply myself unto philosophy. Him also I must thank, that ever I heard first Bacchius[5], then Tandasis[6] and Marcianus[7], and that I did write dialogues in my youth; and that I took liking to the philosophers' little couch and skins, and such other things, which by the Grecian discipline are proper to those who profess philosophy."

What Marcus meant (core philosophy)
Marcus credits Diognetus for teaching him to avoid being distracted by vanity, spectacle, and empty fascination with things that appear impressive but lack substance. He warns against believing in false authorities, performers of tricks, or those who promise extraordinary solutions without grounded truth.

The Stoic principle here is intellectual discipline. Do not be easily persuaded by trends, mysticism without substance, or popular opinion simply because it is widely accepted. Instead, cultivate independent thought, philosophical inquiry, and calm curiosity. Allow others the freedom to speak without becoming reactive or

---

[4] In the context of Marcus Aurelius, Diognetus was a philosopher and artist who served as one of the future emperor's most influential childhood tutors. There is a long-standing scholarly debate about whether this same tutor was the recipient of the famous Epistle to Diognetus, a 2nd-century Christian defense.

[5] Bacchius of Paphos was an ancient Greek philosopher, identified as a Platonic philosopher and a teacher to Marcus Aurelius. Bacchius is linked to the philosophical, particularly Cynic-Stoic, influences in the Emperor's life.

[6] Tandasis is known only by this single mention in the *Meditations*. There are no surviving records of his life, his school of thought, or his specific teachings.

[7] Listening to Marcianus was a key step in Marcus's early transition from a typical Roman education to a life of philosophical discipline. Like Tandasis, Marcianus is known to history entirely through this single reference. No surviving texts or other historical records detail his life or school of thought.

offended, and focus your energy on what deepens wisdom rather than what entertains the ego. Marcus is describing the shift from fascination with novelty to devotion to truth.

Dating translation (what this means emotionally/socially)

Modern dating culture is filled with illusion merchants. Dating "rules" presented as universal truths. Viral advice that promises shortcuts to attraction. Personality labels, manifestation rituals, or psychological buzzwords used as substitutes for genuine understanding. Emotional maturity requires learning to separate insight from performance. Not every confident voice is wise. Not every popular strategy creates meaningful connection. Not every spiritual or psychological claim deserves belief simply because it sounds profound.

This section also speaks to emotional steadiness. Do not become easily offended by opinions that differ from yours. Strong identity allows space for disagreement without personal collapse. In dating, intellectual independence protects you from manipulation. When you stop chasing magical solutions or external validation, you begin building relationships grounded in reality instead of fantasy.

Savage takeaway

Anyone promising a shortcut to love is usually selling theater, not truth.

Quiet power mantra

"I am not impressed by illusions. I choose depth."

IV. FIX YOURSELF QUIETLY

"To Rusticus[8] I am beholding, that I first entered into the conceit that my life wanted some redress and cure. And then, that I did not fall into the ambition of ordinary sophists[9], either to write tracts concerning the common theorems, or to exhort men unto virtue and the study of philosophy by public orations; as also that I never by way of ostentation did affect to show myself an active able man, for any kind of bodily exercises. And that I gave over the study of rhetoric and poetry, and of elegant neat language. That I did not use to walk about the house in my long robe, nor to do any such things. Moreover I learned of him to write letters without any affectation, or curiosity; such as that was, which by him was written to my mother from Sinuessa: and to be easy and ready to be reconciled, and well pleased again with them that had offended me, as soon as any of them would be content to seek unto me again. To read with diligence; not to rest satisfied with a light and superficial knowledge, nor quickly to assent to things commonly

---

[8] Quintus Junius Rusticus was the most influential Stoic mentor in the life of Marcus Aurelius. While previous tutors like Diognetus introduced Marcus to the philosopher's lifestyle, Rusticus is the man who truly made him a Stoic. Rusticus gave Marcus his own personal copy of the Discourses of Epictetus, which became the foundation of the emperor's private philosophy. He convinced Marcus to abandon rhetorical vanity and the "sophistic" style of writing to focus on practical ethics and moral improvement. He taught Marcus to avoid anger and to be easily reconciled with those who had offended him.

[9] In the 5th century B.C.E., a Sophist was a professional itinerant teacher. They were essentially the first "professors" or "lawyers" of the ancient world. They charged high fees to teach wealthy young men the art of public speaking and persuasion, which was essential for winning cases in Athenian courts.

spoken of: whom also I must thank that ever I lighted upon Epictetus his Hypomnemata[10], or moral commentaries and common-factions: which also he gave me of his own."

What Marcus meant (core philosophy)

Marcus credits Rusticus with awakening his awareness that his life required correction and refinement. This is not self-criticism for its own sake, but honest recognition that growth begins with admitting where improvement is needed.

Rusticus taught him to avoid performative virtue. Not to become a philosopher for applause, not to display discipline as spectacle, and not to hide insecurity behind elegant language or intellectual showmanship. True development happens privately, through serious study, honest reflection, and practical change rather than public performance.

He also emphasizes simplicity and authenticity. Speak plainly. Learn deeply. Avoid superficial agreement with popular ideas. Be willing to reconcile easily when someone genuinely seeks repair. The Stoic ideal here is quiet mastery rather than visible status.

Dating translation (what this means emotionally/socially)

Growth in dating is rarely glamorous. There is a phase where you realize your patterns need adjustment. Not because you are broken, but because awareness reveals blind spots. The temptation during this stage is to perform growth instead of embodying it. Posting wisdom instead of practicing it. Speaking in therapy language without actually changing behavior. Real emotional development is subtle. It looks like:

- learning without announcing it
- communicating simply rather than strategically
- dropping the need to appear evolved
- allowing reconciliation when sincere effort is made, without clinging to pride

Dating maturity also means resisting shallow conclusions about people or situations. Not accepting common narratives just because they are popular. Taking time to understand before deciding. The strongest presence in a room is often the least performative one.

Savage takeaway

If your growth needs an audience, it is still a performance.

Quiet power mantra

"I do not perform transformation. I become it."

---

[10] In English, hypomnemata (plural of *hypomnema*) translates to "reminders," "memoranda," or "personal notebooks." For Stoics like Marcus Aurelius, these notebooks were tools for self-formation. Instead of an intimate diary, they were a collection of "already-said" wisdom intended for re-reading and meditation to prepare the soul for life's challenges.

V. STABILITY IS THE REAL POWER

"From Apollonius[11], true liberty, and unvariable steadfastness, and not to regard anything at all, though never so little, but right and reason: and always, whether in the sharpest pains, or after the loss of a child, or in long diseases, to be still the same man; who also was a present and visible example unto me, that it was possible for the same man to be both vehement and remiss: a man not subject to be vexed, and offended with the incapacity of his scholars and auditors in his lectures and expositions; and a true pattern of a man who of all his good gifts and faculties, least esteemed in himself, that his excellent skill and ability to teach and persuade others the common theorems and maxims of the Stoic philosophy. Of him also I learned how to receive favours and kindnesses (as commonly they are accounted:) from friends, so that I might not become obnoxious unto them, for them, nor more yielding upon occasion, than in right I ought; and yet so that I should not pass them neither, as an unsensible and unthankful man."

What Marcus meant (core philosophy)

Marcus honors Apollonius as a living example of inner freedom and unwavering steadiness. The core lesson is consistency of character regardless of circumstance. Whether facing pain, loss, illness, or frustration, the wise person remains guided by reason rather than emotional volatility.

Apollonius demonstrated that strength does not require rigidity. One can be both firm and flexible, intense when necessary and relaxed when appropriate, without losing integrity. He also modeled humility, possessing great skill without self-importance.

Another key Stoic principle here is balanced reciprocity. Accept kindness without becoming indebted or losing autonomy. Gratitude should not turn into submission, nor independence into cold detachment. The wise person receives and gives in proper proportion, guided by reason rather than obligation or ego.

Dating translation (what this means emotionally/socially)

Emotional steadiness is often mistaken for lack of explained, but it is actually a form of quiet authority. In dating, many people shift their personality depending on circumstances. They become more agreeable to avoid loss, more reactive when hurt, or more guarded when afraid. Marcus is describing a different approach: remain anchored in your values regardless of external changes.

Consistency builds trust, both internally and externally. You do not become a different person because someone texts less, shows interest, withdraws, or disappoints. Your standards remain intact because they are rooted in self-command rather than emotional fluctuation.

This section also speaks to receiving without losing independence. Accept kindness, affection, or support without feeling obligated to overgive in return. Gratitude does not require surrender. At the same time, do not reject care out of

---

[11] Apollonius of Chalcedon was a Greek Stoic philosopher of the 2nd century AD. He was summoned to Rome by Emperor Antoninus Pius specifically to instruct his adoptive sons, Marcus Aurelius and Lucius Verus, in the Stoic discipline.

fear of vulnerability or pride. The balance is simple but rare: appreciate what is offered without abandoning yourself.

Savage takeaway
Emotional stability is not boring. It is unshakable power.

Quiet power mantra
"I remain myself, no matter what changes around me."

VI. KIND WITHOUT PERFORMING KINDNESS
"Of Sextus[12], mildness and the pattern of a family governed with paternal affection; and a purpose to live according to nature: to be grave without affectation: to observe carefully the several dispositions of my friends, not to be offended with idiots, nor unseasonably to set upon those that are carried with the vulgar opinions, with the theorems, and tenets of philosophers: his conversation being an example how a man might accommodate himself to all men and companies; so that though his company were sweeter and more pleasing than any flatterer's cogging and fawning; yet was it at the same time most respected and reverenced: who also had a proper happiness and faculty, rationally and methodically to find out, and set in order all necessary determinations and instructions for a man's life. A man without ever the least appearance of anger, or any other passion; able at the same time most exactly to observe the Stoic Apathia[13], or unpassionateness, and yet to be most tender-hearted: ever of good credit; and yet almost without any noise, or rumour: very learned, and yet making little show."

What Marcus meant (core philosophy)
Marcus praises Sextus as an example of quiet authority grounded in natural ease and emotional balance. Sextus embodied gentleness without weakness and seriousness without pretension. His presence was both warm and respected, showing that true dignity does not rely on performance or self-display.

The Stoic ideal here is harmony between rational control and genuine humanity. He was unreactive without becoming cold, tender-hearted without losing composure. He understood people deeply, adjusting himself to different personalities without abandoning integrity.

Another key lesson is restraint in correcting others. Sextus did not aggressively challenge those who held misguided beliefs, nor did he become irritated by ignorance. Instead, he modeled wisdom through example rather than confrontation. His learning and credibility were evident, yet he made no effort to appear impressive. True mastery does not need advertisement.

---

[12] Sextus refers to Sextus of Chaeronea, a philosopher and teacher who was the nephew (or grandson) of the famous biographer Plutarch.
[13] In the Stoic tradition, Apathia (from the Greek *apatheia*) is the state of being free from irrational passions. While it sounds like the modern word "apathy," it does not mean being cold, indifferent, or lazy. To a Stoic, it means having a mind that is unshakable and no longer a slave to overwhelming emotions like fear, lust, or anger.

Dating translation (what this means emotionally/socially)

Emotional maturity in dating is often misunderstood as either detachment or excessive emotional expression. This section describes a third path: calm warmth. You can be:

- emotionally intelligent without being emotionally dramatic
- kind without overexplaining yourself
- adaptable without becoming a chameleon

Many people feel pressure to prove they are "nice," "deep," or "understanding." Sextus represents the opposite. His presence made people feel safe without him trying to convince anyone of his value. In dating, this translates into observing others carefully without rushing to correct, educate, or fix them. Not every disagreement requires a lecture. Not every difference requires confrontation. Respect grows naturally when kindness is grounded in self-possession rather than approval-seeking.

Savage takeaway

The most powerful energy in a room is calm kindness that does not ask for recognition.

Quiet power mantra

"I am gentle without shrinking, and steady without hardening."

VII. CORRECT WITH CLASS, NOT EGO

"From Alexander the Grammarian[14], to be un-reprovable myself, and not reproachfully to reprehend any man for a barbarism, or a solecism, or any false pronunciation, but dextrously[15] by way of answer, or testimony, or confirmation of the same matter (taking no notice of the word) to utter it as it should have been spoken; or by some other such close and indirect admonition, handsomely and civilly to tell him of it."

What Marcus meant (core philosophy)

Marcus learned from Alexander the Grammarian the art of refinement without humiliation. The lesson was not simply about language, but about character. Rather than publicly correcting or shaming others for mistakes, Alexander modeled subtle guidance. He corrected through example, gentle redirection, or thoughtful response rather than direct reproach.

The Stoic principle here is mastery of ego. The goal is not to demonstrate superiority or expose another's ignorance, but to elevate the conversation while preserving dignity on both sides. This reflects a deeper discipline: ensure your own conduct is beyond reproach while avoiding the impulse to criticize others harshly. True wisdom seeks improvement without creating unnecessary friction.

---

[14] Alexander the Grammarian (also known as Alexander of Cotiaeum) was one of the most distinguished Greek scholars of the 2nd century AD and a personal tutor to Marcus Aurelius. He was considered the leading authority on Homer in his time.

[15] Dextrously (or dexterously) is an adverb describing the act of doing something with great skill, agility, and grace, particularly involving manual coordination.

Dating translation (what this means emotionally/socially)

In modern relationships, many conflicts escalate because correction becomes performance. People use "honesty" as a justification for harshness, believing that bluntness equals authenticity. This section introduces a more sophisticated approach. You do not need to:

- point out every flaw
- expose every inconsistency
- prove that you are right in order to feel secure

Emotional intelligence often means guiding rather than confronting. If someone misunderstands something, you can model clarity instead of issuing criticism. If behavior needs addressing, it can be done with composure rather than superiority. This is not avoidance. It is precision. Respect is preserved when correction feels collaborative rather than accusatory.

Savage takeaway

Correcting someone harshly often reveals more about your ego than their mistake.

Quiet power mantra

"I elevate without humiliating."

VIII. POWER ATTRACTS MASKS

"Of Fronto[16], to how much envy and fraud and hypocrisy the state of a tyrannous king is subject unto, and how they who are commonly called εὐπατρίδαι[17], i.e. nobly born, are in some sort incapable, or void of natural affection."

What Marcus meant (core philosophy)

From Fronto, Marcus learned a sobering truth about status and human behavior. Those in positions of power often become surrounded by envy, deception, and hidden motives. External status attracts performance rather than sincerity. People may flatter, manipulate, or conceal their true intentions when hierarchy is involved.

He also reflects on the idea that those born into privilege or elevated status may lack genuine emotional depth or natural affection, having been shaped more by position than by authentic connection.

The Stoic lesson here is clear-eyed realism. Do not romanticize status, power, or social rank. Recognize that environments shaped by ambition often distort authenticity. Wisdom requires awareness of human nature without becoming cynical or bitter.

---

[16] Marcus Cornelius Fronto was the premier Roman orator of the 2nd century and the beloved rhetoric tutor of Marcus Aurelius. While Rusticus was the Emperor's "spiritual" father, Fronto was his "intellectual" father.

[17] In Greek, εὐπατρίδαι (*eupatridai*) translates to "the well-born" or "those of noble fathers."

Dating translation (what this means emotionally/socially)

Modern dating has its own forms of "power." Social influence, beauty, success, attention, popularity, emotional leverage. When someone holds perceived status, they often attract projection rather than genuine connection.

This section speaks to discernment. Not everyone who appears impressive is emotionally available. Not everyone who offers admiration is sincere. The more someone is idealized, the more likely it becomes that interactions are shaped by performance rather than authenticity.

Dating maturity involves recognizing that attraction to status can cloud judgment. Someone may look exceptional on paper yet lack emotional depth. Conversely, someone with quieter presence may offer genuine connection. Understanding human nature allows you to observe patterns without personalizing them. When you recognize that certain environments encourage masks, you stop expecting emotional transparency from those who are not practiced in giving it.

Savage takeaway

Status attracts attention. It does not guarantee character.

Quiet power mantra

"I see through the performance without becoming bitter toward the players."

IX. BUSY IS NOT A PERSONALITY

"Of Alexander the Platonic[18], not often nor without great necessity to say, or to write to any man in a letter, 'I am not at leisure'; nor in this manner still to put off those duties, which we owe to our friends and acquaintances (to every one in his kind) under pretence of urgent affairs."

What Marcus meant (core philosophy)

Marcus learned from Alexander the Platonic the importance of honoring relationships through presence and responsibility. The lesson was not about abandoning priorities, but about resisting the habit of using busyness as an excuse to neglect meaningful duties toward others.

The Stoic principle here is integrity in relationships. Do not hide behind constant urgency or self-importance to avoid connection, accountability, or care. Time is finite, and relationships require intentional participation. True discipline includes showing up where it matters rather than endlessly postponing what is owed to others. This reflects a deeper ethical stance: respect for others is demonstrated through consistent engagement, not through declarations of importance or perpetual delay.

---

[18] Alexander the Platonic (also known as Alexander of Cotiaeum) was the Greek tutor who taught Marcus Aurelius the art of grammar and literary analysis.

Dating translation (what this means emotionally/socially)

Modern dating often uses "I'm busy" as emotional distance disguised as responsibility. While life demands real commitments, repeated unavailability can signal avoidance rather than necessity.

This section invites discernment in two directions. First, toward others. When someone consistently postpones connection, delays communication, or frames availability as a favor rather than a mutual investment, their priorities are revealing themselves. Respect is shown through effort, not through excuses.

Second, toward yourself. Emotional maturity also means not hiding behind productivity to avoid vulnerability. Some people remain perpetually busy because stillness requires emotional honesty. Dating becomes clearer when you understand that time is rarely the true obstacle. Willingness is.

Savage takeaway

If someone is always too busy for connection, they are either unavailable or uninterested. Both require the same response: clarity.

Quiet power mantra

"I make time for what aligns with my values, and I recognize when others do not."

X. RESPOND WITHOUT DEFENSE

"Of Catulus[19], not to contemn any friend's expostulation, though unjust, but to strive to reduce him to his former disposition: freely and heartily to speak well of all my masters upon any occasion, as it is reported of Domitius[20], and Athenodotus: and to love my children with true affection."

What Marcus meant (core philosophy)

From Catulus, Marcus learned emotional generosity in relationships. The lesson is not to dismiss or belittle a friend's complaint, even if it appears unjust or misguided. Instead of reacting defensively, one should aim to restore harmony and guide the relationship back toward goodwill.

This reflects a Stoic commitment to preserving connection without surrendering reason. The focus is not on proving oneself right but on maintaining the health of the relationship where possible. He also emphasizes gratitude and respect toward those who have contributed to one's growth, as well as sincere affection toward those one cares for deeply.

The underlying principle is emotional steadiness combined with generosity of spirit. Strength does not require winning every disagreement. It requires knowing when restoration matters more than validation.

---

[19] Claudius Severus was a Peripatetic (Aristotelian) philosopher and a powerful Roman statesman.

[20] Domitius is used as a historical example of a student who remained publicly loyal and appreciative of his teacher, Athenodotus, even long after his studies were complete. Some scholars, including biographer Donald Robertson, speculate that this Domitius might have been a member of Marcus's mother's family, suggesting that Stoic values had been a tradition on the maternal side of his house for generations.

Dating translation (what this means emotionally/socially)

In modern relationships, the instinct to defend oneself immediately is strong. When someone expresses hurt or frustration, especially if it feels unfair, the natural response is often to argue facts or establish innocence.

This section introduces a more advanced skill: listening without collapsing into defensiveness. You do not have to agree with every accusation to recognize emotional reality. Sometimes people are responding to perception rather than intention. Addressing the emotional tone first can prevent unnecessary escalation.

Dating maturity involves distinguishing between ego and connection. Not every misunderstanding requires debate. Some require patience, calm clarification, and a willingness to guide the conversation back toward mutual understanding. At the same time, this section also reminds us to appreciate those who have supported us and to express affection openly. Emotional restraint does not mean emotional distance.

Savage takeaway

Being right is rarely as powerful as being steady.

Quiet power mantra

"I protect connection without abandoning clarity."

XI. LOVE CLEARLY, LIVE OPENLY

"From my brother Severus[21], to be kind and loving to all them of my house and family; by whom also I came to the knowledge of Thrasea[22] and Helvidius[23], and Cato[24], and Dio[25], and Brutus[26]. He it was also that did put me in the first conceit and desire of an equal commonwealth, administered by justice and equality; and of a kingdom wherein should be regarded nothing more than the good and welfare of the subjects. Of him also, to observe a constant tenor, (not interrupted, with any other cares and distractions,) in the study and esteem of philosophy: to be bountiful and liberal in the largest measure; always to hope the best; and to be confident that my friends love me. In whom I moreover observed open dealing towards those whom he reproved at any time, and that his friends might without all doubt or much observation know what he would, or would not, so open and plain was he."

---

[21] Claudius Severus is the philosopher-statesman Marcus Aurelius credits with giving him a "vision of a free state"

[22] Thrasea Paetus was a Roman Senator and Stoic martyr who became the ultimate symbol of principled resistance against tyranny.

[23] Helvidius Priscus was a 1st-century Roman Senator and Stoic philosopher who famously died resisting imperial tyranny.

[24] Cato the Younger (95–46 BC) was the "patron saint" of Stoic defiance. While the other heroes Marcus Aurelius mentions were his successors, Cato was the original archetype of the man who would rather die than live without freedom.

[25] Dio refers to Dion of Syracuse (c. 408–354 BC), a philosopher-statesman and disciple of Plato.

[26] Marcus Junius Brutus (85–42 BC) is perhaps the most surprising hero on Marcus Aurelius's list of inspirations. Despite being the world's most powerful monarch, Marcus looked to the man who killed a monarch as a model of political integrity.

What Marcus meant (core philosophy)

From his brother Severus, Marcus learned the balance between personal warmth and principled living. Severus modeled kindness toward family and others while remaining deeply committed to justice, fairness, and philosophical integrity.

The Stoic lesson here is alignment between values and action. A life guided by reason should not be fragmented by distraction or inconsistency. Instead, it should maintain a steady devotion to truth and ethical conduct.

Severus also embodied generosity, optimism toward others, and confidence in the sincerity of friendships. He communicated openly and directly, leaving little ambiguity about his intentions or boundaries. This clarity created trust. His kindness was not passive; it was structured by honesty and fairness.

Dating translation (what this means emotionally/socially)

This section speaks to emotional clarity as a form of strength. Many dating dynamics become complicated because people communicate indirectly. They hint instead of stating, assume instead of asking, and withhold clarity to maintain control or avoid discomfort.

Marcus is describing a different model. Kindness and emotional openness do not weaken boundaries. They strengthen them. When you know what you want, communicate it calmly, and act consistently, relationships become less confusing. Others do not need to guess your intentions.

This also touches on optimism without naivety. Choosing to believe in goodwill does not mean ignoring reality. It means approaching connection without cynicism while still holding firm standards. Dating maturity includes being both generous and direct. Warmth and clarity are not opposites.

Savage takeaway

Confusion is rarely mysterious. It usually means someone is avoiding clarity.

Quiet power mantra

"I am kind, direct, and consistent. My clarity is my respect."

XII. MASTER YOURSELF, NOT THE OUTCOME

"From Claudius Maximus[27], in all things to endeavour to have power of myself, and in nothing to be carried about; to be cheerful and courageous in all sudden chances and accidents, as in sicknesses: to love mildness, and moderation, and gravity: and to do my business, whatsoever it be, thoroughly, and without querulousness. Whatsoever he said, all men believed him that as he spake[28], so he thought, and whatsoever he did, that he did it with a good intent. His manner was, never to wonder at anything; never to be in haste, and yet never slow: nor to be perplexed, or dejected, or at any time unseemly, or excessively

---

[27] Claudius Maximus was a Stoic philosopher and Roman consul whom Marcus Aurelius considered the "perfect model" of a human being.

[28] In English, spake is the archaic (old-fashioned) past tense form of the verb speak.

to laugh: nor to be angry, or suspicious, but ever ready to do good, and to forgive, and to speak truth; and all this, as one that seemed rather of himself to have been straight and right, than ever to have been rectified or redressed; neither was there any man that ever thought himself undervalued by him, or that could find in his heart, to think himself a better man than he. He would also be very pleasant and gracious."

What Marcus meant (core philosophy)

From Claudius Maximus, Marcus learned the highest Stoic discipline: self-command. The goal is not to control circumstances but to maintain sovereignty over one's own reactions, decisions, and character.

Maximus embodied composure in all situations. He remained steady during unexpected challenges, neither overwhelmed nor detached from reality. His strength came from moderation, clarity of intention, and consistent action without complaint.

He demonstrated integrity through alignment between words and behavior. Others trusted him because he was internally consistent. He did not chase drama, react excessively, or allow external events to dictate his inner state.

Another core lesson is emotional balance. He avoided extremes, neither rushing nor hesitating, neither overly suspicious nor naively trusting. Kindness and forgiveness were natural extensions of his character, not performances. His presence made others feel respected without diminishing his own authority.

Dating translation (what this means emotionally/socially)

This section describes emotional sovereignty in relationships. Dating often triggers a desire to control outcomes: how someone feels, how quickly things progress, whether situations resolve in your favor. The Stoic approach shifts focus away from external results and toward internal mastery. You cannot control attraction, timing, or another person's choices. You can control:

- how you respond to uncertainty
- how consistently you uphold your standards
- how calmly you navigate unexpected changes

Self-command creates stability. When you are not easily shaken, others experience your presence as grounded rather than reactive. This also speaks to emotional neutrality. Not coldness, but steadiness. Avoiding dramatic swings between idealization and disappointment. Acting with warmth and grace without surrendering your center. Trust grows naturally when your behavior reflects alignment between intention and action. People believe what they see repeated.

Savage takeaway

The strongest position in dating is not control over others. It is control over yourself.

Quiet power mantra

"I remain steady. My power is in how I respond."

XIII. TRUE STRENGTH DOES NOT NEED TO ANNOUNCE ITSELF

"In my father, I observed his meekness; his constancy without wavering in those things, which after a due examination and deliberation, he had determined. How free from all vanity he carried himself in matter of honour and dignity, (as they are esteemed:) his laboriousness and assiduity, his readiness to hear any man, that had aught to say tending to any common good: how generally and impartially he would give every man his due; his skill and knowledge, when rigour or extremity, or when remissness or moderation was in season; how he did abstain from all unchaste love of youths; his moderate condescending to other men's occasions as an ordinary man, neither absolutely requiring of his friends, that they should wait upon him at his ordinary meals, nor that they should of necessity accompany him in his journeys; and that whensoever any business upon some necessary occasions was to be put off and omitted before it could be ended, he was ever found when he went about it again, the same man that he was before. His accurate examination of things in consultations, and patient hearing of others. He would not hastily give over the search of the matter, as one easy to be satisfied with sudden notions and apprehensions. His care to preserve his friends; how neither at any time he would carry himself towards them with disdainful neglect, and grow weary of them; nor yet at any time be madly fond of them. His contented mind in all things, his cheerful countenance, his care to foresee things afar off, and to take order for the least, without any noise or clamour. Moreover how all acclamations and flattery were repressed by him: how carefully he observed all things necessary to the government, and kept an account of the common expenses, and how patiently he did abide that he was reprehended by some for this his strict and rigid kind of dealing. How he was neither a superstitious worshipper of the gods, nor an ambitious pleaser of men, or studious of popular applause; but sober in all things, and everywhere observant of that which was fitting; no affecter of novelties: in those things which conduced to his ease and convenience, (plenty whereof his fortune did afford him,) without pride and bragging, yet with all freedom and liberty: so that as he did freely enjoy them without any anxiety or affectation when they were present; so when absent, he found no want of them. Moreover, that he was never commended by any man, as either a learned acute man, or an obsequious officious man, or a fine orator; but as a ripe mature man, a perfect sound man; one that could not endure to be flattered; able to govern both himself and others. Moreover, how much he did honour all true philosophers, without upbraiding those that were not so; his sociableness, his gracious and delightful conversation, but never unto satiety; his care of his body within bounds and measure, not as one that desired to live long, or over-studious of neatness, and elegancy; and yet not as one that did not regard it: so that through his own care and providence, he seldom needed any inward physic, or outward applications: but especially how ingeniously he would yield to any that had obtained any peculiar faculty, as either eloquence, or the knowledge of the laws, or of ancient customs, or the like; and how he concurred with them, in his best care and endeavour that every one of them might in his kind, for that wherein he excelled, be regarded and esteemed: and although he did all things carefully after the ancient customs of his forefathers, yet even of this was he not desirous that men should take notice, that he did imitate ancient customs. Again, how he was not easily moved and tossed up and down, but loved to be constant, both in the same places and businesses; and how after his great fits of headache he would return fresh and vigorous to his wonted affairs. Again, that secrets he neither had many, nor often, and such only as concerned public matters: his discretion and moderation, in exhibiting of the public sights and shows for the pleasure and pastime of the people: in public buildings. congiaries, and the like. In all these things, having a respect unto men only as men, and to the equity of the things themselves, and not unto the glory that might follow. Never wont to use the baths at unseasonable hours; no builder; never curious, or solicitous, either about his meat, or about the workmanship, or colour of his clothes, or about anything that belonged to external beauty. In all his conversation, far from all inhumanity, all boldness, and incivility, all greediness and impetuosity; never doing anything with such earnestness, and intention, that a man could say of him, that he did sweat about it: but contrariwise, all things distinctly, as at leisure;

without trouble; orderly, soundly, and agreeably. A man might have applied that to him, which is recorded of Socrates, that he knew how to want, and to enjoy those things, in the want whereof, most men show themselves weak; and in the fruition, intemperate: but to hold out firm and constant, and to keep within the compass of true moderation and sobriety in either estate, is proper to a man, who hath a perfect and invincible soul; such as he showed himself in the sickness of Maximus."

What Marcus meant (core philosophy)

In describing his father, Marcus outlines a complete portrait of quiet mastery. The defining qualities are constancy, humility, discernment, and balance. His father was gentle without weakness, decisive without arrogance, and steady without rigidity.

The Stoic lesson here is the integration of character. Virtue is not expressed through dramatic gestures but through consistent, measured conduct across all areas of life. He examined matters carefully before deciding and remained unwavering once reason had guided him. He treated others fairly, neither neglecting friendships nor becoming overly attached.

He avoided vanity, resisted flattery, and did not pursue admiration or status for its own sake. He enjoyed comforts when available without becoming dependent on them, demonstrating freedom from external attachment.

Another central theme is proportion. Knowing when to apply firmness or leniency, when to speak and when to listen, when to act and when to wait. His authority came not from force or spectacle but from internal coherence. Others trusted him because he was stable, moderate, and aligned with principle. This is the Stoic ideal of a mature and invincible soul: composed, grounded, and quietly powerful.

Dating translation (what this means emotionally/socially)

This section describes emotional maturity at its highest level. In dating, many people confuse intensity with depth or dramatic gestures with commitment. Marcus presents a different model: calm reliability. True emotional strength looks like:

- making thoughtful decisions rather than impulsive ones
- maintaining consistency even when circumstances change
- enjoying connection without becoming dependent on it
- remaining open and sociable without losing discernment

The ability to hold balance is rare. Not becoming cold when disappointed, not becoming consumed when excited. Not chasing validation, not performing status, not allowing external praise or criticism to determine self-worth.

This also reflects relational steadiness. Supporting others without controlling them. Appreciating differences without competition. Returning to yourself after difficulty without losing clarity. Dating maturity is not about appearing impressive. It is about becoming stable enough that others experience safety in your presence.

Savage takeaway

Real maturity is invisible to those who only recognize drama.

Quiet power mantra

"I am steady, balanced, and self-governed. My strength speaks without noise."

XIV. GRATITUDE WITHOUT SELF-DECEPTION

"From the gods I received that I had good grandfathers, and parents, a good sister, good masters, good domestics, loving kinsmen, almost all that I have; and that I never through haste and rashness transgressed against any of them, notwithstanding that my disposition was such, as that such a thing (if occasion had been) might very well have been committed by me, but that It was the mercy of the gods, to prevent such a concurring of matters and occasions, as might make me to incur this blame. That I was not long brought up by the concubine of my father; that I preserved the flower of my youth. That I took not upon me to be a man before my time, but rather put it off longer than I needed. That I lived under the government of my lord and father, who would take away from me all pride and vainglory, and reduce me to that conceit and opinion that it was not impossible for a prince to live in the court without a troop of guards and followers, extraordinary apparel, such and such torches and statues, and other like particulars of state and magnificence; but that a man may reduce and contract himself almost to the state of a private man, and yet for all that not to become the more base and remiss in those public matters and affairs, wherein power and authority is requisite. That I have had such a brother, who by his own example might stir me up to think of myself; and by his respect and love, delight and please me. That I have got ingenuous children, and that they were not born distorted, nor with any other natural deformity. That I was no great proficient in the study of rhetoric and poetry, and of other faculties, which perchance I might have dwelt upon, if I had found myself to go on in them with success. That I did by times prefer those, by whom I was brought up, to such places and dignities, which they seemed unto me most to desire; and that I did not put them off with hope and expectation, that (since that they were yet but young) I would do the same hereafter. That I ever knew Apollonius and Rusticus, and Maximus. That I have had occasion often and effectually to consider and meditate with myself, concerning that life which is according to nature, what the nature and manner of it is: so that as for the gods and such suggestions, helps and inspirations, as might be expected from them, nothing did hinder, but that I might have begun long before to live according to nature; or that even now that I was not yet partaker and in present possession of that life, that I myself (in that I did not observe those inward motions, and suggestions, yea and almost plain and apparent instructions and admonitions of the gods,) was the only cause of it. That my body in such a life, hath been able to hold out so long. That I never had to do with Benedicta and Theodotus, yea and afterwards when I fell into some fits of love, I was soon cured. That having been often displeased with Rusticus, I never did him anything for which afterwards I had occasion to repent. That it being so that my mother was to die young, yet she lived with me all her latter years. That as often as I had a purpose to help and succour any that either were poor, or fallen into some present necessity, I never was answered by my officers that there was not ready money enough to do it; and that I myself never had occasion to require the like succour from any other. That I have such a wife, so obedient, so loving, so ingenuous. That I had choice of fit and able men, to whom I might commit the bringing up of my children. That by dreams I have received help, as for other things, so in particular, how I might stay my casting of blood, and cure my dizziness, as that also that happened to thee in Cajeta, as unto Chryses when he prayed by the seashore. And when I did first apply myself to philosophy, that I did not fall into the hands of some sophists, or spent my time either in reading the manifold volumes of ordinary philosophers, nor in practising myself in the solution of arguments and fallacies, nor dwelt upon the studies of the meteors, and other natural curiosities. All these things without the assistance of the gods, and fortune, could not have been."

What Marcus meant (core philosophy)

In this section, Marcus reflects on the role of fortune, guidance, and circumstance in shaping his life. He acknowledges the people, opportunities, and conditions that supported his development, while also recognizing that he possessed tendencies that could have led him astray had circumstances aligned differently.

The Stoic lesson here is humility through perspective. One must recognize both personal responsibility and the influence of external conditions without falling into arrogance or passivity. Marcus expresses gratitude not only for what he received but also for what he avoided. He understands that character is shaped by environment, timing, mentorship, and restraint as much as by individual effort.

Another key element is simplicity within power. He learned that dignity does not require spectacle or excess, and that true authority can exist without outward display. He values moderation, meaningful relationships, thoughtful decisions, and the ability to live according to nature rather than chasing unnecessary complexity. This section reveals a deep awareness that growth requires recognizing one's advantages and limitations without illusion.

Dating translation (what this means emotionally/socially)

In relationships, many people rewrite their personal narrative to feel either completely self-made or completely unlucky. This section invites a more balanced perspective. Your relationship history is shaped by both choice and circumstance. The people you met, the timing of events, the emotional tools you were given or denied, all influenced how you learned to love and connect. Recognizing this removes shame without removing responsibility.

Gratitude in dating is not about pretending everything was perfect. It is about acknowledging the lessons, protections, and moments of growth that allowed you to evolve. There is also a quiet message about simplicity. You do not need dramatic displays, elaborate validation, or external symbols of success to confirm your worth or the value of a relationship. Real stability often looks unremarkable from the outside.

Finally, Marcus recognizes that ignoring inner guidance delayed his progress. In dating terms, many people already sense when something is misaligned but postpone action. Growth accelerates when you stop ignoring what you already know.

Savage takeaway

Luck may shape your path, but awareness determines whether you repeat it.

Quiet power mantra

"I honor what shaped me, and I choose consciously what shapes me next."

XV. EXPECT HUMAN NATURE, PROTECT YOUR PEACE

"In the country of the Quadi at Granua, these. Betimes in the morning say to thyself, This day I shalt have to do with an idle curious man, with an unthankful man, a railer, a crafty, false, or an envious man; an unsociable uncharitable man. All these ill qualities have happened unto them, through ignorance of that which is truly good and truly bad. But I that understand the nature of that which is good, that it only is to be desired, and of that which is bad, that it only is truly odious and shameful: who know moreover, that this transgressor, whosoever he be, is my kinsman, not by the same blood and seed, but by participation of the same reason, and of the same divine particle; How can I either be hurt by any of those, since it is not in their power to make me incur anything that is truly reproachful? or angry, and ill affected towards him, who by nature is so near unto me? for we are all born to be fellow-workers, as the feet, the hands, and the eyelids; as the rows of the upper and under teeth: for such therefore to be in opposition, is against nature; and what is it to chafe at, and to be averse from, but to be in opposition?"

What Marcus meant (core philosophy)

Marcus advises beginning each day with realistic expectations about human behavior. He lists the types of people one will inevitably encounter: ungrateful, envious, deceitful, ignorant, or difficult. This is not cynicism but preparation.

The Stoic principle is emotional immunity through understanding. People behave poorly because they misunderstand what is truly good or bad. Their actions arise from ignorance, not from a personal mission to harm you. Therefore, their behavior cannot truly damage your character unless you allow it to disturb your own reason. The focus remains on self-governance. Anger and resentment are forms of internal opposition to nature, which calls for cooperation rather than hostility.

Marcus also emphasizes shared humanity. Even those who act poorly remain part of the same rational whole. The goal is not emotional closeness with everyone but recognition that conflict loses power when you stop personalizing ignorance.

Dating translation (what this means emotionally/socially)

Dating becomes significantly calmer when you stop expecting emotional perfection from strangers. You will meet:
- people who lack self-awareness
- people who communicate poorly
- people who project their wounds onto others
- people who do not recognize your value

This is not evidence that something is wrong with you. It is evidence that human beings are imperfect. The mistake many people make is treating disappointing behavior as personal betrayal rather than as information. When you expect flawless conduct, every misstep feels like an attack. When you understand human nature, you maintain emotional distance without becoming cold.

This does not mean tolerating harmful behavior. It means recognizing that another person's ignorance does not define your worth or disturb your internal balance unless you grant it that power. Dating maturity involves responding without emotional collapse. Calm clarity replaces reactive frustration.

Savage takeaway

People will reveal their limitations. Your peace depends on not being shocked by it.

Quiet power mantra

"I expect imperfection without absorbing it."

XVI. YOUR MIND IS THE REAL AUTHORITY

"Whatsoever I am, is either flesh, or life, or that which we commonly call the mistress and overruling part of man; reason. Away with thy books, suffer not thy mind any more to be distracted, and carried to and fro; for it will not be; but as even now ready to die, think little of thy flesh: blood, bones, and a skin; a pretty piece of knit and twisted work, consisting of nerves, veins and arteries; think no more of it, than so. And as for thy life, consider what it is; a wind; not one constant wind neither, but every moment of an hour let out, and sucked in again. The third, is thy ruling part; and here consider; Thou art an old man; suffer not that excellent part to be brought in subjection, and to become slavish: suffer it not to be drawn up and down with unreasonable and unsociable lusts and motions, as it were with wires and nerves; suffer it not any more, either to repine at anything now present, or to fear and fly anything to come, which the destiny hath appointed thee."

What Marcus meant (core philosophy)

Marcus reduces human existence to three components: the physical body, the breath of life, and the ruling faculty, which is reason. The body is temporary and fragile. Breath is fleeting and unstable. Only the rational mind has the capacity for true governance.

The Stoic lesson here is radical clarity about what deserves attention and what does not. Physical concerns and external distractions should not dominate the ruling part of the self. Reason must remain sovereign, free from irrational desires, emotional agitation, or fear of the future.

He urges discipline against mental restlessness. Stop searching endlessly for distraction or external stimulation. Accept mortality and impermanence, and use that awareness to anchor the mind in purpose and calm authority. The highest form of freedom is mastery over one's internal state.

Dating translation (what this means emotionally/socially)

Dating often pulls attention toward the least stable aspects of self: appearance, chemistry, validation, and imagined futures. Marcus reminds us that these elements are temporary and unreliable. Your body may react. Your emotions may fluctuate. Attraction may rise and fall. None of these should govern your decisions. The "ruling part" in dating is your clarity.

When you allow insecurity, fear of loss, or craving for approval to lead, your judgment becomes reactive. You begin negotiating against your own standards. Emotional maturity requires returning authority to reason. This does not mean suppressing emotion. It means refusing to let temporary feelings dictate permanent choices.

There is also a quiet urgency in Marcus' tone. Time is limited. Do not waste energy chasing distractions or performing versions of yourself that are disconnected from your core values. Dating becomes simpler when you stop asking, "How do I feel right now?" and begin asking, "Does this align with who I am becoming?"

Savage takeaway
Attraction is a sensation. Self-command is a decision.

Quiet power mantra
"My mind leads. Everything else follows."

XVII. TRUST THE FLOW, NOT THE OUTCOME

"Whatsoever proceeds from the gods immediately, that any man will grant totally depends from their divine providence. As for those things that are commonly said to happen by fortune, even those must be conceived to have dependence from nature, or from that first and general connection, and concatenation of all those things, which more apparently by the divine providence are administered and brought to pass. All things flow from thence: and whatsoever it is that is, is both necessary, and conducing to the whole (part of which thou art), and whatsoever it is that is requisite and necessary for the preservation of the general, must of necessity for every particular nature, be good and behoveful. And as for the whole, it is preserved, as by the perpetual mutation and conversion of the simple elements one into another, so also by the mutation, and alteration of things mixed and compounded. Let these things suffice thee; let them be always unto thee, as thy general rules and precepts. As for thy thirst after books, away with it with all speed, that thou die not murmuring and complaining, but truly meek and well satisfied, and from thy heart thankful unto the gods."

What Marcus meant (core philosophy)
Marcus reflects on the interconnected nature of existence. Whether events arise through divine providence, nature, or what people call fortune, all things belong to a larger order. Nothing exists in isolation; every occurrence participates in a broader system that serves the whole.

The Stoic lesson is acceptance rooted in understanding. Events may feel random or unfair from a limited perspective, but they are part of a continuous process of change and transformation necessary for the functioning of the greater whole.

Marcus advises simplifying the mind. Stop endlessly searching for answers in external sources or intellectual distractions. Instead, adopt guiding principles that allow you to move through life with calm acceptance. Gratitude and humility emerge when one recognizes that control is limited, but participation in the greater order is inevitable. Peace comes from alignment with reality rather than resistance to it.

Dating translation (what this means emotionally/socially)
Dating often becomes exhausting because people attempt to control outcomes instead of participating in the process. You cannot control:
* timing
* chemistry

- another person's emotional readiness
- whether something meant for you arrives or leaves

What you can control is how you respond to what unfolds. This section encourages releasing the obsession with "why did this happen" and replacing it with "how do I move with what is happening." Some connections serve as catalysts, others as mirrors, others as endings that redirect you toward alignment.

When you stop resisting the flow of events, you begin to see patterns with greater clarity. What once felt like rejection becomes redirection. What once felt like chaos reveals structure. There is also a warning here about overconsumption of advice. Endless analysis can become avoidance. At some point, you must stop searching for more frameworks and begin living with the principles you already understand. Dating becomes lighter when you trust that experiences contribute to your growth even when outcomes differ from expectation.

Savage takeaway
You do not need to control the story to grow from it.

Quiet power mantra
"I move with what is, and I trust that clarity arrives through motion."

THE SECOND BOOK
Get Your Shit Together.
Time Is Not Waiting.

I. STOP POSTPONING YOUR OWN EVOLUTION

"Remember how long thou hast already put off these things, and how often a certain day and hour as it were, having been set unto thee by the gods, thou hast neglected it. It is high time for thee to understand the true nature both of the world, whereof thou art a part; and of that Lord and Governor of the world, from whom, as a channel from the spring, thou thyself didst flow: and that there is but a certain limit of time appointed unto thee, which if thou shalt not make use of to calm and allay the many distempers of thy soul, it will pass away and thou with it, and never after return."

What Marcus meant (core philosophy)

Marcus begins Book Two with urgency. He reminds himself that he has delayed necessary inner work for far too long. Opportunities for growth have already been offered repeatedly, yet he has hesitated, postponed, or allowed distraction to intervene.

The Stoic lesson here is awareness of time. Life is finite, and self-development cannot remain theoretical or endlessly deferred. Understanding one's place within the greater order of existence brings responsibility: to live intentionally, to reduce internal conflict, and to align with reason before time runs out.

He emphasizes that the "distempers of the soul" such as anxiety, resentment, confusion, or emotional turbulence are not permanent conditions. They can be calmed, but only through conscious effort. Delay is the real danger. Time moves forward regardless of readiness.

Dating translation (what this means emotionally/socially)

In dating, many people postpone emotional growth while waiting for the right relationship to fix what feels unresolved. They delay:

- setting boundaries
- releasing past attachments
- trusting their intuition
- choosing clarity over ambiguity

There is often a quiet belief that transformation will happen naturally once the right partner arrives. Marcus challenges this assumption. Growth is not something that begins later. It is something that must begin now. Every time you ignore a misalignment, avoid a necessary conversation, or remain in a situation that drains you, you are postponing your own evolution. Dating becomes more aligned when you stop waiting for external circumstances to create internal readiness. Emotional peace is not a future reward. It is a present responsibility.

25

Savage takeaway
You are not stuck. You are delaying.

Quiet power mantra
"I stop postponing the life I already know I need to live."

II. DO IT CLEAN, DO IT FULLY

"Let it be thy earnest and incessant care as a Roman and a man to perform whatsoever it is that thou art about, with true and unfeigned gravity, natural affection, freedom and justice: and as for all other cares, and imaginations, how thou mayest ease thy mind of them. Which thou shalt do; if thou shalt go about every action as thy last action, free from all vanity, all passionate and wilful aberration from reason, and from all hypocrisy, and self-love, and dislike of those things, which by the fates or appointment of God have happened unto thee. Thou seest that those things, which for a man to hold on in a prosperous course, and to live a divine life, are requisite and necessary, are not many, for the gods will require no more of any man, that shall but keep and observe these things."

What Marcus meant (core philosophy)
Marcus calls for disciplined presence in action. Every task, no matter how small, should be approached with sincerity, seriousness, and integrity. The Stoic ideal is to act as though each moment could be the last, which strips away vanity, distraction, and unnecessary emotional noise. He emphasizes simplicity. A meaningful life does not require endless complexity or elaborate philosophy. It requires consistent alignment with reason, honesty in intention, and acceptance of what cannot be changed.

Marcus warns against the internal habits that distort action: ego, emotional impulsivity, hypocrisy, resentment toward fate, and self-centered thinking. Freedom comes from removing these distortions, allowing actions to be direct, grounded, and purposeful. The path to a "divine life" is not complicated. It is the repeated practice of clear, ethical action without unnecessary mental burden.

Dating translation (what this means emotionally/socially)
In dating, confusion often comes from divided intention. People say one thing but mean another. They act while secretly hoping for different outcomes. They perform interest, detachment, or vulnerability instead of simply showing up as they are.

Marcus' advice translates into emotional integrity. Approach relationships without performance. Speak honestly. Act consistently. Let your behavior reflect your actual values rather than strategies designed to control perception. This also speaks to presence. When you are with someone, be fully there instead of mentally rehearsing outcomes, fears, or future scenarios. Overthinking fractures connection. Dating becomes lighter when you remove unnecessary layers:
- no pretending to be less interested to seem desirable
- no overexplaining to secure approval
- no resisting reality when it reveals itself

You do not need complicated rules to navigate relationships. Clear intention and aligned action are enough.

Savage takeaway
Half-present energy creates half-alive connections.

Quiet power mantra
"I act with clarity, without performance or hesitation."

III. STOP HANDING OUT YOUR POWER
"Do, soul, do; abuse and contemn thyself; yet a while and the time for thee to respect thyself, will be at an end. Every man's happiness depends from himself, but behold thy life is almost at an end, whiles affording thyself no respect, thou dost make thy happiness to consist in the souls, and conceits of other men."

What Marcus meant (core philosophy)
Marcus speaks sharply to himself here, confronting the habit of self-neglect. He recognizes that happiness and fulfillment depend on one's own internal governance, yet he has allowed himself to become overly influenced by external opinions and perceptions.

The Stoic lesson is self-respect through self-command. Time is limited, and a life spent chasing approval or shaping one's identity around the judgments of others is a form of self-abandonment.

Marcus emphasizes urgency. There is only a finite window to reclaim authority over one's own mind and priorities. True dignity arises when one stops measuring worth through external validation and instead builds happiness from internal clarity and reason.

Dating translation (what this means emotionally/socially)
Many people unknowingly outsource their emotional stability to others in dating. They measure their value by:
- response times
- attention levels
- perceived interest
- how desired they feel in someone else's eyes

This creates a fragile emotional foundation. When happiness depends on another person's behavior or approval, self-respect becomes unstable.

Marcus' message is direct: respect yourself before time runs out. Stop shaping your identity around someone else's perception of you. Attraction may fluctuate, relationships may change, but your sense of worth must remain self-directed. Dating maturity means refusing to abandon yourself in exchange for acceptance. When you anchor your happiness internally, connection becomes a choice rather than a necessity for validation.

Savage takeaway
The moment you depend on someone else to define your worth, you have already negotiated against yourself.

Quiet power mantra
"My happiness belongs to me, not to someone else's opinion."

IV. FOCUS IS SELF-RESPECT
"Why should any of these things that happen externally, so much distract thee? Give thyself leisure to learn some good thing, and cease roving and wandering to and fro. Thou must also take heed of another kind of wandering, for they are idle in their actions, who toil and labour in this life, and have no certain scope to which to direct all their motions, and desires."

What Marcus meant (core philosophy)
Marcus questions why external events are allowed to disturb the mind so deeply. The Stoic teaching here is about directing attention intentionally. Distraction is not merely external noise; it is a failure to prioritize what truly matters.

He warns against two forms of wandering. The first is mental distraction, constantly shifting attention without purpose. The second is more subtle: busyness without direction. One may appear productive while lacking a clear guiding aim, which leads to exhaustion without fulfillment.

The Stoic solution is clarity of purpose. Give yourself the space to learn, reflect, and align your actions with meaningful objectives. Without a defined internal compass, effort becomes scattered and the mind remains restless.

Dating translation (what this means emotionally/socially)
In dating, distraction often masquerades as activity. Endless texting, analyzing conversations, cycling through multiple connections, or replaying past interactions can create the illusion of progress while preventing real clarity. Emotional wandering drains energy because it lacks intention. Marcus' advice invites you to pause and ask:
- What am I actually looking for?
- Do my actions reflect that intention?
- Am I moving toward clarity or simply avoiding stillness?

Another form of wandering is staying busy in relationships that have no defined direction. Investing energy without shared purpose leads to confusion and emotional fatigue. Dating becomes calmer when you reduce unnecessary noise. Focus allows you to recognize what aligns and release what does not.

Savage takeaway
Motion without direction is just exhaustion with better marketing.

Quiet power mantra
"My energy follows my purpose, not my distractions."

V. SELF-AWARENESS IS NON-NEGOTIABLE

"For not observing the state of another man's soul, scarce was ever any man known to be unhappy. Tell whosoever they be that intend not, and guide not by reason and discretion the motions of their own souls, they must of necessity be unhappy."

What Marcus meant (core philosophy)

Marcus observes that people rarely become unhappy because they misunderstand others; they become unhappy because they fail to understand themselves. The Stoic focus is inward governance. Those who do not examine and guide the movements of their own mind inevitably lose stability.

The lesson is simple but demanding. External circumstances or other people's behavior are not the primary sources of suffering. The true cause lies in an unexamined inner life. Without reason and awareness directing thoughts and impulses, emotions become chaotic and reactive.

Stoicism calls for continuous observation of one's own mental state. Self-awareness is not self-criticism; it is the foundation of freedom. When reason governs the soul, external events lose their power to destabilize.

Dating translation (what this means emotionally/socially)

Many dating struggles are blamed on others, but emotional patterns often originate within. Without self-awareness, people:

- repeat attraction cycles without understanding why
- misinterpret signals through personal bias
- react impulsively instead of responding intentionally
- seek validation instead of connection

Understanding another person is secondary to understanding yourself. If you do not know your own emotional triggers, boundaries, or desires, you will interpret every interaction through confusion rather than clarity. Dating becomes less painful when you shift focus from controlling others to observing your own reactions. Patterns become visible. Choices become deliberate. Self-awareness is not about becoming perfect. It is about becoming conscious.

Savage takeaway

You do not suffer because you do not understand them. You suffer because you have not examined yourself.

Quiet power mantra

"I observe my inner world before judging the outer one."

VI. KNOW WHO YOU ARE, AND MOVE ACCORDINGLY

"These things thou must always have in mind: What is the nature of the universe, and what is mine—in particular: This unto that what relation it hath: what kind of part, of what kind of universe it is: And that there is nobody that can hinder thee, but that thou mayest always both do and speak those things which are agreeable to that nature, whereof thou art a part."

What Marcus meant (core philosophy)

Marcus reminds himself to remain grounded in perspective. To live well, one must understand both the nature of the universe and one's own place within it. Each individual is a part of a greater whole, governed by natural order and reason.

The Stoic lesson is alignment. Actions and speech should reflect the nature of one's rational self rather than external pressures or passing impulses. Once a person understands their role and values, nothing external can truly prevent them from acting in accordance with that nature. Freedom does not come from controlling circumstances. It comes from knowing who you are and acting consistently with that understanding.

Dating translation (what this means emotionally/socially)

Dating becomes complicated when you forget your own nature. Many people adapt themselves to fit the expectations, desires, or fears of another person. They adjust boundaries, alter communication styles, or suppress parts of themselves to maintain connection. Over time, this creates internal conflict. Marcus offers a different approach: clarity about identity first, connection second. When you know:

- your values
- your emotional capacity
- your standards
- your intentions…

You are no longer easily swayed by external influence. No one can truly stop you from acting with integrity unless you abandon it yourself. External rejection, misunderstanding, or pressure cannot override self-alignment unless you allow it to. Dating becomes calmer when you measure choices against your nature rather than against someone else's approval.

Savage takeaway

Confusion begins the moment you forget who you are trying to be.

Quiet power mantra

"I move in alignment with myself, regardless of external noise."

VII. INTENTION REVEALS CHARACTER

'Theophrastus[29], where he compares sin with sin (as after a vulgar sense such things I grant may be compared:) says well and like a philosopher, that those sins are greater which are committed through lust, than those which are committed through anger. For he that is angry seems with a kind of grief and close contraction of himself, to turn away from reason; but he that sins through lust, being overcome by pleasure, doth in his very sin bewray a more impotent, and unmanlike disposition. Well then and like a philosopher doth he say, that he of the two is the more to be condemned, that sins with pleasure, than he

---

[29] Theophrastus (c. 371–287 BC) was a Greek philosopher who succeeded Aristotle as the head of the Peripatetic school in Athens. While he is often overshadowed by his teacher, he was a massive intellectual figure in his own right, known as the "Father of Botany" and a keen observer of human nature.

that sins with grief. For indeed this latter may seem first to have been wronged, and so in some manner through grief thereof to have been forced to be angry, whereas he who through lust doth commit anything, did of himself merely resolve upon that action."

What Marcus meant (core philosophy)

Marcus reflects on Theophrastus' distinction between two types of wrongdoing: actions driven by anger and those driven by pleasure or desire. While both deviate from reason, the philosopher argues that actions rooted in unchecked desire are more serious. Anger may arise from perceived injury or emotional disturbance, suggesting a reactive loss of control. Lust-driven actions, however, represent a conscious surrender to pleasure despite knowing better.

The Stoic lesson centers on intention and self-mastery. The severity of an action lies not only in what is done but in the state of mind from which it emerges. To knowingly choose pleasure over reason reveals a deeper failure of discipline than reacting impulsively under emotional strain. Marcus encourages examining the motives behind behavior. True philosophy requires understanding not just actions but the internal forces guiding them.

Dating translation (what this means emotionally/socially)

In relationships, people often excuse harmful behavior by focusing only on the outcome rather than the intention behind it. There is a difference between:

- someone who reacts poorly in a moment of hurt or misunderstanding
- someone who knowingly pursues selfish pleasure while disregarding consequences

Both can cause pain, but the underlying character is not the same. Anger-driven mistakes may signal emotional immaturity or unresolved wounds. Pleasure-driven decisions, such as deliberate dishonesty, manipulation, or betrayal, reveal conscious prioritization of self-gratification over integrity.

Understanding this distinction protects you from false equivalence. Not all mistakes carry the same weight. Evaluating intent allows you to discern whether someone is struggling with growth or repeatedly choosing self-serving behavior. Dating maturity involves recognizing patterns of choice, not just isolated incidents.

Savage takeaway

A mistake made in pain can be repaired. A betrayal chosen for pleasure reveals a deeper truth.

Quiet power mantra

"I look beyond actions to the intention that created them."

VIII. ACT LIKE TIME MATTERS

"Whatsoever thou dost affect, whatsoever thou dost project, so do, and so project all, as one who, for aught thou knowest, may at this very present depart out of this life. And as for death, if there be any gods, it is no grievous thing to leave the society of men. The gods will do thee no hurt, thou mayest be sure. But if it

be so that there be no gods, or that they take no care of the world, why should I desire to live in a world void of gods, and of all divine providence? But gods there be certainly, and they take care for the world; and as for those things which be truly evil, as vice and wickedness, such things they have put in a man's own power, that he might avoid them if he would: and had there been anything besides that had been truly bad and evil, they would have had a care of that also, that a man might have avoided it. But why should that be thought to hurt and prejudice a man's life in this world, which cannot any ways make man himself the better, or the worse in his own person? Neither must we think that the nature of the universe did either through ignorance pass these things, or if not as ignorant of them, yet as unable either to prevent, or better to order and dispose them. It cannot be that she through want either of power or skill, should have committed such a thing, so as to suffer all things both good and bad, equally and promiscuously, to happen unto all both good and bad. As for life therefore, and death, honour and dishonour, labour and pleasure, riches and poverty, all these things happen unto men indeed, both good and bad, equally; but as things which of themselves are neither good nor bad; because of themselves, neither shameful nor praiseworthy."

What Marcus meant (core philosophy)

Marcus urges himself to live and act with the awareness that life may end at any moment. This is not meant to create fear but clarity. When one remembers the finite nature of existence, actions become more intentional and less clouded by trivial concerns.

He reflects on the nature of death and fate, arguing that whether guided by divine providence or by natural order, nothing truly harmful can occur to one's character unless one chooses vice. External circumstances such as wealth, status, pleasure, hardship, or even death itself are morally neutral. They do not define a person's goodness or worth.

The Stoic lesson is that virtue resides entirely within one's own control. Life's events are neither inherently good nor bad; what matters is how one responds to them. Living with this understanding removes fear and restores focus on ethical action.

Dating translation (what this means emotionally/socially)

In dating, many people act as though there is endless time to become honest, to set boundaries, or to pursue what truly matters. They delay decisions, stay in ambiguous situations, or hold back authenticity out of fear.

Marcus invites a different mindset: act as if time is meaningful now. When you recognize that life is finite, you stop:
- tolerating prolonged uncertainty
- investing in connections that erode your peace
- postponing difficult conversations that would bring clarity

He also reframes external outcomes. Success or failure in dating, being chosen or rejected, experiencing pleasure or disappointment, are not moral judgments. They do not define your value or diminish your character. What matters is whether you act with integrity, honesty, and alignment with your principles.

Dating becomes lighter when you stop labeling experiences as inherently good or bad and instead view them as neutral events through which your character is revealed.

Savage takeaway
The only real failure is living as though you have unlimited time to betray yourself.

Quiet power mantra
"I act with urgency, but without fear. My character is my only true measure."

IX. NOTHING LASTS LONG ENOUGH TO WORSHIP IT
"Consider how quickly all things are dissolved and resolved: the bodies and substances themselves, into the matter and substance of the world: and their memories into the general age and time of the world. Consider the nature of all worldly sensible things; of those especially, which either ensnare by pleasure, or for their irksomeness are dreadful, or for their outward lustre and show are in great esteem and request, how vile and contemptible, how base and corruptible, how destitute of all true life and being they are."

What Marcus meant (core philosophy)
Marcus reflects on impermanence. Everything material dissolves: physical bodies return to nature, memories fade into time, and even the most admired or feared things eventually lose their significance.

The Stoic lesson is detachment through perspective. Many things that appear powerful or overwhelming such as pleasure, pain, status, or reputation are temporary and ultimately lacking true substance. Their influence exists only because the mind assigns them exaggerated importance.

By recognizing the fleeting nature of worldly experiences, one frees oneself from excessive attachment. Pleasure loses its power to enslave. Fear loses its ability to dominate. External admiration loses its authority over self-worth. This is not nihilism but liberation. When you understand that external things are transient, you stop confusing temporary sensations with lasting truth.

Dating translation (what this means emotionally/socially)
Dating often amplifies illusion. Chemistry feels permanent. Attraction feels absolute. Rejection feels catastrophic. Social validation feels like proof of worth. Yet most of these experiences change quickly once perspective returns. Marcus encourages stepping back from emotional magnification. Consider:
*   how quickly infatuation fades when reality appears
*   how quickly heartbreak softens with time
*   how little external approval matters once your inner stability strengthens
Many people become trapped by surface qualities: beauty, charm, attention, or social status. These elements appear powerful but are inherently temporary. Dating maturity involves recognizing when you are projecting lasting meaning onto something that is fundamentally fleeting. When you stop worshipping temporary

experiences, you regain freedom to choose what truly aligns with your deeper values.

Savage takeaway
What feels overwhelming today is often irrelevant tomorrow.

Quiet power mantra
"I value what endures, not what dazzles."

X. SEE CLEARLY, FEAR LESS

"It is the part of a man endowed with a good understanding faculty, to consider what they themselves are in very deed, from whose bare conceits and voices, honour and credit do proceed: as also what it is to die, and how if a man shall consider this by itself alone, to die, and separate from it in his mind all those things which with it usually represent themselves unto us, he can conceive of it no otherwise, than as of a work of nature, and he that fears any work of nature, is a very child. Now death, it is not only a work of nature, but also conducing to nature."

What Marcus meant (core philosophy)
Marcus encourages rational examination of two powerful forces that often govern human behavior: the opinions of others and the fear of death.

First, he advises questioning the authority we give to external praise or criticism. Honor and reputation come from the judgments of other people, who themselves are imperfect and often guided by shallow perceptions. Understanding who these people truly are strips external validation of its exaggerated power.

Second, he reframes death as a natural process rather than something inherently frightening. Fear arises when imagination adds layers of meaning beyond what death actually is. When examined simply, death is part of nature's cycle and therefore neither shameful nor harmful.

The Stoic lesson is clarity through direct observation. Many fears dissolve when examined without emotional distortion. Wisdom lies in removing unnecessary interpretation and seeing reality as it is.

Dating translation (what this means emotionally/socially)
In dating, two things often control behavior: fear of judgment and fear of loss. People worry about:
- how they appear
- what others think of their choices
- whether rejection will diminish their value
- how the ending of a connection will affect their identity

Marcus challenges these fears by questioning their foundation. External opinions only hold power when you grant them authority. The people whose approval you fear losing are often navigating their own insecurities and limited perspectives.

Similarly, the end of a relationship is often treated as something catastrophic rather than as a natural transition. When you remove the emotional stories attached to endings, you begin to see them as part of growth rather than failure. Dating becomes calmer when you stop dramatizing both judgment and loss. What remains is clarity about what truly matters: your integrity, your growth, and your alignment with yourself.

Savage takeaway
Fear grows in imagination. It weakens under examination.

Quiet power mantra
"I see things as they are, not as fear describes them."

XI. MASTER YOUR INNER WORLD FIRST
"Consider with thyself how man, and by what part of his, is joined unto God, and how that part of man is affected, when it is said to be diffused. There is nothing more wretched than that soul, which in a kind of circuit compasseth all things, searching (as he saith) even the very depths of the earth; and by all signs and conjectures prying into the very thoughts of other men's souls; and yet of this, is not sensible, that it is sufficient for a man to apply himself wholly, and to confine all his thoughts and cares to the tendance of that spirit which is within him, and truly and really to serve him. His service doth consist in this, that a man keep himself pure from all violent passion and evil affection, from all rashness and vanity, and from all manner of discontent, either in regard of the gods or men. For indeed whatsoever proceeds from the gods, deserves respect for their worth and excellency; and whatsoever proceeds from men, as they are our kinsmen, should by us be entertained, with love, always; sometimes, as proceeding from their ignorance, of that which is truly good and bad, (a blindness no less, than that by which we are not able to discern between white and black:) with a kind of pity and compassion also."

What Marcus meant (core philosophy)
Marcus warns against the tendency to obsess over external matters while neglecting one's own inner governance. He describes the soul that exhausts itself analyzing others, searching for hidden motives, or attempting to understand the vast world, yet fails to care for the most important responsibility: tending to one's own ruling spirit.

The Stoic lesson is clear. True wisdom begins with internal discipline. The connection between human reason and the divine lies within the rational faculty, and its proper function is purity of intention, freedom from destructive passions, and acceptance of reality without resentment.

Marcus emphasizes restraint from violent emotion, impulsive reactions, vanity, and dissatisfaction with either fate or other people. Respect what arises from nature and respond to human shortcomings with compassion rather than hostility, recognizing that ignorance often drives harmful behavior. Peace emerges when attention returns inward and aligns with reason.

Dating translation (what this means emotionally/socially)

In dating, many people spend enormous energy trying to decode others. They analyze:

- texts and tone
- hidden meanings behind actions
- possible intentions or emotional states

This outward focus can become a distraction from self-awareness. While understanding others has value, it becomes exhausting when it replaces responsibility for your own emotional state. Marcus invites a shift. Instead of asking, "What are they thinking?" ask:

- Am I acting in alignment with my values?
- Am I reacting from clarity or from insecurity?
- Am I maintaining emotional integrity regardless of their behavior?

This section also encourages compassion without naivety. Recognizing that many people act from confusion or emotional blindness allows you to respond without bitterness. Dating maturity involves understanding that your greatest responsibility is not to decipher another person's inner world but to govern your own.

Savage takeaway

Obsessing over their thoughts is often a way of avoiding your own clarity.

Quiet power mantra

"I care for my inner state first. Everything else becomes clearer from there."

XII. YOU ONLY EVER HAVE THIS MOMENT

"If thou shouldst live three thousand, or as many as ten thousands of years, yet remember this, that man can part with no life properly, save with that little part of life, which he now lives: and that which he lives, is no other, than that which at every instant he parts with. That then which is longest of duration, and that which is shortest, come both to one effect. For although in regard of that which is already past there may be some inequality, yet that time which is now present and in being, is equal unto all men. And that being it which we part with whensoever we die, it doth manifestly appear, that it can be but a moment of time, that we then part with. For as for that which is either past or to come, a man cannot be said properly to part with it. For how should a man part with that which he hath not? These two things therefore thou must remember. First, that all things in the world from all eternity, by a perpetual revolution of the same times and things ever continued and renewed, are of one kind and nature; so that whether for a hundred or two hundred years only, or for an infinite space of time, a man see those things which are still the same, it can be no matter of great moment. And secondly, that that life which any the longest liver, or the shortest liver parts with, is for length and duration the very same, for that only which is present, is that, which either of them can lose, as being that only which they have; for that which he hath not, no man can truly be said to lose."

What Marcus meant (core philosophy)

Marcus reflects on time and mortality with precise clarity. Whether a person lives a short life or an extraordinarily long one, the truth remains the same: we only ever possess the present moment. The past is already gone, and the future has not yet arrived. Death, therefore, does not take away vast stretches of life but only the present instant we are currently experiencing.

The Stoic lesson is liberation from illusion. Humans often fear losing life as though it were a vast possession, yet what we truly have is always limited to now. Recognizing this equalizes all lives. Length of years becomes less important than the quality of presence within each moment.

Marcus also emphasizes the cyclical nature of existence. Events repeat in different forms across time, and nothing truly new or permanent emerges. This perspective reduces attachment to duration, achievement, or legacy and instead focuses attention on how one lives the present moment.

Dating translation (what this means emotionally/socially)
In dating, people often live outside the present. They dwell on:
- the past, replaying old relationships and missed opportunities
- the future, imagining outcomes, labels, or permanence

Both remove you from what is actually happening now. Marcus reminds us that the only relationship you truly experience is the one unfolding in the present moment. Worrying about how long something will last or grieving what has already ended pulls attention away from the only place where connection exists.

This perspective also softens fear of endings. Whether a relationship lasts months or decades, its value lies in the quality of presence within the moments shared, not in the total duration. Dating becomes more grounded when you release the obsession with permanence and instead focus on alignment in the present.

Savage takeaway
You are not losing a lifetime when something ends. You are only ever releasing the present moment.

Quiet power mantra
"I live fully in the moment I actually have."

XIII. YOUR PERCEPTION WRITES THE STORY
"Remember that all is but opinion and conceit, for those things are plain and apparent, which were spoken unto Monimus the Cynic[30]; and as plain and apparent is the use that may be made of those things, if that which is true and serious in them, be received as well as that which is sweet and pleasing."

What Marcus meant (core philosophy)
Marcus reminds himself that much of human suffering arises not from events themselves but from the opinions and interpretations we attach to them. Reality exists, but meaning is largely constructed through perception. Referencing the

---

[30] Monimus of Syracuse (4th century BC) was a prominent Cynic philosopher and a student of Diogenes of Sinope. He is best known for his radical skepticism regarding human perception and social values, noting that "everything is but opinion" (*tuphos*).

Cynic philosopher Monimus, he emphasizes that understanding this principle reveals a powerful freedom. When we recognize that judgments are mental creations rather than absolute truths, we gain the ability to respond differently.

The Stoic lesson is discernment. Not every thought deserves belief. Not every emotional reaction reflects objective reality. Wisdom lies in separating what is actually happening from the narrative we build around it. Marcus also suggests that philosophy should not remain abstract. The value of insight lies in practical application. Truth must be used, not merely admired.

Dating translation (what this means emotionally/socially)
Dating is one of the clearest arenas where perception shapes experience. Two people can experience the same event and interpret it entirely differently:
- a delayed response becomes rejection
- silence becomes disinterest
- independence becomes emotional distance

Many emotional spirals begin not with facts but with assumptions layered onto incomplete information. This section encourages pausing before attaching meaning. Ask:
- What actually happened?
- What am I assuming?
- Is this interpretation helping or harming my clarity?

Understanding that perception influences emotional reality allows you to choose responses more consciously. It does not eliminate feeling, but it prevents imagination from turning uncertainty into suffering. Dating becomes calmer when you stop treating every interpretation as truth.

Savage takeaway
Most emotional chaos begins with a story you told yourself, not with what actually happened.

Quiet power mantra
"I question my interpretations before I believe them."

XIV. BETRAYAL STARTS WITH SELF-BETRAYAL
"A man's soul doth wrong and disrespect itself first and especially, when as much as in itself lies it becomes an aposteme[31], and as it were an excrescency of the world, for to be grieved and displeased with anything that happens in the world, is direct apostacy from the nature of the universe; part of which, all particular natures of the world, are. Secondly, when she either is averse from any man, or led by contrary desires or affections, tending to his hurt and prejudice; such as are the souls of them that are angry. Thirdly, when she is overcome by any pleasure or pain. Fourthly, when she doth dissemble, and covertly

---

[31] In English, aposteme (also spelled apostume) is an archaic medical term for an abscess or a large swelling filled with purulent matter (pus). It comes from the Greek word ἀπόστημα (*apóstēma*), which literally means a "standing away" or "separation," referring to the way an abscess separates the surrounding tissues.

and falsely either doth or saith anything. Fifthly, when she doth either affect or endeavour anything to no certain end, but rashly and without due ratiocination and consideration, how consequent or inconsequent it is to the common end. For even the least things ought not to be done, without relation unto the end; and the end of the reasonable creatures is, to follow and obey him, who is the reason as it were, and the law of this great city, and ancient commonwealth."

What Marcus meant (core philosophy)

Marcus outlines several ways in which the soul harms itself. The deepest wrongdoing is not external failure but internal misalignment.

First, the soul injures itself when it resists reality, becoming bitter or resentful toward the natural unfolding of events. This is a rejection of the larger order to which we belong. Second, the soul fractures itself through hostility toward others, especially when driven by anger or destructive desire. Third, it loses integrity when governed by excessive pleasure or excessive pain, allowing emotion rather than reason to dictate behavior. Fourth, dishonesty damages the soul, whether through deception toward others or self-deception. Finally, acting without clear purpose weakens the rational nature. Every action should be connected to a meaningful end aligned with reason and shared humanity.

The Stoic lesson is alignment. The soul thrives when it acts with clarity, honesty, and harmony with the greater whole. Disorder begins internally long before it appears externally.

Dating translation (what this means emotionally/socially)

In dating, most emotional damage begins long before conflict appears on the surface. Self-betrayal happens when you:

- resist reality instead of accepting what someone's behavior clearly shows
- hold resentment that turns connection into opposition
- let attraction or fear override your values
- pretend to feel or want something you do not
- continue investing without clear intention or direction

Marcus reminds us that misalignment with ourselves is the root of many relational struggles. When actions contradict inner truth, emotional tension grows. Dating maturity means maintaining internal coherence. You do not allow pleasure to override judgment. You do not let pain turn you into someone you do not respect. You do not act without knowing why you are acting. Clarity of purpose protects emotional stability.

Savage takeaway

The fastest way to lose yourself is to ignore what you already know is true.

Quiet power mantra

"I remain aligned with myself, even when it would be easier not to."

XV. EVERYTHING PASSES. YOUR CHARACTER REMAINS.

"The time of a man's life is as a point; the substance of it ever flowing, the sense obscure; and the whole composition of the body tending to corruption. His soul is restless, fortune uncertain, and fame doubtful; to be brief, as a stream so are all things belonging to the body; as a dream, or as a smoke, so are all that belong unto the soul. Our life is a warfare, and a mere pilgrimage. Fame after life is no better than oblivion. What is it then that will adhere and follow? Only one thing, philosophy. And philosophy doth consist in this, for a man to preserve that spirit which is within him, from all manner of contumelies and injuries, and above all pains or pleasures; never to do anything either rashly, or feignedly, or hypocritically: wholly to depend from himself and his own proper actions: all things that happen unto him to embrace contentedly, as coming from Him from whom he himself also came; and above all things, with all meekness and a calm cheerfulness, to expect death, as being nothing else but the resolution of those elements, of which every creature is composed. And if the elements themselves suffer nothing by this their perpetual conversion of one into another, that dissolution, and alteration, which is so common unto all, why should it be feared by any? Is not this according to nature? But nothing that is according to nature can be evil.

Whilst I was at Carnuntum."

What Marcus meant (core philosophy)

Marcus confronts the fleeting nature of life with striking clarity. Human existence is brief and unstable. The body changes and decays, the mind fluctuates, fortune is unpredictable, and fame is unreliable. Everything associated with external life is transient, like a dream or a passing current. Against this impermanence, Marcus identifies one enduring anchor: philosophy, meaning the disciplined care of one's inner spirit.

The Stoic ideal is to preserve the integrity of the ruling self. Do not allow pleasure, pain, praise, or insult to corrupt inner stability. Act without pretense or hypocrisy. Depend on your own actions rather than external validation. Accept events as part of nature's order and face death without fear, recognizing it as a natural transformation rather than a catastrophe. Nothing that follows nature can be truly harmful. Peace comes from alignment with this understanding.

Dating translation (what this means emotionally/socially)

Dating often magnifies things that feel permanent but are not. Attraction fades. Emotional intensity shifts. Status and external approval fluctuate. Even memories soften over time. Much of what feels overwhelming in the moment becomes distant once perspective expands.

Marcus' reminder is grounding: the only thing that truly follows you through every relationship is your character. This changes how you approach connection. Instead of asking:

- Will this last forever?
- Will they remember me?
- How do others perceive this relationship?

You begin asking:

- Am I acting with integrity?

- Am I staying aligned with myself?
- Am I responding with calm clarity rather than emotional chaos?

When you anchor yourself internally, relationships become experiences rather than identities. Endings lose their power to define you because your stability does not depend on permanence. Dating maturity involves accepting that all connections exist within time, but your character remains the constant through them all.

Savage takeaway
Nothing external lasts long enough to build your identity on it.

Quiet power mantra
"I let everything pass except my integrity."

THE THIRD BOOK
Mind Your Own Damn Mind

I. DO NOT WAIT UNTIL YOU KNOW BETTER

"A man must not only consider how daily his life wasteth and decreaseth, but this also, that if he live long, he cannot be certain, whether his understanding shall continue so able and sufficient, for either discreet consideration, in matter of businesses; or for contemplation: it being the thing, whereon true knowledge of things both divine and human, doth depend. For if once he shall begin to dote, his respiration, nutrition, his imaginative, and appetitive, and other natural faculties, may still continue the same: he shall find no want of them. But how to make that right use of himself that he should, how to observe exactly in all things that which is right and just, how to redress and rectify all wrong, or sudden apprehensions and imaginations, and even of this particular, whether he should live any longer or no, to consider duly; for all such things, wherein the best strength and vigour of the mind is most requisite; his power and ability will be past and gone. Thou must hasten therefore; not only because thou art every day nearer unto death than other, but also because that intellective faculty in thee, whereby thou art enabled to know the true nature of things, and to order all thy actions by that knowledge, doth daily waste and decay: or, may fail thee before thou die."

What Marcus meant (core philosophy)

Marcus deepens the urgency introduced in earlier passages. He reminds himself that life does not only diminish through time but also through the gradual weakening of the intellect. Even if the body continues to function, the clarity of judgment, reasoning, and discernment that allow a person to live wisely may fade before death arrives.

The Stoic lesson is not merely awareness of mortality but awareness of diminishing capacity. The ability to perceive truth, make just decisions, and correct oneself depends on mental clarity. Waiting indefinitely to pursue wisdom risks losing the very faculties required to attain it. Marcus urges immediate action. Growth cannot be postponed until a more convenient moment. One must begin now while the mind remains capable of deep reflection and disciplined self-governance.

Dating translation (what this means emotionally/socially)

In dating, many people believe they will change later. Later they will:
- set boundaries
- stop repeating unhealthy patterns
- communicate honestly
- choose alignment over comfort

Marcus challenges this illusion. Emotional clarity is not guaranteed to strengthen automatically with time. Patterns reinforce themselves when left unexamined. The longer you delay self-awareness, the more habitual your reactions become.

This section encourages using your current insight while it is accessible. If you already recognize what is misaligned, waiting only deepens the gap between knowledge and action. Dating maturity involves honoring the intelligence you have now rather than assuming future clarity will rescue you. Time does not automatically create wisdom. Intentional action does.

Savage takeaway
Knowing better and doing nothing is simply slow self-abandonment.

Quiet power mantra
"I act on my clarity while I still have it."

II. BEAUTY LIVES IN IMPERFECTION

"This also thou must observe, that whatsoever it is that naturally doth happen to things natural, hath somewhat in itself that is pleasing and delightful: as a great loaf when it is baked, some parts of it cleave as it were, and part asunder, and make the crust of it rugged and unequal, and yet those parts of it, though in some sort it be against the art and intention of baking itself, that they are thus cleft and parted, which should have been and were first made all even and uniform, they become it well nevertheless, and have a certain peculiar property, to stir the appetite. So figs are accounted fairest and ripest then, when they begin to shrink, and wither as it were. So ripe olives, when they are next to putrefaction, then are they in their proper beauty. The hanging down of grapes—the brow of a lion, the froth of a foaming wild boar, and many other like things, though by themselves considered, they are far from any beauty, yet because they happen naturally, they both are comely, and delightful; so that if a man shall with a profound mind and apprehension, consider all things in the world, even among all those things which are but mere accessories and natural appendices as it were, there will scarce appear anything unto him, wherein he will not find matter of pleasure and delight. So will he behold with as much pleasure the true rictus[32] of wild beasts, as those which by skilful painters and other artificers are imitated. So will he be able to perceive the proper ripeness and beauty of old age, whether in man or woman: and whatsoever else it is that is beautiful and alluring in whatsoever is, with chaste and continent eyes he will soon find out and discern. Those and many other things will he discern, not credible unto every one, but unto them only who are truly and familiarly acquainted, both with nature itself, and all natural things."

What Marcus meant (core philosophy)
Marcus reflects on the quiet beauty present in natural processes, even in moments that appear flawed, broken, or imperfect. A loaf of bread splitting as it bakes, fruit wrinkling at ripeness, or the marks of age and decay all carry their own form of harmony because they arise from nature's unfolding.

The Stoic lesson is perception guided by understanding. When one observes deeply, imperfections cease to feel like errors and instead reveal themselves as expressions of natural order. Beauty is not limited to polished perfection; it exists within change, aging, and transformation. Marcus suggests that wisdom reshapes how we see the world. Those who understand nature intimately begin to find meaning and delight in what others overlook or reject. The capacity to appreciate reality as it is, rather than as we wish it to be, brings a profound sense of peace.

---

[32] In English, a rictus refers to a fixed, grimacing, or unnatural opening of the mouth.

Dating translation (what this means emotionally/socially)

In dating, people often chase idealized versions of beauty, connection, or emotional experience. They look for:

- flawless chemistry
- perfect communication
- effortless compatibility
- unchanging attraction

Marcus invites a different perspective. Real connection contains irregularities. Awkward moments, vulnerability, emotional complexity, and the visible signs of growth or aging are not defects; they are evidence of authenticity.

When you understand this, attraction becomes deeper and more grounded. Instead of chasing polished perfection, you begin to appreciate what feels real. This also applies to self-perception. Many people struggle because they measure themselves against artificial standards rather than recognizing the quiet power of natural presence. Dating maturity means seeing beauty in truth rather than illusion. Imperfection stops feeling like a problem and begins to feel like evidence of life.

Savage takeaway

Perfection is sterile. Real beauty always carries texture.

Quiet power mantra

"I recognize the beauty that comes from what is real."

III. EVERYONE EXITS THE STORY

"Hippocrates having cured many sicknesses, fell sick himself and died. The Chaldeans and Astrologians having foretold the deaths of divers, were afterwards themselves surprised by the fates. Alexander and Pompeius, and Caius Cæsar, having destroyed so many towns, and cut off in the field so many thousands both of horse and foot, yet they themselves at last were fain to part with their own lives. Heraclitus having written so many natural tracts concerning the last and general conflagration of the world, died afterwards all filled with water within, and all bedaubed with dirt and dung without. Lice killed Democritus; and Socrates, another sort of vermin, wicked ungodly men. How then stands the case? Thou hast taken ship, thou hast sailed, thou art come to land, go out, if to another life, there also shalt thou find gods, who are everywhere. If all life and sense shall cease, then shalt thou cease also to be subject to either pains or pleasures; and to serve and tend this vile cottage; so much the viler, by how much that which ministers unto it doth excel; the one being a rational substance, and a spirit, the other nothing but earth and blood."

What Marcus meant (core philosophy)

Marcus lists powerful figures, brilliant thinkers, and accomplished individuals, all of whom ultimately met the same end: death. Achievement, intelligence, influence, or mastery over others does not grant exemption from nature's law.

The Stoic lesson is humility before impermanence. No matter how extraordinary a person may appear, their fate remains shared with all humanity. Death is neither punishment nor injustice but a natural transition.

Marcus reframes mortality not as tragedy but as completion. Life is a journey, like a voyage ending at shore. Whether death leads to continued existence under divine order or to peaceful cessation of sensation, neither outcome should provoke fear. Both remove the burdens of pain, pleasure, and the fragile physical body. This perspective frees the mind from excessive attachment to status, achievement, or physical existence itself.

Dating translation (what this means emotionally/socially)
In dating, people often place certain individuals on pedestals, imagining them as uniquely powerful, irreplaceable, or beyond ordinary limitations. Marcus dissolves this illusion.

Everyone, regardless of charisma, success, beauty, or influence, remains human and temporary. Recognizing this prevents emotional imbalance. You stop elevating others to mythic status or diminishing yourself in comparison. This perspective also softens the fear of endings. Relationships begin and end within the larger flow of life. No connection is exempt from change, and no person holds permanent power over your existence.

Dating becomes more grounded when you remember that no one is larger than the natural cycle of life itself. Attraction remains meaningful, but reverence becomes balanced with realism.

Savage takeaway
No one is too powerful, too beautiful, or too important to be human.

Quiet power mantra
"I meet people as equals within the same fleeting story."

IV. RETURN YOUR ATTENTION TO YOURSELF
"Spend not the remnant of thy days in thoughts and fancies concerning other men, when it is not in relation to some common good, when by it thou art hindered from some other better work. That is, spend not thy time in thinking, what such a man doth, and to what end: what he saith, and what he thinks, and what he is about, and such other things or curiosities, which make a man to rove and wander from the care and observation of that part of himself, which is rational, and overruling. See therefore in the whole series and connection of thy thoughts, that thou be careful to prevent whatsoever is idle and impertinent: but especially, whatsoever is curious and malicious: and thou must use thyself to think only of such things, of which if a man upon a sudden should ask thee, what it is that thou art now thinking, thou mayest answer This, and That, freely and boldly, that so by thy thoughts it may presently appear that in all thee is sincere, and peaceable; as becometh one that is made for society, and regards not pleasures, nor gives way to any voluptuous imaginations at all: free from all contentiousness, envy, and suspicion, and from whatsoever else thou wouldest blush to confess thy thoughts were set upon. He that is such, is he surely that doth not put off to lay hold on that which is best indeed, a very priest and minister of the gods, well acquainted and in good correspondence with him especially that is seated and placed within himself, as in a temple and sacrary: to whom also he keeps and preserves himself unspotted by pleasure, undaunted by pain; free from any manner of wrong, or contumely, by himself offered unto himself: not capable of any evil from others: a wrestler of the best sort, and for the highest prize, that he

may not be cast down by any passion or affection of his own; deeply dyed and drenched in righteousness, embracing and accepting with his whole heart whatsoever either happeneth or is allotted unto him. One who not often, nor without some great necessity tending to some public good, mindeth what any other, either speaks, or doth, or purposeth: for those things only that are in his own power, or that are truly his own, are the objects of his employments, and his thoughts are ever taken up with those things, which of the whole universe are by the fates or Providence destinated and appropriated unto himself. Those things that are his own, and in his own power, he himself takes order, for that they be good: and as for those that happen unto him, he believes them to be so. For that lot and portion which is assigned to every one, as it is unavoidable and necessary, so is it always profitable. He remembers besides that whatsoever partakes of reason, is akin unto him, and that to care for all men generally, is agreeing to the nature of a man: but as for honour and praise, that they ought not generally to be admitted and accepted of from all, but from such only, who live according to nature. As for them that do not, what manner of men they be at home, or abroad; day or night, how conditioned themselves with what manner of conditions, or with men of what conditions they moil and pass away the time together, he knoweth, and remembers right well, he therefore regards not such praise and approbation, as proceeding from them, who cannot like and approve themselves."

What Marcus meant (core philosophy)

Marcus delivers one of his strongest reminders about mental discipline. He warns against wasting thought on the private lives, motives, or imagined intentions of others when such thinking serves no meaningful purpose. Curiosity about others becomes harmful when it distracts from self-governance and purposeful action.

The Stoic lesson is clarity of focus. The rational mind should be occupied with what is within one's control: personal character, ethical action, and alignment with reason. Idle speculation, gossip, suspicion, and envy weaken the inner spirit and scatter attention away from what truly matters.

Marcus emphasizes transparency with oneself. Thoughts should be clean enough that one could openly acknowledge them without shame. The ideal state is sincerity, calmness, and freedom from hidden agendas or restless comparison.

He describes a person whose inner life becomes sacred ground, protected from excess pleasure, reactive emotion, and external distraction. Such a person accepts what fate delivers, acts justly, and values approval only from those who live according to virtue.

Dating translation (what this means emotionally/socially)

This passage speaks directly to one of the most exhausting patterns in modern dating: mental obsession with other people. Overthinking often looks like:

- analyzing what someone meant
- imagining hidden intentions
- replaying conversations repeatedly
- comparing yourself to others
- wondering what they think or feel without direct evidence

Marcus calls this wandering of the mind. Every moment spent decoding someone else beyond what is necessary pulls attention away from your own clarity. Instead of asking, "What are they doing, thinking, or feeling?" the focus returns to:

- What am I choosing?
- What aligns with my values?
- What action is mine to take?

He also reframes validation. Praise or approval from people who lack self-awareness or integrity carries little value. Emotional stability grows when you stop measuring yourself through external perception and instead evaluate yourself through alignment with your principles. Dating becomes dramatically calmer when you withdraw your mental energy from speculation and reinvest it into self-command.

Savage takeaway
Overthinking someone else is often avoidance disguised as insight.

Quiet power mantra
"My attention belongs to what I control: my thoughts, my actions, my alignment."

V. LIVE SO CLEANLY YOU NEED NO WITNESSES
"Do nothing against thy will, nor contrary to the community, nor without due examination, nor with reluctancy. Affect not to set out thy thoughts with curious neat language. Be neither a great talker, nor a great undertaker. Moreover, let thy God that is in thee to rule over thee, find by thee, that he hath to do with a man; an aged man; a sociable man; a Roman; a prince; one that hath ordered his life, as one that expecteth, as it were, nothing but the sound of the trumpet, sounding a retreat to depart out of this life with all expedition. One who for his word or actions neither needs an oath, nor any man to be a witness."

What Marcus meant (core philosophy)
Marcus is describing integrity as inner alignment rather than outward performance. He advises acting only in ways that:

- do not violate your own conscience
- serve the greater community
- are examined carefully before action
- arise without resentment or reluctance

This is a call to simplicity and authenticity. Speech should not be overly polished or performative. Excessive talking and grand undertakings driven by ego are distractions from real virtue. The "God within" refers to the rational ruling faculty. Marcus urges us to live in such a way that this inner guide recognizes dignity, maturity, and readiness. The ideal person carries themselves as if prepared at any moment to leave life without unfinished moral business. True character is so consistent that it does not require proof, witnesses, or elaborate justification. Integrity speaks through action alone.

Dating translation (what this means emotionally/socially)
This passage is essentially the anti-performative dating manual.

47

Marcus is saying: Stop performing versions of yourself designed to impress or secure approval. In modern dating terms:

- Do not say yes when you mean no.
- Do not pretend enthusiasm you don't feel.
- Do not mold yourself into someone else's expectations.
- Do not over-explain or over-justify your character.

He also warns against two common traps:

The Over-Talker

Explaining yourself endlessly, over-sharing early, or trying to persuade someone to understand you instead of simply being consistent.

The Over-Undertaker

Trying to carry the relationship, fix the dynamic, or force momentum through effort alone.

Healthy dating comes from alignment between inner truth and outward behavior. When you live congruently, you do not need to convince anyone of your value. People experience it directly. The idea of being "ready to depart at any moment" translates emotionally into living without clinging or desperation. You show up fully, but you are not dependent on outcomes.

Savage takeaway

If you need to constantly explain your character, your actions probably aren't matching your words.

Quiet power mantra

"I act in alignment with myself. Nothing forced, nothing fake, nothing needing proof."

VI. STAND STRAIGHT BY THINE OWN NATURE

"To be cheerful, and to stand in no need, either of other men's help or attendance, or of that rest and tranquillity, which thou must be beholding to others for. Rather like one that is straight of himself, or hath ever been straight, than one that hath been rectified."

What Marcus meant (core philosophy)

Marcus is describing self-sufficiency of character. To be cheerful is not to deny hardship, but to remain inwardly steady regardless of circumstance. He speaks of a state where a person does not rely upon others to provide their inner peace, stability, or moral alignment. He contrasts two kinds of people:

- One who stands upright by their own nature.
- One who must constantly be corrected, repaired, or supported by external forces to remain upright.

The goal is not isolation or pride, but internal steadiness. True tranquillity should arise from within, not from the approval, reassurance, or constant assistance of others. A person who governs themselves well becomes naturally cheerful because they are not perpetually thrown off balance by external dependency.

Dating translation (what this means emotionally/socially)
This is Marcus describing emotional self-regulation before modern psychology gave it a name.

He is not saying "never need anyone."
He is saying: Do not make another person responsible for stabilizing your inner world.

In dating, this looks like:
- Not needing constant reassurance to feel secure.
- Not outsourcing your mood to someone else's behavior.
- Not expecting a partner to fix wounds you refuse to tend yourself.

The difference between attraction and emotional burden often lies here. Someone who stands straight internally:
- brings warmth without leaning excessively
- chooses connection rather than clinging to it
- remains cheerful because their identity is not dependent on romantic validation

Marcus is also quietly warning against relationships built on rescue dynamics. If someone must continually correct or carry you emotionally, resentment eventually replaces affection.

Savage takeaway
Confidence is not loud independence. It is emotional stability that does not require constant maintenance by others.

Quiet power mantra
"I stand upright from within. My peace is self-rooted."

VII. CHOOSE THE HIGHER STANDARD AND DO NOT NEGOTIATE WITH LESS
"If thou shalt find anything in this mortal life better than righteousness, than truth, temperance, fortitude, and in general better than a mind contented both with those things which according to right and reason she doth, and in those, which without her will and knowledge happen unto thee by the providence; if I say, thou canst find out anything better than this, apply thyself unto it with thy whole heart, and that which is best wheresoever thou dost find it, enjoy freely. But if nothing thou shalt find worthy to be preferred to that spirit which is within thee; if nothing better than to subject unto thee thine own lusts and desires, and not to give way to any fancies or imaginations before thou hast duly considered of them, nothing better than to withdraw thyself (to use Socrates his words) from all sensuality, and submit thyself unto the gods, and to have care of all men in general: if thou shalt find that all other things in comparison of this, are but vile, and of little moment; then give not way to any other thing, which being once though but affected and inclined unto, it will no more be in thy power without all distraction as thou oughtest to prefer and to pursue after that good, which is thine own and thy proper good. For it is not lawful, that anything that is

of another and inferior kind and nature, be it what it will, as either popular applause, or honour, or riches, or pleasures; should be suffered to confront and contest as it were, with that which is rational, and operatively good. For all these things, if once though but for a while, they begin to please, they presently prevail, and pervert a man's mind, or turn a man from the right way. Do thou therefore I say absolutely and freely make choice of that which is best, and stick unto it. Now, that they say is best, which is most profitable. If they mean profitable to man as he is a rational man, stand thou to it, and maintain it; but if they mean profitable, as he is a creature, only reject it; and from this thy tenet and conclusion keep off carefully all plausible shows and colours of external appearance, that thou mayest be able to discern things rightly."

What Marcus meant (core philosophy)

Marcus is drawing a clear philosophical hierarchy of value. He asks: if you can find anything better than virtue, self-governance, reason, and alignment with truth, then pursue it completely. But if nothing surpasses these qualities, then they must become your unwavering anchor. The Stoic position is simple but demanding:

- The highest good is the rational soul governed by virtue.
- External rewards, even appealing ones, are lower goods.
- The danger is not merely choosing lesser things, but allowing them to compete with what is highest.

Marcus warns that once external pleasures begin to charm the mind, they subtly redirect one's priorities. Applause, wealth, sensuality, status. None are evil by nature, but all become corrupting when they are allowed to rival inner integrity. True discipline is not rejecting pleasure blindly. It is refusing to negotiate away your highest self for something temporarily attractive.

Dating translation (what this means emotionally/socially)

This is the dating equivalent of refusing to lower your internal standard just because something feels good in the moment.

Marcus is essentially saying: Once you compromise your core values for attraction, validation, chemistry, or attention, your clarity disappears. Examples in modern dating:

- Ignoring red flags because the chemistry is strong.
- Accepting crumbs because the attention feels flattering.
- Choosing emotional chaos over calm because chaos feels exciting.
- Allowing someone's potential to outweigh their actual behavior.

The rational self knows what is aligned. But external pleasure can seduce you into abandoning it. Marcus is urging you to recognize the difference between:

- What feeds your highest self.
- What simply stimulates your nervous system.

When you prioritize the latter, you begin drifting away from yourself.

Savage takeaway

If it makes you abandon your standards, it was never an upgrade.

Quiet power mantra

"I choose what strengthens my soul, not what temporarily dazzles it."

VIII. NEVER TRADE YOUR DIGNITY FOR PERCEIVED GAIN

"Never esteem of anything as profitable, which shall ever constrain thee either to break thy faith, or to lose thy modesty; to hate any man, to suspect, to curse, to dissemble, to lust after anything, that requireth the secret of walls or veils. But he that preferreth before all things his rational part and spirit, and the sacred mysteries of virtue which issueth from it, he shall never lament and exclaim, never sigh; he shall never want either solitude or company: and which is chiefest of all, he shall live without either desire or fear. And as for life, whether for a long or short time he shall enjoy his soul thus compassed about with a body, he is altogether indifferent. For if even now he were to depart, he is as ready for it, as for any other action, which may be performed with modesty and decency. For all his life long, this is his only care, that his mind may always be occupied in such intentions and objects, as are proper to a rational sociable creature."

What Marcus meant (core philosophy)

Marcus draws a firm boundary around what should never be considered "profitable."

If something requires you to abandon integrity, modesty, honesty, or goodwill toward others, then by definition it is not beneficial, regardless of how attractive it appears. True profit is not external success but internal alignment.

The Stoic ideal is a person governed by reason and virtue. Such a person does not depend on circumstances for peace. They do not cling to solitude or fear company, nor do they chase or flee life itself. They live in a state of readiness because their conscience is clear and their priorities are aligned with their nature as rational and social beings. Freedom comes not from controlling the world, but from refusing to compromise one's inner principles.

Dating translation (what this means emotionally/socially)

Marcus is essentially saying: If a relationship makes you smaller, more secretive, more anxious, or less aligned with yourself, it is not a gain. Modern examples:

- Staying with someone who requires you to hide parts of your life or identity.
- Breaking promises to yourself to maintain someone else's approval.
- Becoming suspicious, jealous, or manipulative because the dynamic is unstable.
- Accepting situations that thrive only in secrecy, ambiguity, or emotional shadows.

A healthy connection does not require you to sacrifice your integrity to maintain attraction. Marcus also touches on emotional independence. When you are aligned with yourself:

- You are not desperate for attention.
- You are not terrified of being alone.
- You are not clinging to outcomes.

You become calm because you are not bargaining with your own values.

Savage takeaway
If you have to betray yourself to keep it, it was never a win.

Quiet power mantra
"My integrity is non-negotiable. Nothing worth having requires me to abandon myself."

IX. CLEAN INNER HOUSE, EXIT WITHOUT REGRET

"In the mind that is once truly disciplined and purged, thou canst not find anything, either foul or impure, or as it were festered: nothing that is either servile, or affected: no partial tie; no malicious averseness; nothing obnoxious; nothing concealed. The life of such an one, death can never surprise as imperfect; as of an actor, that should die before he had ended, or the play itself were at an end, a man might speak."

What Marcus meant (core philosophy)
Marcus describes the condition of a disciplined mind. A purified mind is not perfect in the moralistic sense. It is clear. Nothing hidden, festering, or corrupting beneath the surface. No servility, meaning no dependence on external approval. No affectation, meaning no false persona. No secret grudges or concealed motives.

Such a person lives transparently with themselves. Because of this clarity, death cannot catch them "unfinished." Their life does not feel incomplete, like a play cut off before the final act. They are not waiting for external resolution, validation, or future perfection to feel whole. Completion is an inner state, not a timeline. The Stoic goal is not control over when life ends, but readiness at any moment because one has lived authentically and with integrity.

Dating translation (what this means emotionally/socially)
Marcus is describing emotional closure as a lifestyle, not an event. In dating, many people live in unfinished emotional states:

- unresolved resentment
- hidden agendas
- pretending to be someone else to maintain attraction
- lingering attachment to past wounds or unfinished stories

A disciplined inner life means:

- no secret self-betrayals
- no pretending to be "cool" when you are hurting
- no staying in dynamics that make you feel smaller or dishonest

When you are internally clean, relationships become lighter because you are not carrying hidden emotional debris into them. You stop waiting for someone else to give you closure or completeness. And ironically, this is what makes you emotionally magnetic. There is nothing sticky, desperate, or unfinished in your energy.

Savage takeaway
Closure is not something you get from them. It is something you create by refusing to live half-truths.

Quiet power mantra
"I live cleanly within myself. Nothing in me waits unfinished."

X. MASTER YOUR MIND, MINIMIZE THE NOISE

"Use thine opinative faculty with all honour and respect, for in her indeed is all: that thy opinion do not beget in thy understanding anything contrary to either nature, or the proper constitution of a rational creature. The end and object of a rational constitution is, to do nothing rashly, to be kindly affected towards men, and in all things willingly to submit unto the gods. Casting therefore all other things aside, keep thyself to these few, and remember withal that no man properly can be said to live more than that which is now present, which is but a moment of time. Whatsoever is besides either is already past, or uncertain. The time therefore that any man doth live, is but a little, and the place where he liveth, is but a very little corner of the earth, and the greatest fame that can remain of a man after his death, even that is but little, and that too, such as it is whilst it is, is by the succession of silly mortal men preserved, who likewise shall shortly die, and even whiles they live know not what in very deed they themselves are: and much less can know one, who long before is dead and gone."

What Marcus meant (core philosophy)
Marcus is placing sacred responsibility on the "opinative faculty," the mind's ability to judge, interpret, and assign meaning. Everything depends on how you interpret reality. The Stoic principle here is radical: events themselves are neutral. What disturbs us is the opinion we form about them. Therefore:

- Guard your interpretations carefully.
- Do nothing rashly.
- Maintain goodwill toward others.
- Accept what unfolds beyond your control.

He also collapses the illusion of permanence. Life is brief. Fame is fragile. Reputation fades quickly. Even those who remember you barely understand themselves. What remains meaningful is not external legacy, but how you use your rational mind in the present moment.

Dating translation (what this means emotionally/socially)
Marcus is basically telling you: Stop assigning dramatic meaning to temporary situations. Dating often becomes exhausting because we over-interpret:

- A delayed text becomes rejection.
- Ambiguity becomes betrayal.
- Silence becomes personal failure.

Your interpretation creates emotional turbulence far more than the event itself. This section is also quietly savage about fame and perception. The opinions of others, their approval, their judgment, their memory of you. None of it lasts. So why distort yourself trying to control how someone perceives you? In relationships, emotional peace comes from:

- responding thoughtfully instead of reacting impulsively
- assuming neutrality instead of worst-case narratives
- recognizing that most social "stakes" are temporary illusions

Your power lies in choosing interpretations that align with reason and self-respect.

Savage takeaway

Most of your suffering is not caused by what happened. It is caused by the story you told yourself about it.

Quiet power mantra

"I govern my interpretations. The present moment is enough."

XI. SEE THINGS CLEARLY, STRIP THEM OF ILLUSION

"To these ever-present helps and mementoes, let one more be added, ever to make a particular description and delineation as it were of every object that presents itself to thy mind, that thou mayest wholly and throughly contemplate it, in its own proper nature, bare and naked; wholly, and severally; divided into its several parts and quarters: and then by thyself in thy mind, to call both it, and those things of which it doth consist, and in which it shall be resolved, by their own proper true names, and appellations. For there is nothing so effectual to beget true magnanimity, as to be able truly and methodically to examine and consider all things that happen in this life, and so to penetrate into their natures, that at the same time, this also may concur in our apprehensions: what is the true use of it? and what is the true nature of this universe, to which it is useful? how much in regard of the universe may it be esteemed? how much in regard of man, a citizen of the supreme city, of which all other cities in the world are as it were but houses and families?"

What Marcus meant (core philosophy)

Marcus teaches a mental discipline of precise observation. He advises breaking every experience down into its essential components. See it "bare and naked," without exaggeration, projection, or emotional distortion. Name things accurately. Understand what they are made of, what purpose they serve, and how they fit into the larger structure of existence. This is not cold detachment. It is clarity. Magnanimity, or greatness of spirit, comes from seeing reality as it truly is rather than as imagination or desire paints it. When you analyze events in their true proportions:

- Nothing appears overwhelmingly powerful.
- Nothing feels falsely catastrophic.
- Everything returns to its rightful scale.

By understanding where something belongs in the greater order of life, you reduce emotional distortion and gain freedom from illusion.

Dating translation (what this means emotionally/socially)

Marcus is essentially telling you: Stop romanticizing what does not deserve mythology. In dating, many problems arise from inflated perception:

- A charming date becomes "the one."
- Mixed signals become a mysterious love story.
- Breadcrumbing becomes destiny.
- Basic attraction becomes cosmic meaning.

Stoic clarity means stripping the situation down: What actually happened? What did they actually do? What is the practical reality of their behavior? When you see clearly:

- Red flags stop looking like puzzles.
- Ambiguity stops looking like depth.
- Inconsistency stops looking like chemistry.

This also works in reverse. You avoid over-demonizing situations too. Not every disappointment is a tragedy. Sometimes it is simply two people not aligned. Clarity removes both fantasy and unnecessary suffering.

Savage takeaway
Call things by their real names. Illusion loses power the moment it is described accurately.

Quiet power mantra
"I see clearly. I name reality as it is, not as I wish it to be."

XII. PAUSE, IDENTIFY, RESPOND WITH THE RIGHT VIRTUE

"What is this, that now my fancy is set upon? of what things doth it consist? how long can it last? which of all the virtues is the proper virtue for this present use? as whether meekness, fortitude, truth, faith, sincerity, contentation[33], or any of the rest? Of everything therefore thou must use thyself to say, This immediately comes from God, this by that fatal connection, and concatenation of things, or (which almost comes to one) by some coincidental casualty. And as for this, it proceeds from my neighbour, my kinsman, my fellow: through his ignorance indeed, because he knows not what is truly natural unto him: but I know it, and therefore carry myself towards him according to the natural law of fellowship; that is kindly, and justly. As for those things that of themselves are altogether indifferent, as in my best judgment I conceive everything to deserve more or less, so I carry myself towards it."

What Marcus meant (core philosophy)
Marcus is teaching deliberate awareness before reaction. Instead of being carried away by impulse, he recommends a disciplined internal dialogue:

- What is this thing I am experiencing?
- What is it made of?
- How long will it last?
- Which virtue is required here?

He reframes events through three lenses:

1. Everything ultimately arises from the larger order of existence.
2. Other people act from ignorance rather than inherent malice.
3. Most external things are neutral. Their meaning depends on how we relate to them.

The aim is to respond consciously rather than emotionally. Each moment becomes an opportunity to practice a specific virtue suited to the situation. Stoicism is not suppression of emotion. It is intelligent selection of response.

---

[33] In English, contentation is an archaic term for contentment, satisfaction, or the act of being satisfied.

Dating translation (what this means emotionally/socially)

Marcus is basically giving you a relationship superpower: slow down before assigning meaning. Instead of reacting immediately:

- What exactly just happened?
- Is this permanent or temporary?
- Which version of myself do I want to bring here?

Examples:

They cancelled a date. Instead of spiraling:

- Is this a pattern or a single event?
- Does this call for patience, boundaries, or detachment?

Someone says something triggering. Instead of escalating:

- Do I respond with truth?
- With calm?
- With firm clarity?

Marcus also reframes how we view others' behavior. Most people are not villains. They are simply unaware, immature, or acting from their own confusion. That does not mean you tolerate bad treatment. It means you respond without unnecessary emotional poisoning. You choose your virtue. You do not let circumstances choose it for you.

Savage takeaway

Your power is not controlling what happens. It is choosing who you become in response.

Quiet power mantra

"I pause. I see clearly. I answer with the right virtue."

XIII. FOCUS ONLY ON WHAT IS RIGHT NOW

"If thou shalt intend that which is present, following the rule of right and reason carefully, solidly, meekly, and shalt not intermix any other businesses, but shall study this only to preserve thy spirit unpolluted, and pure, and shall cleave unto him without either hope or fear of anything, in all things that thou shalt either do or speak, contenting thyself with heroical truth, thou shalt live happily; and from this, there is no man that can hinder thee."

What Marcus meant (core philosophy)

Marcus returns to one of the central pillars of Stoicism: presence governed by reason. He argues that happiness is not achieved through grand accomplishments or external outcomes, but through disciplined attention to the present moment guided by virtue. His instructions are precise:

- Do what is before you according to reason.
- Act with steadiness and gentleness.
- Avoid mental fragmentation by mixing in unnecessary concerns.
- Preserve inner purity by refusing to contaminate your spirit with fear or excessive hope.

Hope and fear are paired intentionally. Both pull the mind away from the present into imagined futures. The Stoic ideal is a person fully rooted in the present action, aligned with truth, and unconcerned with outcomes beyond their control. Such a person cannot be prevented from living well, because their happiness does not depend on external circumstances.

Dating translation (what this means emotionally/socially)
Marcus is basically saying: Stop trying to control the entire relationship timeline. Just show up well in the moment you are actually in. Dating becomes exhausting when people:
- obsess over future outcomes
- analyze where things are going instead of experiencing where they are
- act from fear of loss or hope for validation rather than authenticity

Presence in dating looks like:
- responding honestly instead of strategically
- engaging without trying to manipulate the outcome
- staying aligned with your character regardless of whether the connection succeeds

When you act from hope or fear, you start performing.
When you act from clarity and truth, you remain grounded.

Marcus is also quietly radical here: no one can stop you from living with integrity. Not rejection, not ghosting, not misunderstanding. Your power lies entirely within how you choose to show up.

Savage takeaway
The only thing you control is how you behave right now. That is enough.

Quiet power mantra
"I act with truth in this moment. Nothing else is required."

XIV. KEEP YOUR INNER PRINCIPLES READY AT ALL TIMES
"As physicians and chirurgeons have always their instruments ready at hand for all sudden cures; so have thou always thy dogmata in a readiness for the knowledge of things, both divine and human: and whatsoever thou dost, even in the smallest things that thou dost, thou must ever remember that mutual relation, and connection that is between these two things divine, and things human. For without relation unto God, thou shalt never speed in any worldly actions; nor on the other side in any divine, without some respect had to things human."

What Marcus meant (core philosophy)
Marcus compares philosophy to a physician's tools. Just as a healer keeps instruments ready for immediate use, a disciplined person keeps guiding principles prepared for any situation. These "dogmata" are not rigid rules but deeply internalized truths about how to live:
- understanding the nature of reality
- recognizing one's place within a larger order
- balancing divine perspective with practical human responsibility

He emphasizes the unity between what is spiritual and what is practical. One cannot succeed fully in worldly action without alignment with higher principles, and one cannot pursue higher ideals without engagement in ordinary human life. Wisdom is not theoretical. It must be immediately accessible and applicable.

Dating translation (what this means emotionally/socially)

Marcus is basically saying: Do not wait until chaos hits to decide who you are. Many dating mistakes happen because people improvise their values in the moment instead of living from established principles. Examples:

- Saying yes when you know you mean no because you haven't pre-decided your boundaries.
- Reacting emotionally because you haven't practiced emotional regulation.
- Losing clarity under pressure because your standards were never internalized.

Having your "tools ready" means:

- knowing your non-negotiables
- understanding your emotional patterns
- having pre-set principles for communication, boundaries, and self-respect

Marcus also reminds us that relationships exist at the intersection of the spiritual and the practical. You cannot be spiritually evolved while behaving poorly in everyday interactions. And you cannot build meaningful relationships if you ignore deeper values. Alignment means both.

Savage takeaway

If you only remember your standards after you are hurt, you waited too long.

Quiet power mantra

"My principles are ready before the moment arrives."

XV. STOP PREPARING TO LIVE AND START LIVING NOW

"Be not deceived; for thou shalt never live to read thy moral commentaries, nor the acts of the famous Romans and Grecians; nor those excerpta from several books; all which thou hadst provided and laid up for thyself against thine old age. Hasten therefore to an end, and giving over all vain hopes, help thyself in time if thou carest for thyself, as thou oughtest to do."

What Marcus meant (core philosophy)

Marcus delivers a sharp reminder about procrastination disguised as preparation. He acknowledges the human tendency to delay true living by believing there will always be more time later. We gather books, plans, ideals, and intentions, imagining a future version of ourselves who will finally live wisely. Marcus cuts through this illusion. You may never reach that imagined future. The Stoic message is not urgency driven by panic, but clarity about time:

- Life is finite.
- Preparation without action becomes avoidance.
- Wisdom exists to be practiced, not merely collected.

He urges immediate alignment between knowledge and action. Philosophy is not meant for someday. It is meant for now.

Dating translation (what this means emotionally/socially)
Marcus is essentially saying: Stop waiting to become the perfect version of yourself before living honestly in relationships. Common delays in dating:
- "I'll start setting boundaries when I'm more confident."
- "I'll say what I really want once things feel safer."
- "I'll choose better partners after I fully heal."

This creates an endless loop of postponement. Growth does not happen before experience. It happens through aligned action within experience.

Another layer here: Many people spend more time-consuming advice about relationships than actually practicing healthier behavior. Reading, learning, analyzing. All useful. But without action, they become avoidance mechanisms. Marcus calls you forward: You do not need more preparation to begin living with integrity.

Savage takeaway
You are not waiting for the right moment. You are avoiding the moment you already have.

Quiet power mantra
"I act on what I know now. Life does not wait."

XVI. SEE BEYOND WHAT IS OBVIOUS
"To steal, to sow, to buy, to be at rest, to see what is to be done (which is not seen by the eyes, but by another kind of sight:) what these words mean, and how many ways to be understood, they do not understand. The body, the soul, the understanding. As the senses naturally belong to the body, and the desires and affections to the soul, so do the dogmata to the understanding."

What Marcus meant (core philosophy)
Marcus distinguishes between different levels of perception. The body sees through physical senses. The soul experiences through emotions and desires. But the understanding, the rational faculty, perceives through principles. He is describing a deeper form of vision. Not merely observing what appears externally, but recognizing meaning, intention, and truth beneath appearances. Many people interpret actions only at the surface level. They understand words literally, behaviors immediately, without grasping underlying causes or principles. The disciplined mind learns to interpret through reason rather than instinct or impulse. This is what allows a person to act wisely instead of reactively.

Dating translation (what this means emotionally/socially)
Marcus is basically telling you: Stop judging relationships only by what you see on the surface. In dating, people often rely only on:
- physical attraction (body)
- emotional intensity (soul)

But neglect rational understanding (mind).

Examples:

Someone texts constantly. Emotion says: they care deeply. Reason asks: is this consistency or insecurity?

Someone speaks beautifully. Emotion says: connection. Reason asks: do their actions align?

Someone withdraws. Emotion says: rejection. Reason asks: is this pattern, personality, or circumstance?

Marcus is encouraging a third layer of perception. Not cynicism, but clarity. When you operate from understanding:

- You see patterns earlier.
- You interpret behavior more accurately.
- You respond thoughtfully instead of emotionally.

You begin seeing the structure behind the experience, not just the experience itself.

Savage takeaway

Attraction shows you what you feel. Understanding shows you what is real.

Quiet power mantra

"I look beyond appearances. My understanding sees clearly."

XVII. BE GOOD EVEN WHEN NO ONE SEES OR BELIEVES IT

"To be capable of fancies and imaginations, is common to man and beast. To be violently drawn and moved by the lusts and desires of the soul, is proper to wild beasts and monsters, such as Phalaris and Nero were. To follow reason for ordinary duties and actions is common to them also, who believe not that there be any gods, and for their advantage would make no conscience to betray their own country; and who when once the doors be shut upon them, dare do anything. If therefore all things else be common to these likewise, it follows, that for a man to like and embrace all things that happen and are destinated unto him, and not to trouble and molest that spirit which is seated in the temple of his own breast, with a multitude of vain fancies and imaginations, but to keep him propitious and to obey him as a god, never either speaking anything contrary to truth, or doing anything contrary to justice, is the only true property of a good man. And such a one, though no man should believe that he liveth as he doth, either sincerely and conscionably, or cheerful and contentedly; yet is he neither with any man at all angry for it, nor diverted by it from the way that leadeth to the end of his life, through which a man must pass pure, ever ready to depart, and willing of himself without any compulsion to fit and accommodate himself to his proper lot and portion."

What Marcus meant (core philosophy)

Marcus distinguishes between what is common and what is truly rare. Many qualities are shared across humanity:

- imagination
- desire
- even rational thinking used for practical purposes

But the defining trait of a truly good person is deeper:

- accepting what happens without inner turmoil
- maintaining truth and justice regardless of circumstances
- keeping the inner spirit calm, aligned, and undisturbed

Virtue is not validated by recognition or approval. A good person remains steady even if misunderstood, doubted, or unseen. Marcus also emphasizes independence from external validation. The worth of a life is not determined by whether others recognize its sincerity. True integrity is quiet, internal, and self-sustaining.

Dating translation (what this means emotionally/socially)

Marcus is essentially saying: Your character is not proven by how others respond to you. In dating, people often abandon their best self when they feel unseen or unappreciated:

- becoming colder because someone did not reciprocate
- acting out because attention was withdrawn
- compromising values to gain approval

Marcus rejects this. You do not become truthful because someone rewards honesty. You do not become kind because someone deserves it. You act according to who you are. This also addresses a powerful emotional trap: The need for someone to acknowledge your goodness before you feel secure in it.

Marcus says your alignment is internal. Whether someone understands you or not does not change the value of your actions. And when you live this way:

- rejection loses its sting
- misunderstanding loses its power
- approval becomes irrelevant rather than addictive

Savage takeaway

If your goodness depends on being recognized, it was never fully yours.

Quiet power mantra

"I live by truth and justice, whether seen or unseen."

THE FOURTH BOOK
Nothing Is Personal (But Your Growth Is)

I. BECOME THE FIRE THAT ADAPTS AND CONSUMES

"That inward mistress part of man if it be in its own true natural temper, is towards all worldly chances and events ever so disposed and affected, that it will easily turn and apply itself to that which may be, and is within its own power to compass, when that cannot be which at first it intended. For it never doth absolutely addict and apply itself to any one object, but whatsoever it is that it doth now intend and prosecute, it doth prosecute it with exception and reservation; so that whatsoever it is that falls out contrary to its first intentions, even that afterwards it makes its proper object. Even as the fire when it prevails upon those things that are in his way; by which things indeed a little fire would have been quenched, but a great fire doth soon turn to its own nature, and so consume whatsoever comes in his way: yea by those very things it is made greater and greater."

What Marcus meant (core philosophy)

Marcus describes the ideal state of the inner ruling faculty, the rational core of a person. When the mind is aligned with its true nature, it does not become shattered by obstacles. Instead, it adapts fluidly. It pursues intentions without rigid attachment to outcomes. The Stoic does not cling to specific results. They act with purpose but maintain flexibility, allowing unexpected events to become part of the path rather than disruptions to it. Marcus uses the metaphor of fire:

- A weak flame is extinguished by resistance.
- A strong fire absorbs whatever stands in its way and transforms it into fuel.

Strength of character means transforming adversity into material for growth. Nothing that happens externally has the power to defeat a disciplined mind. Instead, it becomes something that strengthens it.

Dating translation (what this means emotionally/socially)

Marcus is describing emotional resilience in relationships. Many people attach themselves not only to a person but to a specific imagined outcome:

- This must become a relationship.
- This must lead to commitment.
- This must unfold according to my timeline.

When reality deviates, they collapse emotionally because their identity was attached to the outcome. The Stoic approach:

- pursue connection sincerely
- hold intentions lightly
- adapt when reality changes

Examples: A connection fades.

Weak fire says: I failed. Something is wrong with me.

Strong fire says: This becomes experience, clarity, growth. I redirect without losing myself.

Rejection, misunderstanding, unexpected change. All become fuel when you refuse to let them define your worth. Marcus is not teaching emotional detachment from caring. He is teaching detachment from rigidity.

Savage takeaway
The stronger your inner fire, the less anything can stop you. It only becomes more fuel.

Quiet power mantra
"I transform obstacles into strength. Nothing wastes me."

II. MOVE WITH INTENTION, NOT IMPULSE
"Let nothing be done rashly, and at random, but all things according to the most exact and perfect rules of art."

What Marcus meant (core philosophy)
Marcus emphasizes deliberate action guided by reason and mastery. Nothing should be done carelessly or without conscious intention. The Stoic ideal is to live as an artist or craftsman of life, where every action reflects skill, discipline, and awareness.

The "rules of art" do not refer to rigid formulas but to the cultivated wisdom that comes from understanding human nature, virtue, and the proper use of reason. To act randomly is to surrender control to impulse, distraction, or external pressure. To act according to art is to move with clarity, precision, and inner alignment. Stoicism treats living well as a practiced discipline rather than a spontaneous accident.

Dating translation (what this means emotionally/socially)
Marcus is basically saying: Stop treating your emotional life like a reaction. Treat it like a craft. Many dating mistakes come from impulsive decisions:
- texting out of anxiety
- agreeing to things you do not truly want
- escalating emotionally before trust is built
- reacting defensively instead of responding thoughtfully

Intentional dating means:
- speaking deliberately
- choosing actions aligned with your values
- moving at a pace that reflects self-respect rather than urgency

This does not mean being cold or calculating. It means being conscious. When you act without awareness, you often regret your behavior later. When you act with intention, even mistakes become part of growth rather than sources of shame.

Savage takeaway
Chemistry is spontaneous. Character is deliberate.

Quiet power mantra
"I move with purpose. My actions reflect intention, not impulse."

III. YOUR PEACE IS NOT A PLACE, IT IS A PRACTICE

"They seek for themselves private retiring places, as country villages, the sea-shore, mountains; yea thou thyself art wont to long much after such places. But all this thou must know proceeds from simplicity in the highest degree. At what time soever thou wilt, it is in thy power to retire into thyself, and to be at rest, and free from all businesses. A man cannot any whither retire better than to his own soul; he especially who is beforehand provided of such things within, which whensoever he doth withdraw himself to look in, may presently afford unto him perfect ease and tranquillity. By tranquillity I understand a decent orderly disposition and carriage, free from all confusion and tumultuousness. Afford then thyself this retiring continually, and thereby refresh and renew thyself. Let these precepts be brief and fundamental, which as soon as thou dost call them to mind, may suffice thee to purge thy soul throughly, and to send thee away well pleased with those things whatsoever they be, which now again after this short withdrawing of thy soul into herself thou dost return unto. For what is it that thou art offended at? Can it be at the wickedness of men, when thou dost call to mind this conclusion, that all reasonable creatures are made one for another? and that it is part of justice to bear with them? and that it is against their wills that they offend? and how many already, who once likewise prosecuted their enmities, suspected, hated, and fiercely contended, are now long ago stretched out, and reduced unto ashes? It is time for thee to make an end. As for those things which among the common chances of the world happen unto thee as thy particular lot and portion, canst thou be displeased with any of them, when thou dost call that our ordinary dilemma to mind, either a providence, or Democritus his atoms; and with it, whatsoever we brought to prove that the whole world is as it were one city? And as for thy body, what canst thou fear, if thou dost consider that thy mind and understanding, when once it hath recollected itself, and knows its own power, hath in this life and breath (whether it run smoothly and gently, or whether harshly and rudely), no interest at all, but is altogether indifferent: and whatsoever else thou hast heard and assented unto concerning either pain or pleasure? But the care of thine honour and reputation will perchance distract thee? How can that be, if thou dost look back, and consider both how quickly all things that are, are forgotten, and what an immense chaos of eternity was before, and will follow after all things: and the vanity of praise, and the inconstancy and variableness of human judgments and opinions, and the narrowness of the place, wherein it is limited and circumscribed? For the whole earth is but as one point; and of it, this inhabited part of it, is but a very little part; and of this part, how many in number, and what manner of men are they, that will commend thee? What remains then, but that thou often put in practice this kind of retiring of thyself, to this little part of thyself; and above all things, keep thyself from distraction, and intend not anything vehemently, but be free and consider all things, as a man whose proper object is Virtue, as a man whose true nature is to be kind and sociable, as a citizen, as a mortal creature. Among other things, which to consider, and look into thou must use to withdraw thyself, let those two be among the most obvious and at hand. One, that the things or objects themselves reach not unto the soul, but stand without still and quiet, and that it is from the opinion only which is within, that all the tumult and all the trouble doth proceed. The next, that all these things, which now thou seest, shall within a very little while be changed, and be no more: and ever call to mind, how many changes and alterations in the world thou thyself hast already been an eyewitness of in thy time. This world is mere change, and this life, opinion."

What Marcus meant (core philosophy)

Marcus challenges the human desire to escape outwardly in order to find inner peace. People long for retreats. Mountains, oceans, solitude. But Marcus says the greatest retreat is always available within the disciplined mind. True tranquility is not withdrawal from life. It is an orderly inner state, free from chaos and emotional turbulence. He offers a method:

- Withdraw into yourself regularly.

- Recall essential principles.
- Reframe disturbance through reason.

He dismantles common sources of agitation:

- anger toward others (remembering shared human nature and mortality)
- resentment toward circumstances (seeing the world as governed by order or necessity)
- fear of bodily discomfort (recognizing the independence of the rational mind)
- obsession with reputation (recognizing the fleeting nature of praise)

The Stoic retreat is not avoidance. It is recalibration. Peace comes from recognizing two truths:

1. External events do not touch the soul. Only our opinions about them do.
2. Everything is constantly changing. Nothing remains long enough to justify lasting turmoil.

Dating translation (what this means emotionally/socially)

Marcus is basically saying: Stop believing that emotional peace will arrive when the external situation changes. Many people think:

- When I meet the right person, I'll feel calm.
- When this relationship stabilizes, I'll feel secure.
- When they finally understand me, I'll be at peace.

Marcus says peace is internal practice, not relational outcome. In dating, this looks like:

- grounding yourself instead of seeking constant reassurance
- recognizing that someone's behavior cannot disturb you unless your interpretation allows it
- stepping back mentally instead of reacting immediately to emotional triggers

He also dismantles reputation anxiety. Worrying about how you are perceived, whether someone approves of you, or how a relationship reflects on you. All temporary illusions. And perhaps most powerful: Everything changes. Feelings, people, situations. When you accept this fully, you stop gripping so tightly.

Savage takeaway

You do not need to escape your life to find peace. You need to stop abandoning yourself inside it.

Quiet power mantra

"My refuge is within me. I return to myself and become clear."

IV. WE BELONG TO ONE HUMAN CITY

"If to understand and to be reasonable be common unto all men, then is that reason, for which we are termed reasonable, common unto all. If reason is general, then is that reason also, which prescribeth what is to be done and what not, common unto all. If that, then law. If law, then are we fellow-citizens. If so, then are we partners in some one commonweal. If so, then the world is as it were a city. For which other

65

commonweal is it, that all men can be said to be members of? From this common city it is, that understanding, reason, and law is derived unto us, for from whence else? For as that which in me is earthly I have from some common earth; and that which is moist from some other element is imparted; as my breath and life hath its proper fountain; and that likewise which is dry and fiery in me: (for there is nothing which doth not proceed from something; as also there is nothing that can be reduced unto mere nothing;) so also is there some common beginning from whence my understanding hath proceeded."

What Marcus meant (core philosophy)

Marcus builds a logical chain to demonstrate humanity's shared nature. If all humans possess reason, then reason itself must be universal. If reason is shared, then the principles governing right action are also shared. From this comes law, and from law comes citizenship in a greater common society.

Marcus expands the idea of citizenship beyond nation or tribe. The true "city" is the universe itself. Humanity forms one interconnected community bound by shared rational nature. Just as the physical elements of our bodies come from nature, our ability to think and understand arises from a common source.

The Stoic implication is profound: We are not isolated individuals competing against one another. We are participants in a shared moral ecosystem. Therefore, our actions toward others should reflect cooperation, justice, and mutual respect.

Dating translation (what this means emotionally/socially)

Marcus is essentially saying: Relationships are not battles between opposing sides. They are interactions between fellow citizens of the same human experience. Dating often becomes adversarial:

- men vs. women
- avoidant vs. anxious
- power struggles disguised as attraction

Marcus dissolves this. If we share reason and human nature, then:

- understanding becomes more powerful than judgment
- compassion becomes more effective than resentment
- cooperation becomes more meaningful than control

This does not mean tolerating harmful behavior. It means recognizing that others act from the same human condition, even when misguided. Seeing relationships through shared humanity shifts you from: "What do I gain or lose here?" to "How do we meet as equals within the same human story?" And ironically, this mindset creates stronger boundaries because it removes the need for manipulation or dominance.

Savage takeaway

Dating stops feeling like war when you stop treating other humans like enemies.

Quiet power mantra

"I meet others as fellow citizens of the same human world."

V. ACCEPT THE CYCLE AND RELEASE THE FEAR

"As generation is, so also death, a secret of nature's wisdom: a mixture of elements, resolved into the same elements again, a thing surely which no man ought to be ashamed of: in a series of other fatal events and consequences, which a rational creature is subject unto, not improper or incongruous, nor contrary to the natural and proper constitution of man himself."

What Marcus meant (core philosophy)

Marcus reflects on death as a natural process rather than a tragedy or disgrace. Just as birth is a transformation of elements into form, death is their return. Nothing is lost. Nothing unnatural occurs. It is simply another stage within the larger order of nature.

For a rational being, fear or shame surrounding death arises from misunderstanding its place within the natural cycle. Marcus emphasizes that death is neither a punishment nor an anomaly. It belongs to the same chain of events that governs all existence. To accept death is to accept life as it truly is: finite, changing, and part of a continuous transformation. This acceptance frees the mind from unnecessary dread and allows a person to live with greater clarity and dignity.

Dating translation (what this means emotionally/socially)

Marcus is not only talking about physical death. He is also describing endings. In relationships, people resist endings as though they are unnatural failures:

- the end of a connection
- the loss of attraction
- the closing of a chapter

But endings are not violations of life. They are part of its structure. When you accept this:

- breakups become transitions instead of personal defeats
- change becomes evolution rather than abandonment
- emotional closure becomes possible without bitterness

Many people cling to relationships because they fear the symbolic "death" of the story they imagined. Marcus reminds us: Nothing in life stays fixed. Transformation is not the enemy. It is the rule.

Savage takeaway

Not every ending is a loss. Some are simply the next phase of nature doing its work.

Quiet power mantra

"I accept endings as part of life's natural rhythm."

VI. STOP RESISTING WHAT IS INEVITABLE

"Such and such things, from such and such causes, must of necessity proceed. He that would not have such things to happen, is as he that would have the fig-tree grow without any sap or moisture. In sum, remember this, that within a very little while, both thou and he shall both be dead, and after a little while more, not so much as your names and memories shall be remaining."

What Marcus meant (core philosophy)

Marcus speaks about causality and acceptance. Everything that happens arises from prior causes. Events unfold according to the nature of things. To resist what must occur is as irrational as wishing a tree to grow without nourishment. This is not fatalism. It is recognition of reality's structure. He reinforces this perspective by reminding us of mortality:

- You will die.
- Others will die.
- Even memory and reputation fade.

The purpose is not pessimism but liberation. When you understand how brief and transient everything is, you stop wasting energy resisting the unavoidable or obsessing over temporary disturbances. Acceptance allows clarity. Resistance prolongs suffering.

Dating translation (what this means emotionally/socially)

Marcus is basically saying: Stop fighting reality when it shows you what is happening. In dating, people often resist obvious patterns:

- Someone shows inconsistency, yet you try to force stability.
- Someone is emotionally unavailable, yet you try to create intimacy alone.
- A relationship ends, yet you keep replaying alternate outcomes in your mind.

Wanting reality to be different does not change it. The Stoic response is not resignation but intelligent alignment: See clearly. Accept what is. Move accordingly. Marcus also reminds us of perspective. The conflict, the disappointment, the ego wound that feels enormous today. In time, both people involved will be gone, and the moment will fade into silence. This perspective dissolves unnecessary drama.

Savage takeaway

Reality is not cruel for being honest. Fighting what is only exhausts you.

Quiet power mantra

"I accept what is real and move with clarity."

VII. REMOVE THE STORY, REMOVE THE SUFFERING

"Let opinion be taken away, and no man will think himself wronged. If no man shall think himself wronged, then is there no more any such thing as wrong. That which makes not man himself the worse, cannot make his life the worse, neither can it hurt him either inwardly or outwardly. It was expedient in nature that it should be so, and therefore necessary."

What Marcus meant (core philosophy)

Marcus is making one of the most radical Stoic claims: Injury does not exist independently of opinion. Events occur. Words are spoken. Actions happen. But the feeling of being wronged arises from the interpretation assigned by the mind.

68

If the opinion of injury is removed, the internal experience of harm dissolves. This does not deny that injustice exists in the world. Rather, Marcus distinguishes between external events and internal damage. Nothing external can corrupt the soul unless we allow it through our judgment. If something does not make you morally worse, then it has not truly harmed you. Nature has structured things this way so that inner freedom remains possible regardless of external circumstances.

Dating translation (what this means emotionally/socially)

Marcus is essentially saying: Being hurt and being harmed are not always the same thing. In dating, many emotional wounds come from interpretation:
- "They rejected me" becomes "I am unworthy."
- "They lied" becomes "I am a fool."
- "They chose someone else" becomes "I lost value."

But the external action does not define your inner state unless you attach meaning that diminishes yourself. This does not mean suppressing emotions or excusing bad behavior. It means reclaiming authority over how deeply something penetrates your identity. Someone's actions can disappoint you without defining you. When you remove the story that turns an event into a personal injury, emotional freedom returns.

Savage takeaway

They can act badly. Only you can decide whether it defines you.

Quiet power mantra

"I release the story of harm. Nothing outside me diminishes my worth."

VIII. ACT AS THE PERSON YOU CLAIM TO BE

"Whatsoever doth happen in the world, doth happen justly, and so if thou dost well take heed, thou shalt find it. I say not only in right order by a series of inevitable consequences, but according to justice and as it were by way of equal distribution, according to the true worth of everything. Continue then to take notice of it, as thou hast begun, and whatsoever thou dost, do it not without this proviso, that it be a thing of that nature that a good man (as the word good is properly taken) may do it. This observe carefully in every action."

What Marcus meant (core philosophy)

Marcus urges us to see events not as random injustices but as parts of a larger order governed by nature's balance. He is not claiming that every outcome feels fair from a human perspective. Rather, he suggests that events unfold within a rational structure where cause and consequence operate continuously.

The practical takeaway is not passive acceptance but ethical responsibility. Since the world unfolds according to its nature, the only true control lies in how we act within it.

Marcus therefore gives a simple standard: Before acting, ask whether this is something a truly good person would do. Virtue becomes the compass. Not emotional reaction, not social approval, but alignment with character.

Dating translation (what this means emotionally/socially)

Marcus is essentially saying: Stop asking, "Did they deserve this?" and start asking, "Does this align with who I want to be?"

In relationships, people often justify behavior based on circumstance:
- They hurt me, so I will hurt them back.
- They ghosted me, so I will play games too.
- They lied, so honesty no longer matters.

Marcus rejects reactive morality. Your behavior should not fluctuate based on someone else's character.

Examples:
- Communicating clearly even when frustrated.
- Leaving with dignity rather than revenge.
- Setting boundaries without cruelty.

This is not weakness. It is strength rooted in identity. You become stable because your actions are guided by internal standards rather than external chaos.

Savage takeaway

Do not let someone else's behavior downgrade your character.

Quiet power mantra

"I act in alignment with who I choose to be."

IX. SEE THE TRUTH, NOT THEIR NARRATIVE

"Conceit no such things, as he that wrongeth thee conceiveth, or would have thee to conceive, but look into the matter itself, and see what it is in very truth."

What Marcus meant (core philosophy)

Marcus warns against adopting another person's interpretation of reality. When someone acts wrongly toward you, they often carry their own internal story, justification, or projection. The danger lies in unconsciously accepting their version of events as truth. The Stoic task is to return to the thing itself. Strip away intention, accusation, emotional coloring, and social drama. Examine the reality directly:
- What actually happened?
- What is objectively present?

Truth exists independent of someone's framing or your emotional reaction. By seeing clearly, the rational mind remains free from manipulation, confusion, or distortion.

Dating translation (what this means emotionally/socially)

Marcus is basically saying: Do not accept someone else's narrative if it contradicts reality. In dating, this happens constantly:
- Someone behaves poorly but reframes it as your fault.

- Someone withdraws but calls it "needing space" while continuing inconsistent behavior.
- Someone minimizes your feelings by redefining events to suit their perspective.

If you adopt their interpretation without examination, you begin doubting your own perception. Stoic clarity requires stepping back and asking: What actually happened, independent of explanation?

Example:
They cancelled repeatedly.
Their narrative: "You're too demanding."

Reality: repeated lack of consistency. Seeing the truth removes confusion and restores self-trust.

Savage takeaway
Reality is not what someone says it is. Reality is what actually happens.

Quiet power mantra
"I trust clear seeing. I return to truth, not interpretation."

X. HOLD STRONG PRINCIPLES, KEEP A FLEXIBLE MIND

"These two rules, thou must have always in a readiness. First, do nothing at all, but what reason proceeding from that regal and supreme part, shall for the good and benefit of men, suggest unto thee. And secondly, if any man that is present shall be able to rectify thee or to turn thee from some erroneous persuasion, that thou be always ready to change thy mind, and this change to proceed, not from any respect of any pleasure or credit thereon depending, but always from some probable apparent ground of justice, or of some public good thereby to be furthered; or from some other such inducement."

What Marcus meant (core philosophy)
Marcus gives two governing rules for a rational life. First, act only according to reason, guided by the highest part of the self, and directed toward the good of humanity. Actions should not be impulsive or self-serving but aligned with justice and collective well-being. Second, remain open to correction.

True strength is not rigid stubbornness. If someone presents a clearer understanding rooted in justice or truth, the wise person adapts willingly. Changing one's mind is not weakness when it arises from reason rather than vanity. Marcus distinguishes between:
- changing for approval, pleasure, or reputation (which weakens integrity)
- changing because truth becomes clearer (which strengthens integrity)
The ideal is firmness of principle combined with humility of understanding.

Dating translation (what this means emotionally/socially)
Marcus is basically saying: Know your values, but do not confuse ego with conviction. In dating, people often swing between extremes:

- bending too easily to keep peace
- refusing to reconsider anything out of pride

Healthy emotional intelligence looks like:

- acting from clear principles such as honesty, respect, and kindness
- being willing to adjust when presented with genuine new understanding

Examples:

A partner gives feedback that reveals a blind spot. Instead of defending immediately, you consider whether truth exists in what they say.

Or:

Someone pressures you to compromise your boundaries. You remain firm because the change would be driven by approval-seeking rather than truth. Marcus teaches discernment. Change for clarity, not for validation.

Savage takeaway

Strength is not refusing to change. Strength is changing only when truth demands it.

Quiet power mantra

"I stand firm in principle and flexible in understanding."

XI. USE THE REASON YOU ALREADY HAVE

"Hast thou reason? I have. Why then makest thou not use of it? For if thy reason do her part, what more canst thou require?"

What Marcus meant (core philosophy)

Marcus cuts directly to simplicity. Humans possess reason, the faculty that allows discernment, judgment, and wise action. If reason is available, then excuses become unnecessary.

The Stoic question becomes: If you know what is right, why do you hesitate to do it? Marcus suggests that many of our struggles arise not from lack of knowledge, but from failure to apply what we already understand. The rational faculty is sufficient for living well. Once reason is engaged, external complications lose their power. This is a call to self-responsibility. Stop searching endlessly for new answers when you already possess the capacity to see clearly.

Dating translation (what this means emotionally/socially)

Marcus is essentially saying: You already know more than you pretend not to know. In dating, clarity often exists long before action:

- You know when someone is inconsistent.
- You know when you are being treated below your standard.
- You know when you are ignoring your own needs.

Yet people delay because they want different outcomes than reality offers. Reason quietly observes while emotion negotiates. Marcus invites you back to your own discernment.

Instead of asking: "What should I do?"

Ask: "What do I already know is true?"

The answer is usually present. The challenge is choosing to follow it.

Savage takeaway

You do not need more signs. You need the courage to act on what you already see.

Quiet power mantra

"My reason is enough. I trust what I already know."

XII. ALL RETURNS TO THE SAME SOURCE

"As a part hitherto thou hast had a particular subsistence: and now shalt thou vanish away into the common substance of Him, who first begot thee, or rather thou shalt be resumed again into that original rational substance, out of which all others have issued, and are propagated. Many small pieces of frankincense are set upon the same altar, one drops first and is consumed, another after; and it comes all to one."

What Marcus meant (core philosophy)

Marcus reflects on individuality within the larger whole. Each person exists as a temporary expression of a greater universal substance. Just as pieces of incense burn at different times upon the same altar, individuals live and fade at different moments, yet all belong to the same process.

The Stoic view removes hierarchy from timing. It does not matter whether one "ends" earlier or later. The outcome is identical. All return to the same origin. This perspective dissolves fear and comparison. Death is not loss of meaning. It is reintegration into the greater order from which life emerged. The metaphor emphasizes humility and unity:

- no life stands apart from the whole
- no ending is singularly tragic in the universal sense

Acceptance of this truth allows one to live without clinging or resentment toward the inevitability of change.

Dating translation (what this means emotionally/socially)

Marcus is also describing emotional endings and transitions. In relationships, people often compare:

- Why did theirs last longer?
- Why did this end sooner than I hoped?
- Why did I not get more time?

The incense metaphor says: Duration does not determine value. Some connections burn briefly yet profoundly. Others linger without depth. The timing does not define the worth of the experience. Letting go becomes easier when you understand that every relationship is part of a larger unfolding rather than a permanent possession. You are not losing something that belonged exclusively to you. You are participating in a shared human experience that naturally changes form.

Savage takeaway
Longer does not mean better. Every flame returns to the same fire.

Quiet power mantra
"I belong to the greater whole. I release comparison and accept the cycle."

XIII. DO NOT LIVE BY THEIR PRAISE OR THEIR DISMISSAL
"Within ten days, if so happen, thou shalt be esteemed a god of them, who now if thou shalt return to the dogmata and to the honouring of reason, will esteem of thee no better than of a mere brute, and of an ape."

What Marcus meant (core philosophy)
Marcus exposes the instability of public opinion. The same people who elevate someone today may dismiss them tomorrow. Reputation fluctuates rapidly, shaped by perception rather than truth. He warns against grounding identity in external approval.

If you abandon reason and integrity to satisfy others, you become subject to their shifting judgments. Their praise does not make you greater, and their dismissal does not make you lesser. The Stoic ideal is independence from the emotional swings caused by public perception. Character must be rooted in reason, not in reputation.

Dating translation (what this means emotionally/socially)
Marcus is basically saying: Do not change who you are based on how someone temporarily perceives you. In dating:
- Someone idealizes you early and calls you perfect.
- Later, they withdraw or criticize, and suddenly you feel diminished.

Nothing essential about you changed. Only their perception shifted. People project:
- They may pedestalize you.
- They may devalue you.
- They may alternate between both.

If your self-worth follows their opinion, you become emotionally unstable. The Stoic approach:
- Let praise pass without inflation.
- Let criticism pass without collapse.

Stay anchored to your own reasoned understanding of yourself.

Savage takeaway
If someone's opinion can make you feel like a god today and worthless tomorrow, you gave them too much authority.

Quiet power mantra
"I remain steady regardless of praise or dismissal."

74

XIV. DO NOT DELAY BECOMING WHO YOU ARE
"Not as though thou hadst thousands of years to live. Death hangs over thee: whilst yet thou livest, whilst thou mayest, be good."

What Marcus meant (core philosophy)
Marcus delivers one of his most direct reminders: Time is limited. Human beings behave as if life stretches endlessly ahead, postponing virtue, clarity, and meaningful action for some imagined future. Marcus interrupts this illusion.

Death is not distant. It accompanies us constantly. Therefore, the task is simple: Be good now. Virtue is not something reserved for old age, retirement, or after circumstances improve. It belongs to the present moment. The Stoic focus is not on fearing death, but on allowing the awareness of mortality to sharpen intention and eliminate procrastination.

Dating translation (what this means emotionally/socially)
Marcus is essentially saying: Stop postponing your authentic self. In dating, people delay integrity:
- waiting to express needs until the relationship feels safer
- tolerating misalignment instead of leaving early
- pretending to be less intense, less honest, less clear to maintain attraction

Life does not guarantee a later opportunity to live truthfully. Being "good" in relationships means:
- communicating honestly now
- treating others with respect now
- respecting yourself now

Not after clarity arrives. Not after certainty appears. Now. Because the time you assume you have may not exist.

Savage takeaway
You are not preparing to become your best self. You are either living it or postponing it.

Quiet power mantra
"I choose integrity now. There is no later promised."

XV. STOP WATCHING THEM AND WALK YOUR OWN LINE
"Now much time and leisure doth he gain, who is not curious to know what his neighbour hath said, or hath done, or hath attempted, but only what he doth himself, that it may be just and holy? or to express it in Agathos'[34] words, Not to look about upon the evil conditions of others, but to run on straight in the line, without any loose and extravagant agitation."

---

[34] n ancient Greek, agathos (ἀγαθός) primarily means "good." While simple on the surface, its meaning shifted significantly across different eras and philosophical schools.

What Marcus meant (core philosophy)

Marcus points to a powerful source of wasted energy: preoccupation with other people. Curiosity about what others are doing, saying, or intending pulls attention away from one's own moral path. The Stoic ideal is focused self-governance. Instead of scanning outward for comparison, judgment, or distraction, the disciplined person asks: Is what I am doing just? Is it aligned with virtue?

The metaphor of running straight in a line captures unwavering attention toward one's own conduct. Distraction arises from looking sideways. Progress comes from maintaining direction. Peace increases when we release the urge to monitor others' behavior and redirect attention inward.

Dating translation (what this means emotionally/socially)

Marcus is basically saying: Stop tracking what they are doing and start anchoring in what you are doing. Dating anxiety often grows from outward focus:

- checking their activity
- analyzing what they said to someone else
- comparing yourself to perceived competition
- wondering how they feel instead of examining your own boundaries

This outward scanning creates agitation because it places your emotional stability in someone else's actions.

Stoic clarity asks: Am I behaving with integrity? Am I showing up honestly? Am I aligned with my standards?

When you return to your own path, much of the mental noise disappears. You gain time, energy, and emotional freedom because you are no longer running someone else's race.

Savage takeaway

Your peace begins the moment you stop tracking them and start leading yourself.

Quiet power mantra

"I stay in my lane. My focus is my own conduct."

XVI. PRAISE DOES NOT ADD VALUE

"He who is greedy of credit and reputation after his death, doth not consider, that they themselves by whom he is remembered, shall soon after every one of them be dead; and they likewise that succeed those; until at last all memory, which hitherto by the succession of men admiring and soon after dying hath had its course, be quite extinct. But suppose that both they that shall remember thee, and thy memory with them should be immortal, what is that to thee? I will not say to thee after thou art dead; but even to thee living, what is thy praise? But only for a secret and politic consideration, which we call οἰκονομίαν[35], or dispensation. For as for that, that it is the gift of nature, whatsoever is commended in thee, what might be

---

[35] In Greek, οἰκονομίαν (*oikonomían*) is the accusative form of the noun οἰκονομία (*oikonomía*). It primarily translates to "management," "stewardship," or "administration."

objected from thence, let that now that we are upon another consideration be omitted as unseasonable. That which is fair and goodly, whatsoever it be, and in what respect soever it be, that it is fair and goodly, it is so of itself, and terminates in itself, not admitting praise as a part or member: that therefore which is praised, is not thereby made either better or worse. This I understand even of those things, that are commonly called fair and good, as those which are commended either for the matter itself, or for curious workmanship. As for that which is truly good, what can it stand in need of more than either justice or truth; or more than either kindness and modesty? Which of all those, either becomes good or fair, because commended; or dispraised suffers any damage? Doth the emerald become worse in itself, or more vile if it be not commended? Doth gold, or ivory, or purple? Is there anything that doth though never so common, as a knife, a flower, or a tree?"

What Marcus meant (core philosophy)

Marcus dismantles the human obsession with reputation and legacy. He reminds us that those who praise us will themselves soon disappear, along with the memory of their praise. Even if recognition were eternal, it would still add nothing essential to the thing being praised. True goodness, like an emerald or gold, possesses intrinsic value. It does not become better through admiration or worse through neglect. Praise is external. Virtue is internal.

The Stoic insight is that worth does not arise from recognition. Justice, truth, kindness, and integrity stand complete within themselves. They require no audience to validate them. Freedom comes when one stops seeking external confirmation for internal value.

Dating translation (what this means emotionally/socially)

Marcus is essentially saying: Your worth does not increase when someone admires you, and it does not decrease when someone overlooks you. In dating, people often measure value through attention:

- compliments become proof of worth
- silence becomes proof of inadequacy
- validation becomes emotional currency

This creates instability because your identity rises and falls with another person's perception.

Marcus reframes it: A good person remains good whether praised or ignored. A strong connection does not make you more valuable. A rejection does not make you less.

Examples:

- Someone calls you amazing. Nothing essential changed.
- Someone loses interest. Nothing essential changed.

When you internalize this, you stop chasing praise and start embodying self-respect.

Savage takeaway

Attention is not proof of value. Value exists before anyone notices it.

Quiet power mantra

"My worth stands complete within itself."

XVII. EVERYTHING CHANGES FORM, NOTHING IS LOST

"If so be that the souls remain after death (say they that will not believe it); how is the air from all eternity able to contain them? How is the earth (say I) ever from that time able to Contain the bodies of them that are buried? For as here the change and resolution of dead bodies into another kind of subsistence (whatsoever it be;) makes place for other dead bodies: so the souls after death transferred into the air, after they have conversed there a while, are either by way of transmutation, or transfusion, or conflagration, received again into that original rational substance, from which all others do proceed: and so give way to those souls, who before coupled and associated unto bodies, now begin to subsist single. This, upon a supposition that the souls after death do for a while subsist single, may be answered. And here, (besides the number of bodies, so buried and contained by the earth), we may further consider the number of several beasts, eaten by us men, and by other creatures. For notwithstanding that such a multitude of them is daily consumed, and as it were buried in the bodies of the eaters, yet is the same place and body able to contain them, by reason of their conversion, partly into blood, partly into air and fire. What in these things is the speculation of truth? to divide things into that which is passive and material; and that which is active and formal."

What Marcus meant (core philosophy)
Marcus explores transformation through nature's continual processes. He reflects on the question of what happens after death, not to argue theology, but to emphasize the constant movement and conversion within existence. Bodies return to elements. Souls, if they persist, return to a larger rational source. Nature continuously makes space through transformation. Nothing remains fixed. Everything shifts form, dissolves, and re-enters the larger system. He distinguishes between:

- the passive, material aspect of existence
- the active, rational or organizing principle

Understanding this removes fear of change. What appears as ending is simply transition. The Stoic lesson is not metaphysical certainty but intellectual humility and acceptance of natural processes.

Dating translation (what this means emotionally/socially)
Marcus is also describing emotional transformation. Relationships end, identities evolve, feelings shift. Nothing remains static. Many people resist emotional change because they interpret transformation as loss:

- The relationship changed, therefore something broke.
- Attraction faded, therefore something failed.
- A chapter ended, therefore it was wasted.

Marcus reframes this: Nothing is wasted. Everything transforms. Experiences become insight. Connection becomes memory. Emotion becomes wisdom. Even heartbreak becomes material that reshapes who you are. When you accept transformation as natural, you stop clinging to fixed forms and begin trusting the process of growth.

Savage takeaway
Nothing disappears. It only changes shape.

Quiet power mantra
"I accept transformation. Everything evolves into something new."

XVIII. STAY CENTERED AND SEE CLEARLY

"Not to wander out of the way, but upon every motion and desire, to perform that which is just: and ever to be careful to attain to the true natural apprehension of every fancy, that presents itself."

What Marcus meant (core philosophy)

Marcus gives two guiding disciplines: First, do not wander. Maintain alignment with justice in every action, intention, and desire. The Stoic life is not scattered or reactive but directed and grounded in virtue. Second, examine every impression carefully. Thoughts and perceptions arrive constantly, but not all are accurate or worthy of belief. The rational mind must pause and assess:

- Is this true?
- Is this aligned with nature?
- Is this leading toward justice?

Clarity comes from disciplined attention. The Stoic ideal is steadiness. One neither drifts aimlessly nor becomes controlled by unchecked impulses or misinterpretations.

Dating translation (what this means emotionally/socially)

Marcus is basically saying: Stay aligned with yourself and question your emotional assumptions. In dating, people often "wander" emotionally:

- abandoning their standards when attraction appears
- chasing mixed signals instead of honoring clarity
- acting from impulse rather than grounded intention

At the same time, unchecked assumptions create chaos:

- assuming rejection without evidence
- interpreting silence as judgment
- projecting stories onto neutral situations

Stoic clarity means: Act justly according to your values. Pause before believing every emotional narrative.

This creates emotional stability because you are guided by principles rather than momentary feelings.

Savage takeaway

Not every feeling is truth. Your job is to discern before you react.

Quiet power mantra

"I remain centered. I act justly and see clearly."

XIX. TRUST THE TIMING OF LIFE

"Whatsoever is expedient unto thee, O World, is expedient unto me; nothing can either be 'unseasonable unto me, or out of date, which unto thee is seasonable. Whatsoever thy seasons bear, shall ever by me be esteemed as happy fruit, and increase. O Nature! from thee are all things, in thee all things subsist, and to thee all tend. Could he say of Athens, Thou lovely city of Cecrops; and shalt not thou say of the world, Thou lovely city of God?"

What Marcus meant (core philosophy)

Marcus expresses radical alignment with nature and the greater order of existence. He suggests that what is beneficial for the whole is ultimately beneficial for the individual, even when it does not immediately appear so.

Rather than resisting circumstances as mistimed or unfair, the Stoic accepts that events unfold according to a larger rhythm beyond personal preference. The metaphor of the world as a "city" highlights belonging. Humans are not separate from nature but citizens within it. Everything arises from nature, exists within it, and returns to it. Acceptance of this relationship cultivates gratitude rather than resistance.

Dating translation (what this means emotionally/socially)

Marcus is basically saying: Stop believing you are out of sync with life just because something did not happen when you wanted it to. In relationships, people often feel:

- I met them at the wrong time.
- I am behind everyone else.
- Love should have happened by now.
- This ending ruined my timeline.

Stoic perspective reframes timing: What happens is part of your path, not evidence that life is against you. Acceptance does not mean passivity. It means trusting that:

- lessons arrive when needed
- connections appear and leave according to larger patterns
- growth often comes disguised as disruption

When you see life as a shared unfolding rather than a personal misfortune, bitterness softens into curiosity. You stop fighting the season you are in.

Savage takeaway

Life is not late or early. It is simply unfolding.

Quiet power mantra

"I move with life's timing. What comes now belongs to me."

XX. DO LESS, LIVE CLEARER

"They will say commonly, Meddle not with many things, if thou wilt live cheerfully. Certainly there is nothing better, than for a man to confine himself to necessary actions; to such and so many only, as reason in a creature that knows itself born for society, will command and enjoin. This will not only procure that cheerfulness, which from the goodness, but that also, which from the paucity of actions doth usually proceed. For since it is so, that most of those things, which we either speak or do, are unnecessary; if a man shall cut them off, it must needs follow that he shall thereby gain much leisure, and save much trouble, and therefore at every action a man must privately by way of admonition suggest unto himself, What? may not this that now I go about, be of the number of unnecessary actions? Neither must he use himself to cut off actions only, but thoughts and imaginations also, that are unnecessary for so will unnecessary consequent actions the better be prevented and cut off."

What Marcus meant (core philosophy)

Marcus teaches disciplined simplicity. Cheerfulness does not arise from doing more, knowing more, or managing more. It comes from reducing life to what is necessary and aligned with reason. He identifies two sources of peace:

- the goodness of right action
- the lightness that comes from fewer unnecessary burdens

Most human activity is excess. Unnecessary speech, unnecessary tasks, unnecessary worries. The Stoic practice is continuous discernment: Is this necessary? Is this aligned with my purpose as a rational, social being? By cutting away excess actions, one gains time, clarity, and calm. But Marcus goes deeper. Not only actions must be reduced. Thoughts must also be examined. Unnecessary thoughts generate unnecessary actions. Simplify the mind, and life becomes simpler.

Dating translation (what this means emotionally/socially)

Marcus is basically saying: Your dating life becomes lighter the moment you stop engaging in emotional overproduction.

Examples of unnecessary actions:

- overanalyzing every text
- having conversations that go nowhere
- explaining yourself repeatedly to someone who refuses to understand
- continuing connections that clearly lack alignment

Examples of unnecessary thoughts:

- replaying conversations endlessly
- imagining worst-case scenarios
- creating stories about someone's intentions without evidence

When you remove the unnecessary:

- emotional energy returns
- boundaries become clearer
- attraction feels more grounded instead of chaotic

Cheerfulness comes not from finding the perfect person, but from removing what drains you.

Savage takeaway

Peace is not gained by adding more. It is gained by removing what never needed to be there.

Quiet power mantra

"I release the unnecessary. Simplicity brings me peace."

XXI. CHOOSE THE SIMPLER WAY OF BEING

"Try also how a good man's life; (of one, who is well pleased with those things whatsoever, which among the common changes and chances of this world fall to his own lot and share; and can live well contented and fully satisfied in the justice of his own proper present action, and in the goodness of his disposition for

the future:) will agree with thee. Thou hast had experience of that other kind of life: make now trial of this also. Trouble not thyself any more henceforth, reduce thyself unto perfect simplicity. Doth any man offend? It is against himself that he doth offend: why should it trouble thee? Hath anything happened unto thee? It is well, whatsoever it be, it is that which of all the common chances of the world from the very beginning in the series of all other things that have, or shall happen, was destinated and appointed unto thee. To comprehend all in a few words, our life is short; we must endeavour to gain the present time with best discretion and justice. Use recreation with sobriety."

What Marcus meant (core philosophy)

Marcus invites a deliberate shift in how one lives. Instead of continuing a life filled with agitation, resistance, and unnecessary complexity, he proposes an experiment: try living as a good person grounded in acceptance, justice, and simplicity. The good life, as he defines it, rests on three pillars:

- acceptance of whatever happens as part of the natural order
- satisfaction with acting justly in the present moment
- trust that a virtuous disposition toward the future is enough

He reduces suffering by reframing events: If someone acts wrongly, they harm themselves through their own character. Why carry the burden of their actions within yourself? If something happens to you, it belongs to the unfolding pattern of life. Resistance adds unnecessary suffering.

The conclusion is concise: Life is brief. Use your present wisely. Live simply. Rest moderately. Act justly.

Dating translation (what this means emotionally/socially)

Marcus is essentially saying: You already know what chaos feels like. Try peace instead. Many people repeat emotional patterns:

- chasing unavailable partners
- overthinking every outcome
- carrying resentment toward others' behavior

Marcus suggests another path: Focus on your conduct, not their mistakes. If someone behaves poorly, that reflects their character, not your worth. If something ends or changes, it becomes part of your story without needing to become your suffering. Simplifying your dating life means:

- choosing clarity over drama
- acting with integrity regardless of outcome
- letting go of emotional excess that does not serve growth

He also adds a gentle reminder: joy and recreation are allowed, but with balance. Emotional health includes rest and lightness.

Savage takeaway

You do not need a new life. You need a simpler way of living the one you already have.

Quiet power mantra

"I choose simplicity. I act justly and release what is not mine to carry."

XXII. TRUST THE ORDER, EVEN WHEN YOU CANNOT SEE IT

"Either this world is a κόσμος[36], or comely piece, because all disposed and governed by certain order: or if it be a mixture, though confused, yet still it is a comely piece. For is it possible that in thee there should be any beauty at all, and that in the whole world there should be nothing but disorder and confusion? and all things in it too, by natural different properties one from another differenced and distinguished; and yet all through diffused, and by natural sympathy, one to another united, as they are?"

What Marcus meant (core philosophy)

Marcus considers whether the universe is perfectly ordered or partially chaotic. Regardless of which is true, he argues that the world must contain some form of inherent harmony.

His reasoning is simple: If beauty, reason, and coherence exist within us, they must originate from something greater than ourselves. It would be irrational for the individual to possess order while the whole remains entirely disordered.

Even apparent chaos participates in a deeper structure. Diversity and difference do not negate unity. Instead, everything exists in relationship, connected through natural sympathy. The Stoic perspective encourages trust in the underlying coherence of existence, even when events appear confusing or fragmented.

Dating translation (what this means emotionally/socially)

Marcus is basically saying: Just because something feels messy does not mean it is meaningless. Relationships often feel chaotic:

- timing seems wrong
- connections appear and disappear unexpectedly
- emotions conflict with logic

From the inside, dating can feel like disorder. Marcus reframes this: Even confusing experiences may belong to a larger pattern shaping growth and understanding. If you possess the capacity for love, clarity, and depth, it suggests that connection itself is not random or meaningless.

This does not mean every relationship is destined or perfect. It means that the process itself has coherence, even when the individual moments feel scattered. Instead of assuming life is broken because something did not work out, consider that complexity may still be part of a larger harmony.

Savage takeaway

Just because you cannot see the pattern yet does not mean there is none.

Quiet power mantra

"I trust that life holds order beyond my current view."

---

[36] In Greek, κόσμος (*kósmos*) primarily translates to "order," "ornament," or "the world/universe."

XXIII. DO NOT BE SURPRISED BY HUMAN NATURE

"A black or malign disposition, an effeminate disposition; an hard inexorable disposition, a wild inhuman disposition, a sheepish disposition, a childish disposition; a blockish, a false, a scurril[37], a fraudulent, a tyrannical: what then? If he be a stranger in the world, that knows not the things that are in it; why not be a stranger as well, that wonders at the things that are done in it?"

What Marcus meant (core philosophy)

Marcus lists many flawed human dispositions: cruel, childish, deceptive, tyrannical, weak, foolish. His point is not condemnation but recognition. Human nature contains a wide spectrum of character. These traits are not anomalies; they are recurring expressions within humanity.

He then asks: If someone is ignorant of how the world works, we call them a stranger to reality. So why should someone be surprised when people behave according to flawed human tendencies? To be shocked by human imperfection is, in a sense, to misunderstand the nature of humanity itself. Wisdom lies not in expecting perfection, but in understanding what people are capable of, both good and bad.

Dating translation (what this means emotionally/socially)

Marcus is saying: Stop being shocked when people act like people. In dating, many frustrations come from expecting others to behave according to our internal standards rather than their actual character. You encounter:

*   emotionally unavailable people
*   manipulators
*   avoiders
*   immature communicators
*   kind but confused souls
*   selfish or wounded individuals

None of these are new phenomena. The real suffering begins when we treat predictable human behavior as if it were shocking betrayal by the universe. Understanding human nature does not mean tolerating bad behavior. It means recognizing patterns without losing your equilibrium. When you understand reality, you respond strategically rather than emotionally collapsing into surprise.

Savage takeaway

You cannot be endlessly shocked by predictable behavior and still claim wisdom.

Quiet power mantra

"I expect humanity to be human, and I remain steady anyway."

---

[37] In English, scurril is an archaic or rare form of the word scurrilous. It describes something that is vulgar, grossly abusive, or foul-mouthed.

XXIV. TO ABANDON REASON IS TO ABANDON YOUR PLACE IN THE WORLD

"He is a true fugitive, that flies from reason, by which men are sociable. He blind, who cannot see with the eyes of his understanding. He poor, that stands in need of another, and hath not in himself all things needful for this life. He an aposteme of the world, who by being discontented with those things that happen unto him in the world, doth as it were apostatise[38], and separate himself from common nature's rational administration. For the same nature it is that brings this unto thee, whatsoever it be, that first brought thee into the world. He raises sedition in the city, who by irrational actions withdraws his own soul from that one and common soul of all rational creatures."

What Marcus meant (core philosophy)

Marcus defines several forms of true poverty and exile, not as material conditions, but as inner states:

- The true fugitive is not one who runs from places, but one who runs from reason.
- The truly blind are not those without sight, but those who refuse understanding.
- The truly poor are those who depend entirely on others for inner stability.
- The true rebel against nature is the one who resents reality itself.

To reject reason is to reject the shared bond that connects all rational beings. Human society exists because of a common rational nature. When someone abandons reason and acts purely from impulse, resentment, or irrationality, they separate themselves from this shared order. Such a person becomes like an infection within the whole, disrupting harmony rather than contributing to it.

Dating translation (what this means emotionally/socially)

Marcus is drawing a sharp line: The real problem is not external chaos. The problem is abandoning your own rational center. In modern emotional life:

- When someone rejects logic and accountability, they disconnect from relational harmony.
- When someone refuses reflection and lives only through reaction, they become unpredictable and destabilizing.
- When someone constantly resists reality instead of working with it, they isolate themselves emotionally and socially.

You cannot build stability with someone who has fled reason. And equally important: When *you* abandon your rational clarity, chasing emotional storms, over-identifying with rejection, or resisting what is clearly happening, you temporarily exile yourself from your own strength. Marcus is not asking for cold detachment. He is asking for alignment with reality.

Savage takeaway

Drama begins where reason ends.

Quiet power mantra

"I remain aligned with reason, and therefore I remain whole."

---

[38] Apostatise means to abandon or renounce one's religious faith, political party, or principles.

XXV. PHILOSOPHY DOES NOT REQUIRE PERFECT CONDITIONS

"There is, who without so much as a coat; and there is, who without so much as a book, doth put philosophy in practice. I am half naked, neither have I bread to eat, and yet I depart not from reason, saith one. But I say; I want the food of good teaching, and instructions, and yet I depart not from reason."

What Marcus meant (core philosophy)
Here Marcus reminds us that philosophy is not an intellectual luxury reserved for comfort or privilege. Some practice wisdom without material security:
- without clothing,
- without food,
- without external resources.

And yet they remain aligned with reason. He then expands the idea: Even without ideal teachers, perfect guidance, or structured instruction, one can still remain faithful to reason. The essence of philosophy is not possession of tools or circumstances. It is the internal commitment to live according to understanding, integrity, and rational awareness regardless of external lack. True wisdom is self-sustaining.

Dating translation (what this means emotionally/socially)
Applied to modern emotional life: You do not need perfect conditions to show up as your highest self. You do not need:
- the perfect partner
- perfect healing
- perfect timing
- perfect understanding from others to remain grounded in your values.

Many people wait for ideal circumstances before acting wisely.

Marcus says: Wisdom is demonstrated precisely when conditions are imperfect. If someone can only act with integrity when life feels easy, they are not anchored in reason; they are dependent on comfort. And for yourself: Even when you feel under-resourced emotionally, unsupported, misunderstood, or tired, your inner clarity remains available. You may lack many things. But you never lack the capacity to choose alignment.

Savage takeaway
Integrity is not a luxury item.

Quiet power mantra
"I remain aligned with reason, even when nothing around me is ideal."

XXVI. MASTER YOUR CRAFT, RELEASE CONTROL

"What art and profession soever thou hast learned, endeavour to affect it, and comfort thyself in it; and pass the remainder of thy life as one who from his whole heart commits himself and whatsoever belongs unto him, unto the gods: and as for men, carry not thyself either tyrannically or servilely towards any."

What Marcus meant (core philosophy)

Marcus reminds us to remain rooted in the discipline we have chosen. Whatever skill, calling, or profession one has learned:

- practice it sincerely,
- embody it fully,
- take comfort in the steadiness it provides.

But alongside mastery comes surrender. Commit yourself and your life to the larger order of existence, to fate, nature, or the divine as you understand it. This is not passive resignation but peaceful acceptance that not everything rests within personal control. And in dealing with others:

- do not dominate,
- do not submit in weakness.

Neither tyranny nor servility belongs to a rational person. The balanced soul stands upright, neither crushing nor collapsing.

Dating translation (what this means emotionally/socially)

In modern relational life: Become deeply rooted in who you are and what you do well. Your craft may be:

- your work,
- your voice,
- your creativity,
- your emotional intelligence.

Let it anchor you. People often abandon themselves when relationships enter the picture. They try to control outcomes or surrender their autonomy entirely. Marcus offers a third path: Commit to your path, release the outcome. And in relationships:

- do not attempt to control another person's will or behavior.
- do not shrink yourself to avoid discomfort.

Healthy connection lives in the middle: Standing fully in yourself without overpowering or disappearing.

Savage takeaway

Master yourself. Release the need to control everyone else.

Quiet power mantra

"I walk my path fully, neither above others nor beneath them."

XXVII. ALL AGES ARE THE SAME PLAY

"Consider in my mind, for example's sake, the times of Vespasian[39]: thou shalt see but the same things: some marrying, some bringing up children, some sick, some dying, some fighting, some feasting, some

---

[39] Vespasian (reigned 69–79 AD) was a Roman Emperor of relatively humble origins who founded the Flavian Dynasty and restored stability to Rome after the chaotic Year of the Four Emperors. He commissioned Rome's most famous landmark, originally known as the Flavian Amphitheatre, using funds from the spoils of the Jewish War.

merchandising, some tilling, some flattering, some boasting, some suspecting, some undermining, some wishing to die, some fretting and murmuring at their present estate, some wooing, some hoarding, some seeking after magistracies, and some after kingdoms. And is not that their age quite over, and ended? Again, consider now the times of Trajan[40]. There likewise thou seest the very self-same things, and that age also is now over and ended. In the like manner consider other periods, both of times and of whole nations, and see how many men, after they had with all their might and main intended and prosecuted some one worldly thing or other did soon after drop away, and were resolved into the elements. But especially thou must call to mind them, whom thou thyself in thy lifetime hast known much distracted about vain things, and in the meantime neglecting to do that, and closely and unseparably (as fully satisfied with it) to adhere unto it, which their own proper constitution did require. And here thou must remember, that thy carriage in every business must be according to the worth and due proportion of it, for so shalt thou not easily be tired out and vexed, if thou shalt not dwell upon small matters longer than is fitting."

What Marcus meant (core philosophy)

Marcus invites you to step outside the illusion of historical importance. Think of past eras:

- Vespasian's time
- Trajan's time
- any empire, any generation

What do you see? People:

- marrying
- arguing
- working
- chasing status
- worrying
- competing
- longing
- hoarding
- fearing death while wasting life

Different names. Same patterns. And every one of those lives felt urgent while they lived it. Yet now? Gone. Dissolved into history. The point is not nihilism. It is perspective. Most human agitation revolves around things that do not endure. So, Marcus advises: Act in proportion. Give each task only the weight it deserves. Exhaustion comes when we treat small matters as if they were eternal battles.

Dating translation (what this means emotionally/socially)

Zoom out. Every modern drama feels uniquely catastrophic:

- dating apps
- ghosting
- social status
- "winning" relationships

---

[40] Trajan (reigned 98–117 AD) was one of Rome's most successful and beloved emperors, officially bestowed with the title *Optimus Princeps* ("Best Ruler") by the Senate.

- proving something to someone

But look at history honestly. Humans have always:
- chased approval
- pursued love poorly
- obsessed over reputation
- feared missing out

And then they vanished. This is not depressing. It is liberating.

It means: You do not need to over-invest emotional energy into temporary social noise. Especially in dating:
- Don't dwell endlessly on small interactions.
- Don't build epic narratives around minor disappointments.
- Don't lose yourself chasing validation that will not matter even five years from now.

Stay aligned with your true nature instead of chasing temporary applause.

Savage takeaway
Most of what feels urgent is just recycled human drama. Don't give small things epic energy.

Quiet power mantra
"History repeats the same distractions. I choose what is worthy of my attention."

XXVIII. FAME FADES. CHARACTER REMAINS.
"Those words which once were common and ordinary, are now become obscure and obsolete; and so the names of men once commonly known and famous, are now become in a manner obscure and obsolete names. Camillus, Cæso, Volesius, Leonnatus; not long after, Scipio, Cato, then Augustus, then Adrianus, then Antoninus Pius: all these in a short time will be out of date, and, as things of another world as it were, become fabulous. And this I say of them, who once shined as the wonders of their ages, for as for the rest, no sooner are they expired, than with them all their fame and memory. And what is it then that shall always be remembered? all is vanity. What is it that we must bestow our care and diligence upon? even upon this only: that our minds and wills be just; that our actions be charitable; that our speech be never deceitful, or that our understanding be not subject to error; that our inclination be always set to embrace whatsoever shall happen unto us, as necessary, as usual, as ordinary, as flowing from such a beginning, and such a fountain, from which both thou thyself and all things are. Willingly therefore, and wholly surrender up thyself unto that fatal concatenation, yielding up thyself unto the fates, to be disposed of at their pleasure."

What Marcus meant (core philosophy)
Marcus is dismantling one of humanity's deepest illusions: The belief that recognition lasts. He lists powerful figures whose names once dominated the world:
- Camillus
- Scipio
- Cato
- Augustus

- Hadrian
- Antoninus Pius

Men who shaped history. Leaders whose reputations filled entire empires.

And yet: Even they drift toward obscurity. Even greatness dissolves into myth, then into silence. So, he asks the essential question: If fame itself disappears… what actually matters? His answer is simple and severe: Not legacy. Not applause. Only:

- a just mind
- charitable action
- honest speech
- clear understanding
- acceptance of reality as it unfolds

Everything else is vanity.

Dating translation (modern emotional lens)

This hits especially hard in a world obsessed with visibility. Followers. Likes. Perception. Winning narratives.

Marcus would say: The people you are trying to impress will be forgotten. The standards you are trying to meet will evolve. The social games will reset endlessly. So, stop shaping yourself around external recognition. Instead:

- Speak truthfully.
- Act kindly but without self-abandonment.
- Keep your internal compass clean.

Because reputation fades. Character is the only thing that travels with you.

Deep emotional layer

There is something deeply freeing here. You do not need to control how you are remembered. You only need to control how you live now.

Marcus calls this: "Yielding to the concatenation of fate."

Not passive surrender. Alignment. Trusting that life flows from a larger source, and moving with it instead of fighting every current.

Savage takeaway

History forgets almost everyone. So, stop living for memory. Live for integrity.

Quiet power mantra

"I release the need to be remembered. I choose to be true."

XXIX. ALL THINGS ARE SEEDS OF CHANGE

"Whatsoever is now present, and from day to day hath its existence; all objects of memories, and the minds and memories themselves, incessantly consider, all things that are, have their being by change and alteration. Use thyself therefore often to meditate upon this, that the nature of the universe delights in

nothing more, than in altering those things that are, and in making others like unto them. So that we may say, that whatsoever is, is but as it were the seed of that which shall be. For if thou think that that only is seed, which either the earth or the womb receiveth, thou art very simple."

What Marcus meant (core philosophy)

Marcus reminds himself that change is not an interruption of life. Change is the fundamental mechanism of existence itself. Everything that exists is already in motion toward transformation:

- memories change
- minds change
- circumstances change
- identities change

Nothing is static. Even what feels solid is simply a stage within an ongoing process of becoming. He expands the metaphor of "seed" beyond literal reproduction. A seed is not only something planted physically; every moment, every condition, every state of being contains within it the beginning of what comes next.

The universe delights in transformation. Resistance to change is resistance to nature itself. To believe that only obvious beginnings count as seeds is naïve. Every present reality is already the origin of the future.

Dating translation (what this means emotionally/socially)

Applied to emotional and relational life: What you are experiencing right now is not the final form. It is the seed. The relationship you thought was permanent becomes the catalyst for independence. The heartbreak becomes emotional clarity. The situationship becomes the moment you finally choose yourself. People often cling to the present as if it must remain fixed. They mourn endings as failures rather than recognizing them as transitions.

Marcus is saying: Nothing is just happening to you. Everything is becoming something through you. The version of you that entered a connection is not the version that leaves it. Every interaction is shaping the next phase of your identity, your standards, and your emotional intelligence. Even confusion is a seed. Even disappointment is a seed. The question is not whether change will occur. The question is whether you will recognize what is being planted inside you as it happens.

Savage takeaway

Nothing stays. That includes the version of you that tolerated less.

Quiet power mantra

"I allow change to shape me into what comes next."

XXX. SIMPLICITY IS EMOTIONAL MASTERY

"Thou art now ready to die, and yet hast thou not attained to that perfect simplicity: thou art yet subject to many troubles and perturbations; not yet free from all fear and suspicion of external accidents; nor yet either so meekly disposed towards all men, as thou shouldest; or so affected as one, whose only study and only wisdom is, to be just in all his actions."

What Marcus meant (core philosophy)

Marcus confronts himself with uncomfortable honesty. He reminds himself that even though death is always near, he has not yet reached true simplicity of character. For him, simplicity does not mean naïveté or minimalism. It means internal clarity:

- freedom from unnecessary fear
- release from suspicion and emotional turbulence
- steadiness toward external events
- genuine kindness toward others
- unwavering commitment to justice in action

He is acknowledging that wisdom is not intellectual understanding alone. It is emotional refinement. A person may understand philosophy and still be reactive, defensive, or internally unsettled. True simplicity is the absence of internal noise.

Dating translation (what this means emotionally/socially)

Applied to relationships, this speaks directly to emotional maturity. You may believe you are healed, wise, or evolved. Then someone triggers you and you realize:

- you still fear abandonment
- you still assume hidden motives
- you still brace for disappointment
- you still carry suspicion shaped by past wounds

Marcus is not shaming himself. He is observing where emotional reactions still exist so he can refine them. In dating, simplicity looks like:

- Responding instead of reacting.
- Seeing someone clearly without projecting past partners onto them.
- Maintaining kindness without losing boundaries.
- Choosing justice and integrity even when hurt.

Many people chase complicated emotional dynamics because chaos feels familiar. Simplicity feels almost foreign because it removes drama as identity. But emotional simplicity is power. It is the ability to stand grounded without being hardened.

Savage takeaway

Healing is not proven by what you understand. It is proven by what no longer triggers you.

Quiet power mantra

"I move toward clarity, kindness, and steady inner calm."

XXXI. WATCH WHAT PEOPLE CHASE AND WHAT THEY FEAR

"Behold and observe, what is the state of their rational part; and those that the world doth account wise, see what things they fly and are afraid of; and what things they hunt after."

What Marcus meant (core philosophy)

Marcus urges himself to study people not by their reputation, but by observing the state of their rational mind. True understanding comes from noticing:

92

- what people avoid
- what they pursue
- what triggers fear
- what drives desire

Even those considered wise by society reveal their real character through their attachments and aversions. Reputation and titles mean little compared to behavior. By observing without judgment, one sees clearly what governs another person's internal world.

Dating translation (what this means emotionally/socially)
In dating, listen less to what someone says about themselves and more to what their patterns reveal. Watch:
- what they run from (commitment, accountability, vulnerability)
- what they chase (validation, novelty, control, status)
- what makes them anxious
- what they prioritize when choices become difficult

People tell you who they are through motion, not language.
- Someone may claim emotional maturity but panic at intimacy.
- Someone may present confidence but constantly seek external approval.
- Someone may say they want partnership yet pursue only excitement.

Observation without projection saves emotional energy. You stop trying to interpret potential and instead recognize patterns.

Savage takeaway
Believe behavior. Titles like "emotionally intelligent" are self-assigned.

Quiet power mantra
"I see clearly by watching actions, not words."

XXXII. SUFFERING LIVES IN INTERPRETATION, NOT EVENTS
"In another man's mind and understanding thy evil Cannot subsist, nor in any proper temper or distemper of the natural constitution of thy body, which is but as it were the coat or cottage of thy soul. Wherein then, but in that part of thee, wherein the conceit, and apprehension of any misery can subsist? Let not that part therefore admit any such conceit, and then all is well. Though thy body which is so near it should either be cut or burnt, or suffer any corruption or putrefaction, yet let that part to which it belongs to judge of these, be still at rest; that is, let her judge this, that whatsoever it is, that equally may happen to a wicked man, and to a good man, is neither good nor evil. For that which happens equally to him that lives according to nature, and to him that doth not, is neither according to nature, nor against it; and by consequent, neither good nor bad."

What Marcus meant (core philosophy)
Marcus separates external reality from internal judgment. He argues that harm does not exist inside other people's thoughts, nor solely within the body itself. Painful events may happen to the physical form, but suffering arises from the part of us that interprets those events as misfortune or injustice. The rational mind has the power to decide:

- whether something is good or bad
- whether something is worth distress
- whether an event defines us

If something can happen equally to both a virtuous person and a flawed one, it cannot inherently be good or evil. It is simply part of existence. Peace comes from refusing to label neutral events as personal tragedy.

Dating translation (what this means emotionally/socially)

In relationships, much of the pain people carry comes from the story they attach to events rather than the events themselves.

- Rejection happens to everyone.
- Miscommunication happens to everyone.
- Breakups happen to everyone.

The suffering begins when the mind adds meaning:

- "This means I'm not enough."
- "This proves love isn't safe."
- "This always happens to me."

Marcus is not denying pain. He is separating physical or emotional experience from identity-level interpretation. Someone's behavior may hurt, but the narrative you attach determines whether it becomes trauma or information. When you stop assigning moral meaning to every outcome, emotional resilience grows.

Savage takeaway

What hurts is often the story you told yourself about what it meant.

Quiet power mantra

"I release interpretations that turn experience into suffering."

XXXIII. ALL THINGS ARE INTERCONNECTED

"Ever consider and think upon the world as being but one living substance, and having but one soul, and how all things in the world, are terminated into one sensitive power; and are done by one general motion as it were, and deliberation of that one soul; and how all things that are, concur in the cause of one another's being, and by what manner of connection and concatenation all things happen."

What Marcus meant (core philosophy)

Marcus encourages himself to see the universe as a single living organism. Everything exists within one shared system:

- one living substance
- one unified soul or rational order
- one interconnected movement

Nothing happens in isolation. Every event contributes to another. Every cause is linked to other causes through an intricate chain of connection. To understand reality is to recognize interdependence. Each action, thought, and moment participates in a larger unfolding beyond individual perception. This perspective reduces ego-centered thinking and invites acceptance of the broader flow of existence.

Dating translation (what this means emotionally/socially)

Applied to relationships, nothing happens randomly or independently from the larger story of your life. Every person you meet:

- shapes your standards
- refines your awareness
- reveals patterns you carry
- prepares you for future alignment

The connection that felt like a detour becomes preparation. The heartbreak becomes boundary-setting. The unexpected encounter becomes redirection. When you see relationships as isolated failures or successes, you miss the larger narrative arc. Marcus reminds you that experiences are interconnected threads, not standalone mistakes. Even endings contribute to beginnings you cannot yet see.

Savage takeaway

Nothing was wasted. Every connection moved you somewhere.

Quiet power mantra

"I trust that every experience is part of a greater unfolding."

XXXIV. YOU ARE THE MIND, NOT THE BODY YOU CARRY

"What art thou, that better and divine part excepted, but as Epictetus said well, a wretched soul, appointed to carry a carcass up and down?"

What Marcus meant (core philosophy)

Marcus echoes Epictetus to remind himself of the distinction between the higher rational self and the physical body. The body is temporary, vulnerable, and subject to decay. It is not the true seat of identity. The divine or rational part, the mind capable of reason and moral choice, is the higher aspect of human existence. He uses stark language intentionally. By calling the body a "carcass," he strips away attachment to vanity, comfort, or physical obsession. The goal is not self-loathing but perspective. You are not defined by flesh alone. You are defined by the consciousness that directs it.

Dating translation (what this means emotionally/socially)

In dating, people often collapse their entire worth into physical desirability:

- how attractive they appear
- how they compare to others
- whether someone chooses them sexually or romantically

Marcus would say this is a misplacement of identity. Your body is part of your experience, but it is not your essence. Attraction may open doors, but character determines whether connection survives. When someone reduces you to appearance, they are interacting with the surface. When you reduce yourself to appearance, you abandon your deeper power. True attraction grows from the rational and emotional self:

- integrity

- self-respect
- clarity
- presence

The right person recognizes the mind that carries the body, not just the body itself.

Savage takeaway
You are not competing as a body. You are revealing yourself as a mind.

Quiet power mantra
"My worth lives in who I am, not only in how I appear."

XXXV. CHANGE IS NEITHER LOSS NOR GAIN
"To suffer change can be no hurt; as no benefit it is, by change to attain to being. The age and time of the world is as it were a flood and swift current, consisting of the things that are brought to pass in the world. For as soon as anything hath appeared, and is passed away, another succeeds, and that also will presently out of sight."

What Marcus meant (core philosophy)
Marcus reminds himself that change itself is neutral. Transformation is neither inherently harmful nor beneficial. It simply is. The world moves like a constant current:
- things arise
- things pass
- new things replace what was

Nothing remains fixed long enough to define permanent success or failure. Even what feels monumental quickly dissolves into the ongoing flow of existence. By seeing life as a swift river, Marcus reduces attachment to outcomes. Change does not diminish you, nor does it automatically elevate you. It is simply the natural movement of reality.

Dating translation (what this means emotionally/socially)
In relationships, people often interpret change as proof of something deeply personal:
- a breakup becomes "I failed"
- someone moving on becomes "I was replaceable"
- feelings fading becomes "it wasn't real"

Marcus would challenge that interpretation. Change in connection does not automatically mean loss or gain. It means movement. People grow. Dynamics shift. Attraction evolves. Timing changes. The emotional meaning you assign is separate from the fact itself. When you understand that relationships exist within a current, you stop trying to freeze moments that were never meant to stay still. What leaves is not always loss. What arrives is not always victory. Both are part of motion.

Savage takeaway
Not everything that ends was taken from you. Some things simply moved on.

Quiet power mantra
"I move with change without attaching identity to it."

XXXVI. NOTHING IS RANDOM, EVERYTHING FOLLOWS A PATTERN

"Whatsoever doth happen in the world, is, in the course of nature, as usual and ordinary as a rose in the spring, and fruit in summer. Of the same nature is sickness and death; slander, and lying in wait, and whatsoever else ordinarily doth unto fools use to be occasion either of joy or sorrow. That, whatsoever it is, that comes after, doth always very naturally, and as it were familiarly, follow upon that which was before.
For thou must consider the things of the world, not as a loose independent number, consisting merely of necessary events; but as a discreet connection of things orderly and harmoniously disposed. There is then to be seen in the things of the world, not a bare succession, but an admirable correspondence and affinity."

What Marcus meant (core philosophy)
Marcus urges himself to see events as natural expressions of an ordered universe. Just as roses bloom in spring and fruit grows in summer, so too do:
- sickness
- death
- deception
- joy
- disappointment

These are not anomalies. They are ordinary components of existence. He rejects the idea that life is a chaotic series of disconnected events. Instead, everything unfolds within an intricate chain of cause and effect, forming a harmonious structure even when individual moments feel painful or confusing. Wisdom lies in recognizing the pattern rather than resisting the inevitability of events.

Dating translation (what this means emotionally/socially)
In relationships, people often treat difficult experiences as shocking exceptions:
- betrayal feels unnatural
- misalignment feels unfair
- heartbreak feels like a cosmic mistake

Marcus would say: these experiences are part of the human pattern. Just as love appears, so do misunderstandings. Just as connection forms, endings follow. This does not mean pain is meaningless. It means pain is not evidence that something went wrong with existence itself. When you understand that emotional highs and lows belong to the natural rhythm of relationships, you stop personalizing every difficulty as a unique tragedy. Patterns reveal growth:
- The wrong partner clarifies your standards.
- The miscommunication teaches emotional precision.
- The ending creates space for alignment.

Life moves through sequences, not accidents.

Savage takeaway

What shocked you may simply be part of the pattern you hadn't recognized yet.

Quiet power mantra

"I see the pattern beneath the moment."

XXXVII. WAKE UP AND LIVE BY REASON, NOT INHERITED HABITS

"Let that of Heraclitus[41] never be out of thy mind, that the death of earth, is water, and the death of water, is air; and the death of air, is fire; and so on the contrary. Remember him also who was ignorant whither the way did lead, and how that reason being the thing by which all things in the world are administered, and which men are continually and most inwardly conversant with: yet is the thing, which ordinarily they are most in opposition with, and how those things which daily happen among them, cease not daily to be strange unto them, and that we should not either speak, or do anything as men in their sleep, by opinion and bare imagination: for then we think we speak and do, and that we must not be as children, who follow their father's example; for best reason alleging their bare καθότι παρειλήφαμεν[42]; or, as by successive tradition from our forefathers we have received it."

What Marcus meant (core philosophy)

Marcus reflects on Heraclitus' teaching that everything transforms into something else. Death is not disappearance but transition:

- earth becomes water
- water becomes air
- air becomes fire

Change is constant transformation. He then shifts deeper. Even though reason governs the universe and exists within every human, people resist it. They move through life half-asleep, guided by inherited beliefs, unconscious habits, and unquestioned traditions. He warns against living mechanically:

- speaking without awareness
- acting from imitation rather than understanding
- following patterns simply because they were passed down

True wisdom requires conscious participation. One must wake up from automatic living and align actions with reason rather than conditioning.

Dating translation (what this means emotionally/socially)

In relationships, many people operate from inherited scripts:

- "This is just how dating works."
- "Men always do this."
- "Women always behave like that."
- "I should accept this because it's normal."

---

[41] Heraclitus of Ephesus (c. 535–475 BC) was a pre-Socratic Greek philosopher whose ideas on change and the Logos became foundational to Stoic philosophy.

[42] The Greek phrase καθότι παρειλήφαμεν (kathoti pareilēphamen) translates to English as "inasmuch as/since we have received" or "because we have received."

Marcus challenges this unconscious repetition. Are you choosing consciously, or replaying patterns learned from past relationships, family dynamics, or cultural expectations? Many dating struggles come from moving through emotional life asleep:

- Chasing familiar chaos because it feels normal.
- Accepting breadcrumbs because you were taught to tolerate less.
- Following traditional timelines that don't align with your truth.

Awareness interrupts repetition. When you wake up to your patterns, transformation begins.

Savage takeaway
If you don't question your patterns, you will call familiarity destiny.

Quiet power mantra
"I move through love awake, conscious, and self-directed."

XXXVIII. TIME DOES NOT CHANGE THE NATURE OF DEATH
"Even as if any of the gods should tell thee, Thou shalt certainly die to-morrow, or next day, thou wouldst not, except thou wert extremely base and pusillanimous[43], take it for a great benefit, rather to die the next day after, than to-morrow; (for alas, what is the difference!) so, for the same reason, think it no great matter to die rather many years after, than the very next day."

What Marcus meant (core philosophy)
Marcus challenges the illusion that more time fundamentally changes the reality of mortality. If someone were told they would die tomorrow or the day after, only a deeply fearful person would see a meaningful difference between the two. The point is not to rush toward death, but to recognize that time itself does not alter the nature of existence or its ending. Life is finite regardless of duration.

The Stoic lesson is this: Do not cling desperately to "more time" as if quantity alone gives life meaning. Instead, focus on the quality of how you live now. Whether death comes soon or later, the essential task remains the same: live aligned with reason and virtue in the present moment.

Dating translation (what this means emotionally/socially)
In relationships, people often delay truth because they believe time will fix uncertainty:

- "Maybe if I give it more time, they'll change."
- "Maybe next year will be different."
- "I just need to wait a little longer."

Marcus would question this mindset. More time does not automatically create clarity, compatibility, or commitment. Time only amplifies what already exists. Waiting is not progress if nothing fundamentally changes. This does not mean rushing decisions. It means recognizing that postponing honesty with yourself is

---

[43] In English, pusillanimous means cowardly, timid, or lacking in courage.

rarely wisdom. Whether a relationship ends today or years from now, what matters is whether you lived authentically within it.

Savage takeaway
More time does not turn misalignment into destiny.

Quiet power mantra
"I value presence over postponement."

XXXIX. EVERYONE PASSES, SO HOLD LIFE LIGHTLY

"Let it be thy perpetual meditation, how many physicians who once looked so grim, and so theatrically shrunk their brows upon their patients, are dead and gone themselves. How many astrologers, after that in great ostentation they had foretold the death of some others, how many philosophers after so many elaborate tracts and volumes concerning either mortality or immortality; how many brave captains and commanders, after the death and slaughter of so many; how many kings and tyrants, after they had with such horror and insolency[44] abused their power upon men's lives, as though themselves had been immortal; how many, that I may so speak, whole cities both men and towns: Helice, Pompeii, Herculaneum, and others innumerable are dead and gone. Run them over also, whom thou thyself, one after another, hast known in thy time to drop away. Such and such a one took care of such and such a one's burial, and soon after was buried himself. So one, so another: and all things in a short time. For herein lieth all indeed, ever to look upon all worldly things, as things for their continuance, that are but for a day: and for their worth, most vile, and contemptible, as for example, What is man? That which but the other day when he was conceived was vile snivel; and within few days shall be either an embalmed carcass, or mere ashes. Thus must thou according to truth and nature, throughly consider how man's life is but for a very moment of time, and so depart meek and contented: even as if a ripe olive falling should praise the ground that bare her, and give thanks to the tree that begat her."

What Marcus meant (core philosophy)

Marcus walks through history to remind himself of a humbling truth: no status, skill, or power exempts anyone from mortality. Physicians who saved lives, philosophers who debated eternity, kings who ruled nations, conquerors who commanded armies, entire cities that once thrived. All gone. He strips away illusion by listing examples across every domain of human achievement. The purpose is not nihilism but clarity. Everything we treat as monumental is temporary:

- reputation fades
- power dissolves
- bodies decay
- memory itself disappears

By recognizing this, Marcus seeks freedom from attachment to ego, fear, or worldly obsession. Life becomes simpler when seen as brief. The ideal response is acceptance, leaving life gently and gratefully, like a ripe olive falling naturally from a tree.

---

[44] In English, insolency (an archaic variation of insolence) means rude, disrespectful, or overbearing behavior.

Dating translation (what this means emotionally/socially)

In relationships, people often assign overwhelming importance to moments that, within the vast arc of life, are temporary. The rejection that felt catastrophic. The betrayal that felt defining. The relationship that seemed like the entire story. Marcus invites a larger perspective. Everyone moves through cycles:

- People who once felt unforgettable fade into memory.
- Dynamics that felt permanent become chapters.
- The person who once consumed your thoughts becomes someone you barely recall.

This perspective is not meant to minimize emotion. It is meant to soften attachment to drama and ego. When you remember that everything passes, you stop gripping relationships as proof of identity or worth. You become more present, less desperate, less afraid of endings. You begin to love with appreciation instead of possession.

Savage takeaway

Even the people you thought defined your life will someday be stories you barely revisit.

Quiet power mantra

"I hold life gently, grateful for each moment without clinging."

XL. BE THE STILL POINT AMID THE STORM

"Thou must be like a promontory of the sea, against which though the waves beat continually, yet it both itself stands, and about it are those swelling waves stilled and quieted."

What Marcus meant (core philosophy)

Marcus uses the image of a rocky promontory standing firm against relentless waves. The sea continues its motion, but the rock remains unmoved. The lesson is emotional steadiness. External events will continue:

- praise and criticism
- loss and gain
- chaos and calm

The goal is not to stop the waves. The goal is to develop inner stability so that external forces do not disturb your center. Strength is quiet endurance. By remaining grounded, you transform turbulence into calm rather than becoming part of the disturbance.

Dating translation (what this means emotionally/socially)

Relationships often bring emotional waves:

- Mixed signals.
- Unexpected conflict.
- Shifting dynamics.
- Intense attraction followed by uncertainty.

101

Many people react by matching the chaos:
- They chase when ignored.
- They panic when energy changes.
- They lose their internal balance trying to control external behavior.

Marcus invites another path. Be the emotional anchor, not the storm. This does not mean tolerating disrespect or suppressing feelings. It means maintaining your center regardless of another person's inconsistency. When you stop reacting to every emotional wave, clarity emerges. People either meet your steadiness or reveal that they cannot.

Savage takeaway
Calm is power. Chaos loses influence when you stop dancing with it.

Quiet power mantra
"I remain steady while the waves move around me."

XLI. THE EVENT IS NOT THE MISFORTUNE. YOUR RESPONSE DEFINES IT.

"Oh, wretched I, to whom this mischance is happened! nay, happy I, to whom this thing being happened, I can continue without grief; neither wounded by that which is present, nor in fear of that which is to come. For as for this, it might have happened unto any man, but any man having such a thing befallen him, could not have continued without grief. Why then should that rather be an unhappiness, than this a happiness? But however, canst thou, O man! term that unhappiness, which is no mischance to the nature of man I Canst thou think that a mischance to the nature of man, which is not contrary to the end and will of his nature? What then hast thou learned is the will of man's nature? Doth that then which hath happened unto thee, hinder thee from being just? or magnanimous? or temperate? or wise? or circumspect? or true? or modest? or free? or from anything else of all those things in the present enjoying and possession whereof the nature of man, (as then enjoying all that is proper unto her,) is fully satisfied? Now to conclude; upon all occasion of sorrow remember henceforth to make use of this dogma, that whatsoever it is that hath happened unto thee, is in very deed no such thing of itself, as a misfortune; but that to bear it generously, is certainly great happiness."

What Marcus meant (core philosophy)
Marcus reframes suffering through radical perspective. Instead of saying, "This terrible thing happened to me", he challenges himself to say: "Something happened, and I remained whole."

The core Stoic principle here is that external events do not determine happiness or misery. What matters is whether the event prevents you from living according to your nature. He asks, does this stop you from being:
- Just
- Wise
- Calm
- Truthful
- Free in spirit
- Aligned with virtue?

102

If the answer is no, then the event itself is not truly a misfortune. The true victory is not avoiding hardship. The victory is meeting hardship without losing your character.

Dating translation (what this means emotionally/socially)
In relationships, people often define themselves by what happened to them:
- "I was betrayed."
- "I was ghosted."
- "I was rejected."
- "I was blindsided."

Marcus invites a different lens: Yes, something happened. But did it destroy your ability to be grounded, kind, wise, and self-respecting? If you remain aligned with yourself, the experience becomes strength instead of damage. Heartbreak is not proof of loss of worth. It is an event. Your power lies in how you carry it:
- Do you grow clearer?
- Do you become more honest?
- Do you remain compassionate without losing boundaries?

The event does not define you. The way you bear it does.

Savage takeaway
The pain isn't your identity. Your response is your legacy.

Quiet power mantra
"I transform hardship into strength through how I meet it."

XLII. LONGER LIFE DOES NOT MEAN DEEPER LIFE
"It is but an ordinary coarse one, yet it is a good effectual remedy against the fear of death, for a man to consider in his mind the examples of such, who greedily and covetously (as it were) did for a long time enjoy their lives. What have they got more, than they whose deaths have been untimely? Are not they themselves dead at the last? as Cadiciant's, Fabius, Julianus Lepidus, or any other who in their lifetime having buried many, were at the last buried themselves. The whole space of any man's life, is but little; and as little as it is, with what troubles, with what manner of dispositions, and in the society of how wretched a body must it be passed! Let it be therefore unto thee altogether as a matter of indifferency. For if thou shalt look backward; behold, what an infinite chaos of time doth present itself unto thee; and as infinite a chaos, if thou shalt look forward. In that which is so infinite, what difference can there be between that which liveth but three days, and that which liveth three ages?"

What Marcus meant (core philosophy)
Marcus dismantles the fear of death by confronting a simple truth: living longer does not fundamentally change the outcome. Those who chased long life, clung to time, or tried to extend their existence beyond others ultimately reached the same destination. The difference between a short life and a long life becomes insignificant when placed against the vast scale of eternity.

Time before birth was infinite. Time after death will be infinite. Against that backdrop, whether someone lives three days or three decades longer loses meaning. The Stoic insight is not nihilistic. It is freeing. If duration does not define value, then fear of limited time loses its power. What matters is how life is lived, not how long it lasts.

Dating translation (what this means emotionally/socially)

In relationships, people often believe that longevity equals success. A long relationship feels like a victory. A short one feels like failure. Marcus would challenge that assumption. A relationship that lasted years but drained your spirit did not necessarily hold more value than a brief connection that transformed your understanding. Time invested is not proof of meaning. Many people stay because of duration:

- "We've been together so long."
- "I don't want to waste the time."
- "I need this to last to justify everything."

But length does not equal alignment. A short, honest connection can shape you more deeply than a long, misaligned one.

Savage takeaway

Time spent is not proof of value. Depth matters more than duration.

Quiet power mantra

"I measure life by presence and truth, not by length."

XLIII. THE SIMPLEST PATH IS THE TRUEST ONE

"Let thy course ever be the most compendious way. The most compendious, is that which is according to nature: that is, in all both words and deeds, ever to follow that which is most sound and perfect. For such a resolution will free a man from all trouble, strife, dissembling, and ostentation."

What Marcus meant (core philosophy)

Marcus advises himself to choose the most direct and natural path in all actions and speech. The "most compendious way" means the shortest, simplest route. Not shortcuts rooted in avoidance, but clarity aligned with nature and reason. When a person consistently acts according to what is sound and true:

- unnecessary complications disappear
- internal conflict reduces
- deception becomes unnecessary
- performative behavior falls away

Complexity often arises from resisting truth. Simplicity emerges when actions and intentions align naturally. Living according to reason creates ease because there is nothing to hide, defend, or overcomplicate.

Dating translation (what this means emotionally/socially)

In relationships, people frequently avoid the direct path.

- They hint instead of communicate.
- They tolerate confusion instead of asking for clarity.
- They perform versions of themselves instead of showing up honestly.

Marcus would call this unnecessary detouring. The most direct path in dating is:

- saying what you actually want
- asking the question you're afraid to ask
- leaving when alignment isn't present
- acting in ways that feel internally clean rather than strategically manipulative

When you move naturally and honestly, drama loses fuel. Dissembling, chasing, and emotional games dissolve because you are no longer participating in them.

Savage takeaway
Confusion often exists because someone avoided the simple truth.

Quiet power mantra
"I choose the clear and honest path without unnecessary complication."

THE FIFTH BOOK
Do The Thing Even When You Don't Feel Like It

I. RISE BECAUSE PURPOSE IS YOUR NATURE

"In the morning when thou findest thyself unwilling to rise, consider with thyself presently, it is to go about a man's work that I am stirred up. Am I then yet unwilling to go about that, for which I myself was born and brought forth into this world? Or was I made for this, to lay me down, and make much of myself in a warm bed? 'O but this is pleasing.' And was it then for this that thou wert born, that thou mightest enjoy pleasure? Was it not in very truth for this, that thou mightest always be busy and in action? Seest thou not how all things in the world besides, how every tree md plant, how sparrows and ants, spiders and bees: how all in their kind are intent as it were orderly to perform whatsoever (towards the preservation of this orderly universe) naturally doth become and belong unto thin? And wilt not thou do that, which belongs unto a man to do? Wilt not thou run to do that, which thy nature doth require? 'But thou must have some rest.' Yes, thou must. Nature hath of that also, as well as of eating and drinking, allowed thee a certain stint. But thou guest beyond thy stint, and beyond that which would suffice, and in matter of action, there thou comest short of that which thou mayest. It must needs be therefore, that thou dost not love thyself, for if thou didst, thou wouldst also love thy nature, and that which thy nature doth propose unto herself as her end. Others, as many as take pleasure in their trade and profession, can even pine themselves at their works, and neglect their bodies and their food for it; and doest thou less honour thy nature, than an ordinary mechanic his trade; or a good dancer his art? than a covetous man his silver, and vainglorious man applause? These to whatsoever they take an affection, can be content to want their meat and sleep, to further that every one which he affects: and shall actions tending to the common good of human society, seem more vile unto thee, or worthy of less respect and intention?"

What Marcus meant (core philosophy)

Marcus confronts the resistance to action that arises when comfort competes with purpose. When he feels unwilling to rise, he reminds himself: he was born to fulfill human work. Not merely to seek pleasure or remain in ease, but to participate actively in life. Nature itself demonstrates this principle:

- trees grow
- ants labor
- bees build
- every living thing fulfills its function

Humans are no exception. To live according to nature means to engage, contribute, and act in alignment with one's purpose. Rest is natural and necessary, but excess comfort that replaces meaningful action is a form of self-neglect. To avoid one's purpose is to disconnect from one's own nature. Marcus argues that people who love something deeply willingly sacrifice comfort for it. Therefore, reluctance toward meaningful work suggests a lack of alignment with one's deeper self.

106

Dating translation (what this means emotionally/socially)

Emotionally and relationally, this passage speaks to showing up fully rather than retreating into avoidance. It is easy to stay in emotional comfort:

- avoiding difficult conversations
- delaying decisions
- remaining passive instead of intentional

But healthy relationships require participation. To love well is to engage:

- communicate honestly
- take emotional risks when aligned with truth
- pursue growth rather than hide in safety

Many people mistake emotional avoidance for self-care. Marcus would say that true self-love includes honoring your nature, which is active, relational, and purposeful. When you stop shrinking from what you are meant to do emotionally, clarity emerges.

Savage takeaway

Comfort is not always self-love. Sometimes it is avoidance dressed as peace.

Quiet power mantra

"I rise to meet my purpose instead of retreating into comfort."

II. PEACE IS ONE DECISION AWAY

"How easy a thing is it for a man to put off from him all turbulent adventitious imaginations, and presently to be in perfect rest and tranquillity!"

What Marcus meant (core philosophy)

Marcus reminds himself that mental disturbance often comes from "adventitious imaginations" — thoughts that attach themselves unnecessarily to reality. These are not events themselves but interpretations, assumptions, fears, and projections layered on top of what is happening.

The Stoic insight: The mind has the power to release these intrusive constructions immediately. Peace is not something slowly built from external conditions. It is something restored when unnecessary mental noise is removed. Tranquility exists beneath turbulence. The work is simply letting go of what the mind adds unnecessarily.

Dating translation (what this means emotionally/socially)

In relationships, much of emotional chaos comes from imagined narratives rather than actual events:

- "They didn't text back quickly. Something must be wrong."
- "They sounded different. Maybe they're losing interest."
- "What if this means I'm about to be rejected?"

These thoughts feel real, but they are often self-generated turbulence. Marcus suggests that emotional calm is accessible the moment you stop feeding imagined scenarios. When you return to observable reality instead of imagined futures, the nervous system settles. This does not mean ignoring real red flags. It means refusing to create suffering from stories that have no evidence yet.

Savage takeaway
Most emotional chaos is fan fiction your brain wrote without permission.

Quiet power mantra
"I release imagined turbulence and return to calm clarity."

III. DO WHAT IS RIGHT WITHOUT SEEKING PERMISSION

"Think thyself fit and worthy to speak, or to do anything that is according to nature, and let not the reproach, or report of some that may ensue upon it, ever deter thee. If it be right and honest to be spoken or done, undervalue not thyself so much, as to be discouraged from it. As for them, they have their own rational over-ruling part, and their own proper inclination: which thou must not stand and look about to take notice of, but go on straight, whither both thine own particular, and the common nature do lead thee; and the way of both these, is but one."

What Marcus meant (core philosophy)
Marcus reminds himself to act according to nature and reason without fear of criticism or external judgment. If something is truly right:
*   Honest
*   Just
*   aligned with reason

then the possibility of reproach should not deter action. Each person operates according to their own rational faculty and inclinations. Their opinions belong to them, not to you. Watching others for approval or hesitation disrupts alignment with your own nature. The path of individual integrity and the common good ultimately converge. When you act rightly, you serve both yourself and the greater order. The lesson is simple: do not undervalue yourself by shrinking from truth.

Dating translation (what this means emotionally/socially)
In relationships, people often silence themselves out of fear:
*   fear of being "too much"
*   fear of rejection
*   fear of appearing needy or difficult
*   fear of how others might interpret honesty

Marcus would say that when your words or actions come from clarity and integrity, hesitation is self-betrayal.
*   Say what is true.
*   Set the boundary.
*   Express the need.
*   Ask the question.

Other people will interpret your actions according to their own mindset. That is not your responsibility. When you wait for universal approval before acting authentically, you abandon yourself.

Savage takeaway
If it's honest and aligned, say it anyway.

Quiet power mantra
"I act with integrity without waiting for permission or approval."

IV. LIVE IN ALIGNMENT UNTIL THE VERY END

"I continue my course by actions according to nature, until I fall and cease, breathing out my last breath into that air, by which continually breathed in I did live; and falling upon that earth, out of whose gifts and fruits my father gathered his seed, my mother her blood, and my nurse her milk, out of which for so many years I have been provided, both of meat and drink. And lastly, which beareth me that tread upon it, and beareth with me that so many ways do abuse it, or so freely make use of it, so many ways to so many ends."

What Marcus meant (core philosophy)
Marcus reflects on the continuity between life and nature. He sees existence as a cycle:
- breath comes from the air and returns to it
- the body is nourished by the earth and returns to it
- life is sustained by countless natural processes beyond individual control

Rather than fearing death, he frames it as a natural transition within the same system that gave life. The core teaching is quiet acceptance: Continue acting according to nature, fulfilling your role with integrity, until the natural moment of cessation arrives. There is no need for resistance, dramatization, or clinging. Life is participation in a larger order, and death is simply returning to it.

Dating translation (what this means emotionally/socially)
In relationships, this passage speaks to showing up fully without grasping for permanence. Many people try to control outcomes:
- forcing longevity
- resisting natural endings
- holding onto connections past their natural life

Marcus reminds us that relationships, like life itself, exist within cycles. Your role is to act in alignment:
- love honestly
- show up authentically
- participate fully while it exists

But do not cling to permanence as proof of success. Some connections nourish you for a season. Some teach you what you needed at that moment. Letting something complete its natural course is not failure.

Savage takeaway
Your job is to show up fully, not to force forever.

Quiet power mantra
"I move through life and love in harmony with what is natural."

V. MASTER WHAT YOU CAN CONTROL

"No man can admire thee for thy sharp acute language, such is thy natural disability that way. Be it so: yet there be many other good things, for the want of which thou canst not plead the want or natural ability. Let them be seen in thee, which depend wholly from thee; sincerity, gravity, laboriousness, contempt of pleasures; be not querulous, be Content with little, be kind, be free; avoid all superfluity, all vain prattling; be magnanimous. Doest not thou perceive, how many things there be, which notwithstanding any pretence of natural indisposition and unfitness, thou mightest have performed and exhibited, and yet still thou doest voluntarily continue drooping downwards? Or wilt thou say that it is through defect of thy natural constitution, that thou art constrained to murmur, to be base and wretched to flatter; now to accuse, and now to please, and pacify thy body: to be vainglorious, to be so giddy-headed., and unsettled in thy thoughts? nay (witnesses be the Gods) of all these thou mightest have been rid long ago: only, this thou must have been contented with, to have borne the blame of one that is somewhat slow and dull, wherein thou must so exercise thyself, as one who neither doth much take to heart this his natural defect, nor yet pleaseth himself in it."

What Marcus meant (core philosophy)
Marcus accepts that certain abilities may not come naturally to him. Instead of resisting this reality, he shifts focus to what remains fully within his power. Natural limitations are not excuses for neglecting character. Even if someone lacks certain talents or strengths, they can still cultivate:
- sincerity
- discipline
- humility
- restraint
- kindness
- contentment
- magnanimity

Marcus challenges self-pity and avoidance. He questions whether negative behaviors truly come from natural limitation or from voluntary indulgence. The core Stoic message is accountability. You may not control your natural gifts, but you control your character. Growth requires accepting imperfection without using it as justification for remaining stagnant.

Dating translation (what this means emotionally/socially)
In relationships, people often hide behind identity narratives:
- "I'm just bad at communication."
- "I'm not good with emotions."
- "That's just how I am."

Marcus would call this self-excusing. You may not be naturally smooth, emotionally expressive, or socially effortless. But you can still embody:
- Honesty
- Respect
- Consistency
- Emotional responsibility

Relationships thrive on character more than charisma. Someone may not be naturally eloquent yet still communicate sincerely. Someone may not be effortlessly charming yet still show up with integrity. The real question is not what you lack. It is whether you are using perceived limitations as permission to avoid growth.

Savage takeaway
Your weaknesses explain your starting point. They do not excuse your behavior.

Quiet power mantra
"I focus on strengthening what is within my control."

VI. DO GOOD WITHOUT KEEPING SCORE

"Such there be, who when they have done a good turn to any, are ready to set them on the score for it, and to require retaliation. Others there be, who though they stand not upon retaliation, to require any, yet they think with themselves nevertheless, that such a one is their debtor, and they know as their word is what they have done. Others again there be, who when they have done any such thing, do not so much as know what they have done; but are like unto the vine, which beareth her grapes, and when once she hath borne her own proper fruit, is contented and seeks for no further recompense. As a horse after a race, and a hunting dog when he hath hunted, and a bee when she hath made her honey, look not for applause and commendation; so neither doth that man that rightly doth understand his own nature when he hath done a good turn: but from one doth proceed to do another, even as the vine after she hath once borne fruit in her own proper season, is ready for another time. Thou therefore must be one of them, who what they do, barely do it without any further thought, and are in a manner insensible of what they do. 'Nay but,' will some reply perchance, 'this very thing a rational man is bound unto, to understand what it is, that he doeth.' For it is the property, say they, of one that is naturally sociable, to be sensible, that he doth operate sociably: nay, and to desire, that the party him self that is sociably dealt with, should be sensible of it too. I answer, That which thou sayest is true indeed, but the true meaning of that which is said, thou dost not understand. And therefore art thou one of those first, whom I mentioned. For they also are led by a probable appearance of reason. But if thou dost desire to understand truly what it is that is said, fear not that thou shalt therefore give over any sociable action."

What Marcus meant (core philosophy)
Marcus describes three types of people when they do good for others:
1. Those who keep accounts and expect repayment.
2. Those who do not openly demand repayment but internally remember the debt.
3. Those who give naturally, like a vine bearing fruit, without self-congratulation or expectation.

The highest form of virtue belongs to the third. True goodness is not transactional. It flows from nature itself. Just as:
- a horse runs
- a bee makes honey
- a vine produces grapes

the virtuous person acts well simply because it is their nature to do so. Marcus warns that even subtle self-awareness ("I did something good") can become ego. The goal is not unconsciousness but freedom from self-centered accounting. Act rightly. Move on.

111

Dating translation (what this means emotionally/socially)

In relationships, many people operate from invisible ledgers:

- "I texted first three times."
- "I gave more emotionally."
- "I supported them more than they supported me."

Even when not spoken aloud, this scorekeeping creates resentment. Marcus suggests a different approach: Give authentically because it aligns with who you are, not because you expect equal exchange in the moment. This does not mean tolerating imbalance forever. Boundaries still matter. But kindness and generosity should not feel like strategic investments waiting for return. Healthy love comes from natural expression, not silent accounting. When you stop tracking every action, emotional freedom increases.

Savage takeaway

If you're keeping receipts, you're negotiating, not loving.

Quiet power mantra

"I give from alignment, not from expectation."

VII. PRAY FOR THE WHOLE, NOT JUST FOR YOURSELF

"The form of the Athenians' prayer did run thus: 'O rain, rain, good Jupiter, upon all the grounds and fields that belong to the Athenians.' Either we should not pray at all, or thus absolutely and freely; and not every one for himself in particular alone."

What Marcus meant (core philosophy)

Marcus reflects on a simple Athenian prayer asking for rain not for individuals but for the collective land. The lesson is about perspective and intention. Prayer, or any desire directed toward the future, should align with the common good rather than narrow personal gain. He suggests two paths:

- either do not pray at all
- or pray simply, openly, and for the benefit of the whole

True wisdom avoids overly specific demands rooted in personal attachment. Instead, it trusts the broader order of nature and seeks harmony with it. The Stoic ideal is humility: wanting what serves the greater whole rather than attempting to control outcomes for personal advantage.

Dating translation (what this means emotionally/socially)

In relationships, people often focus on highly specific outcomes:

- "Let this person choose me."
- "Let this relationship work exactly how I want."
- "Let this go my way."

Marcus invites a shift. Instead of wishing for a specific person or outcome, align with what serves mutual growth and truth. Ask for:

- clarity over attachment
- alignment over control
- connection that benefits both people, not just your desire

When you release hyper-specific expectations, you reduce suffering created by forcing outcomes that may not serve your deeper well-being.

Savage takeaway
Stop praying for a person. Start aligning with what is truly right for you.

Quiet power mantra
"I align my desires with what serves the greater good and my true nature."

VIII. ACCEPT WHAT IS PRESCRIBED AS PART OF THE WHOLE

"As we say commonly, The physician hath prescribed unto this man, riding; unto another, cold baths; unto a third, to go barefoot: so it is alike to say, The nature of the universe hath prescribed unto this man sickness, or blindness, or some loss, or damage or some such thing. For as there, when we say of a physician, that he hath prescribed anything, our meaning is, that he hath appointed this for that, as subordinate and conducing to health: so here, whatsoever doth happen unto any, is ordained unto him as a thing subordinate unto the fates, and therefore do we say of such things, that they do συμβαίνειν[45], that is, happen, or fall together; as of square stones, when either in walls, or pyramids in a certain position they fit one another, and agree as it were in an harmony, the masons say, that they do συμβαίνειν; as if thou shouldest say, fall together: so that in the general, though the things be divers that make it, yet the consent or harmony itself is but one. And as the whole world is made up of all the particular bodies of the world, one perfect and complete body, of the same nature that particular bodies; so is the destiny of particular causes and events one general one, of the same nature that particular causes are. What I now say, even they that are mere idiots are not ignorant of: for they say commonly τοῦτο ἔφερεν αὐτῷ[46], that is, This his destiny hath brought upon him. This therefore is by the fates properly and particularly brought upon this, as that unto this in particular is by the physician prescribed. These therefore let us accept of in like manner, as we do those that are prescribed unto us our physicians. For them also in themselves shall We find to contain many harsh things, but we nevertheless, in hope of health, and recovery, accept of them. Let the fulfilling and accomplishment of those things which the common nature hath determined, be unto thee as thy health. Accept then, and be pleased with whatsoever doth happen, though otherwise harsh and un-pleasing, as tending to that end, to the health and welfare of the universe, and to Jove's happiness and prosperity. For this whatsoever it be, should not have been produced, had it not conduced to the good of the universe. For neither doth any ordinary particular nature bring anything to pass, that is not to whatsoever is within the sphere of its own proper administration and government agreeable and subordinate. For these two considerations then thou must be well pleased with anything that doth happen unto thee. First, because that for thee properly it was brought to pass, and unto thee it was prescribed; and that from the very beginning by the series and connection of the first causes, it hath ever had a reference unto thee. And secondly, because the good success and perfect welfare, and indeed the very continuance of Him, that is the

---

[45] The Greek word συμβαίνειν (*symbainein*) is the present infinitive of the verb συμβαίνω (*symbainō*). In English, it primarily translates to "to happen" or "to come to pass."
[46] The Greek phrase τοῦτο ἔφερεν αὐτῷ (*touto epheren autō*) translates to "this was bringing (it) to him" or "this brought (it) to him."

Administrator of the whole, doth in a manner depend on it. For the whole (because whole, therefore entire and perfect) is maimed, and mutilated, if thou shalt cut off anything at all, whereby the coherence, and contiguity as of parts, so of causes, is maintained and preserved. Of which certain it is, that thou doest (as much as lieth in thee) cut off, and in some sort violently take somewhat away, as often as thou art displeased with anything that happeneth."

What Marcus meant (core philosophy)

Marcus compares life's events to a physician's prescription. Just as a doctor prescribes treatments that may feel unpleasant yet serve healing, nature assigns circumstances that contribute to the harmony of the whole. What happens to us is not random chaos but part of an interconnected chain:

- individual events serve larger patterns
- hardships may function like medicine
- everything fits together like stones in a structure

Acceptance does not mean passive suffering. It means recognizing that events are part of a broader order beyond individual preference. Resisting reality fractures internal peace. Acceptance restores harmony with the larger system.

Dating translation (what this means emotionally/socially)

In relationships, people often interpret painful experiences as mistakes or punishments:

- "Why did this happen to me?"
- "This ruined everything."
- "This shouldn't have occurred."

Marcus reframes difficulty as prescription rather than misfortune. A breakup may clarify boundaries you never enforced. Rejection may redirect you toward alignment you could not yet see. Conflict may reveal truths that comfort was hiding.

The emotional medicine may feel harsh, but its function is growth. When you resist every uncomfortable experience, you disconnect from the larger process shaping your evolution. Acceptance does not mean tolerating harm indefinitely. It means trusting that experiences serve development even when they are difficult.

Savage takeaway

Not everything painful is wrong. Some things are medicine.

Quiet power mantra

"I accept what comes as part of my growth and the greater harmony."

IX. RETURN AGAIN AND AGAIN WITHOUT SELF-JUDGMENT

"Be not discontented, be not disheartened, be not out of hope, if often it succeed not so well with thee punctually and precisely to do all things according to the right dogmata, but being once cast off, return unto them again: and as for those many and more frequent occurrences, either of worldly distractions, or human infirmities, which as a man thou canst not but in some measure be subject unto, be not thou

discontented with them; but however, love and affect that only which thou dust return unto: a philosopher's life, and proper occupation after the most exact manner. And when thou dust return to thy philosophy, return not unto it as the manner of some is, after play and liberty as it were, to their schoolmasters and pedagogues; but as they that have sore eyes to their sponge and egg: or as another to his cataplasm; or as others to their fomentations: so shalt not thou make it a matter of ostentation at all to obey reason but of ease and comfort. And remember that philosophy requireth nothing of thee, but what thy nature requireth, and wouldest thou thyself desire anything that is not according to nature? for which of these sayest thou; that which is according to nature or against it, is of itself more kind and pleasing? Is it not for that respect especially, that pleasure itself is to so many men's hurt and overthrow, most prevalent, because esteemed commonly most kind, and natural? But consider well whether magnanimity rather, and true liberty, and true simplicity, and equanimity, and holiness; whether these be not most kind and natural? And prudency itself, what more kind and amiable than it, when thou shalt truly consider with thyself, what it is through all the proper objects of thy rational intellectual faculty currently to go on without any fall or stumble? As for the things of the world, their true nature is in a manner so involved with obscurity, that unto many philosophers, and those no mean ones, they seemed altogether incomprehensible, and the Stoics themselves, though they judge them not altogether incomprehensible, yet scarce and not without much difficulty, comprehensible, so that all assent of ours is fallible, for who is he that is infallible in his conclusions? From the nature of things, pass now unto their subjects and matter: how temporary, how vile are they I such as may be in the power and possession of some abominable loose liver, of some common strumpet, of some notorious oppressor and extortioner. Pass from thence to the dispositions of them that thou doest ordinarily converse with, how hardly do we bear, even with the most loving and amiable! that I may not say, how hard it is for us to bear even with our own selves, in such obscurity, and impurity of things: in such and so continual a flux both of the substances and time; both of the motions themselves, and things moved; what it is that we can fasten upon; either to honour, and respect especially; or seriously, and studiously to seek after; I cannot so much as conceive For indeed they are things contrary."

What Marcus meant (core philosophy)

Marcus speaks directly to the reality of imperfection. Even when striving to live according to reason, a person will fail:

- distractions arise
- emotions overwhelm
- habits resurface
- clarity slips

The solution is not frustration or despair. It is return. Each time one falls away from alignment, the task is simple: come back. Philosophy is not punishment or rigid discipline. It is medicine. Marcus compares returning to reason to a wounded person returning to treatment with relief and gratitude. He reminds himself:

- philosophy requires nothing unnatural
- virtue aligns with human nature itself
- progress is not perfection but repeated correction

The world is complex, unstable, and often unclear. Therefore, humility and steady recommitment matter more than flawless execution.

Dating translation (what this means emotionally/socially)

Emotionally, this passage is about self-compassion during growth. In relationships, people often expect themselves to evolve perfectly:

- never fall into old patterns
- never get triggered again
- never make emotional mistakes

But growth is cyclical. You may:

- Fall for the wrong person again.
- React from insecurity.
- Lose clarity temporarily.

Marcus says the power is not in avoiding every misstep. The power is in returning to yourself without shame.

- Come back to your standards.
- Come back to your boundaries.
- Come back to self-respect.

And when you return, do not treat growth like punishment or obligation. Treat it like relief. Like returning to something that restores you.

Savage takeaway

Falling off track isn't failure. Staying away from yourself is.

Quiet power mantra

"I return to alignment gently, again and again."

X. TRUST THE TIMING AND PROTECT YOUR INNER SELF

"Thou must comfort thyself in the expectation of thy natural dissolution, and in the meantime not grieve at the delay; but rest contented in those two things. First, that nothing shall happen unto thee, which is not according to the nature of the universe. Secondly, that it is in thy power, to do nothing against thine own proper God, and inward spirit. For it is not in any man's power to constrain thee to transgress against him."

What Marcus meant (core philosophy)

Marcus encourages acceptance of both life's ending and its unfolding pace. Two truths bring peace: First, nothing that happens falls outside the nature of the universe. Events arise within a larger order, even when they feel difficult or delayed. Second, external circumstances cannot force you to betray your inner self. Your rational spirit, your guiding principle, remains within your control. The world may shape conditions around you, but it cannot compel you to act against your deepest values unless you consent. This realization removes fear:

- death comes when it comes
- life unfolds as it unfolds
- your integrity remains sovereign

Dating translation (what this means emotionally/socially)

In relationships, people often feel trapped by timing or circumstance:

- waiting for commitment
- fearing that time is running out
- worrying that something meaningful is delayed

Marcus reminds you that delay is not disaster. Nothing arrives outside the larger rhythm of life. The timeline may not match your expectations, but it does not remove your agency. The real question is not when things happen, but whether you remain aligned with yourself while waiting. No partner, no situation, no emotional pressure can force you to violate your inner standards unless you allow it. Your power lies in staying true to your values regardless of external timing.

Savage takeaway
Life's timing is not your enemy. Self-betrayal is.

Quiet power mantra
"I trust the unfolding while remaining loyal to my inner truth."

XI. CHECK WHO IS DRIVING YOUR SOUL
"What is the use that now at this present I make of my soul? Thus from time to time and upon all occasions thou must put this question to thyself; what is now that part of mine which they call the rational mistress part, employed about? Whose soul do I now properly possess? a child's? or a youth's? a woman's? or a tyrant's? some brute, or some wild beast's soul?"

What Marcus meant (core philosophy)
Marcus calls for constant self-examination.

He asks himself repeatedly: What is my rational mind doing right now? This is not abstract philosophy. It is practical awareness. He challenges himself to identify which "soul" is currently operating:
- a childish soul driven by impulse
- a fearful or reactive soul
- a tyrannical soul seeking control
- a rational soul guided by reason

The Stoic goal is conscious alignment. The rational faculty must lead, not be overtaken by emotional extremes or unconscious habits. Self-awareness becomes the gatekeeper of virtue.

Dating translation (what this means emotionally/socially)
Emotionally, this passage is about recognizing who you become in relationships. Ask:
- Am I acting from insecurity right now?
- Am I reacting like my younger self seeking validation?
- Am I trying to control instead of connect?
- Am I abandoning logic because emotion feels intense?

Relationships often activate different versions of us. You may feel grounded alone but become anxious with someone unavailable. You may become overly accommodating with someone dominant. You may become defensive when triggered.

Marcus invites you to pause and ask: Who is driving right now? Awareness allows you to shift back into your highest self instead of reacting from old patterns.

Savage takeaway

Not every version of you deserves the steering wheel.

Quiet power mantra

"I lead with my highest self, not my reactive impulses."

XII. REAL GOODNESS IS CHARACTER, NOT STATUS

"What those things are in themselves, which by the greatest part are esteemed good, thou mayest gather even from this. For if a man shall hear things mentioned as good, which are really good indeed, such as are prudence, temperance, justice, fortitude, after so much heard and conceived, he cannot endure to hear of any more, for the word good is properly spoken of them. But as for those which by the vulgar are esteemed good, if he shall hear them mentioned as good, he doth hearken for more. He is well contented to hear, that what is spoken by the comedian, is but familiarly and popularly spoken, so that even the vulgar apprehend the difference. For why is it else, that this offends not and needs not to be excused, when virtues are styled good: but that which is spoken in commendation of wealth, pleasure, or honour, we entertain it only as merrily and pleasantly spoken? Proceed therefore, and inquire further, whether it may not be that those things also which being mentioned upon the stage were merrily, and with great applause of the multitude, scoffed at with this jest, that they that possessed them had not in all the world of their own, (such was their affluence and plenty) so much as a place where to avoid their excrements. Whether, I say, those ought not also in very deed to be much respected, and esteemed of, as the only things that are truly good."

What Marcus meant (core philosophy)

Marcus distinguishes between what is truly good and what society merely calls good. True goods are virtues:

- Prudence
- Justice
- Temperance
- Fortitude

These qualities need no exaggeration or embellishment. When they are named, they stand complete in themselves. By contrast, wealth, pleasure, and honor require constant reinforcement and praise to maintain their perceived value. People keep talking about them because their worth is unstable and dependent on opinion. Marcus points out that even popular culture often mocks these external goods, recognizing their emptiness beneath the surface.

The Stoic insight is clear: Only virtue is inherently good. External things may be preferred or useful, but they are not the foundation of true fulfillment.

Dating translation (what this means emotionally/socially)

In relationships, many people chase what appears desirable instead of what is genuinely good. They prioritize:

- status
- attractiveness
- social approval
- wealth
- charisma

Yet these qualities do not guarantee emotional safety, respect, or alignment. Marcus reminds you to shift your definition of "good."

Instead of asking:
- Is this person impressive?
- Is this relationship exciting?
- Is this connection socially enviable?

Ask:
- Is there integrity?
- Is there consistency?
- Is there kindness and wisdom?

Many relationships fail because people pursue what looks valuable instead of what actually sustains connection.

Savage takeaway
Charm, status, and attraction are not proof of goodness.

Quiet power mantra
"I value character over appearance and substance over status."

XIII. YOU TRANSFORM, YOU DO NOT DISAPPEAR
"All that I consist of, is either form or matter. No corruption can reduce either of these unto nothing: for neither did I of nothing become a subsistent creature. Every part of mine then will by mutation be disposed into a certain part of the whole world, and that in time into another part; and so in infinitum; by which kind of mutation, I also became what I am, and so did they that begot me, and they before them, and so upwards in infinitum. For so we may be allowed to speak, though the age and government of the world, be to some certain periods of time limited, and confined."

What Marcus meant (core philosophy)
Marcus reflects on the fundamental nature of existence: everything is composed of form and matter, and nothing truly becomes nothing. Change is transformation, not annihilation. Each part of us:
- Shifts
- Reorganizes
- Returns to the greater whole

Just as we came into being through endless chains of transformation, we will continue within that same cycle after dissolution. The Stoic view removes fear by reframing death and change as natural mutation rather than loss. Nothing is isolated. Everything belongs to a continuous process of becoming and re-becoming.

Dating translation (what this means emotionally/socially)
Emotionally, this passage speaks to identity within relationships. People often feel like they lose themselves after heartbreak or major change:
- "I'm not who I was."
- "That relationship changed me completely."
- "I feel broken."

Marcus would say: you are not destroyed. You are transformed. Every experience reshapes you:

- lessons become boundaries
- pain becomes awareness
- love becomes wisdom

You are part of an ongoing evolution, not a fixed identity that can be permanently ruined. Even relationships that end become material for who you are becoming next.

Savage takeaway

Nothing truly ends. It becomes something else.

Quiet power mantra

"I embrace transformation as part of my continual becoming."

XIV. YOUR VALUE IS IN HOW YOU ACT, NOT WHAT YOU ACHIEVE

"Reason, and rational power, are faculties which content themselves with themselves, and their own proper operations. And as for their first inclination and motion, that they take from themselves. But their progress is right to the end and object, which is in their way, as it were, and lieth just before them: that is, which is feasible and possible, whether it be that which at the first they proposed to themselves, or no. For which reason also such actions are termed κατορθώσεις[47], to intimate the directness of the way, by which they are achieved. Nothing must be thought to belong to a man, which doth not belong unto him as he is a man. These, the event of purposes, are not things required in a man. The nature of man doth not profess any such things. The final ends and consummations of actions are nothing at all to a man's nature. The end therefore of a man, or the summum bonum whereby that end is fulfilled, cannot consist in the consummation of actions purposed and intended. Again, concerning these outward worldly things, were it so that any of them did properly belong unto man, then would it not belong unto man, to condemn them and to stand in opposition with them. Neither would he be praiseworthy that can live without them; or he good, (if these were good indeed) who of his own accord doth deprive himself of any of them. But we see contrariwise, that the more a man doth withdraw himself from these wherein external pomp and greatness doth consist, or any other like these; or the better he doth bear with the loss of these, the better he is accounted."

What Marcus meant (core philosophy)

Marcus clarifies the nature of rational action. Reason does not depend on external outcomes. It begins within itself and moves toward what is possible and aligned with nature.

The key Stoic insight: The value of an action lies in the intention and execution, not in its final result. External outcomes:

- success
- recognition
- completion
- material gain

---

[47] The Greek word κατορθώσεις (*katorthōseis*) most commonly translates to "successes," "achievements," or "accomplishments."

do not belong to us fully because they depend on factors beyond our control. Therefore, they cannot define the highest good. What belongs to us as humans is:
- choosing rightly
- acting with integrity
- directing effort toward what is feasible and virtuous

If external achievements were truly essential goods, a person could not be praised for living without them. Yet history honors those who detach from status and endure loss with dignity. The true end of human life lies in right action itself, not in the outcome.

Dating translation (what this means emotionally/socially)
In relationships, people often judge themselves by results:
- whether the relationship lasts
- whether someone chooses them
- whether love turns into commitment

Marcus would shift the focus entirely. You are not defined by whether a relationship succeeds externally. You are defined by how you show up within it:
- Did you communicate honestly?
- Did you maintain integrity?
- Did you act with kindness and self-respect?

Outcome is not proof of worth. Sometimes the healthiest, most aligned actions still lead to endings. That does not diminish their value. The true measure of emotional maturity is how you love, not whether the story ends in permanence.

Savage takeaway
You are responsible for your actions, not for the outcome.

Quiet power mantra
"I focus on right action and release attachment to results."

XV. YOUR MIND BECOMES WHAT YOU THINK ABOUT MOST
"Such as thy thoughts and ordinary cogitations are, such will thy mind be in time. For the soul doth as it were receive its tincture from the fancies, and imaginations. Dye it therefore and thoroughly soak it with the assiduity of these cogitations. As for example. Wheresoever thou mayest live, there it is in thy power to live well and happy. But thou mayest live at the Court, there then also mayest thou live well and happy. Again, that which everything is made for, he is also made unto that, and cannot but naturally incline unto it. That which anything doth naturally incline unto, therein is his end. Wherein the end of everything doth consist, therein also doth his good and benefit consist. Society therefore is the proper good of a rational creature. For that we are made for society, it hath long since been demonstrated. Or can any man make any question of this, that whatsoever is naturally worse and inferior, is ordinarily subordinated to that which is better? and that those things that are best, are made one for another? And those things that have souls, are better than those that have none? and of those that have, those best that have rational souls?"

What Marcus meant (core philosophy)

Marcus emphasizes that the soul takes its shape from repeated thoughts. The mind absorbs and reflects whatever it consistently dwells upon. Thoughts are not neutral. They are formative. Therefore:

- what you repeatedly imagine becomes your internal reality
- what you focus on becomes your disposition
- what you dwell on shapes your character

He encourages deliberate mental practice. If you want a steady, virtuous mind, you must intentionally "dye" it with thoughts aligned with reason and nature. He also reinforces that humans are social beings. The natural good of a rational creature lies in cooperation, connection, and participation within society. Living well is not dependent on circumstance. Wherever you are, you can live in alignment with your nature.

Dating translation (what this means emotionally/socially)

Emotionally, this passage is about mental patterns shaping relationship experiences. If your internal dialogue is:

- fear of abandonment
- suspicion
- replaying past hurts
- expecting disappointment

your emotional world begins to mirror those expectations. But if your thoughts cultivate:

- clarity
- grounded self-worth
- openness balanced with discernment

your relational energy shifts. Marcus also reminds us that humans are meant for connection. Independence is powerful, but isolation is not the ultimate goal. Healthy relationships align with our natural inclination toward meaningful social bonds. The key is intentional thinking: Your emotional life is colored by the narratives you rehearse daily.

Savage takeaway

Your love life often reflects your dominant thought patterns.

Quiet power mantra

"I shape my inner world through the thoughts I choose to repeat."

XVI. DO NOT EXPECT THE IMPOSSIBLE FROM IMPERFECT PEOPLE

"To desire things impossible is the part of a mad man. But it is a thing impossible, that wicked man should not commit some such things. Neither doth anything happen to any man, which in the ordinary course of nature as natural unto him doth not happen. Again, the same things happen unto others also. And truly, if either he that is ignorant that such a thing hath happened unto him, or he that is ambitious to be commended for his magnanimity, can be patient, and is not grieved: is it not a grievous thing, that

either ignorance, or a vain desire to please and to be commended, should be more powerful and effectual than true prudence? As for the things themselves, they touch not the soul, neither can they have any access unto it: neither can they of themselves any ways either affect it, or move it. For she herself alone can affect and move herself, and according as the dogmata and opinions are, which she doth vouchsafe herself; so are those things which, as accessories, have any co-existence with her."

What Marcus meant (core philosophy)

Marcus reminds himself that expecting impossibilities leads to suffering. One impossibility is expecting flawed people never to act wrongly. Human nature includes ignorance, weakness, and moral failure. Therefore, encountering wrongdoing should not feel shocking or unnatural. Events themselves do not wound the soul. The soul is affected only by its own judgments. External actions:

- insults
- betrayal
- injustice

cannot directly harm the rational mind unless it interprets them as harm. Patience grounded in wisdom is stronger than patience born from ignorance or a desire for praise. True strength comes from understanding reality as it is.

Dating translation (what this means emotionally/socially)

In relationships, people often suffer because they expect others to behave in ways they are not capable of. Expecting:

- emotional maturity from someone emotionally unavailable
- honesty from someone who avoids accountability
- consistency from someone who thrives on chaos

creates unnecessary pain.

Marcus would say: Stop being shocked when people reveal their nature. This does not mean accepting mistreatment. It means recognizing reality quickly and responding wisely rather than resisting what is clearly shown.

Another key insight: Other people's actions do not define your inner state. Your reaction shapes your emotional experience. You can choose clarity instead of devastation.

Savage takeaway

Your suffering often begins where unrealistic expectations end.

Quiet power mantra

"I accept reality as it is and choose my response wisely."

XVII. TURN OBSTACLES INTO THE PATH FORWARD

"After one consideration, man is nearest unto us; as we are bound to do them good, and to bear with them. But as he may oppose any of our true proper actions, so man is unto me but as a thing indifferent: even as the sun, or the wind, or some wild beast. By some of these it may be, that some operation or other of mine, may be hindered; however, of my mind and resolution itself, there can be no let or impediment, by reason of that ordinary constant both exception (or reservation wherewith it inclineth) and ready

conversion of objects; from that which may not be, to that which may be, which in the prosecution of its inclinations, as occasion serves, it doth observe. For by these the mind doth turn and convert any impediment whatsoever, to be her aim and purpose. So that what before was the impediment, is now the principal object of her working; and that which before was in her way, is now her readiest way."

What Marcus meant (core philosophy)

Marcus recognizes two truths about other people. First, humans are naturally close to us. We are meant to cooperate, help, and tolerate one another. Second, people may oppose or obstruct our actions. When this happens, they should be viewed like any external force:

- the wind
- the sun
- a wild animal

They are conditions, not enemies. The rational mind remains free because it can redirect itself. When something prevents one course of action, reason converts the obstacle into a new path. The Stoic principle here is adaptability. Nothing external can block your inner intention or resolution unless you allow it. The obstacle itself becomes material for action.

Dating translation (what this means emotionally/socially)

In relationships, people often treat resistance or conflict as total failure:

- rejection feels like the end
- incompatibility feels like personal defeat
- misunderstanding feels like proof that connection is impossible

Marcus would say: Other people may block specific outcomes, but they cannot block your growth.

- A person who cannot meet you becomes clarity.
- A breakup becomes direction.
- A boundary becomes self-definition.

Instead of seeing obstacles as barriers, see them as redirection.

The healthiest mindset is flexible: If this path closes, what becomes possible instead? Your emotional agency remains intact even when someone else changes the circumstances.

Savage takeaway

The obstacle isn't stopping you. It's redirecting you.

Quiet power mantra

"I transform resistance into forward movement."

XVIII. HONOUR THE PART OF YOU THAT LEADS

"Honour that which is chiefest and most powerful in the world, and that is it, which makes use of all things, and governs all things. So also in thyself; honour that which is chiefest, and most powerful; and is of one kind and nature with that which we now spake of. For it is the very same, which being in thee, turneth all other things to its own use, and by whom also thy life is governed."

What Marcus meant (core philosophy)

Marcus directs attention to what is highest and most powerful both in the universe and within ourselves. In the world, there exists a governing rational principle, something that orders and uses all things toward coherence and function. Within the individual, this same principle exists as the rational faculty:

- the guiding intelligence
- the decision-maker
- the inner authority that directs life

This rational part is meant to lead. It interprets experience, shapes action, and determines alignment with nature. To live well is to honor this inner governing force rather than surrender control to impulse, fear, or external pressure.

Dating translation (what this means emotionally/socially)

Emotionally, this passage asks: Are you letting your highest self lead, or are you letting emotion, attraction, or insecurity take control? In relationships, many people abandon their internal authority:

- ignoring intuition
- silencing boundaries
- prioritizing validation over clarity

Marcus reminds you that your inner compass is the most powerful guide you possess. Your rational self can observe feelings without being ruled by them. It can choose alignment over intensity. When you honor that part of yourself, relationships become choices rather than compulsions.

Savage takeaway

Your inner authority should lead. Attraction and emotion are passengers, not drivers.

Quiet power mantra

"I honor the wise and steady part of myself that guides my life."

XIX. WHAT DOES NOT HARM THE WHOLE DOES NOT TRULY HARM YOU

"That which doth not hurt the city itself; cannot hurt any citizen. This rule thou must remember to apply and make use of upon every conceit and apprehension of wrong. If the whole city be not hurt by this, neither am I certainly. And if the whole be not, why should I make it my private grievance? consider rather what it is wherein he is overseen that is thought to have done the wrong. Again, often meditate how swiftly all things that subsist, and all things that are done in the world, are carried away, and as it were conveyed out of sight: for both the substance themselves, we see as a flood, are in a continual flux; and all actions in a perpetual change; and the causes themselves, subject to a thousand alterations, neither is there anything almost, that may ever be said to be now settled and constant. Next unto this, and which follows upon it, consider both the infiniteness of the time already past, and the immense vastness of that which is to come, wherein all things are to be resolved and annihilated. Art not thou then a very fool, who for these things, art either puffed up with pride, or distracted with cares, or canst find in thy heart to make such moans as for a thing that would trouble thee for a very long time? Consider the whole universe whereof thou art but a very little part, and the whole age of the world together, whereof but a short and very

momentary portion is allotted unto thee, and all the fates and destinies together, of which how much is it that comes to thy part and share! Again: another doth trespass against me. Let him look to that. He is master of his own disposition, and of his own operation. I for my part am in the meantime in possession of as much, as the common nature would have me to possess: and that which mine own nature would have me do, I do."

What Marcus meant (core philosophy)

Marcus reframes perceived personal injury through the lens of the larger whole. If something does not damage the greater order, it cannot truly destroy the individual. Much of what feels like personal harm is a judgment layered on top of events rather than actual injury to one's rational nature. He adds several reminders:

- everything is in constant flux
- time sweeps all events away quickly
- pride and distress both arise from overestimating the importance of temporary things

Another person's wrongdoing belongs to them. Their actions reflect their character and choices. Your responsibility lies only with your own conduct and alignment.

The Stoic aim is perspective: Remain grounded in the bigger picture rather than inflating temporary disturbances into permanent wounds.

Dating translation (what this means emotionally/socially)

In relationships, people often internalize another person's behavior as personal damage:

- someone ghosts and you feel diminished
- someone lies and you feel broken
- someone rejects you and you question your worth

Marcus would say: Their actions belong to them. Your integrity remains untouched unless you abandon it. Many perceived injuries are wounds to ego or expectation, not to your core self. Zoom out:

- Will this matter in five years?
- Does this truly change who you are?
- Does this prevent you from living well?

When you stop making every interaction a personal catastrophe, emotional resilience grows. The focus shifts from "What did they do to me?" to "How will I respond in alignment with myself?"

Savage takeaway

Their behavior reveals them. Your reaction reveals you.

Quiet power mantra

"I release personalizing what does not truly diminish me."

XX. LET YOUR MIND LEAD, NOT YOUR SENSATIONS

"Let not that chief commanding part of thy soul be ever subject to any variation through any corporal either pain or pleasure, neither suffer it to be mixed with these, but let it both circumscribe itself, and confine those affections to their own proper parts and members. But if at any time they do reflect and rebound upon the mind and understanding (as in an united and compacted body it must needs;) then must thou not go about to resist sense and feeling, it being natural. However let not thy understanding to this natural sense and feeling, which whether unto our flesh pleasant or painful, is unto us nothing properly, add an opinion of either good or bad and all is well."

What Marcus meant (core philosophy)
Marcus teaches emotional and physical detachment through clarity of roles within the self. Pain and pleasure belong to the body. They are natural sensations and should not be denied or suppressed. However, the rational mind must remain sovereign. The danger arises when the mind adds judgment:
*   labeling pleasure as ultimate good
*   labeling pain as ultimate evil

Sensation itself is neutral. It becomes disturbing only when interpretation attaches value or identity to it. The Stoic task is not to eliminate feeling but to prevent the ruling faculty from becoming enslaved by it. Allow sensations to exist within their proper sphere without letting them dictate the mind's stability.

Dating translation (what this means emotionally/socially)
In relationships, emotional highs and lows often dominate decision-making.
*   Intense attraction feels like destiny.
*   Discomfort feels like disaster.
*   Pleasure feels like proof of compatibility.
*   Pain feels like proof of failure.

Marcus invites separation: Feelings are signals, not rulers. You can experience:
*   chemistry without losing discernment
*   disappointment without losing self-respect
*   longing without abandoning clarity

The problem is not feeling deeply. The problem is allowing feeling to override reason. When you stop labeling emotional sensations as ultimate truth, you regain freedom.

Savage takeaway
Just because you feel something intensely does not mean it's right for you.

Quiet power mantra
"My mind observes my feelings without surrendering to them."

XXI. LIVE SO YOUR SOUL FEELS AT HOME WITH THE DIVINE

"To live with the Gods. He liveth with the Gods, who at all times affords unto them the spectacle of a soul, both contented and well pleased with whatsoever is afforded, or allotted unto her; and performing whatsoever is pleasing to that Spirit, whom (being part of himself) Jove hath appointed to every man as his overseer and governor."

What Marcus meant (core philosophy)
Marcus defines what it means to "live with the gods."

It is not about rituals or outward displays. It is about inner alignment. A person lives in harmony with the divine when:
- they remain content with what is given by nature
- they accept circumstances without inner rebellion
- they act in accordance with the guiding rational spirit within them

The "overseer" Marcus speaks of is the rational faculty, the inner guide aligned with universal reason. To live well is to live in agreement with this inner spirit. When thoughts, actions, and acceptance align with nature, the soul becomes peaceful and self-sufficient.

Dating translation (what this means emotionally/socially)
Emotionally, this passage asks: Do your choices bring you into alignment with your highest self, or away from it? In relationships, you know when you are living "with the gods" because:
- you feel internally settled, not constantly anxious
- your actions match your values
- you do not abandon yourself to maintain connection

Many people chase relationships that create internal conflict. Marcus would say that true alignment feels like inner approval. When your soul feels calm and steady with your choices, you are living in harmony with your deeper nature. Relationships should not require you to betray your inner compass.

Savage takeaway
Peace is the sign you are aligned with yourself.

Quiet power mantra
"I live in alignment with my inner guide and accept what is given."

XXII. CORRECT WITH REASON, NOT ANGER
"Be not angry neither with him whose breath, neither with him whose arm holes, are offensive. What can he do? such is his breath naturally, and such are his arm holes; and from such, such an effect, and such a smell must of necessity proceed. 'O, but the man (sayest thou) hath understanding in him, and might of himself know, that he by standing near, cannot choose but offend.' And thou also (God bless thee!) hast understanding. Let thy reasonable faculty, work upon his reasonable faculty; show him his fault, admonish him. If he hearken unto thee, thou hast cured him, and there will be no more occasion of anger."

What Marcus meant (core philosophy)
Marcus uses a simple example to illustrate a deeper principle. If something unpleasant comes naturally from someone, like a bodily smell, anger serves no purpose. It is simply part of their current condition. When someone has the capacity for reason, the appropriate response is not emotional outrage but rational engagement:

- explain
- guide
- correct calmly

If they understand and change, harmony is restored. If not, anger still adds nothing useful. The Stoic lesson is that anger arises when we demand reality be different than it is. Wisdom responds with clarity and proportion.

Dating translation (what this means emotionally/socially)

In relationships, people often become angry at behaviors that reflect another person's current capacity.

- Someone avoids communication.
- Someone lacks emotional awareness.
- Someone repeats patterns they don't yet recognize.

Marcus would say: If the person is capable of growth, communicate directly and calmly. Offer clarity instead of resentment. If they receive it, the issue resolves. If they don't, anger still does not improve the outcome. Anger often masks frustration that someone isn't meeting expectations. But emotional maturity lies in responding intentionally rather than reacting impulsively. Correction rooted in respect preserves your own peace.

Savage takeaway

Anger doesn't fix people. Clear communication does.

Quiet power mantra

"I respond with clarity and calm instead of reactive anger."

XXIII. STAY FREE WHERE YOU ARE, OR LEAVE WITHOUT RESENTMENT

'Where there shall neither roarer be, nor harlot.' Why so? As thou dost purpose to live, when thou hast retired thyself to some such place, where neither roarer nor harlot is: so mayest thou here. And if they will not suffer thee, then mayest thou leave thy life rather than thy calling, but so as one that doth not think himself anyways wronged. Only as one would say, Here is a smoke; I will out of it. And what a great matter is this! Now till some such thing force me out, I will continue free; neither shall any man hinder me to do what I will, and my will shall ever be by the proper nature of a reasonable and sociable creature, regulated and directed.

What Marcus meant (core philosophy)

Marcus describes two options when facing unpleasant surroundings or people: First, remain where you are and live according to your nature without being internally disturbed. Second, if conditions truly prevent you from living in alignment, leave calmly, without bitterness or feeling wronged.

The metaphor of smoke is important. If a space fills with smoke, you simply step out. No drama, no outrage. Just clear action. Freedom is internal first. No external environment can prevent you from acting according to reason unless you surrender that power.

Dating translation (what this means emotionally/socially)
In relationships, this passage speaks to boundaries and autonomy. If someone's behavior is irritating but does not compromise your values, you can remain steady and unbothered internally. But if the environment becomes misaligned with your nature:

- disrespect
- emotional chaos
- lack of integrity

you have permission to leave. And Marcus adds something powerful: Leave without resentment. You do not need to frame yourself as a victim or carry emotional baggage to justify departure. Sometimes the healthiest choice is simply: "This no longer serves my nature. I step away."

Freedom is not waiting for others to change. It is choosing alignment with yourself.

Savage takeaway
If the room fills with smoke, walk out. Don't argue with the air.

Quiet power mantra
"I remain free within myself and leave calmly when alignment ends."

XXIV. YOU ARE MADE FOR CONNECTION AND COOPERATION

"That rational essence by which the universe is governed, is for community and society; and therefore hath it both made the things that are worse, for the best, and hath allied and knit together those which are best, as it were in an harmony. Seest thou not how it hath sub-ordinated, and co-ordinated? and how it hath distributed unto everything according to its worth? and those which have the pre-eminency and superiority above all, hath it united together, into a mutual consent and agreement."

What Marcus meant (core philosophy)
Marcus reflects on the rational order governing the universe. Nature arranges everything in relation:

- what is lesser supports what is greater
- different parts cooperate toward harmony
- the highest faculties are brought together in unity

Nothing exists in isolation. The rational essence of the universe is inherently communal. Human beings, as rational creatures, share this nature. Our highest good lies in mutual cooperation, shared purpose, and alignment with others through reason and understanding. Harmony is not accidental. It is the intended structure of existence.

Dating translation (what this means emotionally/socially)
Emotionally, this passage reminds you that connection is not weakness. It is natural. Humans are built for partnership, collaboration, and shared growth. But Marcus also implies discernment. Not every connection creates harmony. True alignment happens when two people operate from their highest selves:

- mutual respect
- shared values
- cooperative energy rather than competition

Healthy relationships feel like collaboration, not constant struggle for control. When you align with someone who is also guided by reason and integrity, connection feels cohesive rather than chaotic.

Savage takeaway
Love is not meant to feel like opposition. It's meant to feel like alignment.

Quiet power mantra
"I seek connection rooted in mutual harmony and shared growth."

XXV. REVIEW YOUR LIFE WITH HONESTY, NOT REGRET
"How hast thou carried thyself hitherto towards the Gods? towards thy parents? towards thy brethren? towards thy wife? towards thy children? towards thy masters? thy foster-fathers? thy friends? thy domestics? thy servants? Is it so with thee, that hitherto thou hast neither by word or deed wronged any of them? Remember withal through how many things thou hast already passed, and how many thou hast been able to endure; so that now the legend of thy life is full, and thy charge is accomplished. Again, how many truly good things have certainly by thee been discerned? how many pleasures, how many pains hast thou passed over with contempt? how many things eternally glorious hast thou despised? towards how many perverse unreasonable men hast thou carried thyself kindly, and discreetly?"

What Marcus meant (core philosophy)
Marcus calls for self-examination. He encourages himself to look back and ask:
- How have I treated others?
- Have I acted with justice and kindness?
- Have I endured challenges with dignity?

This is not meant to induce guilt but awareness. He reminds himself to recognize:
- the hardships already overcome
- the wisdom gained through experience
- the ability to withstand pleasure and pain without losing integrity

The reflection serves two purposes: First, accountability. Second, gratitude for progress already made. Life is not measured only by achievements but by the quality of conduct toward others and oneself.

Dating translation (what this means emotionally/socially)
In relationships, people often focus on what went wrong without acknowledging how much they have grown. Marcus invites a different lens. Look at how you have shown up:
- Did you love honestly?
- Did you learn from mistakes?
- Did you remain kind even when hurt?

Growth is visible when you recognize the evolution of your own behavior. Instead of obsessing over who wronged you or who left, consider:

- How did you act?
- Where did you show strength?
- Where did you remain compassionate?

This reflection builds self-trust rather than self-blame.

Savage takeaway

You are not just the relationships that ended. You are the strength you showed inside them.

Quiet power mantra

"I honor my growth and the integrity I have carried forward."

XXVI. DO NOT LET UNWISE MINDS DISTURB A WISE ONE

"Why should imprudent unlearned souls trouble that which is both learned, and prudent? And which is that that is so? she that understandeth the beginning and the end, and hath the true knowledge of that rational essence, that passeth through all things subsisting, and through all ages being ever the same, disposing and dispensing as it were this universe by certain periods of time."

What Marcus meant (core philosophy)

Marcus asks why irrational or unlearned minds should disturb the rational and understanding soul. The wise mind recognizes:

- the beginning and end of things
- the larger order governing existence
- the rational structure running through all time and events

Because of this broader perspective, it remains steady. Disturbance occurs when we allow lesser perspectives to penetrate the rational faculty. But wisdom sees beyond temporary reactions and limited understanding. The Stoic teaching is clear: the more deeply you understand the nature of reality, the less you are shaken by the behavior or opinions of those who do not.

Dating translation (what this means emotionally/socially)

In relationships, people often allow emotionally immature behavior to destabilize their inner world.

- Someone reacts impulsively.
- Someone speaks carelessly.
- Someone lacks emotional awareness.

Marcus would ask: Why allow limited understanding to disrupt clarity you have worked hard to build? This does not mean becoming cold or superior. It means recognizing that not everyone operates from the same level of awareness. You can respond with patience without abandoning your stability. Your peace should not depend on whether others understand as deeply as you do.

Savage takeaway

Don't downgrade your peace to match someone else's chaos.

Quiet power mantra

"My clarity remains steady regardless of others' confusion."

XXVII. LET GO OF ILLUSIONS AND LIVE SIMPLY

"Within a very little while, thou wilt be either ashes, or a sceletum; and a name perchance; and perchance, not so much as a name. And what is that but an empty sound, and a rebounding echo? Those things which in this life are dearest unto us, and of most account, they are in themselves but vain, putrid, contemptible. The most weighty and serious, if rightly esteemed, but as puppies, biting one another: or untoward children, now laughing and then crying. As for faith, and modesty, and justice, and truth, they long since, as one of the poets hath it, have abandoned this spacious earth, and retired themselves unto heaven. What is it then that doth keep thee here, if things sensible be so mutable and unsettled? and the senses so obscure, and so fallible? and our souls nothing but an exhalation of blood? and to be in credit among such, be but vanity? What is it that thou dost stay for? an extinction, or a translation; either of them with a propitious and contented mind. But still that time come, what will content thee? what else, but to worship and praise the Gods; and to do good unto men. To bear with them, and to forbear to do them any wrong. And for all external things belonging either to this thy wretched body, or life, to remember that they are neither thine, nor in thy power."

What Marcus meant (core philosophy)
Marcus confronts the temporary nature of life with stark honesty. Everything fades:
- the body becomes dust
- reputation becomes an echo
- what seems precious reveals its fragility

He strips away attachment to external things by reminding himself that most worldly pursuits are fleeting and unstable. Yet this is not despair. It is liberation. If nothing external truly belongs to us or remains permanent, then the focus shifts toward what endures within our control:
- honoring the divine order
- doing good to others
- living truthfully and justly
- accepting what lies beyond personal ownership

Peace comes from recognizing what is truly ours: our character and our actions.

Dating translation (what this means emotionally/socially)
In relationships, people often treat external factors as ultimate:
- social status of the partner
- appearance
- public validation
- romantic narratives

Marcus reminds you that much of what feels urgent now will fade quickly. Arguments that felt defining become memories. People who felt irreplaceable become chapters. What remains is how you lived:
- Did you act with integrity?
- Did you treat others well?
- Did you remain aligned with yourself?

When you release attachment to external validation, relationships become less about proving worth and more about authentic connection.

Savage takeaway
Most things you worry about today won't matter long enough to define you.

Quiet power mantra
"I release attachment to what fades and focus on what endures within me."

XXVIII. PROGRESS IS ALWAYS AVAILABLE THROUGH RIGHT ACTION

"Thou mayest always speed, if thou wilt but make choice of the right way; if in the course both of thine opinions and actions, thou wilt observe a true method. These two things be common to the souls, as of God, so of men, and of every reasonable creature, first that in their own proper work they cannot be hindered by anything: and secondly, that their happiness doth consist in a disposition to, and in the practice of righteousness; and that in these their desire is terminated."

What Marcus meant (core philosophy)
Marcus reminds himself that forward movement is always possible if one chooses the right path. Two truths define rational beings: First, their true work cannot be obstructed. External events may block specific outcomes, but they cannot prevent the practice of virtue. Second, happiness lies not in results but in the disposition toward righteousness:
- choosing what is just
- acting with integrity
- aligning thought and action with reason

Desire should terminate in right action itself, not in external reward or success. The rational soul finds fulfillment in practicing virtue, not in achieving external milestones.

Dating translation (what this means emotionally/socially)
In relationships, people often feel stuck when circumstances don't go their way:
- someone pulls away
- communication breaks down
- expectations aren't met

Marcus reframes this entirely. You are never blocked from doing your true work:
- communicating honestly
- maintaining boundaries
- showing kindness without losing self-respect

Even if a relationship does not progress externally, your internal growth continues. Your happiness does not depend on whether someone chooses you. It depends on whether you remain aligned with your own values while engaging.

Savage takeaway
No one can block your growth unless you abandon your own path.

Quiet power mantra
"I move forward through right action, regardless of external outcomes."

XXIX. DO NOT LET PUBLIC OPINION DEFINE YOUR PEACE

"If this neither be my wicked act, nor an act anyways depending from any wickedness of mine, and that by it the public is not hurt; what doth it concern me? And wherein can the public be hurt? For thou must not altogether be carried by conceit and common opinion: as for help thou must afford that unto them after thy best ability, and as occasion shall require, though they sustain damage, but in these middle or worldly things; but however do not thou conceive that they are truly hurt thereby: for that is not right. But as that old foster-father in the comedy, being now to take his leave doth with a great deal of ceremony, require his foster-child's rhombus, or rattle-top, remembering nevertheless that it is but a rhombus; so here also do thou likewise. For indeed what is all this pleading and public bawling for at the courts? O man, hast thou forgotten what those things are! yea but they are things that others much care for, and highly esteem of. Wilt thou therefore be a fool too? Once I was; let that suffice."

What Marcus meant (core philosophy)
Marcus urges himself to examine whether something truly matters. If:
- the act is not morally wrong
- it does not arise from personal vice
- it does not harm the greater whole

then it should not disturb him. He warns against being carried away by common opinion or public noise. Many people become emotionally invested in external matters simply because others care deeply about them. Marcus compares this to a child's toy. People argue passionately over things that, from a higher perspective, hold little true importance. Wisdom lies in recognizing what is genuinely meaningful and refusing to be pulled into collective illusions of significance.

Dating translation (what this means emotionally/socially)
In relationships, external pressures often create unnecessary distress:
- what others think about your relationship
- social expectations about timelines
- public narratives about success or failure in love

Marcus would ask: Is this truly harming your integrity or your deeper values? Or is it simply noise created by opinion? Many people suffer because they internalize societal judgments:
- "You should be married by now."
- "You stayed too long."
- "You left too soon."

These are often "rhombus toys" — things loudly valued but not truly essential. Your task is to remain grounded in what is genuinely right for you, while still helping others kindly without absorbing their emotional chaos.

Savage takeaway
Just because others panic about something doesn't mean you should.

Quiet power mantra
"I distinguish real concerns from collective noise and remain steady."

XXX. HAPPINESS DOES NOT DEPEND ON WHEN LIFE ENDS

"Let death surprise me when it will, and where it will, I may be εὔμοιρος[48], or a happy man, nevertheless.
For he is a happy man, who in his lifetime dealeth unto himself a happy lot and portion. A happy lot and portion is, good inclinations of the soul, good desires, good actions."

What Marcus meant (core philosophy)

Marcus affirms that true happiness is independent of the timing or circumstances of death. A person who lives aligned with reason and virtue remains fulfilled regardless of when life ends. External timing:

- early death
- late death
- sudden endings

does not determine whether a life was good. Happiness is internal. It arises from living well in the present moment, not from extending time indefinitely. If one has lived with integrity, acceptance, and clarity, death cannot take away what truly matters.

Dating translation (what this means emotionally/socially)

Emotionally, this speaks to the fear of endings in relationships. People often believe that a relationship must last forever to be meaningful or successful. Marcus challenges that idea. A connection can be complete even if it ends. Its value comes from:

- how you showed up
- what you learned
- how authentically you lived within it

An ending does not erase fulfillment. You can walk away from chapters of life still whole, still happy, still aligned.

Savage takeaway

Endings do not erase meaning. They reveal completion.

Quiet power mantra

"My happiness comes from how I live, not how long things last."

---

[48] The Greek word εὔμοιρος (*eumoiros*) translates to "lucky," "fortunate," or "blessed."

THE SIXTH BOOK
Stay Kind Without Becoming Stupid

I. THE UNIVERSE MOVES WITHOUT MALICE
"The matter itself, of which the universe doth consist, is of itself very tractable and pliable. That rational essence that doth govern it, hath in itself no cause to do evil. It hath no evil in itself; neither can it do anything that is evil: neither can anything be hurt by it. And all things are done and determined according to its will and prescript."

What Marcus meant (core philosophy)
Marcus begins by describing the nature of the universe as ordered by a rational governing principle. The material world itself is flexible and constantly shaped by this rational essence. This governing force does not act with cruelty or evil intention. It does not seek harm, nor does it produce evil as a purpose. Everything unfolds according to a natural order. From the Stoic perspective:
- events are not personal attacks
- the universe does not conspire against individuals
- what happens follows a larger rational pattern beyond human judgment

Peace arises when we stop interpreting events as morally hostile and instead see them as part of a neutral, unfolding system.

Dating translation (what this means emotionally/socially)
In relationships, people often interpret events through a lens of personal harm:
- "This happened to hurt me."
- "The universe is against me."
- "Why is this happening to me?"

Marcus reframes this entirely. Not everything painful is malicious. Sometimes:
- someone leaves because alignment isn't there
- timing shifts because growth is needed
- endings occur without intention to wound

When you stop viewing experiences as targeted attacks, emotional clarity increases. This does not excuse harmful behavior from individuals. But it removes the belief that life itself is hostile.

Savage takeaway
Not everything painful is personal. Sometimes it's just movement.

Quiet power mantra
"I release the belief that life is against me and trust the larger unfolding."

II. DO YOUR DUTY REGARDLESS OF CONDITIONS

"Be it all one unto thee, whether half frozen or well warm; whether only slumbering, or after a full sleep; whether discommended or commended thou do thy duty: or whether dying or doing somewhat else; for that also 'to die,' must among the rest be reckoned as one of the duties and actions of our lives."

What Marcus meant (core philosophy)

Marcus emphasizes constancy. External conditions:

- comfort or discomfort
- fatigue or rest
- praise or criticism
- life or death

should not determine whether one fulfills their role. The Stoic ideal is steady alignment with duty. Circumstances fluctuate, but the rational soul remains consistent in its purpose. Even death itself is framed as part of life's natural sequence, another action within the broader order rather than something separate or terrifying.

The teaching is simple: Do what is right regardless of how you feel or how others respond.

Dating translation (what this means emotionally/socially)

In relationships, people often let external factors dictate their behavior:

- acting differently depending on approval
- withdrawing when tired or emotionally unsettled
- changing values to maintain praise or avoid criticism

Marcus would advise consistency. Show up aligned with who you are whether:

- someone is loving or distant
- you feel confident or vulnerable
- others applaud or misunderstand you

Emotional maturity is the ability to remain grounded even when conditions are imperfect.

Savage takeaway

Integrity doesn't depend on mood, comfort, or validation.

Quiet power mantra

"I remain consistent with my values regardless of external conditions."

III. LOOK DEEPLY BEFORE YOU JUDGE

"Look in, let not either the proper quality, or the true worth of anything pass thee, before thou hast fully apprehended it."

What Marcus meant (core philosophy)

Marcus advises deliberate perception. Do not allow appearances to decide your judgment before you have truly understood the nature and value of something. The rational mind pauses:

- to examine essence rather than surface
- to understand before reacting
- to see clearly beyond first impressions

Many disturbances arise from incomplete understanding. Wisdom requires slowing perception long enough to grasp reality as it truly is.

Dating translation (what this means emotionally/socially)
In relationships, people often react to surface-level signals:

- instant attraction mistaken for compatibility
- early conflict mistaken for incompatibility
- charm mistaken for character

Marcus encourages deeper seeing. Ask:

- What is this person really showing over time?
- What is the true nature of this connection beyond initial emotion?
- Am I responding to reality or projection?

Clarity grows when you allow understanding to deepen before forming conclusions.

Savage takeaway
First impressions are loud. Truth is quieter and reveals itself over time.

Quiet power mantra
"I look deeper before deciding what something truly means."

IV. ACCEPT WHAT YOU DO NOT FULLY UNDERSTAND
"All substances come soon to their change, and either they shall be resolved by way of exhalation (if so be that all things shall be reunited into one substance), or as others maintain, they shall be scattered and dispersed. As for that Rational Essence by which all things are governed, as it best understandeth itself, both its own disposition, and what it doth, and what matter it hath to do with and accordingly doth all things; so we that do not, no wonder, if we wonder at many things, the reasons whereof we cannot comprehend."

What Marcus meant (core philosophy)
Marcus reflects on the constant transformation of all things. Everything changes:

- Dissolving
- Transforming
- Dispersing into new forms

The rational order governing the universe understands its own processes fully, but human understanding remains limited. Therefore, confusion and wonder are natural. Wisdom lies not in demanding complete comprehension but in accepting that many events exceed our current perspective. The Stoic lesson is humility. The universe moves according to reason even when we cannot perceive the full logic behind it.

Dating translation (what this means emotionally/socially)
In relationships, people often suffer because they need full explanations:

- Why did they change?
- Why did this end?
- Why did this happen now?

Marcus reminds you that not everything will make sense from your current vantage point. Some endings lack clear answers. Some behaviors remain mysterious. Some timing feels irrational. You may never fully understand another person's internal world. Peace comes when you accept incomplete understanding without forcing meaning.

Savage takeaway
Not understanding everything doesn't mean something went wrong.

Quiet power mantra
"I allow uncertainty without needing total explanation."

V. THE BEST REVENGE IS NOT BECOMING THEM
"The best kind of revenge is, not to become like unto them."

What Marcus meant (core philosophy)
Marcus offers a simple but powerful rule. When wronged, the instinct may be retaliation or imitation of harmful behavior. True strength lies in refusing to adopt the same faults as those who cause harm. The greatest victory is preserving one's character. Revenge that corrupts your nature is self-defeat. Remaining aligned with virtue keeps the soul intact and free from bitterness.

Dating translation (what this means emotionally/socially)
In relationships, people often mirror behavior they dislike:
- becoming distant after being ghosted
- becoming manipulative after being manipulated
- shutting down emotionally after being hurt

Marcus reminds you that healing is not imitation. You do not need to become cold because someone else was careless. You do not need to abandon integrity because someone else lacked it. Your power lies in staying true to who you are.

Savage takeaway
Winning isn't hurting them back. Winning is staying aligned with yourself.

Quiet power mantra
"I keep my character intact regardless of others' actions."

VI. FIND JOY IN CONTINUOUS RIGHT ACTION
"Let this be thy only joy, and thy only comfort, from one sociable kind action without intermission to pass unto another, God being ever in thy mind."

What Marcus meant (core philosophy)
Marcus defines joy as the steady practice of sociable and virtuous actions. Happiness is not found in isolated achievements but in continuous alignment:

- moving from one good action to another
- serving the common good
- maintaining awareness of the divine or rational order

The rhythm of virtue itself becomes comfort.

Dating translation (what this means emotionally/socially)

Emotionally, this speaks to consistency in how you show up. Rather than seeking dramatic highs or perfect outcomes, focus on:

- steady kindness
- honest communication
- intentional connection

Joy grows through repeated alignment, not through grand gestures or intense moments alone. Healthy relationships are built through small, continuous acts of integrity.

Savage takeaway

Lasting fulfillment comes from consistency, not emotional fireworks.

Quiet power mantra

"I find joy in steady, aligned actions that reflect my true nature."

VII. THE RATIONAL MIND SHAPES ITS OWN REALITY

"The rational commanding part, as it alone can stir up and turn itself; so it maketh both itself to be, and everything that happeneth, to appear unto itself, as it will itself."

What Marcus meant (core philosophy)

Marcus emphasizes the autonomy of the rational faculty. The ruling part of the soul:

- moves itself
- directs its own orientation
- determines how events are perceived

External events do not dictate meaning. The mind interprets, assigns value, and shapes experience through its own judgments. Reality is encountered through perception, and perception is governed by reason when properly cultivated. Therefore, mastery of the self begins with mastery of interpretation.

Dating translation (what this means emotionally/socially)

Emotionally, this passage highlights the power of perspective in relationships. Two people can experience the same event differently:

- rejection can feel like devastation or redirection
- silence can feel like abandonment or information
- conflict can feel like threat or opportunity for clarity

Your internal narrative determines your emotional experience. This does not mean denying reality. It means recognizing that your interpretation is shaping how deeply something affects you. When you strengthen your rational perspective, you regain agency over your emotional world.

Savage takeaway

Events don't control your experience. Your interpretation does.

Quiet power mantra

"I choose the meaning I give to what happens."

VIII. TRUST ORDER OR ACCEPT CHAOS, BUT FIND PEACE EITHER WAY

"According to the nature of the universe all things particular are determined, not according to any other nature, either about compassing and containing; or within, dispersed and contained; or without, depending. Either this universe is a mere confused mass, and an intricate context of things, which shall in time be scattered and dispersed again: or it is an union consisting of order, and administered by Providence. If the first, why should I desire to continue any longer in this fortuit[49] confusion and commixtion[50]? or why should I take care for anything else, but that as soon as may be I may be earth again? And why should I trouble myself any more whilst I seek to please the Gods? Whatsoever I do, dispersion is my end, and will come upon me whether I will or no. But if the latter be, then am not I religious in vain; then will I be quiet and patient, and put my trust in Him, who is the Governor of all."

What Marcus meant (core philosophy)

Marcus presents two possible views of existence:
1. The universe is random chaos.
2. The universe is ordered and guided by reason or providence.

His conclusion is radical in its simplicity: Either way, anxiety is unnecessary. If everything is chaos, worrying is pointless because dissolution awaits regardless. If everything is ordered, then trust and patience are appropriate because events unfold within a rational design. In both cases, inner disturbance serves no purpose. Peace comes from accepting the nature of reality rather than resisting it.

Dating translation (what this means emotionally/socially)

Emotionally, this passage speaks to uncertainty in relationships. People often obsess over meaning:
- Was this meant to be?
- Is there a higher reason?
- Is this random or destiny?

Marcus suggests freedom regardless of the answer. If life is chaotic, you lose nothing by releasing attachment and moving forward. If life is guided by deeper order, then trust the unfolding even when you do not understand it. Either way, clinging to control or overthinking outcomes does not bring peace. You can live calmly whether events feel random or purposeful.

Savage takeaway

Whether life is destiny or chaos, stressing over it changes nothing.

Quiet power mantra

"I release control and rest in acceptance of what unfolds."

---

[49] Fortuit means happening by chance or accidental, rather than by design or necessity.
[50] In English, commixtion is an archaic or formal term for mixture, blending, or intermingling.

IX. RETURN TO YOURSELF QUICKLY

"Whensoever by some present hard occurrences thou art constrained to be in some sort troubled and vexed, return unto thyself as soon as may be, and be not out of tune longer than thou must needs. For so shalt thou be the better able to keep thy part another time, and to maintain the harmony, if thou dost use thyself to this continually; once out, presently to have recourse unto it, and to begin again."

What Marcus meant (core philosophy)
Marcus acknowledges that disturbance is inevitable. Even a disciplined mind will sometimes be shaken by circumstances. The goal is not perfection but recovery. When you lose harmony:
- recognize it quickly
- return to your center
- restore alignment without delay

The more often you practice returning, the more stable you become. Resilience is not the absence of disruption but the speed of recalibration.

Dating translation (what this means emotionally/socially)
Emotionally, this is about emotional regulation within relationships.
- You will get triggered.
- You will feel hurt, anxious, or reactive at times.

Marcus does not demand emotional numbness. He encourages quick return to clarity. Instead of spiraling: Pause. Ground yourself. Reconnect with your values. Healthy emotional maturity is not never losing balance. It is learning how to come back faster each time. This prevents temporary disturbances from becoming long-term chaos.

Savage takeaway
Getting triggered isn't the problem. Staying there is.

Quiet power mantra
"I return to my center quickly and begin again."

X. RETURN TO PHILOSOPHY AS YOUR TRUE HOME

"If it were that thou hadst at one time both a stepmother, and a natural mother living, thou wouldst honour and respect her also; nevertheless to thine own natural mother would thy refuge, and recourse be continually. So let the court and thy philosophy be unto thee. Have recourse unto it often, and comfort thyself in her, by whom it is that those other things are made tolerable unto thee, and thou also in those things not intolerable unto others."

What Marcus meant (core philosophy)
Marcus compares worldly life to a stepmother and philosophy to a true mother. External obligations and environments deserve respect, but inner philosophy is the true refuge. Philosophy provides:
- grounding
- clarity
- emotional stability
- perspective

143

By returning frequently to rational understanding, external pressures become more bearable, and one's own presence becomes more balanced and tolerable to others. The teaching emphasizes cultivating an internal home rather than relying on external conditions for peace.

Dating translation (what this means emotionally/socially)

Emotionally, relationships and environments can feel overwhelming or destabilizing. Marcus suggests maintaining an internal anchor:

- Your values.
- Your self-awareness.
- Your personal philosophy.

Partners, social expectations, or dating dynamics may fluctuate. But your inner compass remains your true refuge. When you regularly return to yourself:

- you don't lose identity inside relationships
- you remain emotionally steady
- you stop expecting others to regulate your peace

This inner grounding allows you to move through relationships with clarity instead of dependence.

Savage takeaway

Your safe place isn't a person. It's your inner alignment.

Quiet power mantra

"I return to my inner wisdom as my constant refuge."

XI. SEE THROUGH ILLUSION AND REMOVE FALSE GLAMOUR

"How marvellous useful it is for a man to represent unto himself meats, and all such things that are for the mouth, under a right apprehension and imagination! as for example: This is the carcass of a fish; this of a bird; and this of a hog. And again more generally; This phalernum, this excellent highly commended wine, is but the bare juice of an ordinary grape. This purple robe, but sheep's hairs, dyed with the blood of a shellfish. So for coitus, it is but the attrition of an ordinary base entrail, and the excretion of a little vile snivel, with a certain kind of convulsion: according to Hippocrates his opinion. How excellent useful are these lively fancies and representations of things, thus penetrating and passing through the objects, to make their true nature known and apparent! This must thou use all thy life long, and upon all occasions: and then especially, when matters are apprehended as of great worth and respect, thy art and care must be to uncover them, and to behold their vileness, and to take away from them all those serious circumstances and expressions, under which they made so grave a show. For outward pomp and appearance is a great juggler; and then especially art thou most in danger to be beguiled by it, when (to a man's thinking) thou most seemest to be employed about matters of moment."

What Marcus meant (core philosophy)

Marcus teaches a powerful Stoic technique: strip things down to their basic nature to remove illusion. Many things appear impressive or desirable because of:

- language
- social framing
- emotional projection
- cultural meaning

But when examined plainly, they reveal ordinary components. This practice reduces attachment by dissolving exaggerated value. It does not mean rejecting pleasure or beauty. It means preventing oneself from being hypnotized by appearance. Clear seeing protects the mind from deception.

Dating translation (what this means emotionally/socially)
In relationships, people often idealize:
- attractiveness
- status
- sexual chemistry
- romantic fantasy

Marcus would suggest mentally removing the glamour:
- The "perfect partner" becomes a human with flaws.
- The intoxicating attraction becomes biology and projection.
- The impressive lifestyle becomes ordinary material circumstances.

This helps prevent:
- pedestal-building
- ignoring red flags
- confusing intensity with compatibility

Seeing clearly allows attraction without losing discernment.

Savage takeaway
What dazzles you often loses power when you see it plainly.

Quiet power mantra
"I see things as they truly are, not as illusion makes them appear."

XII. LEARN FROM THOSE WHO SEE CLEARLY
"See what Crates pronounceth concerning Xenocrates himself."

What Marcus meant (core philosophy)
Marcus briefly references the value of observing wise individuals and their judgments about others. The Stoic practice includes:
- studying examples of virtue
- learning from those who possess clarity
- examining character rather than reputation

By observing how wise people evaluate others, we refine our own standards and avoid being misled by appearances or social prestige. Wisdom grows through conscious imitation of what is genuinely admirable.

Dating translation (what this means emotionally/socially)
In relationships, people often rely on popular opinion or superficial markers to decide who is desirable. Marcus suggests instead looking toward:
- those who demonstrate emotional maturity
- people who consistently act with integrity
- examples of relationships grounded in mutual respect

Rather than following trends or external validation, learn from models that embody the qualities you want to cultivate. Who you admire shapes who you become.

Savage takeaway
Choose your role models carefully. They silently shape your standards.

Quiet power mantra
"I learn from examples that reflect wisdom and integrity."

XIII. HONOUR REASON AND SOCIABILITY ABOVE ALL ELSE

"Those things which the common sort of people do admire, are most of them such things as are very general, and may be comprehended under things merely natural, or naturally affected and qualified: as stones, wood, figs, vines, olives. Those that be admired by them that are more moderate and restrained, are comprehended under things animated: as flocks and herds. Those that are yet more gentle and curious, their admiration is commonly confined to reasonable creatures only; not in general as they are reasonable, but as they are capable of art, or of some craft and subtile invention: or perchance barely to reasonable creatures; as they that delight in the possession of many slaves. But he that honours a reasonable soul in general, as it is reasonable and naturally sociable, doth little regard anything else: and above all things is careful to preserve his own, in the continual habit and exercise both of reason and sociableness: and thereby doth co-operate with him, of whose nature he doth also participate; God."

What Marcus meant (core philosophy)
Marcus outlines levels of admiration. People admire:
- material things
- living creatures
- talent or cleverness
- power over others

But the highest admiration belongs to reason itself. To honour the rational soul means valuing:
- wisdom
- moral character
- sociability
- alignment with universal reason

The wise person prioritizes cultivating their own rational nature above external possessions or status.

Dating translation (what this means emotionally/socially)
In relationships, admiration often centers on surface qualities:
- attractiveness
- success
- charisma
- talent

Marcus suggests looking deeper. The most valuable trait is a rational and socially grounded soul:
- someone who communicates thoughtfully

- someone capable of empathy and cooperation
- someone who values growth over performance

When you prioritize character over spectacle, relationships become more stable and meaningful.

Savage takeaway
Charm and talent impress. Character sustains.

Quiet power mantra
"I honor reason, kindness, and true character above appearances."

XIV. EVERYTHING PASSES, SO HOLD LIGHTLY

"Some things hasten to be, and others to be no more. And even whatsoever now is, some part thereof hath already perished. Perpetual fluxes and alterations renew the world, as the perpetual course of time doth make the age of the world (of itself infinite) to appear always fresh and new. In such a flux and course of all things, what of these things that hasten so fast away should any man regard, since among all there is not any that a man may fasten and fix upon? as if a man would settle his affection upon some ordinary sparrow living by him, who is no sooner seen, than out of sight. For we must not think otherwise of our lives, than as a mere exhalation of blood, or of an ordinary respiration of air. For what in our common apprehension is, to breathe in the air and to breathe it out again, which we do daily: so much is it and no more, at once to breathe out all thy respirative faculty into that common air from whence but lately (as being but from yesterday, and to-day), thou didst first breathe it in, and with it, life."

What Marcus meant (core philosophy)
Marcus emphasizes the constant flow of existence. Everything:
- arises
- changes
- dissolves

Nothing remains fixed long enough to justify deep attachment as permanent. Life itself is compared to breath: temporary, rhythmic, fleeting. Understanding impermanence reduces unnecessary clinging and allows one to move through life with calm acceptance rather than desperate grasping.

Dating translation (what this means emotionally/socially)
In relationships, people often try to freeze moments:
- perfect chemistry
- early excitement
- emotional highs

Marcus reminds us that relationships, like everything else, exist within change. Trying to hold someone or a moment permanently creates suffering. Instead:
- Appreciate without gripping.
- Experience without ownership.
- Allow evolution without fear.

Attachment becomes healthier when you recognize that nothing is meant to remain static.

147

Savage takeaway
You suffer when you try to hold still what is designed to move.

Quiet power mantra
"I experience deeply without clinging to permanence."

XV. HONOUR YOUR MIND ABOVE ALL EXTERNAL PRAISE

"Not vegetative spiration, it is not surely (which plants have) that in this life should be so dear unto us; nor sensitive respiration, the proper life of beasts, both tame and wild; nor this our imaginative faculty; nor that we are subject to be led and carried up and down by the strength of our sensual appetites; or that we can gather, and live together; or that we can feed: for that in effect is no better, than that we can void the excrements of our food. What is it then that should be dear unto us? to hear a clattering noise? if not that, then neither to be applauded by the tongues of men. For the praises of many tongues, is in effect no better than the clattering of so many tongues. If then neither applause, what is there remaining that should be dear unto thee? This I think: that in all thy motions and actions thou be moved, and restrained according to thine own true natural constitution and Construction only… But if thou shalt honour and respect thy mind only, that will make thee acceptable towards thyself…"

What Marcus meant (core philosophy)
Marcus strips away false sources of value:
- pleasure
- appetite
- social approval
- applause

None of these define a meaningful life. The only thing truly worthy of devotion is alignment with one's rational nature. When the mind governs actions according to its highest nature:
- self-contentment arises
- inner freedom grows
- harmony with the larger order emerges

External admiration becomes irrelevant.

Dating translation (what this means emotionally/socially)
In relationships, people often seek validation:
- being chosen
- being praised
- being admired publicly

Marcus dismantles this. Applause is just noise if it pulls you away from yourself. When you prioritize your inner alignment:
- you stop chasing approval
- jealousy decreases
- emotional stability increases

You become less dependent on how others perceive your relationship or your desirability.

Savage takeaway
Approval is loud but empty. Self-alignment is quiet and powerful.

Quiet power mantra
"I honor my inner integrity above external validation."

XVI. VIRTUE MOVES ON A HIGHER PATH
"Under, above, and about, are the motions of the elements; but the motion of virtue, is none of those motions, but is somewhat more excellent and divine. Whose way (to speed and prosper in it) must be through a way, that is not easily comprehended."

What Marcus meant (core philosophy)
Marcus distinguishes virtue from natural physical motion. Physical forces follow predictable patterns, but virtue operates differently. It is:
- subtle
- inward
- elevated beyond material movement

The path of virtue is not obvious or easily understood because it requires inner discipline rather than external force. True progress often looks invisible from the outside.

Dating translation (what this means emotionally/socially)
Emotionally, choosing virtue in relationships may feel counterintuitive:
- choosing calm instead of reacting
- choosing honesty instead of manipulation
- choosing self-respect instead of attachment

These choices may not look dramatic, but they are powerful. Growth in love often happens through invisible internal shifts rather than visible grand gestures.

Savage takeaway
Real growth isn't flashy. It's quiet alignment.

Quiet power mantra
"I move along the higher path even when it is unseen."

XVII. STOP SEEKING PRAISE FROM PEOPLE WHO AREN'T HERE
"Who can choose but wonder at them? They will not speak well of them that are at the same time with them, and live with them; yet they themselves are very ambitious, that they they that shall follow, whom they have never seen, nor shall ever see, should speak well of them. As if a man should grieve that he hath not been commended by them, that lived before him."

What Marcus meant (core philosophy)
Marcus exposes the absurdity of chasing reputation. People neglect appreciating those around them yet obsess over how future generations might judge them. This reveals the emptiness of fame or legacy as motivation. Seeking approval from unseen or imagined audiences distracts from living virtuously in the present. Focus should remain on right action now, not imagined future praise.

Dating translation (what this means emotionally/socially)
In relationships, people sometimes perform for imaginary audiences:
- trying to look like the perfect couple
- worrying about how others will judge their choices
- staying in situations to maintain appearances

Marcus would call this misplaced energy. Your relationship exists between you and the person involved, not for hypothetical observers. Authenticity matters more than optics.

Savage takeaway
Stop living for applause from people who aren't even in the room.

Quiet power mantra
"I live authentically, not for imagined approval."

XVIII. WHAT IS POSSIBLE FOR HUMANS IS POSSIBLE FOR YOU
"Do not ever conceive anything impossible to man, which by thee cannot, or not without much difficulty be effected; but whatsoever in general thou canst Conceive possible and proper unto any man, think that very possible unto thee also."

What Marcus meant (core philosophy)
Marcus challenges the tendency to label things as impossible simply because they are difficult. If something belongs to human capability — if another person can achieve or embody it — then it exists within the realm of possibility for you as well. Difficulty is not evidence of impossibility. The Stoic view:
- human nature contains shared potential
- virtue, discipline, courage, and growth are universal capacities
- limitation often comes from belief rather than reality

The rational mind expands when it stops excluding itself from what is humanly attainable.

Dating translation (what this means emotionally/socially)
Emotionally, people often create internal ceilings:
- "I'm not capable of healthy love."
- "I'll never break this pattern."
- "I can't set boundaries like other people do."

Marcus reframes this. If emotional maturity exists in humans, then it exists as a potential within you. You may need practice, time, or discomfort, but you are not excluded from growth. Stop treating growth like something other people are built for.

Savage takeaway
Just because it's hard for you doesn't mean it's not yours to achieve.

Quiet power mantra
"If it belongs to human nature, it belongs to me too."

XIX. PROTECT YOURSELF WITHOUT HATRED

"Suppose that at the palestra somebody hath all to-torn thee with his nails, and hath broken thy head. Well, thou art wounded. Yet thou dost not exclaim; thou art not offended with him. Thou dost not suspect him for it afterwards, as one that watcheth to do thee a mischief. Yea even then, though thou dost thy best to save thyself from him, yet not from him as an enemy. It is not by way of any suspicious indignation, but by way of gentle and friendly declination. Keep the same mind and disposition in other parts of thy life also. For many things there be, which we must conceit and apprehend, as though we had had to do with an antagonist at the palestra. For as I said, it is very possible for us to avoid and decline, though we neither suspect, nor hate."

What Marcus meant (core philosophy)

Marcus uses the metaphor of athletic training. During sparring, injury may occur without malicious intent. The rational response is not outrage but calm adjustment. The lesson:

- defend yourself without emotional hostility
- avoid harm without demonizing the other person
- maintain internal composure even during conflict

Protection does not require resentment.

Dating translation (what this means emotionally/socially)

In relationships, people often believe boundaries must come with anger. Marcus suggests otherwise. You can:

- step back
- decline engagement
- create distance

without turning someone into a villain. Not every painful interaction is a betrayal. Sometimes it is simply misalignment. Healthy detachment protects your peace more than reactive hostility.

Savage takeaway

Boundaries don't require bitterness.

Quiet power mantra

"I protect myself calmly without creating enemies."

XX. LOVE TRUTH MORE THAN BEING RIGHT

"If anybody shall reprove me, and shall make it apparent unto me, that in any either opinion or action of mine I do err, I will most gladly retract. For it is the truth that I seek after, by which I am sure that never any man was hurt; and as sure, that he is hurt that continueth in any error, or ignorance whatsoever."

What Marcus meant (core philosophy)

Marcus embraces intellectual humility. The aim is truth, not ego preservation. When correction reveals error:

- welcome it
- adjust willingly
- grow without defensiveness

Error is not harmful; attachment to error is. Wisdom requires flexibility of mind.

151

Dating translation (what this means emotionally/socially)

Many relationship conflicts escalate because both people defend their position instead of pursuing truth. Growth demands:

- listening without immediate defense
- acknowledging mistakes
- choosing understanding over winning

A relationship strengthens when truth matters more than pride.

Savage takeaway

Being right feeds ego. Being truthful builds growth.

Quiet power mantra

"I welcome truth even when it challenges me."

XXI. DO YOUR PART AND RELEASE THE REST

"I for my part will do what belongs unto me; as for other things, whether things unsensible or things irrational; or if rational, yet deceived and ignorant of the true way, they shall not trouble or distract me. For as for those creatures which are not endued with reason and all other things and-matters of the world whatsoever I freely, and generously, as one endued with reason, of things that have none, make use of them. And as for men, towards them as naturally partakers of the same reason, my care is to carry myself sociably. But whatsoever it is that thou art about, remember to call upon the Gods. And as for the time how long thou shalt live to do these things, let it be altogether indifferent unto thee, for even three such hours are sufficient."

What Marcus meant (core philosophy)

Marcus separates responsibility from control. Your role:

- act rationally
- treat others sociably
- fulfill your nature

Everything else:

- others' ignorance
- external outcomes
- lifespan

belongs outside your concern. Meaning comes from doing what is yours to do, regardless of duration.

Dating translation (what this means emotionally/socially)

In relationships, emotional suffering often arises from trying to control:

- someone else's readiness
- how long love lasts
- how others behave

Marcus says: Show up fully. Act with integrity. Release the rest. Freedom comes from focusing on your contribution, not the outcome.

Savage takeaway

You control effort, not results.

Quiet power mantra

"I give my best and release what is not mine to govern."

XXII. DEATH ERASES STATUS AND DIFFERENCE

"Alexander of Macedon[51], and he that dressed his mules, when once dead both came to one. For either they were both resumed into those original rational essences from whence all things in the world are propagated; or both after one fashion were scattered into atoms."

What Marcus meant (core philosophy)
Marcus reminds himself of the ultimate equality of all people. Whether emperor or servant, greatness or obscurity, death reduces all distinctions. Two possibilities remain:
* reunion with universal reason
* dissolution into matter

Either way, status, achievement, and hierarchy lose significance. This perspective humbles ambition and dissolves pride. True worth lies not in rank but in how one lives.

Dating translation (what this means emotionally/socially)
In relationships, people often elevate or diminish others based on:
* status
* success
* attractiveness
* perceived social value

Marcus strips this away. Underneath titles and appearances, everyone shares the same human condition. Seeing this clearly helps you:
* stop placing others on pedestals
* stop feeling inferior or superior
* relate from grounded equality

Real connection begins when illusion of hierarchy dissolves.

Savage takeaway
Titles fade. Character remains.

Quiet power mantra
"I meet others as equals beneath all appearances."

XXIII. MANY THINGS CAN EXIST TOGETHER AT ONCE

"Consider how many different things, whether they concern our bodies, or our souls, in a moment of time come to pass in every one of us, and so thou wilt not wonder if many more things or rather all things that are done, can at one time subsist, and coexist in that both one and general, which we call the world."

What Marcus meant (core philosophy)
Marcus points to complexity and simultaneity. Within a single person, countless processes unfold simultaneously:

---

[51] Alexander of Macedon, better known to history as Alexander the Great (356–323 BC), was the King of Macedon who created one of the largest empires in history by the age of thirty. Marcus Aurelius is stating he is not a hero to be emulated, but as a cautionary tale about the vanity of worldly ambition

- physical changes
- thoughts
- emotions
- perceptions

Therefore, it should not surprise us that the universe contains immense layers of concurrent activity. Understanding this reduces confusion and resistance when life feels complex or contradictory. Reality is multifaceted by nature.

Dating translation (what this means emotionally/socially)

Emotionally, this teaches tolerance for complexity in relationships. Someone can:

- care for you and struggle emotionally
- feel attraction and uncertainty
- grow while still being imperfect

Human beings are not singular or simple. Accepting complexity reduces the urge to oversimplify people into "good" or "bad."

Healthy relationships allow multiple truths to exist simultaneously.

Savage takeaway

People are complicated. Stop demanding simple narratives.

Quiet power mantra

"I allow complexity without needing everything to be simple."

XXIV. FULFILL YOUR ROLE WITHOUT ARGUMENT

"If any should put this question unto thee, how this word Antoninus is written, wouldst thou not presently fix thine intention upon it, and utter out in order every letter of it? And if any shall begin to gainsay thee, and quarrel with thee about it; wilt thou quarrel with him again, or rather go on meekly as thou hast begun, until thou hast numbered out every letter? Here then likewise remember, that every duty that belongs unto a man doth consist of some certain letters or numbers as it were, to which without any noise or tumult keeping thyself thou must orderly proceed to thy proposed end, forbearing to quarrel with him that would quarrel and fall out with thee."

What Marcus meant (core philosophy)

Marcus compares life duties to spelling a word letter by letter. The wise person:

- focuses on the task
- proceeds steadily
- ignores unnecessary conflict

Argumentation and distraction do not advance purpose. The key is calm persistence. Fulfill your role without being pulled into others' emotional turbulence.

Dating translation (what this means emotionally/socially)

In relationships, people often get pulled into arguments that derail clarity. Marcus advises: Stay focused on your values. Communicate calmly. Do not abandon your direction because someone seeks conflict. You don't need to win every argument. You need to stay aligned.

Savage takeaway
Not every argument deserves your participation.

Quiet power mantra
"I move steadily toward my purpose without engaging unnecessary conflict."

XXV. TEACH WITHOUT ANGER
"Is it not a cruel thing to forbid men to affect those things, which they conceive to agree best with their own natures, and to tend most to their own proper good and behoof? But thou after a sort deniest them this liberty, as often as thou art angry with them for their sins. For surely they are led unto those sins whatsoever they be, as to their proper good and commodity. But it is not so (thou wilt object perchance). Thou therefore teach them better, and make it appear unto them: but be not thou angry with them."

What Marcus meant (core philosophy)
Marcus encourages compassion toward human error. People pursue actions believing they are beneficial. Anger assumes malicious intent, but often ignorance drives behavior. The Stoic response:
- educate gently
- clarify truth
- remove hostility

Correction should arise from reason, not emotional reaction.

Dating translation (what this means emotionally/socially)
Emotionally, this speaks to understanding in relationships. When someone behaves poorly, they may believe they are protecting themselves or pursuing happiness. This does not mean accepting harmful behavior. It means responding without rage. Healthy communication:
- explains boundaries
- offers clarity
- avoids contempt

You can correct without dehumanizing.

Savage takeaway
You don't need anger to hold someone accountable.

Quiet power mantra
"I respond with clarity and compassion instead of anger."

XXVI. DEATH RELEASES YOU FROM ALL BURDENS
"Death is a cessation from the impression of the senses, the tyranny of the passions, the errors of the mind, and the servitude of the body."

What Marcus meant (core philosophy)
Marcus reframes death not as something terrifying, but as release. Death ends:
- sensory overwhelm
- emotional turbulence

- mental error
- bodily limitations

Rather than viewing death as loss, he presents it as freedom from the struggles tied to human existence. This perspective reduces fear and encourages acceptance of mortality as part of nature's order.

Dating translation (what this means emotionally/socially)

Emotionally, this teaches detachment from fear of endings. In relationships, people often cling out of fear:

- fear of loss
- fear of loneliness
- fear of starting again

Marcus reminds us that endings are not enemies. They are transitions. Recognizing impermanence allows you to release situations that no longer align without panic or despair.

Savage takeaway

Endings are not punishment. They are release.

Quiet power mantra

"I accept endings as natural transitions rather than threats."

XXVII. DO NOT LOSE YOURSELF TO ENVIRONMENT OR STATUS

"If in this kind of life thy body be able to hold out, it is a shame that thy soul should faint first, and give over, take heed, lest of a philosopher thou become a mere Cæsar in time, and receive a new tincture from the court… Worship the Gods, procure the welfare of men, this life is short. Charitable actions, and a holy disposition, is the only fruit of this earthly life."

What Marcus meant (core philosophy)

Marcus warns against losing philosophical integrity due to external influence. Environment, power, or social pressures can slowly reshape character. He urges:

- simplicity
- sincerity
- justice
- kindness
- resilience

The body may endure hardship, but the true danger lies in the soul losing its alignment. Life is short, and its true fruit lies in virtue and service.

Dating translation (what this means emotionally/socially)

Relationships and environments can subtly change who you are. You may begin compromising:

- values
- boundaries
- authenticity

156

Marcus reminds you to remain grounded in your core identity regardless of influence. A healthy relationship should not require you to abandon who you are at your best.

Savage takeaway
Never trade your character for acceptance or proximity.

Quiet power mantra
"I remain true to my values regardless of environment."

XXVIII. STUDY EXAMPLES OF TRUE CHARACTER

"Do all things as becometh the disciple of Antoninus Pius… All these things of him remember, that whensoever thy last hour shall come upon thee, it may find thee, as it did him, ready for it in the possession of a good conscience."

What Marcus meant (core philosophy)
Marcus reflects on the virtues of Antoninus Pius as a model for living. He highlights:
- steadiness
- patience
- humility
- absence of vanity
- openness to correction
- simplicity
- endurance

Studying examples of lived virtue helps guide one's own behavior. The goal is to live so that death finds you with a clear conscience.

Dating translation (what this means emotionally/socially)
In relationships, who you model yourself after matters. Rather than imitating dramatic or toxic dynamics, look toward examples of:
- calm strength
- emotional maturity
- generosity without ego

Healthy love grows when you emulate stability rather than chaos. Choose role models who embody the qualities you want to become.

Savage takeaway
You become what you consistently admire.

Quiet power mantra
"I shape my life through the virtues I choose to emulate."

XXIX. SEE THE WORLD AS YOU SEE A DREAM AFTER WAKING

"Stir up thy mind, and recall thy wits again from thy natural dreams, and visions, and when thou art perfectly awoken… look upon these worldly things with the same mind as thou didst upon those, that thou sawest in thy sleep."

What Marcus meant (core philosophy)

Marcus invites a shift in perception. Just as dreams feel real until awakening, worldly concerns often appear more significant than they truly are. Philosophical awakening allows one to see:

- emotional exaggeration
- illusion of permanence
- misplaced importance

This perspective creates distance from unnecessary attachment.

Dating translation (what this means emotionally/socially)

Emotionally, past relationships or current worries can feel overwhelming, like vivid dreams. With perspective, many intense experiences lose their grip. Marcus encourages stepping back and observing life with clarity: What feels overwhelming now may later appear small or transient. Awareness reduces emotional over-identification with temporary experiences.

Savage takeaway

What feels huge today may look like a dream once you wake up.

Quiet power mantra

"I observe life with awakened clarity rather than emotional illusion."

XXX. FOCUS ONLY ON WHAT BELONGS TO YOUR MIND

"I consist of body and soul. Unto my body all things are indifferent, for of itself it cannot affect one thing more than another with apprehension of any difference; as for my mind, all things which are not within the verge of her own operation, are indifferent unto her, and for her own operations, those altogether depend of her; neither does she busy herself about any, but those that are present; for as for future and past operations, those also are now at this present indifferent unto her."

What Marcus meant (core philosophy)

Marcus separates body and rational mind to clarify control. The body reacts passively, but the rational faculty governs interpretation and action. Key Stoic insight:

- External events are indifferent.
- Only your own thoughts and actions belong to you.
- The present moment is the only field of operation.

Past and future lose power when the mind returns to present agency.

Dating translation (what this means emotionally/socially)

In relationships, suffering often comes from focusing on:

- past conversations
- imagined future outcomes
- others' reactions

Marcus reminds you that your power exists only in how you act now. You cannot control their response, but you can control your integrity in the moment.

Savage takeaway
Your peace lives in the present, not in hypothetical timelines.

Quiet power mantra
"I return to what is mine to govern right now."

XXXI. DO WHAT BELONGS TO YOUR NATURE

"As long as the foot doth that which belongeth unto it to do, and the hand that which belongs unto it, their labour, whatsoever it be, is not unnatural. So a man as long as he doth that which is proper unto a man, his labour cannot be against nature; and if it be not against nature, then neither is it hurtful unto him. But if it were so that happiness did consist in pleasure: how came notorious robbers, impure abominable livers, parricides, and tyrants, in so large a measure to have their part of pleasures?"

What Marcus meant (core philosophy)
Marcus argues that pleasure cannot define happiness, since even immoral people experience pleasure. True fulfillment comes from fulfilling one's proper function:
* rationality
* virtue
* right action
When actions align with nature, effort strengthens rather than harms.

Dating translation (what this means emotionally/socially)
Emotional intensity or pleasure does not equal compatibility. Chemistry can exist without alignment. Healthy relationships support your deeper nature:
* growth
* stability
* integrity
Not just excitement.

Savage takeaway
Pleasure proves nothing about long-term alignment.

Quiet power mantra
"I choose alignment over momentary pleasure."

XXXII. HONOUR YOUR HUMAN NATURE AS YOUR TRUE CRAFT

"Dost thou not see, how even those that profess mechanic arts, though in some respect they be no better than mere idiots, yet they stick close to the course of their trade, neither can they find in their heart to decline from it: and is it not a grievous thing that an architect, or a physician shall respect the course and mysteries of their profession, more than a man the proper course and condition of his own nature, reason, which is common to him and to the Gods?"

What Marcus meant (core philosophy)
Marcus compares human life to a craft. Workers honor their disciplines, yet many neglect the highest discipline: living according to reason. Human nature itself is sacred work. To ignore reason is to abandon your highest vocation.

Dating translation (what this means emotionally/socially)
People often invest effort into external achievements but neglect emotional growth. Healthy relationships require intentional practice:
- communication
- self-awareness
- boundary-setting

Living wisely is a skill that must be trained.

Savage takeaway
You train your career more seriously than your character.

Quiet power mantra
"I treat self-mastery as my greatest practice."

XXXIII. SEE LIFE FROM THE LARGEST PERSPECTIVE
"Asia, Europe; what are they, but as corners of the whole world; of which the whole sea, is but as one drop; and the great Mount Athos, but as a clod, as all present time is but as one point of eternity. All, petty things; all things that are soon altered, soon perished. And all things come from one beginning; either all severally and particularly deliberated and resolved upon, by the general ruler and governor of all; or all by necessary consequence. So that the dreadful hiatus of a gaping lion, and all poison, and all hurtful things, are but (as the thorn and the mire) the necessary consequences of goodly fair things. Think not of these therefore, as things contrary to those which thou dost much honour, and respect; but consider in thy mind the true fountain of all."

What Marcus meant (core philosophy)
Marcus zooms out to cosmic scale. What feels large becomes small within:
- infinite time
- vast space
- universal processes

Even harmful things arise as natural consequences within a larger order. Perspective dissolves fear and attachment.

Dating translation (what this means emotionally/socially)
Relationship struggles can feel overwhelming when viewed narrowly. Zooming out helps:
- this moment is temporary
- this story is one chapter
- pain exists within a larger growth arc

Distance restores calm without denying emotion.

Savage takeaway
Most problems shrink when you stop standing nose-to-nose with them.

Quiet power mantra
"I widen my perspective and regain calm."

XXXIV. ALL THINGS REPEAT IN DIFFERENT FORMS

"He that seeth the things that are now, hath Seen all that either was ever, or ever shall be, for all things are of one kind; and all like one unto another. Meditate often upon the connection of all things in the world; and upon the mutual relation that they have one unto another. For all things are after a sort folded and involved one within another, and by these means all agree well together. For one thing is consequent unto another, by local motion, by natural conspiration and agreement, and by substantial union, or, reduction of all substances into one."

What Marcus meant (core philosophy)

Marcus reflects on the repeating nature of human existence. History, behavior, emotions, and outcomes cycle through familiar patterns because they emerge from the same underlying human nature. Nothing is entirely new; it only appears new from a limited perspective.

The Stoic lesson is clarity through pattern recognition. When you recognize that experiences follow recurring structures, you stop interpreting events as uniquely personal or uniquely catastrophic. Instead, you understand them as part of a larger interconnected flow where cause leads to effect and all things relate to one another. Seeing the bigger pattern removes emotional exaggeration and restores rational awareness.

Dating translation (what this means emotionally/socially)

Dating often feels intensely personal when it is actually deeply predictable. The "once-in-a-lifetime connection," the confusing mixed signals, the sudden withdrawal, the magnetic chemistry followed by distance. These dynamics repeat across people and generations. Understanding this removes the illusion that your situation is uniquely doomed or magically destined.

Instead of asking, "Why is this happening to me," you begin asking, "What pattern is unfolding here?"
Recognizing patterns gives you emotional leverage. You stop reacting blindly and start observing strategically.

Savage takeaway

You're not experiencing a cosmic exception. You're witnessing a familiar pattern wearing a new face.

Quiet power mantra

"I see the pattern, and I choose consciously."

XXXV. LOVE WHAT IS GIVEN, BUT LOVE WITH TRUTH

"Fit and accommodate thyself to that estate and to those occurrences, which by the destinies have been annexed unto thee; and love those men whom thy fate it is to live with; but love them truly. An instrument, a tool, an utensil, whatsoever it be, if it be fit for the purpose it was made for, it is as it should be though he perchance that made and fitted it, be out of sight and gone. But in things natural, that power which hath framed and fitted them, is and abideth within them still: for which reason she ought also the more to be respected, and we are the more obliged (if we may live and pass our time according to her purpose and intention) to think that all is well with us, and according to our own minds. After this manner also, and in this respect it is, that he that is all in all doth enjoy his happiness."

What Marcus meant (core philosophy)

Marcus encourages alignment with reality rather than resistance against it. Acceptance is not passive resignation but intelligent cooperation with what is present. To "love those whom fate brings" means engaging fully and sincerely with the people and circumstances already within your life. True happiness arises when you work with the nature of things rather than against them. Nature contains an inherent order. When you align with that order and live authentically within it, peace becomes possible.

Dating translation (what this means emotionally/socially)

Dating maturity means loving what is real, not what you wish someone would become. Many people fall in love with potential, projection, or imagined futures rather than the person standing in front of them. Marcus reminds you to love truly. That means:

- seeing someone clearly
- accepting what is genuinely present
- not forcing destiny into fantasy

Acceptance does not mean settling. It means removing illusion so that your choices are grounded in truth rather than longing.

Savage takeaway

Love the reality, not the edit you created in your head.

Quiet power mantra

"I meet what is real and respond with clarity."

XXXVI. ONLY YOUR WILL DEFINES GOOD OR BAD

"What things soever are not within the proper power and jurisdiction of thine own will either to compass or avoid, if thou shalt propose unto thyself any of those things as either good, or evil; it must needs be that according as thou shalt either fall into that which thou dost think evil, or miss of that which thou dost think good, so wilt thou be ready both to complain of the Gods, and to hate those men, who either shall be so indeed, or shall by thee be suspected as the cause either of thy missing of the one, or falling into the other. And indeed we must needs commit many evils, if we incline to any of these things, more or less, with an opinion of any difference. But if we mind and fancy those things only, as good and bad, which wholly depend of our own wills, there is no more occasion why we should either murmur against the Gods, or be at enmity with any man."

What Marcus meant (core philosophy)

Marcus draws a strict line between what belongs to you and what does not. External events, outcomes, and other people's actions are outside your control. Only your will, choices, and responses belong fully to you. Suffering increases when we label uncontrollable outcomes as "good" or "bad" instead of recognizing them as neutral events. Freedom comes from shifting judgment away from externals and toward internal character.

Dating translation (what this means emotionally/socially)

You cannot control attraction, timing, compatibility, or whether someone chooses you. When you define your happiness by outcomes you cannot control, you create unnecessary suffering.

Examples:
- "If he chooses me, I win."
- "If she leaves, I fail."
- "If this works out, I'm worthy."

Marcus reframes the game. Your only real measure is how you show up:
- Did you communicate honestly?
- Did you maintain your standards?
- Did you act with integrity?

When your focus shifts inward, resentment toward others dissolves.

Savage takeaway

Rejection isn't a failure of your worth. It's just something outside your jurisdiction.

Quiet power mantra

"My power lives in my choices, not in their response."

XXXVII. CHOOSE HOW YOU PARTICIPATE IN THE STORY

"We all work to one effect, some willingly, and with a rational apprehension of what we do: others without any such knowledge. As I think Heraclitus in a place speaketh of them that sleep, that even they do work in their kind, and do confer to the general operations of the world. One man therefore doth co-operate after one sort, and another after another sort; but even he that doth murmur, and to his power doth resist and hinder; even he as much as any doth co-operate. For of such also did the world stand in need. Now do thou consider among which of these thou wilt rank thyself. For as for him who is the Administrator of all, he will make good use of thee whether thou wilt or no, and make thee (as a part and member of the whole) so to co-operate with him, that whatsoever thou doest, shall turn to the furtherance of his own counsels, and resolutions. But be not thou for shame such a part of the whole, as that vile and ridiculous verse (which Chrysippus[52] in a place doth mention) is a part of the comedy."

What Marcus meant (core philosophy)

Marcus emphasizes that everyone contributes to the unfolding of life, whether consciously or unconsciously. Even resistance becomes part of the greater movement. The real question is not whether you participate but how you participate. Wisdom lies in choosing conscious cooperation rather than blind reaction.

Dating translation (what this means emotionally/socially)

In dating, you are always shaping the dynamic, even when you think you are powerless.
- Silence is participation.
- Avoidance is participation.
- Complaining without change is participation.

---

[52] Chrysippus of Soli (c. 279–206 BC) was the third head of the Stoic school and is often called the "Second Founder of Stoicism." It was said in antiquity that "if there were no Chrysippus, there would be no Stoa."

You can either move through dating consciously with intention and awareness or unconsciously through reaction and habit. The outcome is shaped either way. The difference is whether you evolve through the process.

Savage takeaway
You're always part of the story. Decide whether you're the author or just the drama.

Quiet power mantra
"I participate consciously in my own evolution."

XXXVIII. STAY IN YOUR LANE, SERVE THE WHOLE

"Doth either the sun take upon him to do that which belongs to the rain? or his son Aesculapius[53] that, which unto the earth doth properly belong? How is it with every one of the stars in particular? Though they all differ one from another, and have their several charges and functions by themselves, do they not all nevertheless concur and co-operate to one end?"

What Marcus meant (core philosophy)
Marcus points to natural order. Every element in nature has its own role and function. The sun does not attempt to become rain. Each force fulfills its purpose while contributing to a larger unified system.

The Stoic lesson is alignment with one's own nature. Harmony arises not when everything becomes the same, but when each part performs its proper function without comparison or interference. Trying to assume roles that are not yours creates imbalance. Cooperation happens through authenticity, not imitation.

Dating translation (what this means emotionally/socially)
Dating chaos often begins when people abandon their own role and try to become something else to secure connection.

Examples:
- becoming overly accommodating to avoid rejection
- performing masculinity or femininity instead of embodying it
- trying to "fix," parent, or rescue a partner
- competing instead of complementing

Healthy dynamics emerge when both people remain rooted in who they are while contributing naturally to the relationship. You are not meant to be everything. You are meant to be fully yourself.

Savage takeaway
Stop trying to be the rain when you were born to be the sun.

Quiet power mantra
"I fulfill my role without abandoning my nature."

---

[53] Aesculapius is the Roman name for the Greek god of medicine, Asclepius.

XXXIX. ACCEPT WHAT ARRIVES, CHOOSE HOW YOU RESPOND

"If so be that the Gods have deliberated in particular of those things that should happen unto me, I must stand to their deliberation, as discrete and wise. For that a God should be an imprudent God, is a thing hard even to conceive: and why should they resolve to do me hurt? for what profit either unto them or the universe (which they specially take care for) could arise from it? But if so be that they have not deliberated of me in particular, certainly they have of the whole in general, and those things which in consequence and coherence of this general deliberation happen unto me in particular, I am bound to embrace and accept of. But if so be that they have not deliberated at all... yet God be thanked, that of those things that concern myself, it is lawful for me to deliberate myself... My nature is, to be rational in all my actions and... towards my fellow members ever to be sociably and kindly disposed and affected."

What Marcus meant (core philosophy)
Marcus explores three possibilities:
1. Events are guided by divine intelligence.
2. Events follow universal order rather than personal design.
3. Events are random.

In all scenarios, the conclusion is the same: your responsibility lies in how you respond. You cannot guarantee outcomes, but you always retain authority over your character, choices, and conduct. Peace comes from accepting reality while directing your own actions wisely.

Dating translation (what this means emotionally/socially)
Dating outcomes rarely unfold according to personal expectations. Someone may leave. Timing may fail. Chemistry may not align. Marcus removes the need to interpret these events as personal injustice. Whether relationships unfold through fate, circumstance, or randomness, your task remains unchanged:
- act with integrity
- remain kind without self-betrayal
- maintain rational perspective

You don't control the storyline. You control your role within it.

Savage takeaway
You don't need to understand why it happened to decide who you are afterward.

Quiet power mantra
"I cannot control outcomes. I can always choose my response."

XL. WHAT HAPPENS TO YOU SERVES THE WHOLE
"Whatsoever in any kind doth happen to any one, is expedient to the whole... whatsoever doth happen to any one man or men... I am content that the word expedient should more generally be understood... as health, wealth, and the like."

What Marcus meant (core philosophy)
Marcus emphasizes that events contribute to the larger system even when they appear neutral or inconvenient from an individual perspective. Many experiences are neither truly good nor bad. They are simply events that serve broader processes beyond immediate understanding. Stoicism reframes life's occurrences as components of a larger unfolding rather than isolated personal judgments.

Dating translation (what this means emotionally/socially)

Not every dating experience exists for romance. Some exist for growth, redirection, or clarity. A relationship ending may feel like loss but function as alignment. A disappointing date may refine your standards. A mismatch may save you from long-term incompatibility. When you stop labeling experiences immediately as success or failure, you gain emotional flexibility.

Savage takeaway

Just because it didn't become forever doesn't mean it wasn't necessary.

Quiet power mantra

"What happens refines me, even when it redirects me."

XLI. THE SHOW REPEATS UNTIL YOU WAKE UP

"As the ordinary shows of the theatre and of other such places… the same things still seen… make the sight ingrateful and tedious; so must all the things that we see all our life long affect us. For all things… are still the same… When then will there be an end?"

What Marcus meant (core philosophy)

Marcus reflects on repetition and boredom as a path toward philosophical insight. When life's patterns begin to feel repetitive, it reveals the predictable structure underlying existence. The lesson is not despair but awakening. When you see repetition clearly, you stop chasing novelty blindly and begin seeking deeper understanding. The cycle ends when awareness changes.

Dating translation (what this means emotionally/socially)

If you keep meeting the same type of partner, facing the same conflicts, or feeling the same disappointment, it may not be coincidence. Patterns repeat until perception evolves. You may notice:
- similar emotional dynamics with different faces
- recurring attraction to unavailable people
- repeated communication breakdowns

The question shifts from "Why does this keep happening?" to "What am I meant to see now that I couldn't see before?"

Savage takeaway

The cast changes. The script stays the same until you rewrite your role.

Quiet power mantra

"I recognize repetition and choose transformation."

XLII. EVEN LEGENDS FADE, SO STOP OVERWORSHIPPING MOMENTS

"Let the several deaths of men of all sorts, and of all sorts of professions, and of all sort of nations, be a perpetual object of thy thoughts,… so that thou mayst even come down to Philistio, Phœbus, and Origanion. Pass now to other generations. Thither shall we after many changes, where so many brave

orators are; where so many grave philosophers; Heraclitus, Pythagoras, Socrates. Where so many heroes of the old times; and then so many brave captains of the latter times; and so many kings. After all these, where Eudoxus, Hipparchus, Archimedes; where so many other sharp, generous, industrious, subtile, peremptory dispositions; and among others, even they, that have been the greatest scoffers and deriders of the frailty and brevity of this our human life; as Menippus, and others, as many as there have been such as he. Of all these consider, that they long since are all dead, and gone. And what do they suffer by it! Nay they that have not so much as a name remaining, what are they the worse for it? One thing there is, and that only, which is worth our while in this world, and ought by us much to be esteemed; and that is, according to truth and righteousness, meekly and lovingly to converse with false, and unrighteous men."

What Marcus meant (core philosophy)

Marcus dismantles the illusion of lasting importance by listing great figures across history and reminding us that all of them eventually disappeared. Fame fades. Power dissolves. Legacy becomes distant memory.

The Stoic lesson is perspective. If even the greatest individuals are eventually reduced to silence, then external recognition cannot be the foundation of meaning. What endures is character. Specifically, living truthfully and kindly even among imperfect people.

Dating translation (what this means emotionally/socially)

Dating often elevates moments or people into exaggerated significance. Someone becomes "the one who changed everything" or "the heartbreak that defined me."

Marcus pulls you back into proportion. Years from now, the emotional intensity fades. What remains is how you behaved:
- Did you stay true to yourself?
- Did you treat others with dignity?
- Did you maintain clarity instead of drama?

The relationship may vanish. Your integrity does not.

Savage takeaway

If history forgets kings, stop acting like one breakup defines your destiny.

Quiet power mantra

"I measure my life by integrity, not emotional intensity."

XLIII. TRAIN YOURSELF TO SEE VIRTUE

"When thou wilt comfort and cheer thyself, call to mind the several gifts and virtues of them, whom thou dost daily converse with; as for example, the industry of the one; the modesty of another; the liberality of a third; of another some other thing. For nothing can so much rejoice thee, as the resemblances and parallels of several virtues, visible and eminent in the dispositions of those who live with thee; especially when, all at once, as near as may be, they represent themselves unto thee. And therefore thou must have them always in a readiness."

What Marcus meant (core philosophy)

Marcus teaches intentional perception. Instead of defaulting to criticism or irritation, consciously notice the virtues in others. The mind can be trained to recognize goodness as readily as it notices flaws. This practice creates emotional stability and strengthens connection to humanity.

Dating translation (what this means emotionally/socially)

Modern dating culture pushes hyper-vigilance toward red flags. While discernment is necessary, constant scanning for problems breeds cynicism. Marcus suggests balance:

- Notice kindness.
- Notice effort.
- Notice emotional maturity.

Seeing virtues clearly allows you to engage without becoming hardened or detached.

Savage takeaway

If you only look for reasons to reject people, you'll eventually reject connection itself.

Quiet power mantra

"I see goodness clearly without losing discernment."

XLIV. ACCEPT YOUR MEASURE, INCLUDING YOUR TIME

"Dost thou grieve that thou dost weigh but so many pounds, and not three hundred rather? Just as much reason hast thou to grieve that thou must live but so many years, and not longer. For as for bulk and substance thou dost content thyself with that proportion of it that is allotted unto thee, so shouldst thou for time."

What Marcus meant (core philosophy)

Marcus compares physical limits with temporal limits. People accept physical boundaries easily but resist the reality that time is finite. The Stoic lesson is acceptance of proportion. Life has boundaries. Peace comes from working fully within those limits rather than wishing endlessly for more.

Dating translation (what this means emotionally/socially)

Many dating anxieties come from imagined timelines:

- "I should be married by now."
- "I'm behind."
- "I don't have enough time."

Marcus reframes this. Your timeline is not wrong simply because it differs from expectation. Acceptance removes panic. And without panic, you make clearer choices.

Savage takeaway

You're not late. You're just living your actual timeline instead of someone else's fantasy.

Quiet power mantra

"I honor my timing without comparison."

XLV. WHEN BLOCKED, CHANGE THE EXPRESSION, NOT THE VIRTUE

"Let us do our best endeavours to persuade them; but however, if reason and justice lead thee to it, do it, though they be never so much against it. But if any shall by force withstand thee, and hinder thee in it, convert thy virtuous inclination from one object unto another, from justice to contented equanimity, and cheerful patience: so that what in the one is thy hindrance, thou mayst make use of it for the exercise of another virtue: and remember that it was with due exception, and reservation, that thou didst at first incline and desire. For thou didst not set thy mind upon things impossible. Upon what then? that all thy desires might ever be moderated with this due kind of reservation. And this thou hast, and mayst always obtain, whether the thing desired be in thy power or no. And what do I care for more, if that for which I was born and brought forth into the world (to rule all my desires with reason and discretion) may be?"

What Marcus meant (core philosophy)

Marcus teaches adaptive virtue. You act according to reason and justice, but you release attachment to specific outcomes. When obstacles arise, redirect your energy toward another expression of virtue rather than abandoning virtue itself. The goal is internal alignment, not external control.

Dating translation (what this means emotionally/socially)

You can show up honestly, communicate clearly, and pursue connection. Another person may still resist or walk away.

Marcus's guidance: Keep your values. Change your direction.
- If openness isn't received, practice self-respect.
- If effort isn't matched, practice detachment.
- If connection ends, practice grace.

Savage takeaway

When someone blocks the path, pivot the lesson. Never downgrade yourself.

Quiet power mantra

"My character adapts without losing itself."

XLVI. WISDOM MEASURES SUCCESS BY ACTION, NOT VALIDATION

"The ambitious supposeth another man's act, praise and applause, to be his own happiness; the voluptuous his own sense and feeling; but he that is wise, his own action."

What Marcus meant (core philosophy)

Marcus distinguishes between three ways people define happiness.
- The ambitious person depends on external approval.
- The pleasure-seeker depends on sensation and feeling.
- The wise person grounds happiness in their own actions.

Stoicism teaches that external praise and emotional highs are unstable foundations. Only your own conduct lies fully within your control. Therefore, true satisfaction comes from acting rightly rather than being rewarded or emotionally gratified.

Dating translation (what this means emotionally/socially)
Many people unknowingly define dating success through external signals:
- being chosen
- receiving attention
- getting validation from others

Others chase emotional intensity, mistaking strong feelings for meaningful connection. Marcus reframes this completely. Dating wisdom is not:
- "Did they like me?"
- "Did I feel butterflies?"

It is: "Did I act in alignment with my values?"

If you showed up honestly, communicated clearly, and respected yourself, you succeeded regardless of outcome.

Savage takeaway
Stop measuring your worth by their reaction. Measure it by your behavior.

Quiet power mantra
"My actions define my success."

XLVII. EVENTS DO NOT CREATE SUFFERING, INTERPRETATION DOES
"It is in thy power absolutely to exclude all manner of conceit and opinion, as concerning this matter; and by the same means, to exclude all grief and sorrow from thy soul. For as for the things and objects themselves, they of themselves have no such power, whereby to beget and force upon us any opinion at all."

What Marcus meant (core philosophy)
Marcus emphasizes the Stoic principle that events themselves do not generate emotional suffering. Interpretation creates emotional response. External situations remain neutral until the mind assigns meaning. Freedom arises when you recognize that your internal narrative, not external reality, shapes your emotional state.

Dating translation (what this means emotionally/socially)
Dating triggers many automatic interpretations:
- "They didn't text back, so I must not be enough."
- "They chose someone else, so I lost."

Marcus would say: The event is neutral. The story is optional. Someone not responding is simply behavior. The pain comes from the meaning you attach to it. When you separate event from interpretation, emotional intensity decreases dramatically.

Savage takeaway
Rejection hurts less when you stop writing tragic stories about neutral events.

Quiet power mantra
"I control the meaning I assign."

XLVIII. LISTEN AS IF YOU ARE ENTERING THEIR INNER WORLD

"Use thyself when any man speaks unto thee, so to hearken unto him, as that in the interim thou give not way to any other thoughts; that so thou mayst (as far as is possible) seem fixed and fastened to his very soul, whosoever he be that speaks unto thee."

What Marcus meant (core philosophy)

Marcus encourages full presence in conversation. True listening requires suspending internal chatter and giving complete attention to the speaker. This is not passive hearing but active immersion. By listening deeply, you connect to another person's perspective without distraction or self-centered interpretation. Presence becomes a form of respect and understanding.

Dating translation (what this means emotionally/socially)

Modern dating is filled with partial attention: thinking about what to say next, analyzing attraction in real time, or comparing or judging internally. Marcus suggests radical presence. Listen to understand, not to perform. Deep listening:

- reveals compatibility faster
- builds emotional safety
- reduces misunderstanding

Presence is one of the most attractive qualities because it communicates genuine interest.

Savage takeaway

Most people wait to speak. Very few actually listen. Be rare.

Quiet power mantra

"I give my full attention without distraction."

XLIX. WHAT HARMS THE WHOLE WILL HARM YOU TOO

"That which is not good for the bee-hive, cannot be good for the bee."

What Marcus meant (core philosophy)

Marcus uses the hive as a metaphor for collective existence. Individuals thrive when the whole system thrives. Actions that harm the collective eventually harm the individual. Stoicism emphasizes interconnectedness. Personal good cannot truly exist in opposition to communal good.

Dating translation (what this means emotionally/socially)

Relationships are ecosystems. Behavior that undermines trust, honesty, or mutual respect may feel beneficial in the short term but ultimately damages connection.

Examples:

- manipulation
- emotional games
- avoidance instead of communication

If the relationship environment becomes unhealthy, both people suffer. Long-term fulfillment requires choices that strengthen the relational "hive."

Savage takeaway
If the dynamic is toxic for the relationship, it will eventually be toxic for you.

Quiet power mantra
"I build connection in ways that strengthen us both."

L. TRUST THE PROCESS WHEN THE PURPOSE IS BEING MET

"Will either passengers, or patients, find fault and complain, either the one if they be well carried, or the others if well cured? Do they take care for any more than this; the one, that their shipmaster may bring them safe to land, and the other, that their physician may effect their recovery?"

What Marcus meant (core philosophy)
Marcus reminds us to focus on the true purpose of any situation rather than secondary discomforts or expectations. A passenger cares about arriving safely, not whether every moment of the journey felt pleasant. A patient cares about healing, not whether every treatment was enjoyable.

The Stoic lesson is clarity of objective. When the essential outcome aligns with your true good, complaints about minor inconveniences lose importance. Wisdom is knowing what truly matters and measuring success accordingly.

Dating translation (what this means emotionally/socially)
In dating, people often judge situations by how easy, smooth, or immediately gratifying they feel. But Marcus asks:
*   What is the real purpose?
*   Growth?
*   Alignment?
*   Emotional clarity?
*   Learning what actually works for you?
Sometimes a connection feels challenging because it is refining you, not failing you. The question becomes: Are you moving toward emotional health and truth? If yes, the process is working even if it is uncomfortable.

Savage takeaway
Stop judging the journey by comfort. Judge it by whether it's taking you somewhere real.

Quiet power mantra
"I measure progress by alignment, not ease."

LI. TIME MOVES EVERYONE FORWARD

"How many of them who came into the world at the same time when I did, are already gone out of it?"

What Marcus meant (core philosophy)
Marcus reflects on mortality and the constant movement of time. People enter and leave life continuously. This awareness dissolves illusions of permanence and encourages urgency without panic. The Stoic goal is perspective: life is brief and shared, and no one remains forever. This realization sharpens focus on what truly matters.

172

Dating translation (what this means emotionally/socially)

Dating anxiety often revolves around timelines or comparison. Marcus shifts attention toward reality: Time moves everyone forward. Everyone is navigating change, loss, growth, and transition. Instead of obsessing over where you "should" be compared to others, recognize that everyone's path unfolds differently and unpredictably. This awareness can soften comparison and encourage presence.

Savage takeaway

Everyone is moving through time. Stop comparing chapters when everyone's book is different.

Quiet power mantra

"I live fully within the moment I have."

LII. PEOPLE ACT FROM THEIR CONDITION, NOT JUST THEIR CHARACTER

"To them that are sick of the jaundice, honey seems bitter; and to them that are bitten by a mad dog, the water terrible; and to children, a little ball seems a fine thing. And why then should I be angry? or do I think that error and false opinion is less powerful to make men transgress, than either choler, being immoderate and excessive, to cause the jaundice; or poison, to cause rage?"

What Marcus meant (core philosophy)

Marcus compares distorted perception to physical illness. Just as disease alters how someone experiences taste or reality, false beliefs and emotional imbalance distort judgment. The lesson is compassion through understanding. Many harmful behaviors arise from distorted perception rather than deliberate malice. Recognizing this reduces anger and increases emotional distance from others' errors.

Dating translation (what this means emotionally/socially)

People in dating often behave in confusing or hurtful ways:
- emotional unavailability
- avoidance
- inconsistent communication

Marcus reminds you that perception shapes behavior. Someone acting poorly may be operating from:
- unresolved wounds
- fear
- distorted beliefs about relationships

Understanding this does not mean tolerating bad treatment. It simply reduces personalizing their behavior.

Savage takeaway

Not everyone sees reality clearly. Stop expecting clarity from someone living in distortion.

Quiet power mantra

"I respond with clarity, not unnecessary anger."

LIII. LIVE ACCORDING TO YOUR NATURE, NOT EXTERNAL PRESSURE

"No man can hinder thee to live as thy nature doth require. Nothing can happen unto thee, but what the common good of nature doth require."

What Marcus meant (core philosophy)

Marcus emphasizes internal freedom. External circumstances cannot prevent you from living according to your true nature, which for Stoics means living rationally, ethically, and in alignment with universal order. Events may challenge you, but they cannot remove your ability to choose your response. Freedom exists internally, not externally.

Dating translation (what this means emotionally/socially)

Dating culture can pressure people into roles or behaviors that feel unnatural:
- pretending to be less invested
- suppressing emotional needs
- playing strategic games

Marcus reminds you that no external dynamic can force you to abandon your authentic nature unless you choose to. You retain agency over how you show up.

Savage takeaway

No one can stop you from being yourself unless you agree to disappear.

Quiet power mantra

"I remain aligned with my nature regardless of circumstance."

LIV. STOP CHASING APPROVAL THAT TIME WILL ERASE

"What manner of men they be whom they seek to please, and what to get, and by what actions: how soon time will cover and bury all things, and how many it hath already buried!"

What Marcus meant (core philosophy)

Marcus reflects on the futility of chasing approval from others. The people whose opinions we chase are themselves temporary, and time eventually buries all reputations and social hierarchies. This perspective exposes how fleeting external validation truly is. The Stoic aim is to act according to reason and virtue rather than social approval.

Dating translation (what this means emotionally/socially)

Many dating decisions revolve around being liked, chosen, or admired. Marcus asks: Who are you trying to impress? And how long will that validation actually matter? When you prioritize approval over authenticity, you sacrifice long-term peace for short-term acceptance. Dating freedom comes from acting according to your values rather than chasing admiration.

Savage takeaway

Stop auditioning for people whose opinions won't matter in five years.

Quiet power mantra

"I choose authenticity over approval."

THE SEVENTH BOOK
People Are Predictable.
Stop Acting Surprised.

I. NOTHING THAT HAPPENS IS NEW

"What is wickedness? It is that which many time and often thou hast already seen and known in the world. And so oft as anything doth happen that might otherwise trouble thee, let this memento presently come to thy mind, that it is that which thou hast already often Seen and known. Generally, above and below, thou shalt find but the same things. The very same things whereof ancient stories, middle age stories, and fresh stories are full whereof towns are full, and houses full. There is nothing that is new. All things that are, are both usual and of little continuance."

What Marcus meant (core philosophy)

Marcus emphasizes the repetitive nature of human experience. What appears shocking or disturbing in the present is rarely unprecedented. Human behavior, including wrongdoing and suffering, follows familiar patterns across time.

The Stoic lesson is emotional stabilization through perspective. When you recognize that events are recurring expressions of human nature rather than unique catastrophes, you reduce unnecessary shock and distress. Nothing is entirely new. Everything is temporary.

Dating translation (what this means emotionally/socially)

Dating drama often feels uniquely personal:

- ghosting
- mixed signals
- betrayal
- emotional confusion

Marcus reminds you that these patterns have existed for generations. Recognizing this removes the illusion that you are experiencing something uniquely unfair or uniquely devastating. When you see patterns as recurring human behaviors rather than personal attacks, emotional resilience increases.

Savage takeaway

You're not witnessing a once-in-a-lifetime tragedy. You're watching a familiar human pattern play out again.

Quiet power mantra

"I recognize patterns without personalizing them."

II. YOUR THINKING ONLY LOSES POWER IF YOU STOP USING IT

"What fear is there that thy dogmata, or philosophical resolutions and conclusions, should become dead in thee, and lose their proper power and efficacy to make thee live happy, as long as those proper and correlative fancies, and representations of things on which they mutually depend (which continually to stir up and revive is in thy power,) are still kept fresh and alive? It is in my power concerning this thing that is happened, what soever it be, to conceit that which is right and true. If it be, why then am I troubled? Those things that are without my understanding, are nothing to it at all: and that is it only, which doth properly concern me. Be always in this mind, and thou wilt be right."

What Marcus meant (core philosophy)

Marcus reassures himself that philosophical principles do not lose strength unless neglected. Wisdom remains alive through active application. The core Stoic idea is that your interpretation of events remains within your power. External situations cannot disturb your inner stability unless you allow false judgments to take root. Mental clarity requires consistent renewal.

Dating translation (what this means emotionally/socially)

You may know your standards, boundaries, and emotional truths. Yet when emotions intensify, people often abandon their own wisdom.

Marcus says: Your clarity hasn't disappeared. You simply need to apply it. No matter what happens:
- you can choose the interpretation
- you can maintain perspective
- you can decide what meaning to assign

Your emotional stability lives in how you think, not in what happens externally.

Savage takeaway

Your wisdom didn't fail. You just stopped using it for a moment.

Quiet power mantra

"I return to clear thinking whenever I choose."

III. SEE THE WORLD CLEARLY WITHOUT BECOMING BITTER

"That which most men would think themselves most happy for, and would prefer before all things, if the Gods would grant it unto them after their deaths, thou mayst whilst thou livest grant unto thyself; to live again. See the things of the world again, as thou hast already seen them. For what is it else to live again? Public shows and solemnities with much pomp and vanity, stage plays, flocks and herds; conflicts and contentions: a bone thrown to a company of hungry curs; a bait for greedy fishes; the painfulness, and continual burden-bearing of wretched ants, the running to and fro of terrified mice: little puppets drawn up and down with wires and nerves: these be the objects of the world among all these thou must stand steadfast, meekly affected, and free from all manner of indignation; with this right ratiocination and apprehension; that as the worth is of those things which a man doth affect, so is in very deed every man's worth more or less."

What Marcus meant (core philosophy)

Marcus invites radical clarity about the world. Human society contains vanity, competition, struggle, and repetitive behavior. Recognizing this is not meant to create cynicism but steadiness. The Stoic aim is emotional neutrality. You observe reality clearly without becoming angry or disillusioned. Your worth reflects what you choose to value and pursue.

Dating translation (what this means emotionally/socially)

Dating environments can feel chaotic:
- competition for attention
- superficial displays
- performative behavior

Marcus advises seeing these dynamics clearly without resentment. Instead of becoming cynical or reactive, remain steady. Recognize that much of what people chase is driven by instinct or illusion. Your value lies in what you choose to pursue, not in the noise around you.

Savage takeaway

The dating world may be messy, but you don't have to become messy to survive it.

Quiet power mantra

"I see clearly and remain steady."

IV. UNDERSTAND WORDS AND ACTIONS ONE PIECE AT A TIME

"Word after word, every one by itself, must the things that are spoken be conceived and understood; and so the things that are done, purpose after purpose, every one by itself likewise. And as in matter of purposes and actions, we must presently see what is the proper use and relation of every one; so of words must we be as ready, to consider of every one what is the true meaning, and signification of it according to truth and nature, however it be taken in common use."

What Marcus meant (core philosophy)

Marcus emphasizes careful observation and analysis. Each word and action should be examined individually rather than interpreted through assumption or emotional projection. Clarity comes from breaking complex situations into smaller components and understanding their true meaning. Stoicism values precise perception over reactive interpretation.

Dating translation (what this means emotionally/socially)

Miscommunication often happens because people interpret entire situations based on assumptions rather than actual words or behaviors.

Marcus suggests: Listen to the actual words. Observe the actual actions. Separate what happened from what you imagine it means. This prevents overanalysis driven by insecurity or projection.

177

Savage takeaway

Stop writing entire emotional novels based on one ambiguous sentence.

Quiet power mantra

"I understand clearly before I interpret."

V. USE YOUR ABILITY WITHOUT EGO, AND ACCEPT HELP WITHOUT SHAME

"Is my reason, and understanding sufficient for this, or no? If it be sufficient, without any private applause, or public ostentation as of an instrument, which by nature I am provided of, I will make use of it for the work in hand, as of an instrument, which by nature I am provided of. if it be not, and that otherwise it belong not unto me particularly as a private duty, I will either give it over, and leave it to some other that can better effect it: or I will endeavour it; but with the help of some other, who with the joint help of my reason, is able to bring somewhat to pass, that will now be seasonable and useful for the common good. For whatsoever I do either by myself, or with some other, the only thing that I must intend, is, that it be good and expedient for the public. For as for praise, consider how many who once were much commended, are now already quite forgotten, yea they that commended them, how even they themselves are long since dead and gone. Be not therefore ashamed, whensoever thou must use the help of others. For whatsoever it be that lieth upon thee to effect, thou must propose it unto thyself, as the scaling of walls is unto a soldier. And what if thou through either lameness or some other impediment art not able to reach unto the top of the battlements alone, which with the help of another thou mayst; wilt thou therefore give it over, or go about it with less courage and alacrity, because thou canst not effect it all alone?"

What Marcus meant (core philosophy)

Marcus reflects on practical humility. If you can accomplish something with your own reason, do it without seeking praise. If you cannot, seek help without shame. The purpose is not personal glory but effectiveness aligned with the greater good. The Stoic lesson is freedom from ego. Tools exist to be used. Human beings are cooperative by nature, and asking for help is not weakness but wisdom. Praise fades quickly, but meaningful contribution remains.

Dating translation (what this means emotionally/socially)

Dating often pressures people into independence performances:
*   pretending you don't need support
*   refusing advice or collaboration
*   believing you must handle everything alone

Marcus reframes strength as intelligent cooperation. Healthy dating includes:
*   asking for perspective
*   accepting emotional support
*   collaborating toward mutual growth

Your goal is not to prove self-sufficiency but to move toward truth and alignment.

Savage takeaway

Needing help doesn't make you weak. Refusing help out of ego does.

Quiet power mantra

"I use every resource wisely without shame."

VI. THE FUTURE WILL MEET YOU WITH THE SAME STRENGTH YOU HAVE NOW

"Let not things future trouble thee. For if necessity so require that they come to pass, thou shalt (whensoever that is) be provided for them with the same reason, by which whatsoever is now present, is made both tolerable and acceptable unto thee. All things are linked and knitted together, and the knot is sacred, neither is there anything in the world, that is not kind and natural in regard of any other thing, or, that hath not some kind of reference and natural correspondence with whatsoever is in the world besides. For all things are ranked together, and by that decency of its due place and order that each particular doth observe, they all concur together to the making of one and the same κόσμος⁵⁴ or world: as if you said, a comely piece, or an orderly composition. For all things throughout, there is but one and the same order; and through all things, one and the same God, the same substance and the same law. There is one common reason, and one common truth, that belongs unto all reasonable creatures, for neither is there save one perfection of all creatures that are of the same kind, and partakers of the same reason."

What Marcus meant (core philosophy)

Marcus encourages trust in rational capacity. Future difficulties do not require present anxiety because the same reasoning ability that helps you navigate current challenges will be available later. The Stoic worldview emphasizes interconnected order. Everything belongs within a larger structure, and human reason is part of that structure. Peace comes from trusting your ability to meet reality when it arrives.

Dating translation (what this means emotionally/socially)

Dating anxiety often revolves around imagined future pain:
- "What if I get hurt?"
- "What if it doesn't work out?"
- "What if I choose wrong?"

Marcus reminds you that you already possess the tools you need.
- You handled past uncertainty.
- You will handle future uncertainty.
- You don't need to pre-suffer imaginary scenarios.

Savage takeaway

You survived every past uncertainty without knowing the ending. You'll survive the next one too.

Quiet power mantra

"I trust my future self to meet what comes."

VII. EVERYTHING FADES QUICKLY, INCLUDING MEMORY

"Whatsoever is material, doth soon vanish away into the common substance of the whole; and whatsoever is formal, or, whatsoever doth animate that which is material, is soon resumed into the common reason of the whole; and the fame and memory of anything, is soon swallowed up by the general age and duration of the whole."

---

⁵⁴ The Greek word κόσμος (kósmos) primarily means "order," "orderly arrangement," or "adornment."

What Marcus meant (core philosophy)
Marcus reflects on impermanence. Physical form dissolves, consciousness returns to universal reason, and even fame disappears over time. The Stoic aim is liberation from attachment to reputation or permanence. If everything fades, then living rightly now becomes more important than trying to secure lasting recognition.

Dating translation (what this means emotionally/socially)
People often fear how they will be remembered in relationships:
- worrying about legacy with an ex
- replaying moments endlessly
- needing to leave a lasting impression

Marcus suggests release. Most memories fade. Most stories dissolve into time. What matters is not how permanently someone remembers you, but how authentically you lived.

Savage takeaway
You don't need to become unforgettable. You need to become aligned.

Quiet power mantra
"I live fully without clinging to permanence."

VIII. RIGHT ACTION IS NATURAL TO A REASONABLE PERSON
"To a reasonable creature, the same action is both according to nature, and according to reason."

What Marcus meant (core philosophy)
Marcus emphasizes that rationality and natural living are not separate. For human beings, acting according to reason is acting according to nature. Virtue does not require complexity. When reason guides behavior, alignment follows naturally. Stoicism simplifies ethics into clarity: reasoned action equals natural action.

Dating translation (what this means emotionally/socially)
Dating confusion often arises when people ignore clear reasoning in favor of impulse or fear. You already know when something feels aligned:
- honest communication
- respectful boundaries
- consistency between words and actions

When you act from calm clarity rather than emotional chaos, decisions feel natural rather than forced.

Savage takeaway
If you have to twist yourself into confusion, it's probably not aligned.

Quiet power mantra
"My clarity guides my natural action."

IX. TRUE STRAIGHTNESS COMES FROM WITHIN
"Straight of itself, not made straight."

What Marcus meant (core philosophy)
Marcus expresses the Stoic ideal of inner alignment. True virtue does not require external correction or pressure. What is genuinely good is naturally upright by its own nature, not forced into appearance. The Stoic lesson is authenticity. Right character does not rely on external approval, validation, or supervision. Integrity exists internally.

Dating translation (what this means emotionally/socially)
Many people try to adjust themselves in dating to appear desirable:
- modifying personality to attract interest
- suppressing needs to seem easygoing
- performing instead of being

Marcus reminds you that genuine alignment cannot be manufactured through performance. Real compatibility happens when you are straight by your own nature, not reshaped to fit someone else's expectations.

Savage takeaway
If you have to force yourself into alignment, it isn't real alignment.

Quiet power mantra
"I stand upright by my own nature."

X. YOU ARE NOT SEPARATE FROM THE WHOLE
"As several members in one body united, so are reasonable creatures in a body divided and dispersed, all made and prepared for one common operation. And this thou shalt apprehend the better, if thou shalt use thyself often to say to thyself, I am μέλος[55], or a member of the mass and body of reasonable substances. But if thou shalt say I am μέρος[56], or a part, thou dost not yet love men from thy heart. The joy that thou takest in the exercise of bounty, is not yet grounded upon a due ratiocination and right apprehension of the nature of things. Thou dost exercise it as yet upon this ground barely, as a thing convenient and fitting; not, as doing good to thyself, when thou dost good unto others."

What Marcus meant (core philosophy)
Marcus emphasizes interconnectedness. Humans are not isolated units but members of a larger rational whole. True compassion arises when one understands that helping others is not sacrifice but participation in shared existence. The distinction between "member" and "part" highlights emotional depth. Seeing yourself as a true member implies genuine unity rather than detached obligation.

Dating translation (what this means emotionally/socially)
Dating can encourage individualism to the point of emotional separation:
- viewing partners as interchangeable
- treating connection as transactional
- prioritizing self-protection over shared growth

---

[55] In Greek, the word μέλος (mélos) primarily translates to "member" or "limb."
[56] In Greek, μέρος (méros) is a versatile word that most commonly translates to "part", "portion", or "place."

Marcus suggests that genuine connection requires recognizing mutual belonging. Caring for another person is not losing yourself but expanding your sense of self. Healthy relationships are collaborative ecosystems, not competitions.

Savage takeaway
Connection isn't weakness. It's recognition that you were never meant to exist alone.

Quiet power mantra
"I strengthen myself when I strengthen connection."

XI. EVENTS ONLY HURT WHEN YOU LABEL THEM AS HARM
"Of things that are external, happen what will to that which can suffer by external accidents. Those things that suffer let them complain themselves, if they will; as for me, as long as I conceive no such thing, that that which is happened is evil, I have no hurt; and it is in my power not to conceive any such thing."

What Marcus meant (core philosophy)
Marcus reinforces a central Stoic principle: external events do not inherently harm us. Harm arises from judgment and interpretation. The power lies in perception. If you refuse to define an event as damaging, it loses its ability to disturb your internal state. Freedom comes from choosing interpretation consciously.

Dating translation (what this means emotionally/socially)
Dating events frequently feel devastating because of the meanings attached to them:
- "They didn't choose me, so I'm unworthy."
- "It ended, so it was a failure."

Marcus separates event from interpretation. Someone leaving is behavior. The suffering emerges from the narrative added afterward. Choosing a different interpretation restores emotional agency.

Savage takeaway
Pain is real. The story you attach to it is optional.

Quiet power mantra
"I decide what holds power over me."

XII. REMAIN TRUE TO YOUR NATURE REGARDLESS OF OTHERS
"Whatsoever any man either doth or saith, thou must be good; not for any man's sake, but for thine own nature's sake; as if either gold, or the emerald, or purple, should ever be saying to themselves, Whatsoever any man either doth or saith, I must still be an emerald, and I must keep my colour."

What Marcus meant (core philosophy)
Marcus uses precious materials as metaphors for character. Gold remains gold regardless of external conditions. Likewise, virtue should remain consistent regardless of how others behave. Stoicism teaches internal consistency. Goodness is not reactionary but intrinsic. Your character does not change based on others' actions.

Dating translation (what this means emotionally/socially)

Dating often triggers reactive behavior:

- withdrawing kindness when hurt
- becoming guarded after disappointment
- mirroring poor behavior

Marcus advises maintaining your nature regardless of external dynamics. Consistency in character protects self-respect and prevents emotional chaos.

Savage takeaway

Don't downgrade your character just because someone else lacks theirs.

Quiet power mantra

"I remain true to my nature no matter who stands before me."

XIII. YOUR MIND ONLY SUFFERS WHEN IT BETRAYS ITSELF

"This may ever be my comfort and security: my understanding, that ruleth over all, will not of itself bring trouble and vexation upon itself. This I say; it will not put itself in any fear, it will not lead itself into any concupiscence. If it be in the power of any other to compel it to fear, or to grieve, it is free for him to use his power. But sure if itself do not of itself, through some false opinion or supposition incline itself to any such disposition; there is no fear. For as for the body, why should I make the grief of my body, to be the grief of my mind? If that itself can either fear or complain, let it. But as for the soul, which indeed, can only be truly sensible of either fear or grief; to which only it belongs according to its different imaginations and opinions, to admit of either of these, or of their contraries; thou mayst look to that thyself, that it suffer nothing. Induce her not to any such opinion or persuasion. The understanding is of itself sufficient unto itself, and needs not (if itself doth not bring itself to need) any other thing besides itself, and by consequent as it needs nothing, so neither can it be troubled or hindered by anything, if itself doth not trouble and hinder itself."

What Marcus meant (core philosophy)

Marcus asserts that the rational mind has inherent sovereignty. External events cannot force inner disturbance unless the mind consents through false judgments. The Stoic insight is radical responsibility for internal state. Fear, grief, and distress arise not directly from events but from interpretations and beliefs. The mind is self-sufficient when it refuses to generate unnecessary suffering.

Dating translation (what this means emotionally/socially)

Dating triggers powerful emotions, but Marcus reminds you that the deepest suffering often comes from internal narratives rather than external events.

Examples:

- assuming rejection defines your worth
- imagining betrayal before it exists
- attaching meaning that creates fear

Your mind does not have to escalate emotional pain. You can allow physical feelings or disappointment without turning them into identity-level suffering.

Savage takeaway

The event didn't destroy your peace. The story you told yourself did.

Quiet power mantra

"My mind does not harm itself with false stories."

XIV. SEE OPINIONS FOR WHAT THEY ARE, THEN RELEASE THEM

"What is εὐδαιμονία[57], or happiness: but ἀγαθὸς δαίμων[58], or, a good dæmon, or spirit? What then dost thou do here, O opinion? By the Gods I adjure thee, that thou get thee gone, as thou camest: for I need thee not. Thou camest indeed unto me according to thy ancient wonted manner. It is that, that all men have ever been subject unto. That thou camest therefore I am not angry with thee, only begone, now that I have found thee what thou art."

What Marcus meant (core philosophy)

Marcus personifies intrusive thoughts and opinions, recognizing them as recurring mental habits rather than truths. The Stoic lesson is awareness without attachment. Thoughts arise naturally, but you are not obligated to accept or keep them. Happiness emerges from recognizing false opinions and dismissing them calmly rather than fighting them emotionally.

Dating translation (what this means emotionally/socially)

Dating activates familiar mental patterns:
- "I'm not enough."
- "They will leave."
- "I must prove myself."

Marcus suggests treating these thoughts like visitors rather than authorities. Acknowledge them. Recognize their origin. Then release them without anger or shame. You don't need to fight every thought. You only need to stop believing it automatically.

Savage takeaway

Not every thought deserves a seat at your table.

Quiet power mantra

"I recognize thoughts without becoming ruled by them."

XV. CHANGE IS THE CONDITION FOR EVERYTHING THAT EXISTS

"Is any man so foolish as to fear change, to which all things that once were not owe their being? And what is it, that is more pleasing and more familiar to the nature of the universe? How couldst thou thyself use thy ordinary hot baths, should not the wood that heateth them first be changed? How couldst thou receive any nourishment from those things that thou hast eaten, if they should not be changed? Can anything else almost (that is useful and profitable) be brought to pass without change? How then dost not thou perceive, that for thee also, by death, to come to change, is a thing of the very same nature, and as necessary for the nature of the universe?"

What Marcus meant (core philosophy)

Marcus reframes change as the fundamental mechanism of existence. Everything beneficial arises through transformation. Resistance to change is resistance to

---

[57] In Greek, εὐδαιμονία (*eudaimonía*) is most often translated into English as "happiness." In ancient philosophy, it describes a deeper state of being that is more accurately defined as "human flourishing" or "well-being."

[58] In English, ἀγαθὸς δαίμων (*agathos daimōn*) literally translates to "good spirit" or "noble spirit."

nature itself. The Stoic view embraces impermanence as necessary and meaningful. Change is not disruption but continuation.

Dating translation (what this means emotionally/socially)
Dating involves constant transitions:
- Beginnings
- Endings
- emotional shifts
- evolving identities

Fear of change often keeps people stuck in misaligned situations. Marcus reminds you that transformation is not loss but movement. Without change, growth and nourishment would not exist. Relationships ending or evolving is not failure; it is natural process.

Savage takeaway
You can't demand growth while fearing change.

Quiet power mantra
"I welcome transformation as part of my nature."

XVI. LOVE EVEN THOSE WHO ERR, BECAUSE NOTHING LASTS LONG

"Through the substance of the universe, as through a torrent pass all particular bodies, being all of the same nature, and all joint workers with the universe itself as in one of our bodies so many members among themselves. How many such as Chrysippus, how many such as Socrates, how many such as Epictetus, hath the age of the world long since swallowed up and devoured? Let this, be it either men or businesses, that thou hast occasion to think of, to the end that thy thoughts be not distracted and thy mind too earnestly set upon anything, upon every such occasion presently come to thy mind. Of all my thoughts and cares, one only thing shall be the object, that I myself do nothing which to the proper constitution of man, (either in regard of the thing itself, or in regard of the manner, or of the time of doing,) is contrary. The time when thou shalt have forgotten all things, is at hand. And that time also is at hand, when thou thyself shalt be forgotten by all. Whilst thou art, apply thyself to that especially which unto man as he is a mart, is most proper and agreeable, and that is, for a man even to love them that transgress against him. This shall be, if at the same time that any such thing doth happen, thou call to mind, that they are thy kinsmen; that it is through ignorance and against their wills that they sin; and that within a very short while after, both thou and he shall be no more. But above all things, that he hath not done thee any hurt; for that by him thy mind and understanding is not made worse or more vile than it was before."

What Marcus meant (core philosophy)
Marcus combines impermanence with compassion. All individuals pass through existence briefly, including the wise and the flawed alike. Understanding this dissolves excessive attachment and resentment. The Stoic ideal is maintaining virtue regardless of others' behavior, recognizing that wrongdoing often stems from ignorance rather than malice. True harm occurs only when one's own character deteriorates.

Dating translation (what this means emotionally/socially)
Dating inevitably brings encounters with people who disappoint, misunderstand, or act poorly. Marcus suggests:
- recognize shared humanity
- understand that many mistakes arise from ignorance or fear
- avoid allowing resentment to degrade your own character

This does not mean tolerating harmful behavior. It means protecting your inner state from being shaped by bitterness.

Savage takeaway
They can behave badly without turning you into someone worse.

Quiet power mantra
"I protect my character regardless of others' actions."

XVII. FORM CHANGES, SUBSTANCE CONTINUES
'The nature of the universe, of the common substance of all things as it were of so much wax hath now perchance formed a horse; and then, destroying that figure, hath new tempered and fashioned the matter of it into the form and substance of a tree: then that again into the form and substance of a man: and then that again into some other. Now every one of these doth subsist but for a very little while. As for dissolution, if it be no grievous thing to the chest or trunk, to be joined together; why should it be more grievous to be put asunder?"

What Marcus meant (core philosophy)
Marcus uses the metaphor of wax to describe transformation. Matter constantly changes form, but the underlying substance remains part of the larger whole. Creation and dissolution are equal aspects of nature. The Stoic insight is that separation or ending is not inherently tragic. If formation is natural, dissolution must be equally natural. Fear arises when we treat change as loss rather than transformation.

Dating translation (what this means emotionally/socially)
Relationships evolve, reshape, and sometimes end. Marcus reminds you that endings are not unnatural interruptions but part of the same process that allowed connection to begin. A relationship ending is not destruction. It is transformation into something else:
- growth
- clarity
- new identity
- new possibility

Resisting dissolution often creates more suffering than accepting change as part of life's rhythm.

Savage takeaway
If you celebrate beginnings, you must accept endings as part of the same cycle.

Quiet power mantra
"I accept transformation without resistance."

XVIII. ANGER IS AGAINST YOUR OWN NATURE

"An angry countenance is much against nature, and it is oftentimes the proper countenance of them that are at the point of death. But were it so, that all anger and passion were so thoroughly quenched in thee, that it were altogether impossible to kindle it any more, yet herein must not thou rest satisfied, but further endeavour by good consequence of true ratiocination, perfectly to conceive and understand, that all anger and passion is against reason. For if thou shalt not be sensible of thine innocence; if that also shall be gone from thee, the comfort of a good conscience, that thou doest all things according to reason: what shouldest thou live any longer for? All things that now thou seest, are but for a moment. That nature, by which all things in the world are administered, will soon bring change and alteration upon them, and then of their substances make other things like unto them: and then soon after others again of the matter and substance of these: that so by these means, the world may still appear fresh and new."

What Marcus meant (core philosophy)

Marcus teaches that anger contradicts rational nature. Even if anger fades, one must intellectually understand why it is misaligned with reason. True peace is not merely suppressing emotion but comprehending its irrational roots. Because everything is transient, anger toward fleeting situations becomes even more unnecessary.

Dating translation (what this means emotionally/socially)

Dating can trigger anger:
- betrayal
- rejection
- disrespect

Marcus does not say feelings never arise. Instead, he urges deeper reflection:
- Does anger improve clarity?
- Does it align with your values?
- Does it serve your rational self?

Understanding the temporary nature of situations helps dissolve the impulse to cling to resentment.

Savage takeaway

Anger feels powerful, but it rarely makes you wiser.

Quiet power mantra

"I choose clarity over reaction."

XIX. UNDERSTAND THE BELIEF BEHIND THE BEHAVIOR

"Whensoever any man doth trespass against other, presently consider with thyself what it was that he did suppose to be good, what to be evil, when he did trespass. For this when thou knowest, thou wilt pity him thou wilt have no occasion either to wonder, or to be angry. For either thou thyself dust yet live in that error and ignorance, as that thou dust suppose either that very thing that he doth, or some other like worldly thing, to be good; and so thou art bound to pardon him if he have done that which thou in the like case wouldst have done thyself. Or if so be that thou dost not any more suppose the same things to be good or evil, that he doth; how canst thou but be gentle unto him that is in an error?"

187

What Marcus meant (core philosophy)

Marcus encourages examining the internal beliefs driving another person's actions. People act according to what they believe is good or necessary, even when mistaken. Understanding this creates compassion without requiring agreement. The Stoic goal is replacing outrage with insight.

Dating translation (what this means emotionally/socially)

When someone behaves poorly in dating, the instinct is often judgment or anger. Marcus suggests asking: What did they believe they were gaining? What fear or misunderstanding drove their choice? This perspective doesn't excuse harmful behavior, but it reduces emotional shock and personalizing. Seeing behavior as belief-driven makes detachment easier.

Savage takeaway

People don't just act badly. They act according to flawed stories they believe are right.

Quiet power mantra

"I seek understanding before judgment."

XX. ENJOY THE PRESENT WITHOUT CLINGING TO IT

"Fancy not to thyself things future, as though they were present but of those that are present, take some aside, that thou takest most benefit of, and consider of them particularly, how wonderfully thou wouldst want them, if they were not present. But take heed withal, lest that whilst thou dust settle thy contentment in things present, thou grow in time so to overprize them, as that the want of them (whensoever it shall so fall out) should be a trouble and a vexation unto thee. Wind up thyself into thyself. Such is the nature of thy reasonable commanding part, as that if it exercise justice, and have by that means tranquillity within itself, it doth rest fully satisfied with itself without any other thing."

What Marcus meant (core philosophy)

Marcus advises appreciating present blessings while maintaining inner independence. Gratitude should not become attachment so strong that loss becomes devastation. The Stoic balance is appreciation without dependency. True stability arises from internal tranquility rather than external possession.

Dating translation (what this means emotionally/socially)

In relationships, it is easy to either: live in imagined futures or cling too tightly to present happiness.

Marcus recommends a middle path: Enjoy connection deeply. Value what exists now. But do not build your identity entirely upon it. Inner stability ensures that love enriches life rather than becoming the sole foundation of it.

Savage takeaway

Love what you have without turning it into something you cannot survive losing.

Quiet power mantra

"I appreciate deeply without clinging."

XXI. CUT THROUGH ILLUSION AND RETURN TO CLARITY

"Wipe off all opinion stay the force and violence of unreasonable lusts and affections: circumscribe the present time examine whatsoever it be that is happened, either to thyself or to another: divide all present objects, either in that which is formal or material think of the last hour. That which thy neighbour hath committed, where the guilt of it lieth, there let it rest. Examine in order whatsoever is spoken. Let thy mind penetrate both into the effects, and into the causes. Rejoice thyself with true simplicity, and modesty; and that all middle things between virtue and vice are indifferent unto thee. Finally, love mankind; obey God."

What Marcus meant (core philosophy)

Marcus lays out a mental discipline for peace. Remove unnecessary interpretation. Control impulsive desires. Focus only on the present moment. Analyze events clearly by separating cause from effect, and moral value from neutral circumstance.

The Stoic ideal is simplicity: clarity without excess emotional overlay. True good lies only in virtue; everything else is neutral.

Dating translation (what this means emotionally/socially)

Dating becomes chaotic when imagination replaces observation:
- overinterpreting texts
- projecting intentions
- attaching emotional meaning to neutral events

Marcus advises: Return to facts. Stay present. Let others' actions remain their responsibility. Clarity arises when you stop adding layers of narrative that distort reality.

Savage takeaway

Most dating drama is opinion stacked on top of neutral events.

Quiet power mantra

"I see clearly without adding unnecessary story."

XXII. TRUST ORDER, RELEASE FEAR

"All things (saith he) are by certain order and appointment. And what if the elements only. It will suffice to remember, that all things in general are by certain order and appointment: or if it be but few. And as concerning death, that either dispersion, or the atoms, or annihilation, or extinction, or translation will ensue. And as concerning pain, that that which is intolerable is soon ended by death; and that which holds long must needs be tolerable; and that the mind in the meantime (which is all in all) may by way of interclusion, or interception, by stopping all manner of commerce and sympathy with the body, still retain its own tranquillity. Thy understanding is not made worse by it. As for those parts that suffer, let them, if they can, declare their grief themselves. As for praise and commendation, view their mind and understanding, what estate they are in; what kind of things they fly, and what things they seek after: and that as in the seaside, whatsoever was before to be seen, is by the continual succession of new heaps of sand cast up one upon another, soon hid and covered; so in this life, all former things by those which immediately succeed."

What Marcus meant (core philosophy)

Marcus explores acceptance of universal order. Whether events are divinely guided or simply natural processes, everything unfolds within a larger structure. Pain is either brief or bearable. Praise is fleeting. Time continually replaces all things. The Stoic solution is inner independence. External circumstances cannot damage your rational core unless you allow them to.

Dating translation (what this means emotionally/socially)

Dating anxiety often comes from fearing pain or chasing validation. Marcus reframes both: Pain is temporary or manageable. Praise fades quickly. External opinions are unstable. When you understand this, emotional balance returns. You stop chasing approval and fearing rejection because both lose exaggerated importance.

Savage takeaway

Approval fades like footprints in sand. Stop building your identity on it.

Quiet power mantra

"My peace is not dependent on praise or fear."

XXIII. FROM A HIGHER PERSPECTIVE, EVERYTHING SHRINKS

Out of Plato. 'He then whose mind is endowed with true magnanimity, who hath accustomed himself to the contemplation both of all times, and of all things in general; can this mortal life (thinkest thou) seem any great matter unto him? It is not possible, answered he. Then neither will such a one account death a grievous thing? By no means.'

What Marcus meant (core philosophy)

Drawing from Plato, Marcus highlights the power of perspective. When the mind expands to consider all time and existence, individual concerns lose their overwhelming intensity. Magnanimity comes from seeing life as part of a vast continuum rather than a narrow personal drama. Fear diminishes as perspective widens.

Dating translation (what this means emotionally/socially)

Dating experiences can feel enormous in the moment:
- heartbreak feels permanent
- attraction feels destiny-level
- rejection feels catastrophic

Marcus invites you to zoom out. From a wider perspective:
- one connection is not your entire story
- one ending does not define your life

This broader view restores emotional proportion.

Savage takeaway

What feels massive now becomes a footnote when you widen your lens.

Quiet power mantra

"I hold perspective larger than the moment."

XXIV. TRUE POWER IS INNER DISCIPLINE, NOT OUTER IMAGE

Out of Antisthenes[59]. 'It is a princely thing to do well, and to be ill-spoken of. It is a shameful thing that the face should be subject unto the mind, to be put into what shape it will, and to be dressed by it as it will; and that the mind should not bestow so much care upon herself, as to fashion herself, and to dress herself as best becometh her.'

What Marcus meant (core philosophy)

Marcus quotes Antisthenes to emphasize internal refinement over external appearance. People spend immense effort shaping outward presentation but often neglect shaping their character and thoughts. True nobility lies in doing good regardless of reputation. The Stoic ideal is self-governance: cultivate the mind more carefully than the image.

Dating translation (what this means emotionally/socially)

Modern dating encourages focus on presentation:
- curated photos
- crafted personas
- performative confidence

Marcus suggests shifting effort inward: Develop emotional maturity. Strengthen character. Refine thinking. External image attracts attention. Inner discipline sustains meaningful connection.

Savage takeaway

Looking impressive matters less than being internally solid.

Quiet power mantra

"I refine my character more than my image."

XXV. ANGER CHANGES NOTHING EXCEPT YOU

Out of several poets and comics. 'It will but little avail thee, to turn thine anger and indignation upon the things themselves that have fallen across unto thee. For as for them, they are not sensible of it, &c[60]. Thou shalt but make thyself a laughing-stock; both unto the Gods and men, &c. Our life is reaped like a ripe ear of corn; one is yet standing and another is down, &c. But if so be that I and my children be neglected by the gods, there is some reason even for that, &c. As long as right and equity is of my side, &c. Not to lament with them, not to tremble, &c.'

What Marcus meant (core philosophy)

Marcus gathers wisdom from poets to highlight the futility of anger toward events themselves. Circumstances are indifferent to your emotional reaction. Anger does not alter reality; it only disturbs the person who carries it. Life moves quickly and unpredictably, like grain harvested in sequence. Stoic strength lies in maintaining justice and composure regardless of external outcomes.

---

[59] Antisthenes (c. 445–365 BC) was a Greek philosopher, a close pupil of Socrates, and is traditionally regarded as the founder of the Cynic school of philosophy.
[60] In English, &c. is an archaic abbreviation for et cetera.

Dating translation (what this means emotionally/socially)
In dating, anger often arises from unmet expectations:
- someone behaves differently than you hoped
- timing fails
- connection doesn't unfold as imagined

Marcus reminds you that directing anger toward reality itself changes nothing. You may feel justified, but anger rarely improves clarity or outcomes. Maintaining dignity and self-alignment matters more than reacting emotionally to disappointment.

Savage takeaway
Reality doesn't care about your anger. Only you pay the cost of carrying it.

Quiet power mantra
"I release anger that serves no purpose."

XXVI. LIVE WELL, NOT SAFELY

Out of Plato. 'My answer, full of justice and equity, should be this: Thy speech is not right, O man! if thou supposest that he that is of any worth at all, should apprehend either life or death, as a matter of great hazard and danger; and should not make this rather his only care, to examine his own actions, whether just or unjust: whether actions of a good, or of a wicked man, &c. For thus in very truth stands the case, O ye men of Athens. What place or station soever a man either hath chosen to himself, judging it best for himself; or is by lawful authority put and settled in, therein do I think (all appearance of danger notwithstanding) that he should continue, as one who feareth neither death, nor anything else, so much as he feareth to commit anything that is vicious and shameful, &c. But, O noble sir, consider I pray, whether true generosity and true happiness, do not consist in somewhat else rather, than in the preservation either of our, or other men's lives. For it is not the part of a man that is a man indeed, to desire to live long or to make much of his life whilst he liveth: but rather (he that is such) will in these things wholly refer himself unto the Gods, and believing that which every woman can tell him, that no man can escape death; the only thing that he takes thought and care for is this, that what time he liveth, he may live as well and as virtuously as he can possibly, &c. To look about, and with the eyes to follow the course of the stars and planets as though thou wouldst run with them; and to mind perpetually the several changes of the elements one into another. For such fancies and imaginations, help much to purge away the dross and filth of this our earthly life,' &c. That also is a fine passage of Plato's, where he speaketh of worldly things in these words: 'Thou must also as from some higher place look down, as it were, upon the things of this world, as flocks, armies, husbandmen's labours, marriages, divorces, generations, deaths: the tumults of courts and places of judicatures; desert places; the several nations of barbarians, public festivals, mournings, fairs, markets.' How all things upon earth are pell-mell; and how miraculously things contrary one to another, concur to the beauty and perfection of this universe.

What Marcus meant (core philosophy)
Marcus, through Plato, teaches that the highest concern is not survival or safety but virtue. Fear of loss or death should never outweigh commitment to just action. A wide perspective dissolves fear. When you see life as part of a vast and constantly changing universe, individual anxieties lose their overwhelming grip.

Dating translation (what this means emotionally/socially)

Many dating choices are driven by fear:

- fear of rejection
- fear of loneliness
- fear of emotional risk

Marcus reframes the priority: The goal is not emotional safety at all costs. The goal is to act with integrity. Speak honestly. Show up authentically. Make choices aligned with your values rather than avoiding vulnerability to prevent discomfort.

Savage takeaway

Playing safe might protect your ego, but it rarely builds real connection.

Quiet power mantra

"I choose integrity over emotional safety."

XXVII. EVERYTHING FOLLOWS THE SAME PATTERN

To look back upon things of former ages, as upon the manifold changes and conversions of several monarchies and commonwealths. We may also foresee things future, for they shall all be of the same kind; neither is it possible that they should leave the tune, or break the concert that is now begun, as it were, by these things that are now done and brought to pass in the world. It comes all to one therefore, whether a man be a spectator of the things of this life but forty years, or whether he see them ten thousand years together: for what shall he see more? 'And as for those parts that came from the earth, they shall return unto the earth again; and those that came from heaven, they also shall return unto those heavenly places.' Whether it be a mere dissolution and unbinding of the manifold intricacies and entanglements of the confused atoms; or some such dispersion of the simple and incorruptible elements... 'With meats and drinks and divers charms, they seek to divert the channel, that they might not die. Yet must we needs endure that blast of wind that cometh from above, though we toil and labour never so much.'

What Marcus meant (core philosophy)

Marcus emphasizes repetition across history. Human patterns remain consistent regardless of era. Change occurs within recurring structures. Understanding this reduces attachment to novelty or uniqueness. Life unfolds according to rhythms larger than any individual. Acceptance arises when you recognize the continuity of existence.

Dating translation (what this means emotionally/socially)

Dating patterns repeat across generations:

- attraction cycles
- emotional dynamics
- misunderstandings

Recognizing repetition removes the illusion that your experiences are uniquely extraordinary or uniquely doomed. This perspective brings calm. What feels overwhelming becomes understandable as part of larger human patterns.

Savage takeaway

You're not trapped in a unique drama. You're living a timeless human story.

Quiet power mantra

"I observe patterns without losing perspective."

XXVIII. TRUE STRENGTH IS CHARACTER, NOT COMPARISON

"He hath a stronger body, and is a better wrestler than I. What then? Is he more bountiful? is he more modest? Doth he bear all adverse chances with more equanimity: or with his neighbour's offences with more meekness and gentleness than I?"

What Marcus meant (core philosophy)

Marcus challenges comparison based on external traits. Physical strength or external advantage does not determine true worth. Virtue is measured through internal qualities: generosity, modesty, resilience, and gentleness. The Stoic focus shifts evaluation inward rather than outward.

Dating translation (what this means emotionally/socially)

Comparison is common in dating:

- comparing appearance
- comparing status
- comparing desirability

Marcus redirects attention to character. The real question is not who is more attractive or impressive externally, but:

- Who shows integrity?
- Who remains kind under pressure?
- Who maintains emotional steadiness?

These qualities determine long-term compatibility and personal worth.

Savage takeaway

External advantages don't equal deeper value.

Quiet power mantra

"I measure myself by character, not comparison."

XXIX. WHERE REASON LEADS, THERE IS NO REAL LOSS

"Where the matter may be effected agreeably to that reason, which both unto the Gods and men is common, there can be no just cause of grief or sorrow. For where the fruit and benefit of an action well begun and prosecuted according to the proper constitution of man may be reaped and obtained, or is sure and certain, it is against reason that any damage should there be suspected. In all places, and at all times, it is in thy power religiously to embrace whatsoever by God's appointment is happened unto thee, and justly to converse with those men, whom thou hast to do with, and accurately to examine every fancy that presents itself, that nothing may slip and steal in, before thou hast rightly apprehended the true nature of it."

What Marcus meant (core philosophy)

Marcus teaches that when actions align with universal reason and virtue, there is no true harm. Loss is only imagined when we measure outcomes incorrectly. The Stoic path includes three core practices:

- accept what happens
- act justly toward others
- examine impressions carefully before believing them

Peace arises when reasoning replaces emotional assumption.

Dating translation (what this means emotionally/socially)

If you act with integrity in dating, there is no real failure. Even if:

- someone leaves
- timing fails
- attraction fades

If your actions aligned with your values, nothing essential was lost. Marcus reminds you to examine emotional reactions carefully. Many dating fears come from assumptions rather than reality.

Savage takeaway

If you showed up with integrity, you didn't lose. You completed your part.

Quiet power mantra

"I trust the outcome of actions aligned with reason."

XXX. FOLLOW YOUR NATURE, NOT OTHER PEOPLE'S PATHS

"Look not about upon other men's minds and understandings; but look right on forwards whither nature, both that of the universe, in those things that happen unto thee; and thine in particular, in those things that are done by thee: doth lead, and direct thee. Now every one is bound to do that, which is consequent and agreeable to that end which by his true natural constitution he was ordained unto. As for all other things, they are ordained for the use of reasonable creatures: as in all things we see that that which is worse and inferior, is made for that which is better. Reasonable creatures, they are ordained one for another. That therefore which is chief in every man's constitution, is, that he intend the common good. The second is, that he yield not to any lusts and motions of the flesh. For it is the part and privilege of the reasonable and intellective faculty, that she can so bound herself, as that neither the sensitive, nor the appetitive faculties, may not anyways prevail upon her. For both these are brutish. And therefore over both she challengeth mastery, and cannot anyways endure, if in her right temper, to be subject unto either. And this indeed most justly. For by nature she was ordained to command all in the body. The third thing proper to man by his constitution, is, to avoid all rashness and precipitancy; and not to be subject to error. To these things then, let the mind apply herself and go straight on, without any distraction about other things, and she hath her end, and by consequent her happiness."

What Marcus meant (core philosophy)

Marcus urges attention toward one's own path rather than comparison. Humans are designed for reason, self-command, and cooperation with others. Three key principles emerge:

- serve the common good
- govern impulses through reason
- avoid rashness

Happiness comes from alignment with one's natural purpose, not external imitation.

Dating translation (what this means emotionally/socially)

Dating culture encourages comparison:

- comparing timelines
- comparing partners
- comparing desirability

195

Marcus redirects focus inward. Follow your own nature:

- act thoughtfully rather than impulsively
- avoid reactive decisions driven by attraction alone
- seek connection aligned with deeper values

True compatibility arises when both people live authentically rather than perform roles.

Savage takeaway
Stop checking where everyone else is going. Walk your own path with clarity.

Quiet power mantra
"I follow my nature without comparison."

XXXI. LIVE AS IF THIS MOMENT IS BONUS TIME

"As one who had lived, and were now to die by right, whatsoever is yet remaining, bestow that wholly as a gracious overplus upon a virtuous life. Love and affect that only, whatsoever it be that happeneth, and is by the fates appointed unto thee. For what can be more reasonable? And as anything doth happen unto thee by way of cross, or calamity, call to mind presently and set before thine eyes, the examples of some other men, to whom the self-same thing did once happen likewise. Well, what did they? They grieved; they wondered; they complained. And where are they now? All dead and gone. Wilt thou also be like one of them? Or rather leaving to men of the world (whose life both in regard of themselves, and them that they converse with, is nothing but mere mutability; or men of as fickle minds, as fickle bodies; ever changing and soon changed themselves) let it be thine only care and study, how to make a right use of all such accidents. For there is good use to be made of them, and they will prove fit matter for thee to work upon, if it shall be both thy care and thy desire, that whatsoever thou doest, thou thyself mayst like and approve thyself for it. And both these, see, that thou remember well, according as the diversity of the matter of the action that thou art about shall require. Look within; within is the fountain of all good. Such a fountain, where springing waters can never fail, so thou dig still deeper and deeper."

What Marcus meant (core philosophy)
Marcus suggests living as though life beyond this moment is a gift rather than a guarantee. Every remaining moment becomes an opportunity for virtue. Instead of complaining about hardship, transform it into material for growth. The source of goodness lies within, not outside. Self-approval through virtuous action becomes the true measure of life.

Dating translation (what this means emotionally/socially)
Dating often includes disappointment, uncertainty, and change.

Marcus encourages reframing: Instead of asking "Why is this happening to me?" ask "How can I use this well?"

Each experience becomes:

- refinement
- self-knowledge
- deeper alignment

When you stop resisting reality and start using it consciously, even difficult experiences strengthen you.

196

Savage takeaway
Life doesn't owe you ease. It offers material. What you build from it is yours.

Quiet power mantra
"I turn every experience into growth."

XXXII. LET YOUR OUTER PRESENCE REFLECT INNER STEADINESS

"Thou must use thyself also to keep thy body fixed and steady; free from all loose fluctuant either motion, or posture. And as upon thy face and looks, thy mind hath easily power over them to keep them to that which is grave and decent; so let it challenge the same power over the whole body also. But so observe all things in this kind, as that it be without any manner of affectation."

What Marcus meant (core philosophy)
Marcus links physical composure with mental discipline. External presence can reflect internal steadiness when guided naturally rather than artificially. The key is authenticity. True composure is calm and natural, not performative or forced. Self-mastery expresses itself through quiet alignment between mind and body.

Dating translation (what this means emotionally/socially)
In dating, nervous energy or performative behavior often arises from insecurity. Marcus suggests grounded presence:
- calm posture
- natural expression
- emotional steadiness

Attraction often grows from authentic composure rather than exaggerated performance.

Savage takeaway
Confidence isn't loud. It's calm alignment between how you feel and how you move.

Quiet power mantra
"My presence reflects my inner steadiness."

XXXIII. LIFE REQUIRES THE READINESS OF A WRESTLER, NOT THE GRACE OF A DANCER

"The art of true living in this world is more like a wrestler's, than a dancer's practice. For in this they both agree, to teach a man whatsoever falls upon him, that he may be ready for it, and that nothing may cast him down."

What Marcus meant (core philosophy)
Marcus compares life to wrestling rather than dancing. Dancing follows predictable patterns; wrestling demands readiness for the unexpected. Stoicism trains adaptability. Instead of expecting smooth flow, one prepares to meet resistance directly. Strength lies in readiness, resilience, and balance under pressure.

Dating translation (what this means emotionally/socially)
Dating rarely unfolds according to scripts:
- plans change
- feelings shift
- unexpected challenges appear

If you approach dating expecting perfection or choreography, disappointment is inevitable. Instead, approach it like a wrestler:
- grounded
- responsive
- resilient

Emotional strength comes from adaptability rather than control.

Savage takeaway
Dating isn't choreography. It's contact sport.

Quiet power mantra
"I meet whatever comes with readiness."

XXXIV. UNDERSTAND WHOSE APPROVAL YOU ARE CHASING

'Thou must continually ponder and consider with thyself, what manner of men they be, and for their minds and understandings what is their present estate, whose good word and testimony thou dost desire. For then neither wilt thou see cause to complain of them that offend against their wills; or find any want of their applause, if once thou dost but penetrate into the true force and ground both of their opinions, and of their desires. 'No soul (saith he) is willingly bereft of the truth,' and by consequent, neither of justice, or temperance, or kindness, and mildness; nor of anything that is of the same kind. It is most needful that thou shouldst always remember this. For so shalt thou be far more gentle and moderate towards all men."

What Marcus meant (core philosophy)
Marcus advises examining the character and understanding of those whose approval we seek. If you understand their limitations or motivations, their praise or criticism loses exaggerated influence. People act based on their perception of good, even when mistaken. Recognizing this fosters compassion and reduces resentment.

Dating translation (what this means emotionally/socially)
Many dating insecurities come from craving validation:
- wanting someone's approval
- fearing someone's rejection

Marcus asks: Is this person's perspective truly aligned with your values? Does their judgment deserve authority over your self-worth? Understanding who someone is dissolves unnecessary emotional dependency on their opinion.

Savage takeaway
Before craving someone's approval, decide if their perspective is worth wanting.

Quiet power mantra
"I value insight over validation."

XXXV. PAIN DOES NOT DEFINE YOU
"What pain soever thou art in, let this presently come to thy mind, that it is not a thing whereof thou needest to be ashamed, neither is it a thing whereby thy understanding, that hath the government of all, can be made worse. For neither in regard of the substance of it, nor in regard of the end of it (which is, to intend the common good) can it alter and corrupt it. This also of Epicurus mayst thou in most pains find some help of, that it is 'neither intolerable, nor eternal;' so thou keep thyself to the true bounds and limits of reason and give not way to opinion. This also thou must consider, that many things there be, which oftentimes unsensibly trouble and vex thee, as not armed against them with patience, because they go not ordinarily under the name of pains, which in very deed are of the same nature as pain; as to slumber unquietly, to suffer heat, to want appetite: when therefore any of these things make thee discontented, check thyself with these words: Now hath pain given thee the foil; thy courage hath failed thee."

What Marcus meant (core philosophy)
Marcus reframes pain as neutral to character. Pain cannot corrupt the rational mind unless one interprets it as defeat. He also notes that many subtle discomforts create hidden distress because we fail to recognize them as forms of pain requiring patience. Stoicism emphasizes endurance through rational perspective.

Dating translation (what this means emotionally/socially)
Emotional pain in dating often carries shame:
- heartbreak
- rejection
- disappointment

Marcus reminds you: Pain does not diminish your worth. It does not weaken your character unless you interpret it as failure. Recognizing emotional discomfort as part of experience reduces its power.

Savage takeaway
Feeling pain doesn't make you weak. Believing pain defines you does.

Quiet power mantra
"My strength remains intact through discomfort."

XXXVI. DO NOT BECOME HARD LIKE THOSE WHO HARM
"Take heed lest at any time thou stand so affected, though towards unnatural evil men, as ordinary men are commonly one towards another."

What Marcus meant (core philosophy)
Marcus warns against becoming hardened or reactive, even toward those who behave badly. The Stoic goal is to maintain one's own nature rather than mirror negativity. Your character should remain consistent regardless of others' actions.

Dating translation (what this means emotionally/socially)
After negative dating experiences, many people become:
- cynical
- guarded to the point of coldness
- reactive or defensive

Marcus advises maintaining integrity without adopting bitterness. Protect boundaries, yes. But do not let past hurt reshape your character into something unrecognizable.

Savage takeaway
Don't let bad behavior teach you to become someone you don't respect.

Quiet power mantra
"I remain aligned with my nature, not theirs."

XXXVII. JUDGE CHARACTER BY THE SOUL, NOT THE STORY

"How know we whether Socrates were so eminent indeed, and of so extraordinary a disposition? For that he died more gloriously, that he disputed with the Sophists more subtilty; that he watched in the frost more assiduously; that being commanded to fetch innocent Salaminius, he refused to do it more generously; all this will not serve. Nor that he walked in the streets, with much gravity and majesty, as was objected unto him by his adversaries: which nevertheless a man may well doubt of, whether it were so or no, or, which above all the rest, if so be that it were true, a man would well consider of, whether commendable, or dis-commendable. The thing therefore that we must inquire into, is this; what manner of soul Socrates had: whether his disposition was such; as that all that he stood upon, and sought after in this world, was barely this, that he might ever carry himself justly towards men, and holily towards the Gods. Neither vexing himself to no purpose at the wickedness of others, nor yet ever condescending to any man's evil fact, or evil intentions, through either fear, or engagement of friendship. Whether of those things that happened unto him by God's appointment, he neither did wonder at any when it did happen, or thought it intolerable in the trial of it. And lastly, whether he never did suffer his mind to sympathise with the senses, and affections of the body. For we must not think that Nature hath so mixed and tempered it with the body, as that she hath not power to circumscribe herself, and by herself to intend her own ends and occasions."

What Marcus meant (core philosophy)
Marcus challenges superficial judgments. Reputation, stories, or dramatic actions do not define true virtue. The real question is the quality of the soul. True greatness lies in:
- consistent justice
- inner steadiness
- independence from external praise or suffering

Character is revealed through disposition, not spectacle.

Dating translation (what this means emotionally/socially)
Dating culture often evaluates people through:
- grand gestures
- dramatic stories
- curated personas

Marcus suggests looking deeper:
- Does this person act with integrity consistently?
- Do they remain steady under pressure?
- Do they avoid compromising values for approval?

Long-term compatibility depends on inner character, not impressive moments.

Savage takeaway
Charm is loud. Character is consistent.

Quiet power mantra
"I evaluate souls, not performances."

XXXVIII. TRUE GREATNESS CAN REMAIN UNSEEN

"For it is a thing very possible, that a man should be a very divine man, and yet be altogether unknown. This thou must ever be mindful of, as of this also, that a man's true happiness doth consist in very few things. And that although thou dost despair, that thou shalt ever be a good either logician, or naturalist, yet thou art never the further off by it from being either liberal, or modest, or charitable, or obedient unto God."

What Marcus meant (core philosophy)
Marcus reminds us that virtue does not require recognition. A person may live nobly without public acknowledgment. Happiness depends on simple internal qualities:
- Kindness
- Humility
- Generosity
- alignment with higher principles

External achievements are secondary.

Dating translation (what this means emotionally/socially)
Many people seek validation through visibility:
- being chosen publicly
- appearing impressive
- gaining admiration

Marcus reframes value: You do not need to be extraordinary in the eyes of others to live meaningfully. In dating, quiet emotional maturity often outweighs visible status.

Savage takeaway
Being deeply good matters more than being visibly impressive.

Quiet power mantra
"My worth exists even when unseen."

XXXIX. NOTHING CAN DISTURB A CALM MIND WITHOUT PERMISSION

"Free from all compulsion in all cheerfulness and alacrity thou mayst run out thy time, though men should exclaim against thee never so much, and the wild beasts should pull in sunder the poor members of thy pampered mass of flesh. For what in either of these or the like cases should hinder the mind to retain her own rest and tranquillity, consisting both in the right judgment of those things that happen unto her, and in the ready use of all present matters and occasions? So that her judgment may say, to that which is befallen her by way of cross: this thou art in very deed, and according to thy true nature: notwithstanding that in the judgment of opinion thou dust appear otherwise: and her discretion to the present object; thou

201

art that, which I sought for. For whatsoever it be, that is now present, shall ever be embraced by me as a fit and seasonable object, both for my reasonable faculty, and for my sociable, or charitable inclination to work upon. And that which is principal in this matter, is that it may be referred either unto the praise of God, or to the good of men. For either unto God or man, whatsoever it is that doth happen in the world hath in the ordinary course of nature its proper reference; neither is there anything, that in regard of nature is either new, or reluctant and intractable, but all things both usual and easy."

What Marcus meant (core philosophy)
Marcus emphasizes radical internal freedom. Even extreme external adversity cannot disturb the mind unless judgment allows it. Events themselves become opportunities for virtue when interpreted correctly. The Stoic practice is accepting reality as raw material for meaningful action.

Dating translation (what this means emotionally/socially)
Dating experiences can feel destabilizing:
- criticism
- rejection
- unexpected endings

Marcus invites you to reinterpret: Every situation becomes material for growth and kindness. Instead of resisting reality, integrate it into your development.

Savage takeaway
Peace comes from how you interpret events, not from controlling them.

Quiet power mantra
"I meet every moment as material for growth."

XL. LIVE EACH DAY COMPLETE, WITHOUT EXTREMES
Then hath a man attained to the estate of perfection in his life and conversation, when he so spends every day, as if it were his last day: never hot and vehement in his affections, nor yet so cold and stupid as one that had no sense; and free from all manner of dissimulation."

What Marcus meant (core philosophy)
Marcus describes balanced living:
- present awareness of mortality
- emotional moderation
- authenticity without performance

Perfection is not intensity or detachment alone but equilibrium between feeling and reason.

Dating translation (what this means emotionally/socially)
Dating extremes often cause instability:
- over-investing too quickly
- emotional shutdown to avoid vulnerability

Marcus proposes balance: Feel deeply but stay grounded. Care sincerely without losing yourself. Remain honest without performing a role.

Savage takeaway
True emotional power is neither obsession nor numbness. It is balance.

Quiet power mantra
"I live fully, calmly, and honestly each day."

XLI. IF EVEN THE GODS ARE PATIENT, WHY ARE YOU SO QUICK TO JUDGE

"Can the Gods, who are immortal, for the continuance of so many ages bear without indignation with such and so many sinners, as have ever been, yea not only so, but also take such care for them, that they want nothing; and dust thou so grievously take on, as one that could bear with them no longer; thou that art but for a moment of time? yea thou that art one of those sinners thyself? A very ridiculous thing it is, that any man should dispense with vice and wickedness in himself, which is in his power to restrain; and should go about to suppress it in others, which is altogether impossible."

What Marcus meant (core philosophy)
Marcus confronts hypocrisy and impatience toward others. If divine intelligence can tolerate human flaws with patience, it is unreasonable for individuals to become outraged at imperfection. The Stoic lesson:
* focus on correcting yourself
* accept that you cannot control others
* cultivate humility about your own faults

Trying to control others' behavior wastes energy better used for self-mastery.

Dating translation (what this means emotionally/socially)
Dating frustration often arises from trying to change people:
* wishing someone would act differently
* resenting patterns you cannot control

Marcus suggests redirecting effort inward. You cannot force maturity, honesty, or emotional availability. But you can refine:
* your boundaries
* your reactions
* your choices

Patience becomes strength when combined with self-awareness.

Savage takeaway
Fixing yourself is possible. Fixing others is fantasy.

Quiet power mantra
"I focus on mastering myself, not controlling others."

XLII. IF IT SERVES NEITHER REASON NOR KINDNESS, RELEASE IT

"What object soever, our reasonable and sociable faculty doth meet with, that affords nothing either for the satisfaction of reason, or for the practice of charity, she worthily doth think unworthy of herself."

What Marcus meant (core philosophy)
Marcus defines a simple filter for value. Anything that does not support rational clarity or compassionate connection holds little worth. Stoicism prioritizes:

- reason (truth, clarity, understanding)
- sociability (kindness, cooperation)

Distractions that serve neither should be discarded.

Dating translation (what this means emotionally/socially)
Ask two questions when evaluating dating dynamics:
- Does this make me clearer?
- Does this help me act with kindness or integrity?

If the answer is no, the dynamic may be misaligned.

Examples:
- drama without growth
- attention without respect
- attraction without compatibility

Savage takeaway
If it feeds neither clarity nor kindness, it's probably noise.

Quiet power mantra
"I give energy only to what supports reason and compassion."

XLIII. DO GOOD WITHOUT NEEDING APPLAUSE
"When thou hast done well, and another is benefited by thy action, must thou like a very fool look for a third thing besides, as that it may appear unto others also that thou hast done well, or that thou mayest in time, receive one good turn for another? No man useth to be weary of that which is beneficial unto him. But every action according to nature, is beneficial. Be not weary then of doing that which is beneficial unto thee, whilst it is so unto others."

What Marcus meant (core philosophy)
Marcus teaches that virtuous action is its own reward. Seeking recognition or repayment diminishes the purity of action. True benefit lies in the act itself, because acting according to nature strengthens character. Expectation creates unnecessary emotional burden.

Dating translation (what this means emotionally/socially)
Many dating disappointments arise from hidden expectations:
- "I did so much for them."
- "They owe me appreciation."
- "They should reciprocate."

Marcus encourages acting from authenticity rather than transaction. Give when it aligns with who you are, not as an investment expecting return.

Savage takeaway
Kindness becomes heavy when you attach a receipt to it.

Quiet power mantra
"I act well because it aligns with me, not for reward."

204

XLIV. TRUST THE LARGER ORDER TO FIND CALM

"The nature of the universe did once certainly before it was created, whatsoever it hath done since, deliberate and so resolve upon the creation of the world. Now since that time, whatsoever it is, that is and happens in the world, is either but a consequent of that one and first deliberation: or if so be that this ruling rational part of the world, takes any thought and care of things particular, they are surely his reasonable and principal creatures, that are the proper object of his particular care and providence. This often thought upon, will much conduce to thy tranquillity."

What Marcus meant (core philosophy)

Marcus finds peace in the idea that existence unfolds according to a larger rational order. Whether viewed as divine providence or natural structure, events follow meaningful coherence. Trust in this order reduces anxiety about outcomes. Acceptance becomes a pathway to tranquility.

Dating translation (what this means emotionally/socially)

Dating uncertainty often creates anxiety:
- wondering if timing is wrong
- questioning outcomes
- fearing unpredictability

Marcus suggests trusting that experiences unfold within a larger process of growth and alignment. Not every connection is meant to last, but every experience contributes to your development.

Savage takeaway

You don't need to control the path to benefit from walking it.

Quiet power mantra

"I trust the unfolding without forcing control."

THE EIGHTH BOOK
Your Peace Is Not Up For Negotiation

I. LET GO OF IMAGE AND RETURN TO NATURE

'This also, among other things, may serve to keep thee from vainglory; if thou shalt consider, that thou art now altogether incapable of the commendation of one, who all his life long, or from his youth at least, hath lived a philosopher's life. For both unto others, and to thyself especially, it is well known, that thou hast done many things contrary to that perfection of life. Thou hast therefore been confounded in thy course, and henceforth it will be hard for thee to recover the title and credit of a philosopher. And to it also is thy calling and profession repugnant. If therefore thou dost truly understand, what it is that is of moment indeed; as for thy fame and credit, take no thought or care for that: let it suffice thee if all the rest of thy life, be it more or less, thou shalt live as thy nature requireth, or according to the true and natural end of thy making. Take pains therefore to know what it is that thy nature requireth, and let nothing else distract thee. Thou hast already had sufficient experience, that of those many things that hitherto thou hast erred and wandered about, thou couldst not find happiness in any of them. Not in syllogisms[61], and logical subtilties, not in wealth, not in honour and reputation, not in pleasure. In none of all these. Wherein then is it to be found? In the practice of those things, which the nature of man, as he is a man, doth require. How then shall he do those things? if his dogmata, or moral tenets and opinions (from which all motions and actions do proceed), be right and true. Which be those dogmata? Those that concern that which is good or evil, as that there is nothing truly good and beneficial unto man, but that which makes him just, temperate, courageous, liberal; and that there is nothing truly evil and hurtful unto man, but that which causeth the contrary effects.'

What Marcus meant (core philosophy)

Marcus dismantles attachment to reputation. Even if one has failed or wandered, redemption lies not in reclaiming an image but in aligning with nature moving forward. Happiness does not come from:

- reputation
- intellectual pride
- wealth
- pleasure

True good lies in virtue: justice, courage, temperance, generosity.

Dating translation (what this means emotionally/socially)

Dating often pulls people into identity performance:

- trying to appear impressive
- chasing validation
- defining worth through others' approval

Marcus redirects focus: Stop worrying about how you appear. Start living aligned with who you actually are. Past mistakes do not prevent future integrity.

---

[61] In English, syllogisms are a form of logical argument where a conclusion is drawn from two given or assumed premises. This is the cornerstone of Aristotelian logic and was a primary tool used by the Stoics to test the truth of their beliefs.

Savage takeaway

Your reputation isn't your redemption. Your actions are.

Quiet power mantra

"I return to alignment, not image."

II. ACT AS IF YOU WILL JUDGE THIS MOMENT LATER

"Upon every action that thou art about, put this question to thyself; How will this when it is done agree with me? Shall I have no occasion to repent of it? Yet a very little while and I am dead and gone; and all things are at end. What then do I care for more than this, that my present action whatsoever it be, may be the proper action of one that is reasonable; whose end is, the common good; who in all things is ruled and governed by the same law of right and reason, by which God Himself is."

What Marcus meant (core philosophy)

Marcus proposes a simple ethical test: act in ways your future self will approve. Awareness of mortality sharpens moral clarity. Right action aligns with reason and contributes to the common good.

Dating translation (what this means emotionally/socially)

Before acting in dating situations, ask: Will I respect this decision later?

Examples:
- sending that reactive message
- staying where you feel misaligned
- compromising values for approval

Marcus suggests choosing actions that preserve self-respect regardless of outcome.

Savage takeaway

If future-you would cringe, don't do it.

Quiet power mantra

"I act in ways I will respect tomorrow."

III. INNER FREEDOM OUTWEIGHS OUTER POWER

"Alexander, Caius, Pompeius; what are these to Diogenes, Heraclitus, and Socrates? These penetrated into the true nature of things; into all causes, and all subjects: and upon these did they exercise their power and authority. But as for those, as the extent of their error was, so far did their slavery extend."

What Marcus meant (core philosophy)

Marcus contrasts political power with philosophical wisdom. External authority does not equal inner freedom. Those who misunderstand reality become slaves to their own ignorance regardless of status. True power lies in understanding and self-mastery.

Dating translation (what this means emotionally/socially)

In dating, perceived power often comes from:
- status
- attractiveness
- social influence

Marcus reminds us that emotional wisdom matters more than external dominance. Someone may appear powerful but lack inner stability or clarity. Choose depth over surface prestige.

Savage takeaway
External status doesn't equal emotional maturity.

Quiet power mantra
"I value inner clarity over outer power."

IV. OTHERS WILL BE WHO THEY ARE, YOU MUST BE WHO YOU ARE

"What they have done, they will still do, although thou shouldst hang thyself. First; let it not trouble thee. For all things both good and evil: come to pass according to the nature and general condition of the universe, and within a very little while, all things will be at an end; no man will be remembered: as now of Africanus[62] (for example) and Augustus it is already come to pass. Then secondly; fix thy mind upon the thing itself; look into it, and remembering thyself, that thou art bound nevertheless to be a good man, and what it is that thy nature requireth of thee as thou art a man, be not diverted from what thou art about, and speak that which seemeth unto thee most just: only speak it kindly, modestly, and without hypocrisy."

What Marcus meant (core philosophy)
Marcus acknowledges a hard truth: people behave according to their nature, not your wishes. Your task is not to control them but to remain aligned with your own virtue. Justice should be expressed with kindness, modesty, and sincerity.

Dating translation (what this means emotionally/socially)
In dating, people often repeat patterns:
- avoidance
- inconsistency
- emotional unavailability

Marcus advises acceptance: They will act according to who they are. Your responsibility is:
- remain grounded
- speak honestly
- maintain integrity without aggression

Savage takeaway
You don't need them to change to remain true to yourself.

Quiet power mantra
"I stay aligned regardless of others' behavior."

---

[62] Africanus refers to Scipio Africanus the Younger (185–129 BC), the famed Roman general who destroyed Carthage. Marcus Aurelius cites him as part of a recurring Stoic exercise to realize that even the most "highly acclaimed" figures in history eventually become archaic names and faint echoes.

V. CHANGE IS NOT NEW, ONLY CONTINUOUS

"That which the nature of the universe doth busy herself about, is; that which is here, to transfer it thither, to change it, and thence again to take it away, and to carry it to another place. So that thou needest not fear any new thing. For all things are usual and ordinary; and all things are disposed by equality."

What Marcus meant (core philosophy)

Marcus emphasizes that change is the constant function of the universe. Nothing is truly new; everything is part of an ongoing cycle of transformation. Fear often arises from perceiving events as exceptional or unnatural, when in reality they are simply expressions of universal change. Understanding this removes shock and restores acceptance.

Dating translation (what this means emotionally/socially)

Dating transitions feel dramatic:

- beginnings
- endings
- shifting emotions

Marcus reminds you: Nothing you experience is outside the natural order. Relationships evolving or ending are not anomalies; they are normal processes. Accepting change reduces emotional resistance.

Savage takeaway

What feels unprecedented to you is simply another turn of an ancient cycle.

Quiet power mantra

"I move with change instead of fearing it."

VI. PEACE COMES FROM ALIGNMENT WITH REASON, SERVICE, AND ACCEPTANCE

"Every particular nature hath content, when in its own proper course it speeds. A reasonable nature doth then speed, when first in matter of fancies and imaginations, it gives no consent to that which is either false uncertain. Secondly, when in all its motions and resolutions it takes its level at the common good only, and that it desireth nothing, and flieth from nothing, bet what is in its own power to compass or avoid. And lastly, when it willingly and gladly embraceth, whatsoever is dealt and appointed unto it by the common nature. For it is part of it; even as the nature of any one leaf, is part of the common nature of all plants and trees. But that the nature of a leaf, is part of a nature both unreasonable and unsensible, and which in its proper end may be hindered; or, which is servile and slavish: whereas the nature of man is part of a common nature which cannot be hindered, and which is both reasonable and just. From whence also it is, that according to the worth of everything, she doth make such equal distribution of all things, as of duration, substance form, operation, and of events and accidents. But herein consider not whether thou shalt find this equality in everything absolutely and by itself; but whether in all the particulars of some one thing taken together, and compared with all the particulars of some other thing, and them together likewise."

What Marcus meant (core philosophy)

Marcus outlines three foundations of inner contentment:

- reject false impressions

- aim actions toward the common good
- accept what happens as part of universal order

Human beings belong to a rational system that distributes events according to a larger balance beyond individual perception. Peace comes from alignment with this structure.

Dating translation (what this means emotionally/socially)
Dating becomes calmer when you:
- stop believing every emotional story your mind generates
- prioritize mutual respect and growth
- accept outcomes without resistance

You cannot control everything, but you can align with clarity, integrity, and acceptance.

Savage takeaway
Peace isn't found by controlling outcomes. It's found by aligning with truth.

Quiet power mantra
"I reject illusion, serve the good, and accept reality."

VII. YOU MAY LACK TIME FOR STUDY, BUT NEVER FOR VIRTUE

"Thou hast no time nor opportunity to read. What then? Hast thou not time and opportunity to exercise thyself, not to wrong thyself; to strive against all carnal pleasures and pains, and to get the upper hand of them; to contemn honour and vainglory; and not only, not to be angry with them, whom towards thee thou doest find unsensible and unthankful; but also to have a care of them still, and of their welfare?"

What Marcus meant (core philosophy)
Marcus removes excuses for moral growth. Even without intellectual study, one can practice virtue through daily behavior. True philosophy is lived through:
- self-control
- humility
- compassion toward difficult people

Virtue is always available regardless of circumstance.

Dating translation (what this means emotionally/socially)
You don't need perfect self-development or deep theory to date well. Practice virtue through:
- honest communication
- emotional regulation
- kindness even when others are difficult

Growth happens through action, not preparation alone.

Savage takeaway
You don't need more knowledge to act better. You need more alignment.

Quiet power mantra
"I practice virtue through daily action."

VIII. STOP COMPLAINING ABOUT YOUR CIRCUMSTANCES

"Forbear henceforth to complain of the trouble of a courtly life, either in public before others, or in private by thyself."

What Marcus meant (core philosophy)

Marcus advises ending habitual complaint. Constant dissatisfaction drains energy and prevents acceptance. Stoicism encourages focusing on what is within your control rather than resenting unavoidable circumstances.

Dating translation (what this means emotionally/socially)

Complaining about dating culture, apps, or experiences can become a repetitive loop that reinforces frustration.

Marcus suggests: Stop feeding resentment through constant narration. Instead:
- focus on your choices
- refine your approach
- act intentionally

Energy used for complaint could be redirected toward growth.

Savage takeaway

Complaining feels productive but rarely changes anything.

Quiet power mantra

"I focus on what I can shape, not what I can complain about."

IX. REAL REGRET IS FOR VIRTUE NEGLECTED, NOT PLEASURE MISSED

"Repentance is an inward and self-reprehension for the neglect or omission of somewhat that was profitable. Now whatsoever is good, is also profitable, and it is the part of an honest virtuous man to set by it, and to make reckoning of it accordingly. But never did any honest virtuous man repent of the neglect or omission of any carnal pleasure: no carnal pleasure then is either good or profitable."

What Marcus meant (core philosophy)

Marcus defines repentance as regret for neglecting what is truly beneficial. If something is genuinely good, it strengthens character and contributes to a virtuous life. He argues that wise people do not regret missing bodily pleasures. Therefore, those pleasures are not the true "good," because the true good produces lasting benefit rather than fleeting satisfaction.

Dating translation (what this means emotionally/socially)

In dating, people often fear missing out:
- missing a hookup
- missing attention
- missing "chemistry"

Marcus flips the fear. You won't regret not chasing temporary pleasure. You will regret:
- ignoring your standards
- betraying your values
- staying where you knew it was wrong

Savage takeaway
You won't regret missing a thrill. You'll regret abandoning yourself.

Quiet power mantra
"I choose what strengthens me, not what tempts me."

X. QUESTION THE THING UNTIL IT SHRINKS TO ITS TRUE SIZE

"This, what is it in itself, and by itself, according to its proper constitution? What is the substance of it? What is the matter, or proper use? What is the form or efficient cause? What is it for in this world, and how long will it abide? Thus must thou examine all things, that present themselves unto thee."

What Marcus meant (core philosophy)
Marcus teaches analytical clarity. Strip experiences down to their reality:
- what it truly is
- what it is made of
- what purpose it serves
- how long it lasts

This dissolves illusion. Most emotional overwhelm depends on exaggeration and unclear thinking.

Dating translation (what this means emotionally/socially)
Apply this to dating triggers:
- That text you're spiraling over: what is it, really?
- That "chemistry": what is it, really?
- That fear of losing them: what is it, really?

When you examine things precisely, they shrink back into proportion.

Savage takeaway
Interrogate the fantasy until only facts remain.

Quiet power mantra
"I reduce emotion by returning to reality."

XI. GET UP. YOUR PURPOSE IS BIGGER THAN COMFORT

"When thou art hard to be stirred up and awaked out of thy sleep, admonish thyself and call to mind, that, to perform actions tending to the common good is that which thine own proper constitution, and that which the nature of man do require. But to sleep, is common to unreasonable creatures also. And what more proper and natural, yea what more kind and pleasing, than that which is according to nature?"

What Marcus meant (core philosophy)
Marcus uses waking as a metaphor for discipline. Humans are made for purposeful action and contribution, not endless comfort. What is "most pleasing" in the deepest sense is not indulgence but living in alignment with nature and purpose.

Dating translation (what this means emotionally/socially)
Dating can tempt you into comfort-based choices:

- staying in the lukewarm situation
- accepting crumbs because it's familiar
- settling because it's easier than starting over

Marcus reminds you: your nature is built for higher standards and purposeful choices. Get up. Choose what serves your life.

Savage takeaway
Comfort is not a life plan.

Quiet power mantra
"I rise into what is worthy of me."

XII. EXAMINE EVERY IMPRESSION BEFORE YOU BELIEVE IT
"As every fancy and imagination presents itself unto thee, consider (if it be possible) the true nature, and the proper qualities of it, and reason with thyself about it."

What Marcus meant (core philosophy)
Marcus warns against automatic belief in mental impressions. Thoughts are not facts; they are proposals. Stoic discipline requires pausing to examine each impression for truth, usefulness, and proportion.

Dating translation (what this means emotionally/socially)
In dating, the mind generates instant narratives:
- "They didn't text back, they're done."
- "They're perfect, this is destiny."
- "I'm too much."

Marcus says: slow down. Examine. Most dating suffering is an unchecked impression turning into certainty.

Savage takeaway
Not every thought is a prophecy.

Quiet power mantra
"I question impressions before I accept them."

XIII. PEOPLE ACT ACCORDING TO WHAT THEY BELIEVE
"At thy first encounter with any one, say presently to thyself: This man, what are his opinions concerning that which is good or evil? as concerning pain, pleasure, and the causes of both; concerning honour, and dishonour, concerning life and death? thus and thus. Now if it be no wonder that a man should have such and such opinions, how can it be a wonder that he should do such and such things? I will remember then, that he cannot but do as he doth, holding those opinions that he doth. Remember, that as it is a shame for any man to wonder that a fig tree should bear figs, so also to wonder that the world should bear anything, whatsoever it is which in the ordinary course of nature it may bear. To a physician also and to a pilot it is a shame either for the one to wonder, that such and such a one should have an ague[63]; or for the other, that the winds should prove Contrary."

---

[63] In English, ague (pronounced AY-gyoo) is an archaic medical term for a fever, specifically one characterized by shivering, chills, and sweating.

What Marcus meant (core philosophy)

Marcus teaches that behavior flows from belief systems. People act according to what they think is good, bad, desirable, or threatening. Instead of being shocked by behavior, understand the underlying worldview producing it. Just as a fig tree produces figs, people produce actions consistent with their beliefs.

Dating translation (what this means emotionally/socially)

When someone behaves in dating:

- avoids commitment
- seeks validation
- withdraws emotionally

Ask: What must they believe about love, safety, or worth for this to make sense? Understanding removes unnecessary shock and personalizing.

Savage takeaway

Stop being surprised when people behave exactly like who they are.

Quiet power mantra

"I understand behavior through beliefs, not emotion."

XIV. CHANGING YOUR MIND IS A FORM OF STRENGTH

"Remember, that to change thy mind upon occasion, and to follow him that is able to rectify thee, is equally ingenuous, as to find out at the first, what is right and just, without help. For of thee nothing is required, ti[64], is beyond the extent of thine own deliberation and jun. merit, and of thine own understanding."

What Marcus meant (core philosophy)

Marcus rejects stubbornness disguised as strength. Revising your beliefs when presented with truth is not weakness but wisdom. Growth comes through correction and learning. The goal is not being right immediately but being aligned with truth eventually.

Dating translation (what this means emotionally/socially)

In dating, ego often prevents adjustment:

- staying attached to wrong assumptions
- refusing to acknowledge incompatibility
- holding onto outdated narratives about someone

Marcus encourages flexibility. Changing your perspective when new information appears is emotional maturity.

Savage takeaway

Staying wrong out of pride isn't strength. It's fear.

Quiet power mantra

"I evolve when truth becomes clearer."

---

[64] In Greek, the word τι (*ti*) most commonly means "what" or "something." Its exact translation in English depends on whether it is being used to ask a question or to describe something indefinite.

XV. IF YOU CAN FIX IT, FIX IT. IF NOT, RELEASE IT

"If it were thine act and in thine own power, wouldest thou do it? If it were not, whom dost tin accuse? the atoms, or the Gods? For to do either, the part of a mad man. Thou must therefore blame nobody, but if it be in thy power, redress what is amiss; if it be not, to what end is it to complain? For nothing should be done but to some certain end."

What Marcus meant (core philosophy)

Marcus simplifies responsibility:

- If something is within your control, act.
- If not, blaming serves no purpose.

Complaining without actionable purpose wastes energy and disrupts peace. Stoicism emphasizes practical response over emotional protest.

Dating translation (what this means emotionally/socially)

In dating situations:

- If you can communicate, communicate.
- If you can leave, leave.
- If you cannot change the situation, release resistance.

Endless analysis or blame creates suffering without progress.

Savage takeaway

Either take action or let it go. Complaining without change is self-inflicted pain.

Quiet power mantra

"I act where I can and release what I cannot control."

XVI. CHANGE IS NATURAL EVEN IN ENDINGS

"Whatsoever dieth and falleth, however and wheresoever it die and fall, it cannot fall out of the world, here it have its abode and change, here also shall it have its dissolution into its proper elements. The same are the world's elements, and the elements of which thou dost consist. And they when they are changed, they murmur not; why shouldest thou?"

What Marcus meant (core philosophy)

Marcus frames death and dissolution as transformation within a continuous system. Nothing truly leaves existence; it merely changes form. Resistance to change contradicts the nature of reality. Acceptance arises when recognizing oneself as part of this same process.

Dating translation (what this means emotionally/socially)

Relationships ending can feel like loss beyond repair.

Marcus reframes endings: Nothing disappears completely. Experiences transform into growth, memory, and future direction. Resistance prolongs suffering; acceptance allows integration.

Savage takeaway

Everything changes without complaint. You can too.

Quiet power mantra

"I accept endings as transformation, not destruction."

XVII. EVERYTHING EXISTS FOR A PURPOSE

"Whatsoever is, was made for something: as a horse, a vine. Why wonderest thou? The sun itself will say of itself, I was made for something; and so hath every god its proper function. What then were then made for? to disport and delight thyself? See how even common sense and reason cannot brook it."

What Marcus meant (core philosophy)

Marcus reminds us that nothing exists without purpose. Every part of nature serves a function, from the smallest plant to the sun itself. Human beings are no exception. Life is not meant solely for pleasure or distraction. Purpose is tied to contribution, function, and alignment with nature's order.

Dating translation (what this means emotionally/socially)

In relationships, people often fall into entertainment or validation modes:
  * dating for distraction
  * seeking ego boosts
  * chasing emotional highs

Marcus pushes toward intentionality.

Ask: What am I here to build, express, or become through this connection?

Savage takeaway

You were not made just to pass time or chase dopamine.

Quiet power mantra

"I move with purpose, not distraction."

XVIII. THE END IS AS NATURAL AS THE BEGINNING

"Nature hath its end as well in the end and final consummation of anything that is, as in the begin-nine and continuation of it."

What Marcus meant (core philosophy)

Nature values endings as much as beginnings. Completion, dissolution, and closure are not failures; they are necessary stages of existence. Every process includes:
  * emergence
  * growth
  * completion

Resisting endings misunderstands nature itself.

Dating translation (what this means emotionally/socially)

Relationships ending are often treated as failure.

Marcus reframes: The ending may be the fulfillment of its purpose. Some relationships exist to teach, redirect, or complete a phase.

Savage takeaway

An ending does not mean something went wrong. Sometimes it means it finished correctly.

Quiet power mantra

"I respect endings as part of natural completion."

XIX. FAME, DEATH, AND THE ILLUSION OF IMPORTANCE

"As one that tosseth up a ball. And what is a ball the better, if the motion of it be upwards; or the worse if it be downwards; or if it chance to fall upon the ground? So for the bubble; if it continue, what it the better? and if it dissolve, what is it of the worse And so is it of a candle too. And so must thou reason with thyself, both in matter of fame, and in matter of death. For as for the body itself, (the subject of death) wouldest thou know the vileness of it? Turn it about that thou mayest behold it the worst sides upwards as well, as in its more ordinary pleasant shape; how doth it look, when it is old and withered? when sick and pained? when in the act of lust, and fornication? And as for fame. This life is short. Both he that praiseth, and he that is praised; he that remembers, and he that is remembered, will soon be dust and ashes. Besides, it is but in one corner of this part of the world that thou art praised; and yet in this corner, thou hast not the joint praises of all men; no nor scarce of any one constantly. And yet the whole earth itself, what is it but as one point, in regard of the whole world?"

What Marcus meant (core philosophy)
Marcus dismantles attachment to:
* status
* reputation
* physical beauty
* fear of death

He compares life to transient motion, like a tossed ball or dissolving bubble. Upward or downward movement does not change intrinsic worth. Fame is fleeting because:
* those praising you will die
* memory fades
* even the world itself is tiny in the vast universe

Dating translation (what this means emotionally/socially)
Applied to relationships:
* external validation is unstable
* attractiveness fades
* approval from others is temporary

Chasing admiration or fear of loss leads to anxiety. Marcus urges grounding in internal character instead.

Savage takeaway
If your peace depends on applause, you built it on sand.

Quiet power mantra
"I anchor myself in character, not recognition."

XX. KNOW WHAT YOU ARE ACTUALLY LOOKING AT
"That which must be the subject of thy consideration, is either the matter itself, or the dogma, or the operation, or the true sense and signification."

What Marcus meant (core philosophy)
Marcus teaches analytical clarity. Every situation should be examined through four lenses:

- the matter itself (what actually exists)
- the belief or interpretation attached
- the action being taken
- the true meaning behind it

This prevents emotional distortion.

Dating translation (what this means emotionally/socially)
When triggered or confused, separate:
- What actually happened?
- What story am I telling myself about it?
- What action is occurring?
- What does it truly mean, if anything?

This dismantles projection and emotional exaggeration.

Savage takeaway
Most suffering comes from interpretation, not reality.

Quiet power mantra
"I see clearly by separating fact from story."

XXI. STOP POSTPONING WHO YOU SHOULD BE
"Most justly have these things happened unto thee: why dost not thou amend? O but thou hadst rather become good to-morrow, than to be so to-day."

What Marcus meant (core philosophy)
Marcus calls out procrastination of character. People delay growth, virtue, or discipline by promising themselves future transformation. But postponement is avoidance disguised as intention. The only real moment of change is now.

Dating translation (what this means emotionally/socially)
Applied to relationships:
- waiting to set boundaries later
- waiting to become secure later
- waiting to stop tolerating nonsense later

Growth delayed becomes growth denied.

Savage takeaway
You don't become better tomorrow by practicing avoidance today.

Quiet power mantra
"I become who I should be now."

XXII. ACT FOR GOOD, ACCEPT WHAT COMES
"Shall I do it? I will; so the end of my action be to do good unto men. Doth anything by way of cross or adversity happen unto me? I accept it, with reference unto the Gods, and their providence; the fountain of all things, from which whatsoever comes to pass, doth hang and depend."

What Marcus meant (core philosophy)

Two guiding principles:

1. Act for the common good.
2. Accept outcomes beyond control.

Virtue lies in intention and effort, not external results. Acceptance is not passivity; it is alignment with reality.

Dating translation (what this means emotionally/socially)

Show up:

- honestly
- kindly
- with integrity

Then release attachment to how others respond. You control conduct, not reception.

Savage takeaway

Do good because it is right, not because it guarantees reward.

Quiet power mantra

"I control my actions, not outcomes."

XXIII. SEE THROUGH ILLUSION

"By one action judge of the rest: this bathing which usually takes up so much of our time, what is it? Oil, sweat, filth; or the sordes[65] of the body: an excrementitious viscosity, the excrements of oil and other ointments used about the body, and mixed with the sordes of the body: all base and loathsome. And such almost is every part of our life; and every worldly object."

What Marcus meant (core philosophy)

Marcus strips glamour away from appearances. Even luxurious rituals are, at their core, simple physical processes. Seeing through illusion reduces attachment and vanity. He encourages viewing things plainly rather than idealizing them.

Dating translation (what this means emotionally/socially)

Applied to dating:

- romanticizing someone beyond reality
- idolizing status, beauty, or lifestyle
- projecting fantasy onto ordinary human behavior

Seeing clearly prevents emotional overinvestment.

Savage takeaway

When you remove fantasy, clarity appears.

Quiet power mantra

"I see things as they are, not as I wish them to be."

---

[65] In English, sordes (pronounced SOR-deez) is a formal or archaic term for dirt, filth, or foul matter. Marcus Aurelius uses it to describe the uncleanliness of the soul or the "grossness" of material life.

XXIV. EVERYTHING AND EVERYONE PASSES

"Lucilla buried Verus; then was Lucilla herself buried by others. So Secunda Maximus, then Secunda herself. So Epitynchanus, Diotimus; then Epitynchanus himself. So Antoninus Pius, Faustina his wife; then Antoninus himself. This is the course of the world. First Celer, Adrianus; then Adrianus himself. And those austere ones; those that foretold other men's deaths; those that were so proud and stately, where are they now? Those austere ones I mean, such as were Charax, and Demetrius the Platonic, and Eudaemon, and others like unto those. They were all but for one day; all dead and gone long since. Some of them no sooner dead, than forgotten. Others soon turned into fables. Of others, even that which was fabulous, is now long since forgotten. This thereafter thou must remember, that whatsoever thou art compounded of, shall soon be dispersed, and that thy life and breath, or thy soul, shall either be no more or shall ranslated (sp.), and appointed to some certain place and station."

What Marcus meant (core philosophy)

Marcus lists names to show inevitability:

- power fades
- reputation dissolves
- memory disappears

Everyone eventually joins the same end. The purpose is not nihilism but perspective. Knowing everything passes helps:

- release ego
- reduce fear
- prioritize virtue over legacy.

Dating translation (what this means emotionally/socially)

Applied emotionally: The drama that feels permanent today will dissolve. Breakups, rejection, praise, status: All temporary. What remains is how you lived.

Savage takeaway

Time erases almost everything except who you became.

Quiet power mantra

"I invest in character, not permanence."

XXV. THE TRUE JOY OF BEING HUMAN

"The true joy of a man, is to do that which properly belongs unto a man. That which is most proper unto a man, is, first, to be kindly affected towards them that are of the same kind and nature as he is himself to contemn all sensual motions and appetites, to discern rightly all plausible fancies and imaginations, to contemplate the nature of the universe; both it, and things that are done in it. In which kind of contemplation three several relations are to be observed The first, to the apparent secondary cause. The Second to the first original cause, God, from whom originally proceeds whatsoever doth happen in the world. The third and last, to them that we live and converse with: what use may be made of it, to their use and benefit."

What Marcus meant (core philosophy)

Joy is not pleasure. Joy is alignment. Marcus defines true human function as:

- kindness toward others
- mastery over impulses
- clear discernment of illusion vs truth
- contemplation of the larger order of existence

220

He outlines three lenses for understanding events:
1. Immediate causes (what happened physically).
2. Ultimate cause (universal order or divine structure).
3. Human impact (how it serves or harms others).

Joy comes from functioning according to nature, not chasing stimulation.

Dating translation (what this means emotionally/socially)
Applied to relationships:
- act from integrity, not craving
- observe patterns rather than projecting fantasy
- ask: what serves the whole, not just my desire?

Real satisfaction comes from alignment, not emotional chaos.

Savage takeaway
Pleasure excites. Purpose fulfills.

Quiet power mantra
"I live in alignment with my nature."

XXVI. PAIN IS INTERPRETATION
"If pain be an evil, either it is in regard of the body; (and that cannot be, because the body of itself is altogether insensible:) or in regard of the soul But it is in the power of the soul, to preserve her own peace and tranquillity, and not to suppose that pain is evil. For all judgment and deliberation; all prosecution, or aversation is from within, whither the sense of evil (except it be let in by opinion) cannot penetrate."

What Marcus meant (core philosophy)
Pain exists, but suffering depends on judgment. The body experiences sensation. The mind assigns meaning. The soul maintains power by refusing to label sensation as catastrophic. Stoicism does not deny pain; it denies its authority over inner peace.

Dating translation (what this means emotionally/socially)
Applied emotionally:
- rejection hurts
- loss hurts
- disappointment hurts

But interpretation determines whether pain becomes identity. Without the story "this means I am unworthy," pain remains temporary sensation.

Savage takeaway
Pain knocks. Opinion opens the door.

Quiet power mantra
"I feel without surrendering my peace."

XXVII. USE THE POWER YOU ALREADY HAVE
"Wipe off all idle fancies, and say unto thyself incessantly; Now if I will, it is in my power to keep out of this my soul all wickedness, all lust, and concupiscences, all trouble and confusion. But on the contrary to

behold and consider all things according to their true nature, and to carry myself towards everything according to its true worth. Remember then this thy power that nature hath given thee."

What Marcus meant (core philosophy)

The mind possesses sovereign authority over internal acceptance. External events arrive uninvited. Internal interpretation is chosen. Marcus emphasizes:

- remove unnecessary mental noise
- view reality clearly
- respond proportionally to truth.

The reminder: you already possess this power.

Dating translation (what this means emotionally/socially)

Applied to modern dynamics:

- spiraling over texts
- inventing narratives about silence
- emotional projection

Most suffering comes from imagined stories, not actual events. Clear perception reduces unnecessary turmoil.

Savage takeaway

Your mind is not a hostage unless you hand over the keys.

Quiet power mantra

"I choose clarity over fantasy."

XXVIII. SPEAK WITH DIGNITY, NOT DISPLAY

"Whether thou speak in the Senate or whether thou speak to any particular, let thy speech In always grave and modest. But thou must not openly and vulgarly observe that sound and exact form of speaking, concerning that which is truly good and truly civil; the vanity of the world, and of worldly men: which otherwise truth and reason doth prescribe."

What Marcus meant (core philosophy)

Speech should be:

- measured
- modest
- truthful without performative righteousness.

Wisdom does not require theatrical delivery. He warns against:

- moral grandstanding
- intellectual vanity
- preaching truth in a way that becomes ego display.

Dating translation (what this means emotionally/socially)

Applied socially: Strong presence comes from grounded communication, not domination. Truth delivered with calm authority carries more power than dramatic correction.

Savage takeaway
Wisdom whispers; ego announces.

Quiet power mantra
"I speak with clarity, not performance."

XXIX. EVEN EMPIRES DISAPPEAR

"Augustus his court; his wife, his daughter, his nephews, his sons-in-law his sister, Agrippa, his kinsmen, his domestics, his friends; Areus, Mæcenas, his slayers of beasts for sacrifice and divination: there thou hast the death of a whole court together. Proceed now on to the rest that have been since that of Augustus. Hath death dwelt with them otherwise, though so many and so stately whilst they lived, than it doth use to deal with any one particular man? Consider now the death of a whole kindred and family, as of that of the Pompeys, as that also that useth to be written upon some monuments, HE WAS THE LAST OF HIS OWN KINDRED. O what care did his predecessors take, that they might leave a successor, yet behold at last one or other must of necessity be THE LAST. Here again therefore consider the death of a whole kindred."

What Marcus meant (core philosophy)
Even the most powerful dynasties vanish. Marcus lists entire imperial circles to show:
- status does not resist time
- legacy cannot prevent extinction
- collective importance still ends in silence.

The Stoic lesson is scale. Human drama feels enormous while happening, but history reduces everything to dust.

Dating translation (what this means emotionally/socially)
Applied emotionally: The relationship that feels like the center of the universe today will someday be a small memory in a long timeline. This isn't nihilism. It is relief. You do not need to dramatize temporary chapters as eternal destiny.

Savage takeaway
If empires disappear, your situationship will too.

Quiet power mantra
"This moment matters, but it is not permanent."

XXX. LIVE ONE ACTION AT A TIME

"Contract thy whole life to the measure and proportion of one single action. And if in every particular action thou dost perform what is fitting to the utmost of thy power, let it suffice thee. And who can hinder thee, but that thou mayest perform what is fitting? But there may be some outward let and impediment. Not any, that can hinder thee, but that whatsoever thou dost, thou may do it, justly, temperately, and with the praise of God. Yea, but there may be somewhat, whereby some operation or other of thine may be hindered. And then, with that very thing that doth hinder, thou mayest he well pleased, and so by this gentle and equanimious conversion of thy mind unto that which may be, instead of that which at first thou didst intend, in the room of that former action there succeedeth another, which agrees as well with this contraction of thy life, that we now speak of."

What Marcus meant (core philosophy)
Life becomes manageable when reduced to the present action. Focus on:
- what is right now
- what is within your control
- doing it well.

Obstacles do not destroy purpose; they redirect it. Virtue adapts.

Dating translation (what this means emotionally/socially)
Instead of obsessing over outcomes:
- focus on how you show up in each interaction
- act with integrity regardless of result.

Rejection cannot stop you from behaving with dignity.

Savage takeaway
You cannot control outcomes, but you always control your conduct.

Quiet power mantra
"I master this moment."

XXXI. HOLD LIGHTLY, RELEASE EASILY
"Receive temporal blessings without ostentation, when they are sent and thou shalt be able to part with them with all readiness and facility when they are taken from thee again."

What Marcus meant (core philosophy)
Enjoy what comes without clinging. Stoicism is not rejection of pleasure; it is freedom from dependence. Gratitude without attachment creates stability.

Dating translation (what this means emotionally/socially)
Enjoy:
- connection
- attraction
- good moments

without believing they must last forever. Attachment turns gifts into burdens.

Savage takeaway
Possession creates fear. Appreciation creates freedom.

Quiet power mantra
"I receive fully. I release gracefully."

XXXII. SEPARATION FROM THE WHOLE
"If ever thou sawest either a hand, or a foot, or a head lying by itself, in some place or other, as cut off from the rest of the body, such must thou conceive him to make himself, as much as in him lieth, that either is offended with anything that is happened, (whatsoever it be) and as it were divides himself from it: or that commits anything against the natural law of mutual correspondence, and society among men: or, he that, commits any act of uncharitableness. Whosoever thou art, thou art such, thou art cast forth I know not whither out of the general unity, which is according to nature. Thou went born indeed a part,

but now thou hast cut thyself off. However, herein is matter of joy and exultation, that thou mayst be united again. God hath not granted it unto any other part, that once separated and cut off, it might be reunited, and come together again. But, behold, that GOODNESS how great and immense it is! which hath so much esteemed MAN. As at first he was so made, that he needed not, except he would himself, have divided himself from the whole; so once divided and cut off, IT hath so provided and ordered it, that if he would himself, he might return, and grow together again, and be admitted into its former rank and place of a part, as he was before."

What Marcus meant (core philosophy)

To act against reason or kindness is to sever oneself from humanity. Isolation is self-created when:

- resentment dominates
- cruelty replaces cooperation
- ego rejects connection.

The hopeful part: reintegration is always possible. Humans can return to harmony through choice.

Dating translation (what this means emotionally/socially)

When hurt, people often withdraw, harden, or become cynical.

Marcus says: Disconnection is understandable but unnatural long-term. Healing means choosing reconnection without losing wisdom.

Savage takeaway

Bitterness cuts you off from life more than anyone else ever could.

Quiet power mantra

"I choose connection without losing myself."

XXXIII. OBSTACLES BECOME MATERIAL

"As almost all her other faculties and properties the nature of the universe hath imparted unto every reasonable creature, so this in particular we have received from her, that as whatsoever doth oppose itself unto her, and doth withstand her in her purposes and intentions, she doth, though against its will and intention, bring it about to herself, to serve herself of it in the execution of her own destinated ends; and so by this though not intended co-operation of it with herself makes it part of herself whether it will or no. So may every reasonable creature, what crosses and impediments soever it meets with in the course of this mortal life, it may use them as fit and proper objects, to the furtherance of whatsoever it intended and absolutely proposed unto itself as its natural end and happiness."

What Marcus meant (core philosophy)

Nature wastes nothing. Even resistance becomes material for progress. What appears as opposition is absorbed into the larger movement of existence and redirected toward purpose.

The Stoic insight: Obstacles do not stop the process. They become part of it. Reason allows a person to transform setbacks into fuel rather than barriers.

Dating translation (what this means emotionally/socially)

The rejection, the ghosting, the misalignment, the "wrong person" are not detours away from your path. They are part of the shaping process.
- Instead of asking: "Why is this happening to me?"
- Ask: "How does this refine my clarity, boundaries, or self-trust?"

Dating maturity is when nothing is wasted emotionally.

Savage takeaway
The obstacle is not against you. It is training you.

Quiet power mantra
"I turn resistance into direction."

XXXIV. SHRINK THE SUFFERING TO THE PRESENT

"Let not the general representation unto thyself of the wretchedness of this our mortal life, trouble thee. Let not thy mind wander up and down, and heap together in her thoughts the many troubles and grievous calamities which thou art as subject unto as any other. But as everything in particular doth happen, put this question unto thyself, and say: What is it that in this present matter, seems unto thee so intolerable? For thou wilt be ashamed to confess it. Then upon this presently call to mind, that neither that which is future, nor that which is past can hurt thee; but that only which is present. (And that also is much lessened, if thou dost lightly circumscribe it:) and then check thy mind if for so little a while, (a mere instant), it cannot hold out with patience."

What Marcus meant (core philosophy)
Most suffering comes from mental accumulation, not reality itself. We suffer by:
- projecting future pain
- replaying past wounds
- exaggerating scale.

Marcus teaches narrowing experience to the immediate moment. When suffering is reduced to the present instant, it becomes manageable.

Dating translation (what this means emotionally/socially)
Heartbreak becomes overwhelming when the mind stacks:
- "What if I'm alone forever?"
- "This always happens."
- "I wasted years."

But right now, in this moment, the pain is usually smaller than the story around it. Emotional resilience grows when you deal only with what exists now.

Savage takeaway
You are not suffering from the moment. You are suffering from the narrative.

Quiet power mantra
"I meet only this moment."

XXXV. MEMORY DOES NOT SAVE ANYONE

"What? are either Panthea or Pergamus abiding to this day by their masters' tombs? or either Chabrias or Diotimus by that of Adrianus? O foolery! For what if they did, would their masters be sensible of It? or if sensible, would they be glad of it? or if glad, were these immortal? Was not it appointed unto them also (both men and women,) to become old in time, and then to die? And these once dead, what would become of these former? And when all is done, what is all this for, but for a mere bag of blood and corruption?"

What Marcus meant (core philosophy)

Marcus dismantles attachment to legacy, mourning rituals, and external remembrance. Even devotion fades. Memory does not preserve permanence. Physical existence itself is temporary matter. The lesson is liberation from obsession with being remembered or validated after the fact.

Dating translation (what this means emotionally/socially)

People stay emotionally stuck trying to preserve:
*   what once was
*   how they were seen
*   who should have valued them.

Marcus says: Even deep emotional moments fade into time. Clinging to symbolic meaning prolongs suffering. Closure comes from acceptance, not preservation.

Savage takeaway

Nothing becomes permanent just because it felt important.

Quiet power mantra

"I release what time has already released."

XXXVI. TRUE SHARPNESS IS RIGHT JUDGMENT

"If thou beest quick-sighted, be so in matter of judgment, and best discretion, saith he."

What Marcus meant (core philosophy)

Intelligence is not merely perception. It is discernment. Being observant without wise judgment leads to confusion. True sharpness is the ability to interpret reality correctly.

Dating translation (what this means emotionally/socially)

Seeing red flags is not enough. The real skill is:
*   interpreting behavior accurately
*   believing patterns instead of excuses
*   choosing wisely based on what you see.

Awareness without action is wasted insight.

Savage takeaway

Insight means nothing if you ignore what it tells you.

Quiet power mantra

"I trust clear seeing."

XXXVII. CONTINENCE OVER PLEASURE

"In the whole constitution of man, I see not any virtue contrary to justice, whereby it may be resisted and opposed. But one whereby pleasure and voluptuousness may be resisted and opposed, I see: continence."

What Marcus meant (core philosophy)

Justice stands unchallenged because it aligns fully with reason. Pleasure, however, requires restraint. Marcus identifies continence (self-control) as the counterweight to indulgence. The danger is not pleasure itself, but surrendering judgment to it. Virtue is preserved when reason governs desire.

Dating translation (what this means emotionally/socially)

Chemistry, attraction, and emotional highs can overpower discernment. Continence in dating means:

- not confusing intensity with compatibility
- not abandoning standards for attention
- not letting loneliness override wisdom.

Self-control protects long-term alignment from short-term impulse.

Savage takeaway

Attraction is loud. Wisdom is quiet. Choose which one leads.

Quiet power mantra

"I choose alignment over impulse."

XXXVIII. REMOVE THE STORY, REMOVE THE SUFFERING

"If thou canst but withdraw conceit and opinion concerning that which may seem hurtful and offensive, thou thyself art as safe, as safe may be. Thou thyself? and who is that? Thy reason. 'Yea, but I am not reason.' Well, be it so. However, let not thy reason or understanding admit of grief, and if there be anything in thee that is grieved, let that, (whatsoever it be,) conceive its own grief, if it can."

What Marcus meant (core philosophy)

Events do not harm the rational mind. Interpretation creates suffering. By withdrawing opinion, one removes emotional injury at its root. Reason remains untouched unless it consents.

Dating translation (what this means emotionally/socially)

Someone pulling away, rejecting you, or behaving poorly does not automatically wound your core self. The injury comes from meaning assigned:

- "I'm not enough."
- "I failed."
- "This proves something about me."

Separate event from interpretation, and emotional stability returns.

Savage takeaway

Pain happens. Identity damage is optional.

Quiet power mantra

"My reason remains untouched."

XXXIX. NOTHING CAN HARM YOUR REASON

"That which is a hindrance of the senses, is an evil to the sensitive nature. That which is a hindrance of the appetitive and prosecutive faculty, is an evil to the sensitive nature. As of the sensitive, so of the vegetative constitution, whatsoever is a hindrance unto it, is also in that respect an evil unto the same. And so likewise, whatsoever is a hindrance unto the mind and understanding, must needs be the proper evil of the reasonable nature. Now apply all those things unto thyself. Do either pain or pleasure seize on thee? Let the senses look to that. Hast thou met with Some obstacle or other in thy purpose and intention? If thou didst propose without due reservation and exception now hath thy reasonable part received a blow indeed But if in general thou didst propose unto thyself what soever might be, thou art not thereby either hurt, nor properly hindered. For in those things that properly belong unto the mind, she cannot be hindered by any man. It is not fire, nor iron; nor the power of a tyrant nor the power of a slandering tongue; nor anything else that can penetrate into her."

What Marcus meant (core philosophy)

Each part of human nature has its own domain:

- body feels pain
- desire experiences frustration
- reason governs judgment.

The rational mind remains invulnerable unless it abandons its own principles. External forces cannot penetrate inner integrity.

Dating translation (what this means emotionally/socially)

Someone can:

- disappoint you
- reject you
- misunderstand you

but they cannot corrupt your self-worth or character unless you allow it. Emotional strength comes from distinguishing between external events and internal judgment.

Savage takeaway

They can affect your circumstances. They cannot define your mind.

Quiet power mantra

"My center cannot be invaded."

XL. STABILITY CREATES FREEDOM

"If once round and solid, there is no fear that ever it will change."

What Marcus meant (core philosophy)

A fully formed character becomes stable. Integrity creates resilience because identity is grounded internally rather than shaped by external fluctuations. When the self is whole, instability outside loses power.

Dating translation (what this means emotionally/socially)

When you know who you are:

- mixed signals don't destabilize you
- attention doesn't inflate you
- rejection doesn't erase you.

Emotional solidity comes from internal clarity, not external validation.

Savage takeaway
Unshakeable identity ends emotional chaos.

Quiet power mantra
"I stand whole within myself."

XLI. RIGHT UNDERSTANDING IS JOY

"Why should I grieve myself; who never did willingly grieve any other! One thing rejoices one and another thing another. As for me, this is my joy, if my understanding be right and sound, as neither averse from any man, nor refusing any of those things which as a man I am subject unto; if I can look upon all things in the world meekly and kindly; accept all things and carry myself towards everything according to true worth of the thing itself."

What Marcus meant (core philosophy)
True happiness is internal harmony:
- clear judgment
- kindness toward others
- acceptance of reality.

Joy comes not from circumstance but from alignment between reason, compassion, and acceptance.

Dating translation (what this means emotionally/socially)
Peace in dating is not finding the perfect partner. It is becoming:
- grounded in your values
- open without bitterness
- accepting without resignation.

You stop fighting reality and start moving wisely within it.

Savage takeaway
Peace comes from clarity, not control.

Quiet power mantra
"My joy is a clear and steady mind."

XLII. STOP LIVING FOR FUTURE APPLAUSE

"This time that is now present, bestow thou upon thyself. They that rather hunt for fame after death, do not consider, that those men that shall be hereafter, will be even such, as these whom now they can so hardly bear with. And besides they also will be mortal men. But to consider the thing in itself, if so many with so many voices, shall make such and such a sound, or shall have such and such an opinion concerning thee, what is it to thee?"

What Marcus meant (core philosophy)
Chasing reputation is irrational because:
- future audiences are no wiser than present ones
- praise fades with time
- opinions hold no intrinsic power.

Marcus redirects attention to the present moment. Real value lies in living well now, not being admired later.

Dating translation (what this means emotionally/socially)

Trying to "win" someone's approval, prove your worth, or be remembered as unforgettable is a trap. Their perception is not the measure of your value. Live in alignment with yourself rather than performing for imagined validation.

Savage takeaway

Being unforgettable to the wrong people is not success.

Quiet power mantra

"I invest in the present, not imagined applause."

XLIII. INNER STABILITY TRAVELS WITH YOU

"Take me and throw me where thou wilt: I am indifferent. For there also I shall have that spirit which is within me propitious; that is well pleased and fully contented both in that constant disposition, and with those particular actions, which to its own proper constitution are suitable and agreeable."

What Marcus meant (core philosophy)

External location does not determine inner state. Wherever one goes, the governing spirit travels with them. Contentment arises from internal alignment, not circumstance. Freedom is internal portability.

Dating translation (what this means emotionally/socially)

You carry your emotional baseline into every relationship. Changing partners, environments, or dynamics does not fix internal instability. Real security comes from becoming internally steady. When you are grounded, you remain yourself regardless of who stands in front of you.

Savage takeaway

New environments do not create peace. Inner alignment does.

Quiet power mantra

"I bring my stability with me."

XLIV. IS THIS WORTH LOSING YOURSELF?

"Is this then a thing of that worth, that for it my soul should suffer, and become worse than it was? as either basely dejected, or disordinately affected, or confounded within itself, or terrified? What can there be, that thou shouldest so much esteem?"

What Marcus meant (core philosophy)

Before reacting emotionally, examine whether the object deserves such power. Nothing external is worth damaging the integrity of the soul. The Stoic practice is evaluation: do not trade inner dignity for external disturbance.

Dating translation (what this means emotionally/socially)

Ask yourself: Is this person, argument, or situation worth losing self-respect, abandoning calm, becoming anxious or diminished? Most emotional chaos comes from overvaluing things that do not deserve authority.

Savage takeaway
If it costs your peace, it costs too much.

Quiet power mantra
"My integrity is not negotiable."

XLV. NOTHING UNNATURAL HAPPENS TO YOU

"Nothing can happen unto thee, which is not incidental unto thee, as thou art a man. As nothing can happen either to an ox, a vine, or to a stone, which is not incidental unto them; unto every one in his own kind. If therefore nothing can happen unto anything, which is not both usual and natural; why art thou displeased? Sure the common nature of all would not bring anything upon any, that were intolerable. If therefore it be a thing external that causes thy grief, know, that it is not that properly that doth cause it, but thine own conceit and opinion concerning the thing: which thou mayest rid thyself of, when thou wilt. But if it be somewhat that is amiss in thine own disposition, that doth grieve thee, mayest thou not rectify thy moral tenets and opinions. But if it grieve thee, that thou doest not perform that which seemeth unto thee right and just, why doest not thou choose rather to perform it than to grieve? But somewhat that is stronger than thyself doth hinder thee. Let it not grieve thee then, if it be not thy fault that the thing is not performed. 'Yea but it is a thing of that nature, as that thy life is not worth the while, except it may be performed.' If it be so, upon condition that thou be kindly and lovingly disposed towards all men, thou mayest be gone. For even then, as much as at any time, art thou in a very good estate of performance, when thou doest die in charity with those, that are an obstacle unto thy performance."

What Marcus meant (core philosophy)
Nothing happens outside human nature. Events are:
- natural
- survivable
- neutral until judged.

Suffering arises from interpretation, not occurrence. When something cannot be changed, acceptance becomes virtue. When something can be corrected internally, responsibility replaces complaint.

Dating translation (what this means emotionally/socially)
Rejection, misunderstanding, betrayal, disappointment: These are not personal anomalies. They are human experiences. Your power lies in:
- adjusting your perspective
- correcting your own actions
- maintaining kindness even when obstructed.

Peace comes from recognizing that life unfolds within shared human patterns, not personal injustice.

Savage takeaway
It didn't happen *to* you. It happened *within* human life.

Quiet power mantra
"I meet reality without resistance."

XLVI. THE UNCONQUERABLE MIND

"Remember that thy mind is of that nature as that it becometh altogether unconquerable, when once recollected in herself, she seeks no other content than this, that she cannot be forced: yea though it so fall out, that it be even against reason itself, that it cloth bandy. How much less when by the help of reason she is able to judge of things with discretion? And therefore let thy chief fort and place of defence be, a mind free from passions. A stronger place, (whereunto to make his refuge, and so to become impregnable) and better fortified than this, hath no man. He that seeth not this is unlearned. He that seeth it, and betaketh not himself to this place of refuge, is unhappy."

What Marcus meant (core philosophy)
The true fortress is internal. A mind recollected within itself becomes unconquerable because it stops seeking validation, control, or emotional dependence outside itself. Freedom is achieved not by changing circumstances but by mastering response. Reason strengthens this fortress, making the self resistant to emotional siege.

Dating translation (what this means emotionally/socially)
When your center comes from within:
* mixed signals lose power
* rejection does not destabilize identity
* emotional manipulation fails.

Your safety is not in finding the perfect partner. It is in building an inner position that cannot be forced or shaken.

Savage takeaway
Emotional sovereignty is the strongest boundary you can have.

Quiet power mantra
"My center cannot be conquered."

XLVII. SEPARATE FACT FROM STORY

"Keep thyself to the first bare and naked apprehensions of things, as they present themselves unto thee, and add not unto them. It is reported unto thee, that such a one speaketh ill of thee. Well; that he speaketh ill of thee, so much is reported. But that thou art hurt thereby, is not reported: that is the addition of opinion, which thou must exclude. I see that my child is sick. That he is sick, I see, but that he is in danger of his life also, I see it not. Thus thou must use to keep thyself to the first motions and apprehensions of things, as they present themselves outwardly; and add not unto them from within thyself through mere conceit and opinion. Or rather add unto them: but as one that understandeth the true nature of all things that happen in the world."

What Marcus meant (core philosophy)
Events are neutral facts. Suffering arises when imagination expands them beyond reality. Marcus teaches disciplined perception:
* observe what is
* remove projections
* interpret through reason rather than fear.

Clear seeing prevents unnecessary distress.

Dating translation (what this means emotionally/socially)
Example:

Fact: "They didn't text back."

Added story:
- "They lost interest."
- "I'm not enough."
- "Something is wrong."

Dating anxiety often comes from interpretation layered onto simple events. Power returns when you separate reality from narrative.

Savage takeaway
Facts rarely hurt. Stories do.

Quiet power mantra
"I see clearly without adding fear."

XLVIII. ACCEPT AND ADAPT
"Is the cucumber bitter? set it away. Brambles are in the way? avoid them. Let this suffice. Add not presently speaking unto thyself, What serve these things for in the world? For, this, one that is acquainted with the mysteries of nature, will laugh at thee for it; as a carpenter would or a shoemaker, if meeting in either of their shops with some shavings, or small remnants of their work, thou shouldest blame them for it. And yet those men, it is not for want of a place where to throw them that they keep them in their shops for a while: but the nature of the universe hath no such out-place; but herein doth consist the wonder of her art and skill, that she having once circumscribed herself within some certain bounds and limits, whatsoever is within her that seems either corrupted, or old, or unprofitable, she can change it into herself, and of these very things can make new things; so that she needeth not to seek elsewhere out of herself either for a new supply of matter and substance, or for a place where to throw out whatsoever is irrecoverably putrid and corrupt. Thus she, as for place, so for matter and art, is herself sufficient unto herself."

What Marcus meant (core philosophy)
Nature wastes nothing. Imperfection is part of transformation. Instead of questioning why unpleasant things exist, adapt:
- avoid what harms
- accept what cannot change
- recognize transformation as natural law.

Resistance to reality creates suffering.

Dating translation (what this means emotionally/socially)
Not every person or situation needs deep analysis. Sometimes:
- incompatibility = walk away
- misalignment = redirect.

You do not need cosmic meaning behind every failed connection.

Savage takeaway
Not everything requires closure. Some things require distance.

Quiet power mantra
"I adjust without resistance."

XLIX. DISCIPLINE WITHOUT EXTREMES

"Not to be slack and negligent; or loose, and wanton in thy actions; nor contentious, and troublesome in thy conversation; nor to rove and wander in thy fancies and imaginations. Not basely to contract thy soul; nor boisterously to sally out with it, or furiously to launch out as it were, nor ever to want employment."

What Marcus meant (core philosophy)

Virtue lies in balance:
- neither passive nor aggressive
- neither withdrawn nor chaotic
- neither restless nor stagnant.

The disciplined life avoids extremes and maintains steady engagement with reality.

Dating translation (what this means emotionally/socially)

Emotional maturity avoids:
- over-investing too fast
- withdrawing completely
- constant overthinking
- dramatic reactions.

Healthy presence is calm, steady, and intentional.

Savage takeaway

Stability is not boring. It is powerful.

Quiet power mantra

"I move with calm strength."

L. BE THE CLEAR FOUNTAIN

'They kill me, they cut my flesh; they persecute my person with curses.' What then? May not thy mind for all this continue pure, prudent, temperate, just? As a fountain of sweet and clear water, though she be cursed by some stander by, yet do her springs nevertheless still run as sweet and clear as before; yea though either dirt or dung be thrown in, yet is it no sooner thrown, than dispersed, and she cleared. She cannot be dyed or infected by it. What then must I do, that I may have within myself an overflowing fountain, and not a well? Beget thyself by continual pains and endeavours to true liberty with charity, and true simplicity and modesty.

What Marcus meant (core philosophy)

The ideal mind is like a clear spring: self-renewing, unaffected by external contamination. Insults, harm, or hostility cannot corrupt inner character unless one allows them to. True freedom comes from cultivating:
- charity
- simplicity
- modesty
- inner independence.

Dating translation (what this means emotionally/socially)

Someone's behavior:
- ghosting
- criticism
- emotional cruelty

does not have to change who you are. You remain kind, grounded, and clear not because others deserve it, but because it is your nature.

Savage takeaway
Their dirt does not become your identity.

Quiet power mantra
"I remain clear regardless of what is thrown at me."

LI. WHY SEEK APPROVAL FROM THE LOST?

"He that knoweth not what the world is, knoweth not where he himself is. And he that knoweth not what the world was made for, cannot possibly know either what are the qualities, or what is the nature of the world. Now he that in either of these is to seek, for what he himself was made is ignorant also. What then dost thou think of that man, who proposeth unto himself, as a matter of great moment, the noise and applause of men, who both where they are, and what they are themselves, are altogether ignorant? Dost thou desire to be commended of that man, who thrice in one hour perchance, doth himself curse himself? Dost thou desire to please him, who pleaseth not himself? or dost thou think that he pleaseth himself, who doth use to repent himself almost of everything that he doth?"

What Marcus meant (core philosophy)
Seeking validation from those who lack self-knowledge is irrational. People who do not understand themselves cannot offer meaningful judgment about others. Approval from the confused carries no real value.

Dating translation (what this means emotionally/socially)
Many people you date:
- do not know themselves
- cannot regulate their emotions
- are unsure of what they want.

Why measure your worth through their approval?

Savage takeaway
If they cannot approve of themselves, their approval of you means nothing.

Quiet power mantra
"I release the need for unqualified approval."

LII. ALIGN WITH UNIVERSAL REASON

"Not only now henceforth to have a common breath, or to hold correspondency of breath, with that air, that compasseth us about; but to have a common mind, or to hold correspondency of mind also with that rational substance, which compasseth all things. For, that also is of itself, and of its own nature (if a man can but draw it in as he should) everywhere diffused; and passeth through all things, no less than the air doth, if a man can but suck it in."

What Marcus meant (core philosophy)
Just as humans share air, they also share participation in universal reason. Wisdom comes from aligning with rational order rather than personal chaos. Connection exists through shared rational nature.

Dating translation (what this means emotionally/socially)

When you operate from clarity rather than emotional reaction:

- communication becomes cleaner
- choices become calmer
- connection becomes deeper.

Alignment with reason reduces drama and increases meaningful connection.

Savage takeaway

Clarity connects. Chaos isolates.

Quiet power mantra

"I align with clear reason."

LIII. ONLY YOUR OWN WRONGDOING CAN HARM YOU

"Wickedness in general doth not hurt the world. Particular wickedness doth not hurt any other: only unto him it is hurtful, whosoever he be that offends, unto whom in great favour and mercy it is granted, that whensoever he himself shall but first desire it, he may be presently delivered of it. Unto my free-will my neighbour's free-will, whoever he be, (as his life, or his bode), is altogether indifferent. For though we are all made one for another, yet have our minds and understandings each of them their own proper and limited jurisdiction. For else another man's wickedness might be my evil which God would not have, that it might not be in another man's power to make me unhappy: which nothing now can do but mine own wickedness."

What Marcus meant (core philosophy)

Another person's wrongdoing ultimately harms them, not you. Your freedom lies in recognizing that your inner state is governed only by your own will. No external action can make you unhappy unless your own judgment consents.

Dating translation (what this means emotionally/socially)

Someone's dishonesty, inconsistency, or emotional immaturity does not define your value or destroy your stability. Their behavior reflects their character, not your worth. Your power remains in your response.

Savage takeaway

Their dysfunction is their burden, not your identity.

Quiet power mantra

"My peace belongs to me alone."

LIV. BE LIGHT, NOT FORCE

"The sun seemeth to be shed abroad. And indeed it is diffused but not effused. For that diffusion of it is a τάσις[66] or an extension. For therefore are the beams of it called ἀκτῖνες[67] from the word ἐκτείνεσθαι[68] to be stretched out and extended. Now what a sunbeam is, thou mayest know if thou observe the light of the sun, when through some narrow hole it pierceth into some room that is dark. For it is always in a

---

[66] In Greek, τάσις (*tásis*) translates to "tension," "trend," or "strain."

[67] In Greek, ἀκτῖνες (*aktînes*) is the plural form of ἀκτίς (*aktís*), meaning "rays" or "beams."

[68] In Greek, ἐκτείνεσθαι (the infinitive of ἐκτείνεσθα) means "to be stretched out," "to extend," or "to expand."

direct line. And as by any solid body, that it meets with in the way that is not penetrable by air, it is divided and abrupted, and yet neither slides off, or falls down, but stayeth there nevertheless: such must the diffusion in the mind be; not an effusion, but an extension. What obstacles and impediments soever she meeteth within her way, she must not violently, and by way of an impetuous onset light upon them; neither must she fall down; but she must stand, and give light unto that which doth admit of it. For as for that which doth not, it is its own fault and loss, if it bereave itself of her light."

What Marcus meant (core philosophy)
The mind should resemble sunlight:
- steady
- directed
- illuminating without force.

Wisdom does not crash against resistance or collapse when blocked. It remains present and continues to shine where it is received. True strength is persistence without aggression.

Dating translation (what this means emotionally/socially)
You do not need to convince, chase, or force emotional understanding. Show up:
- clear
- honest
- consistent.

If someone cannot receive your presence or clarity, that is their limitation, not your failure.

Savage takeaway
You are not responsible for forcing others to see your light.

Quiet power mantra
"I shine without forcing."

LV. DO NOT FEAR DEATH

"He that feareth death, either feareth that he shall have no sense at all, or that his senses will not be the same. Whereas, he should rather comfort himself, that either no sense at all, and so no sense of evil; or if any sense, then another life, and so no death properly."

What Marcus meant (core philosophy)
Fear of death dissolves when examined logically:
- if there is no sensation, there is no suffering
- if there is continued existence, death is transformation, not annihilation.

Either way, fear is unnecessary.

Dating translation (what this means emotionally/socially)
Emotionally, people fear endings:
- breakups
- change
- transitions.

Marcus reminds us that endings either bring peace or transformation. Fear comes from imagination, not reality.

Savage takeaway
You fear the idea of endings more than endings themselves.

Quiet power mantra
"I accept change without fear."

LVI. TEACH OR TOLERATE

"All men are made one for another: either then teach them better, or bear with them."

What Marcus meant (core philosophy)
Human beings are interconnected. When faced with others' faults, two rational responses exist:
- guide them toward better understanding
- accept and endure without resentment.

Anger and contempt serve no purpose.

Dating translation (what this means emotionally/socially)
When someone behaves poorly:
- communicate clearly if growth is possible
- accept and disengage if it is not.

Remaining frustrated without action traps you in emotional stagnation.

Savage takeaway
Correct, accept, or walk away. Complaining is wasted energy.

Quiet power mantra
"I respond with clarity, not resentment."

LVII. DELIBERATE MOVEMENT IS STILL FORWARD

"The motion of the mind is not as the motion of a dart. For the mind when it is wary and cautelous, and by way of diligent circumspection turneth herself many ways, may then as well be said to go straight on to the object, as when it useth no such circumspection."

What Marcus meant (core philosophy)
Progress is not always linear. Careful consideration, reflection, and adjustment are not delays but part of moving forward wisely. Speed is less important than correctness.

Dating translation (what this means emotionally/socially)
Taking time to:
- reflect after heartbreak
- reassess patterns
- reconsider boundaries

is not regression. It is intelligent movement toward alignment.

Savage takeaway
Slow clarity beats fast mistakes.

Quiet power mantra
"I move forward with wisdom, not haste."

LVIII. SEE CLEARLY AND BE TRANSPARENT

"To pierce and penetrate into the estate of every one's understanding that thou hast to do with: as also to make the estate of thine own open, and penetrable to any other."

What Marcus meant (core philosophy)
Understanding others requires insight into their mindset. Equally, honesty requires making one's own inner state clear and accessible. Mutual clarity builds harmony.

Dating translation (what this means emotionally/socially)
Healthy connection requires:
- seeing people as they truly are, not as you wish them to be
- communicating your own thoughts openly.

Transparency combined with discernment creates real intimacy.

Savage takeaway
Real connection happens when perception is clear and communication is honest.

Quiet power mantra
"I see clearly and speak openly."

THE NINTH BOOK
Detach Without Becoming Bitter

I. JUSTICE IS ALIGNMENT WITH NATURE

"He that is unjust, is also impious. For the nature of the universe, having made all reasonable creatures one for another, to the end that they should do one another good; more or less according to the several persons and occasions but in nowise hurt one another: it is manifest that he that doth transgress against this her will, is guilty of impiety towards the most ancient and venerable of all the deities. For the nature of the universe, is the nature the common parent of all, and therefore piously to be observed of all things that are, and that which now is, to whatsoever first was, and gave it its being, hath relation of blood and kindred. She is also called truth and is the first cause of all truths. He therefore that willingly and wittingly doth lie, is impious in that he doth receive, and so commit injustice: but he that against his will, in that he disagreeth from the nature of the universe, and in that striving with the nature of the world he doth in his particular, violate the general order of the world. For he doth no better than strive and war against it, who contrary to his own nature applieth himself to that which is contrary to truth. For nature had before furnished him with instincts and opportunities sufficient for the attainment of it; which he having hitherto neglected, is not now able to discern that which is false from that which is true. He also that pursues after pleasures, as that which is truly good and flies from pains, as that which is truly evil: is impious. For such a one must of necessity oftentimes accuse that common nature, as distributing many things both unto the evil, and unto the good, not according to the deserts of either: as unto the bad oftentimes pleasures, and the causes of pleasures; so unto the good, pains, and the occasions of pains. Again, he that feareth pains and crosses in this world, feareth some of those things which some time or other must needs happen in the world. And that we have already showed to be impious. And he that pursueth after pleasures, will not spare, to compass his desires, to do that which is unjust, and that is manifestly impious. Now those things which unto nature are equally indifferent (for she had not created both, both pain and pleasure, if both had not been unto her equally indifferent): they that will live according to nature, must in those things (as being of the same mind and disposition that she is) be as equally indifferent. Whosoever therefore in either matter of pleasure and pain; death and life; honour and dishonour, (which things nature in the administration of the world, indifferently doth make use of), is not as indifferent, it is apparent that he is impious. When I say that common nature doth indifferently make use of them, my meaning is, that they happen indifferently in the ordinary course of things, which by a necessary consequence, whether as principal or accessory, come to pass in the world, according to that first and ancient deliberation of Providence, by which she from some certain beginning, did resolve upon the creation of such a world, conceiving then in her womb as it were some certain rational generative seeds and faculties of things future, whether subjects, changes, successions; both such and such, and just so many."

What Marcus meant (core philosophy)

Justice is not merely social behavior; it is alignment with the structure of reality itself. Marcus argues:
- Humans are designed for cooperation, not harm.
- Acting unjustly is acting against nature.
- Truth is sacred because reality itself is grounded in truth.

Impiety, in Stoic terms, is not religious failure but philosophical misalignment:
- Lying

- pursuing pleasure as ultimate good
- fearing pain as ultimate evil
- resisting the natural distribution of fortune and hardship.

Nature treats pleasure and pain, honor and dishonor, life and death as neutral tools within a larger order. The wise person mirrors this neutrality. True freedom comes from understanding: Nothing external defines good or evil. Only virtue does.

Dating translation (what this means emotionally/socially)

In relationships, people become impious toward their own nature when they:
- chase validation or chemistry as ultimate meaning
- avoid discomfort at all costs
- compromise truth for approval
- treat rejection or hardship as cosmic injustice.

Dating maturity means recognizing:
- attraction is neutral
- rejection is neutral
- praise is neutral
- conflict is neutral.

What matters is whether you remain:
- honest
- fair
- aligned with your values.

When someone lies, manipulates, or harms for pleasure or ego, they are not just wrong toward you; they are out of alignment with themselves. And when you abandon your truth for comfort or validation, you do the same.

Savage takeaway

Nothing external corrupts you. Only abandoning truth does.

Quiet power mantra

"I align with truth, not comfort."

II. THE CORRUPTION OF THE MIND IS THE REAL PLAGUE

"It were indeed more happy and comfortable, for a man to depart out of this world, having lived all his life long clear from all falsehood, dissimulation, voluptuousness, and pride. But if this cannot be, yet it is some comfort for a man joyfully to depart as weary, and out of love with those; rather than to desire to live, and to continue long in those wicked courses. Hath not yet experience taught thee to fly from the plague? For a far greater plague is the corruption of the mind, than any certain change and distemper of the common air can be. This is a plague of creatures, as they are living creatures; but that of men as they are men or reasonable."

What Marcus meant (core philosophy)

Marcus is not moralizing. He is diagnosing. External hardships do not destroy a person's nature. Internal corruption does. Falsehood, ego, excess pleasure, and pride slowly distort judgment until a person can no longer recognize truth or act according to reason. The real tragedy is not suffering but becoming comfortable inside behaviors that betray one's nature.

Stoicism views mental corruption as worse than physical illness because it separates a person from their own rational capacity. Once someone normalizes deception or ego-driven behavior, they lose clarity about what is good, what is harmful, and who they are.

Marcus also introduces a powerful idea: even if you have lived among corruption, wisdom begins the moment you become tired of it. Weariness toward falseness is a form of awakening.

Dating translation (what this means emotionally/socially)
In dating, people rarely fall apart because of heartbreak alone. They fall apart because they begin compromising their internal standards to maintain attachment. Mental corruption in dating looks like:
- pretending to be someone you are not to secure interest
- ignoring obvious red flags because attraction feels intoxicating
- tolerating disrespect because loneliness feels worse
- participating in games, manipulation, or emotional dishonesty.

The danger is not the other person's behavior. The danger is adapting to dysfunction until it feels normal. Many people stay longer in toxic dynamics not because they are fooled but because they become gradually desensitized. Each small compromise lowers internal clarity. Dating maturity begins when you become genuinely tired of pretending, chasing, or performing. That exhaustion is not failure. It is clarity arriving.

Savage takeaway
The wrong person cannot corrupt you unless you agree to abandon your own standards. The real red flag is not their behavior. It is the moment you start rationalizing it.

Quiet power mantra
"I walk away from what corrupts my clarity."

III. ACCEPTING ENDINGS AS NATURAL TRANSFORMATION
"Thou must not in matter of death carry thyself scornfully, but as one that is well pleased with it, as being one of those things that nature hath appointed. For what thou dost conceive of these, of a boy to become a young man, to wax old, to grow, to ripen, to get teeth, or a beard, or grey hairs to beget, to bear, or to be delivered; or what other action soever it be, that is natural unto man according to the several seasons of his life; such a thing is it also to be dissolved. It is therefore the part of a wise man, in matter of death, not in any wise to carry himself either violently, or proudly but patiently to wait for it, as one of nature's operations: that with the same mind as now thou dost expect when that which yet is but an embryo in thy wife's belly shall come forth, thou mayst expect also when thy soul shall fall off from that outward coat or skin: wherein as a child in the belly it lieth involved and shut up. But thou desirest a more popular, and though not so direct and philosophical, yet a very powerful and penetrative recipe against the fear of death, nothing can make they more willing to part with thy life, than if thou shalt consider, both what the subjects themselves are that thou shalt part with, and what manner of disposition thou shalt no more have to do with. True it is, that, offended with them thou must not be by no means,

but take care of them, and meekly bear with them However, this thou mayst remember, that whensoever it happens that thou depart, it shall not be from men that held the same opinions that thou dost. For that indeed, (if it were so) is the only thing that might make thee averse from death, and willing to continue here, if it were thy hap to live with men that had obtained the same belief that thou hast. But now, what a toil it is for thee to live with men of different opinions, thou seest: so that thou hast rather occasion to say, Hasten, I thee pray, O Death; lest I also in time forget myself."

What Marcus meant (core philosophy)

Marcus is not focused on death as tragedy but as transition. Everything in nature follows a cycle: growth, maturation, decline, transformation. Dissolution is not failure. It is completion. The wise person does not resist endings with drama, ego, or denial. They understand that endings belong to the same natural order as beginnings.

He also introduces a psychologically sharp insight: much of our fear of endings comes from attachment to familiar environments and identities, even when they no longer align with who we are becoming. Living among people or systems that no longer share your values becomes a quiet erosion of self. Acceptance of endings is not nihilistic. It is clarity about timing.

Dating translation (what this means emotionally/socially)

In dating, many people treat relationship endings as proof of failure instead of recognizing them as natural phases of development. People resist endings because:
- they fear starting over
- they are attached to the identity they built inside the relationship
- they confuse longevity with success
- they believe walking away means something died instead of something completed.

Dating maturity means recognizing when a relationship has fulfilled its purpose, even if that purpose was growth, learning, or clarity rather than permanence. Holding onto something past its natural season requires distortion:
- minimizing incompatibility
- suppressing intuition
- negotiating against reality.

Marcus reminds us that transformation is continuous. The person you were when you entered a relationship may not be the person you are now. Staying out of fear of change becomes a slow betrayal of your evolution.

Savage takeaway

Not every ending is loss. Some endings are alignment finally catching up with truth. Clinging to what has already completed its cycle is how people lose themselves.

Quiet power mantra

"I release what has finished becoming."

IV. EVERY ACTION SHAPES THE SELF

"He that sinneth, sinneth unto himself. He that is unjust, hurts himself, in that he makes himself worse than he was before. Not he only that committeth, but he also that omitteth something, is oftentimes unjust."

What Marcus meant (core philosophy)

Marcus reframes wrongdoing as self-inflicted damage. In Stoicism, injustice is not primarily about breaking external rules. It is about internal degradation. Every dishonest action, every cowardly avoidance, every failure to act when action is required reshapes the character of the person doing it.

Justice is not just about what you actively do. It also includes what you fail to do. Avoidance, silence, and passivity can be forms of injustice because they allow misalignment to continue. Each decision either strengthens integrity or weakens it. The deeper teaching is that no one escapes the consequences of their behavior because those consequences are written into who they become.

Dating translation (what this means emotionally/socially)

In dating, people often believe that someone else's behavior harms them more than it harms the person acting badly. Marcus would argue the opposite. When someone lies, manipulates, ghosts, or acts unfairly, they are reshaping their own character first. They are practicing disconnection from truth, which erodes their capacity for real intimacy. But this teaching applies equally inward. You harm yourself when you:

- stay silent instead of expressing truth
- ignore boundaries you know should exist
- avoid ending something that clearly needs ending
- tolerate dynamics that contradict your values.

Omission is powerful. Not saying no when you mean no. Not leaving when clarity has arrived. Not speaking honestly because you fear losing someone. These are not neutral acts. They slowly distort self-respect. Dating maturity means understanding that every choice trains your nervous system and identity. You become the person you repeatedly choose to be.

Savage takeaway

The greatest betrayal is not what someone else does to you. It is what you allow yourself to become to keep them.

Quiet power mantra

"I protect who I am by how I choose."

V. RIGHT PERCEPTION, RIGHT ACTION, ACCEPTANCE OF WHAT IS

"If my present apprehension of the object be right, and my present action charitable, and this, towards whatsoever doth proceed from God, be my present disposition, to be well pleased with it, it sufficeth."

What Marcus meant (core philosophy)

Marcus simplifies ethical living into three components:

- clear perception
- virtuous action
- acceptance of outcome.

Wisdom is not controlling reality but meeting it correctly. If your understanding is accurate, your behavior aligned with virtue, and your attitude accepting toward what unfolds, nothing more is required. This removes obsession with results. Stoicism measures success by internal alignment, not external outcome.

Dating translation (what this means emotionally/socially)

Dating anxiety often comes from trying to control how things turn out instead of focusing on how you show up. Marcus suggests a radical shift:

- Did you see clearly?
- Did you act with integrity?
- Did you accept the outcome without bitterness?

If yes, then you have succeeded regardless of whether the relationship continues. This dissolves overthinking because the goal becomes alignment, not guarantee. Many people exhaust themselves trying to engineer attraction, timing, or permanence. Stoic dating maturity means releasing control over reception while maintaining responsibility over intention and action.

Savage takeaway

You are responsible for clarity and character, not chemistry or outcome.

Quiet power mantra

"I show up aligned. The rest is not mine to control."

VI. MASTERING THE INNER FIELD

"To wipe away fancy, to use deliberation, to quench concupiscence, to keep the mind free to herself."

What Marcus meant (core philosophy)

Marcus describes mental discipline as liberation.

"Fancy" refers to distorted imagination or impulsive interpretation. Deliberation means pausing before reaction. Quenching desire means not allowing cravings to dominate judgment. The goal is a mind that belongs to itself, not one ruled by impulse, fantasy, or external influence. Freedom is internal sovereignty.

Dating translation (what this means emotionally/socially)

Dating often amplifies projection and fantasy. People build narratives about someone before reality confirms them:

- imagining compatibility based on attraction
- creating future stories before present consistency exists
- mistaking intensity for depth.

246

Marcus teaches that clarity requires removing imagined overlays and responding only to what is real. A sovereign dater does not chase every emotional spike. They observe, deliberate, and choose consciously. Desire is not the enemy. Unexamined desire is. When your mind belongs to itself, you do not lose direction just because someone is attractive or exciting.

Savage takeaway
Chemistry without clarity is just imagination wearing perfume.

Quiet power mantra
"My mind belongs to me."

VII. HUMANS ARE BUILT FOR CONNECTION, NOT ISOLATION

"Of all unreasonable creatures, there is but one unreasonable soul; and of all that are reasonable, but one reasonable soul, divided betwixt them all. As of all earthly things there is but one earth, and but one light that we see by; and but one air that we breathe in, as many as either breathe or see. Now whatsoever partakes of some common thing, naturally affects and inclines unto that whereof it is part, being of one kind and nature with it. Whatsoever is earthly, presseth downwards to the common earth. Whatsoever is liquid, would flow together. And whatsoever is airy, would be together likewise. So that without some obstacle, and some kind of violence, they cannot well be kept asunder. Whatsoever is fiery, doth not only by reason of the elementary fire tend upwards; but here also is so ready to join, and to burn together, that whatsoever doth want sufficient moisture to make resistance, is easily set on fire. Whatsoever therefore is partaker of that reasonable common nature, naturally doth as much and more long after his own kind. For by how much in its own nature it excels all other things, by so much more is it desirous to be joined and united unto that, which is of its own nature. As for unreasonable creatures then, they had not long been, but presently begun among them swarms, and flocks, and broods of young ones, and a kind of mutual love and affection. For though but unreasonable, yet a kind of soul these had, and therefore was that natural desire of union more strong and intense in them, as in creatures of a more excellent nature, than either in plants, or stones, or trees. But among reasonable creatures, begun commonwealths, friendships, families, public meetings, and even in their wars, conventions, and truces. Now among them that were yet of a more excellent nature, as the stars and planets, though by their nature far distant one from another, yet even among them began some mutual correspondency and unity. So proper is it to excellency in a high degree to affect unity, as that even in things so far distant, it could operate unto a mutual sympathy. But now behold, what is now come to pass. Those creatures that are reasonable, are now the only creatures that have forgotten their natural affection and inclination of one towards another. Among them alone of all other things that are of one kind, there is not to be found a general disposition to flow together. But though they fly from nature, yet are they stopt in their course, and apprehended. Do they what they can, nature doth prevail. And so shalt thou confess, if thou dost observe it. For sooner mayst thou find a thing earthly, where no earthly thing is, than find a man that naturally can live by himself alone."

What Marcus meant (core philosophy)
Marcus argues that connection is not optional for humans. It is structural. Everything in nature moves toward its own kind:
- earth settles with earth
- water flows together
- fire joins and spreads.

Human beings, as rational creatures, are naturally inclined toward unity, cooperation, and relationship. The desire for connection is not weakness. It is evidence of our nature. Yet Marcus observes something tragic: humans alone often resist this inclination. We isolate, divide, compete destructively, and forget our shared humanity. Despite this resistance, nature continues to pull us toward each other. Complete isolation contradicts our design. True excellence does not eliminate the need for connection. It deepens the desire for meaningful unity.

Dating translation (what this means emotionally/socially)

Modern dating culture often frames independence as emotional self-sufficiency to the point of detachment. People say:
- "I don't need anyone."
- "I'm better alone."
- "Connection is weakness."

Marcus would call this a misunderstanding of strength. Wanting connection is natural. Seeking partnership is not desperation. The danger lies not in longing for connection but in abandoning discernment to achieve it.

Dating maturity means holding two truths at once: You are complete on your own. You are also built for connection. The healthiest relationships arise when two individuals who are internally stable still allow themselves to move toward union. Isolation as armor may feel powerful, but it often masks fear of vulnerability or disappointment. Humans are designed to move toward resonance. The key is choosing alignment, not just proximity.

Savage takeaway

You are not weak for wanting connection. You are only misaligned when you chase connection that violates your nature.

Quiet power mantra

"I move toward connection that feels like truth."

VIII. REASON BEARS FRUIT THROUGH HOW YOU LIVE

"Man, God, the world, every one in their kind, bear some fruits. All things have their proper time to bear. Though by custom, the word itself is in a manner become proper unto the vine, and the like, yet is it so nevertheless, as we have said. As for reason, that beareth both common fruit for the use of others; and peculiar, which itself doth enjoy. Reason is of a diffusive nature, what itself is in itself, it begets in others, and so doth multiply."

What Marcus meant (core philosophy)

Everything produces according to its nature. Plants bear fruit physically. Humans bear fruit through reason and action. Reason is not passive. It spreads outward through behavior, influence, and example. What you cultivate internally inevitably expresses itself externally and multiplies through interaction with others. Virtue therefore benefits both the individual and the collective. It nourishes others while strengthening the self. Marcus reminds us that growth happens in seasons. Fruit appears when development has matured, not when forced.

Dating translation (what this means emotionally/socially)

In dating, people often focus on what they receive instead of what they embody. But the "fruit" of your character shapes the quality of connections you attract. Your emotional habits create ripple effects:

- clarity attracts clarity
- chaos attracts chaos
- honesty encourages honesty
- avoidance multiplies confusion.

Dating is not just selection. It is cultivation. If you build emotional maturity, discernment, and integrity, those qualities naturally influence the dynamic. You become a stabilizing force rather than someone constantly reacting to external behavior. Timing also matters. Some relationships arrive before emotional readiness exists to sustain them. Growth must precede harvest.

Savage takeaway

You don't attract what you want. You attract what you consistently embody.

Quiet power mantra

"I cultivate the energy I wish to meet."

IX. TEACH IF YOU CAN. IF NOT, PRACTICE PATIENCE

"Either teach them better if it be in thy power; or if it be not, remember that for this use, to bear with them patiently, was mildness and goodness granted unto thee. The Gods themselves are good unto such; yea and in some things, (as in matter of health, of wealth, of honour,) are content often to further their endeavours: so good and gracious are they. And mightest thou not be so too? or, tell me, what doth hinder thee?"

What Marcus meant (core philosophy)

Marcus presents two ethical responses to imperfection in others:

- guide them if they are capable of learning
- accept them calmly if they are not.

Frustration toward others often comes from expecting them to behave according to your level of awareness or values. Stoic goodness is not naive tolerance. It is emotional steadiness. Patience becomes an expression of strength because it reflects control over one's own reactions. You cannot control whether someone changes. You can control whether you remain internally balanced.

Dating translation (what this means emotionally/socially)

Many people enter relationships believing they can reshape someone through effort, love, or persistence. Marcus introduces a sharper boundary: If someone is capable of growth and receptive, clarity and honest communication can help. If they are not, patience does not mean fixing them. It means releasing resentment and adjusting your expectations or your position. Dating maturity means recognizing:

- not every misunderstanding requires correction
- not every flaw is yours to manage
- emotional labor should not become emotional self-abandonment.

Patience is not staying where alignment is absent. It is maintaining calm while deciding your next move.

Savage takeaway
You are not responsible for upgrading someone's consciousness.

Quiet power mantra
"I offer clarity where it is welcomed. I release what resists growth."

X. ACT WITHOUT SEEKING PITY OR PRAISE

"Labour not as one to whom it is appointed to be wretched, nor as one that either would be pitied, or admired; but let this be thine only care and desire; so always and in all things to prosecute or to forbear, as the law of charity, or mutual society doth require."

What Marcus meant (core philosophy)
Marcus warns against performative suffering and performative virtue. Two traps exist:
- seeing oneself as tragic or victimized
- seeking admiration for moral behavior.

Both distort intention because they shift focus away from right action toward external validation. True virtue operates quietly. It does what is right because it is right, not because it generates sympathy or status.

Dating translation (what this means emotionally/socially)
Dating often invites performance:
- presenting yourself as misunderstood to gain emotional investment
- showcasing independence to appear desirable
- acting overly self-sacrificing to earn approval.

Marcus challenges this dynamic. Alignment means acting from internal clarity, not from the desire to be rescued or admired. Healthy relationships grow from authenticity, not emotional theater. When you stop performing strength or suffering, connection becomes simpler and more honest.

Savage takeaway
If you need applause for your effort, you're still negotiating for approval.

Quiet power mantra
"I act from alignment, not performance."

XI. YOUR TROUBLE COMES FROM YOUR OPINIONS

"This day I did come out of all my trouble. Nay I have cast out all my trouble; it should rather be for that which troubled thee, whatsoever it was, was not without anywhere that thou shouldest come out of it, but within in thine own opinions, from whence it must be cast out, before thou canst truly and constantly be at ease."

What Marcus meant (core philosophy)
Marcus delivers one of the most central Stoic ideas: distress originates from interpretation, not events themselves. External situations trigger reactions, but

suffering is amplified or sustained by internal judgments. Freedom arises when one examines and releases distorted beliefs about what is happening. Peace is not found by changing circumstances but by refining perception.

Dating translation (what this means emotionally/socially)
In dating, people often believe their suffering comes from:
- rejection
- mixed signals
- breakups
- unmet expectations.

Marcus would say the deeper source lies in the meaning attached to those events:
- "I wasn't chosen, so I am not enough."
- "This ended, so I failed."
- "They moved on, so I was replaceable."

The event may hurt. The narrative determines whether it becomes suffering. Dating clarity comes from questioning the story you are telling yourself about what happened. When interpretation shifts, emotional freedom follows.

Savage takeaway
The situation didn't trap you. The story you told yourself about it did.

Quiet power mantra
"I release the stories that keep me stuck."

XII. EVERYTHING PASSES AND MOST OF IT WAS NEVER SPECIAL
"All those things, for matter of experience are usual and ordinary; for their continuance but for a day; and for their matter, most base and filthy. As they were in the days of those whom we have buried, so are they now also, and no otherwise."

What Marcus meant (core philosophy)
Marcus strips away romantic illusion. Most events that feel overwhelming in the present are neither rare nor extraordinary. They have happened countless times before and will happen countless times again. Time reduces intensity. What feels monumental now will eventually become ordinary memory. Stoicism uses this perspective not to diminish meaning but to restore proportion. By recognizing the temporary and repetitive nature of human experiences, emotional reactivity softens. Perspective dissolves drama.

Dating translation (what this means emotionally/socially)
Dating often feels intensely personal, as though every rejection, betrayal, or heartbreak is uniquely devastating.

Marcus reminds us: People have loved, lost, misread signals, been ghosted, felt chosen, and felt abandoned across generations. Your experience matters, but it is not unprecedented. This perspective creates emotional resilience:
- rejection stops feeling like a cosmic event

- disappointment stops defining identity
- attraction stops feeling like destiny.

Seeing dating experiences as part of a broader human pattern allows you to stay grounded instead of spiraling into narratives of permanence.

Savage takeaway
What feels extraordinary now is often just another human story repeating itself.

Quiet power mantra
"This moment is temporary, not defining."

XIII. EVENTS HAVE NO VOICE. YOU GIVE THEM MEANING.
"The things themselves that affect us, they stand without doors, neither knowing anything themselves nor able to utter anything unto others concerning themselves. What then is it, that passeth verdict on them? The understanding."

What Marcus meant (core philosophy)
External events are neutral. They carry no inherent judgment, meaning, or intention. The mind assigns interpretation. Stoicism places responsibility not on controlling circumstances but on examining the internal process that labels events as good, bad, unfair, or catastrophic. Understanding becomes the judge. Freedom lies in recognizing that perception shapes experience.

Dating translation (what this means emotionally/socially)
In dating, people often assume situations carry objective emotional meaning:
- a delayed text means rejection
- silence means disinterest
- a breakup means failure.

Marcus would argue that these conclusions arise from interpretation, not from the events themselves. Reality presents information. The mind creates the narrative. When you separate fact from interpretation, emotional clarity increases:
- Fact: they canceled plans.
- Interpretation: "I am not valued."

Learning to distinguish between the two reduces unnecessary suffering and improves decision-making.

Savage takeaway
The event didn't hurt you. The story you attached to it did.

Quiet power mantra
"I respond to reality, not to assumption."

XIV. CHARACTER IS BUILT THROUGH ACTION, NOT FEELING
"As virtue and wickedness consist not in passion, but in action; so neither doth the true good or evil of a reasonable charitable man consist in passion, but in operation and action."

What Marcus meant (core philosophy)
Marcus separates emotion from moral worth. Feeling anger, attraction, fear, or desire is not inherently virtuous or harmful. What matters is how one acts. Stoicism

acknowledges emotional experience but refuses to let it define ethical value. Character is revealed through behavior, not through internal states.

Dating translation (what this means emotionally/socially)
Dating culture often overemphasizes feelings:
- "I feel strongly, so it must be right."
- "I feel disconnected, so it must be wrong."
- "I feel chemistry, so this matters."

Marcus redirects focus toward action:
- Do they follow through?
- Do they act with respect?
- Do you behave in alignment with your values even when emotions fluctuate?

Strong emotions can exist in unhealthy dynamics. Calm emotions can exist in deeply healthy ones. Consistency of action reveals truth more reliably than intensity of feeling.

Savage takeaway
Chemistry is not character. Watch behavior.

Quiet power mantra
"I judge by action, not emotion."

XV. ASCENT AND DESCENT ARE NOT MORAL JUDGMENTS
"To the stone that is cast up, when it comes down it is no hurt unto it; as neither benefit, when it doth ascend."

What Marcus meant (core philosophy)
Marcus challenges the human tendency to label movement as success or failure. The stone rising or falling simply follows natural forces. Neither direction holds moral value. Stoicism teaches neutrality toward external highs and lows. Change itself is not inherently good or bad. Meaning arises from how one responds, not from whether circumstances improve or decline.

Dating translation (what this means emotionally/socially)
Dating is filled with perceived "ups" and "downs":
- early excitement vs. later stability
- intense beginnings vs. gradual endings
- attention gained vs. attention lost.

People often interpret these shifts as personal victories or failures. Marcus invites a calmer perspective:
- Interest increasing is not proof of worth.
- Interest fading is not proof of inadequacy.

Relationships move through phases. External shifts do not define internal value. When you stop assigning identity to every rise or fall, emotional steadiness becomes possible.

Savage takeaway
Momentum is not meaning. Movement is just movement.

Quiet power mantra
"My worth does not rise or fall with circumstance."

XVI. EXAMINE THE JUDGES YOU FEAR
"Sift their minds and understandings, and behold what men they be, whom thou dost stand in fear of what they shall judge of thee, what they themselves judge of themselves."

What Marcus meant (core philosophy)
Marcus challenges the instinct to fear social judgment. He advises stepping back and examining the people whose opinions you fear. What are their values? How clearly do they understand themselves? Are they wise, aligned, or merely reactive? Often, we grant authority to voices that have not earned it. Stoicism teaches that external judgment only holds power when you assign it importance. True evaluation comes from alignment with reason and virtue, not public approval. Fear dissolves when you realize that many who judge are themselves confused, inconsistent, or disconnected from clarity.

Dating translation (what this means emotionally/socially)
Dating creates intense pressure around perception:
*   fear of how others see your relationship choices
*   anxiety about appearing desirable, chosen, or successful
*   hesitation to walk away because of how it might look.

Marcus invites a ruthless question: Who exactly are you trying to impress? Are they emotionally mature? Do they live according to values you respect? Would you genuinely want their internal life? Many people stay in dynamics or perform identities to satisfy imagined audiences whose approval would not actually nourish them. Dating maturity includes auditing the voices influencing your decisions.

Savage takeaway
Stop reshaping your life to impress people who haven't figured out their own.

Quiet power mantra
"I value the opinions of those aligned with truth."

XVII. EVERYTHING CHANGES, INCLUDING YOU
"All things that are in the world, are always in the estate of alteration. Thou also art in a perpetual change, yea and under corruption too, in some part: and so is the whole world."

What Marcus meant (core philosophy)
Change is constant and unavoidable. Nothing remains fixed. Identity, circumstance, relationships, and the world itself exist in continuous transformation. Stoicism encourages acceptance of this reality rather than resistance to it. Stability is not found in permanence but in adaptability. Even decay is part of transformation. What dissolves creates space for new forms.

Understanding this removes shock when things evolve. Change stops feeling like disruption and becomes recognition of natural flow.

Dating translation (what this means emotionally/socially)
People often enter relationships expecting stability to mean sameness. But:
- attraction shifts
- needs evolve
- priorities change
- identities deepen.

Dating conflict frequently arises when one or both partners resist change, trying to preserve an earlier version of the relationship. Marcus reminds us that transformation is not betrayal. It is nature. Dating maturity means allowing both yourself and others to evolve without clinging to outdated expectations. Some relationships grow alongside change. Others complete their purpose when alignment fades.

Savage takeaway
You cannot demand permanence from something designed to evolve.

Quiet power mantra
"I move with change instead of resisting it."

XVIII. THEIR ACTIONS BELONG TO THEM, NOT TO YOU
"…it is not thine, but another man's sin. Why should it trouble thee? Let him look to it, whose sin it is."

What Marcus meant (core philosophy)
Marcus draws a clean boundary between personal responsibility and external behavior. Another person's wrongdoing belongs to them. Carrying emotional burden for their choices creates unnecessary suffering. Stoicism teaches emotional separation between observation and ownership. You may witness injustice, but you do not need to internalize it as self-definition. Peace comes from recognizing what is yours to govern and what is not.

Dating translation (what this means emotionally/socially)
In dating, people often internalize others' harmful behavior:
- "They cheated, so I wasn't enough."
- "They lied, so I must have missed something."
- "They left, so I failed."

Marcus cuts through this distortion. Someone else's character choices reflect their alignment, not your worth. You are responsible for how you respond, not for why they acted the way they did. Releasing ownership of others' behavior restores emotional clarity and prevents unnecessary self-blame.

Savage takeaway
Their behavior is information, not identity.

Quiet power mantra
"I return responsibility to its rightful owner."

XIX. ENDINGS ARE TRANSITIONS, NOT TRAGEDIES

"Of an operation and of a purpose there is an ending, or of an action and of a purpose we say commonly, that it is at an end: from opinion also there is an absolute cessation, which is as it were the death of it. In all this there is no hurt. Apply this now to a man's age, as first, a child; then a youth, then a young man, then an old man; every change from one age to another is a kind of death And all this while here no matter of grief yet. Pass now unto that life first, that which thou livedst under thy grandfather, then under thy mother, then under thy father. And thus when through the whole course of thy life hitherto thou hast found and observed many alterations, many changes, many kinds of endings and cessations, put this question to thyself What matter of grief or sorrow dost thou find in any of these? Or what doest thou suffer through any of these? If in none of these, then neither in the ending and consummation of thy whole life, which is also but a cessation and change."

What Marcus meant (core philosophy)

Marcus reframes endings as neutral transitions. Every stage of life ends: childhood, youth, identities, beliefs, roles. Each "ending" feels significant in the moment but becomes simply another transformation when viewed from distance. The Stoic insight is that cessation does not equal harm. It is part of natural progression. Even the death of ideas, identities, or relationships follows this pattern. Opinions end. Phases close. Self-concepts dissolve. Yet life continues. Grief often arises from resisting the inevitability of change rather than from the change itself.

Dating translation (what this means emotionally/socially)

Dating is full of perceived "losses" that are actually transitions:
- the end of early-stage excitement
- the shift from possibility to clarity
- the ending of relationships that once felt essential.

People mourn the end of a version of themselves as much as they mourn the other person.

Marcus reminds us: You have already survived countless endings of old identities, former relationships, and previous expectations about life. Why treat this ending as uniquely catastrophic? Dating maturity means recognizing that endings are evolutionary checkpoints, not personal failures.

Savage takeaway

You have already outgrown dozens of versions of your life. This is just another evolution.

Quiet power mantra

"I allow endings to become transformation."

XX. RETURN QUICKLY TO ALIGNMENT

"As occasion shall require, either to thine own understanding, or to that of the universe, or to his, whom thou hast now to do with, let thy refuge be with all speed. To thine own, that it resolve upon nothing against justice. To that of the universe, that thou mayest remember, part of whom thou art. Of his, that thou mayest consider whether in the estate of ignorance, or of knowledge. And then also must thou call to mind, that he is thy kinsman."

256

What Marcus meant (core philosophy)

Marcus outlines three rapid checkpoints for regaining clarity:

- Return to your own reason: Are you acting justly?
- Return to perspective: You are part of a larger whole.
- Return to compassion: The other person may act from ignorance rather than malice.

This framework helps prevent impulsive reaction by grounding action in alignment rather than emotion. Stoicism emphasizes speed of internal correction. The longer one remains misaligned, the harder it becomes to return to clarity.

Dating translation (what this means emotionally/socially)

Dating situations often trigger emotional reactions:

- Defensiveness
- Hurt
- Anger
- Overanalysis.

Marcus offers a practical reset:

- First: Am I acting according to my values?
- Second: Is this moment truly as large as it feels, or am I losing perspective?
- Third: Is the other person intentionally harmful, or simply unaware?

This doesn't excuse bad behavior. It prevents you from abandoning your own integrity while responding. Dating maturity is the ability to recalibrate quickly instead of spiraling emotionally.

Savage takeaway

Your power lies in how fast you return to alignment after being triggered.

Quiet power mantra

"I return to clarity without delay."

XXI. EVERY ACTION SHOULD SERVE CONNECTION, NOT DIVISION

"As thou thyself, whoever thou art, were made for the perfection and consummation, being a member of it, of a common society; so must every action of thine tend to the perfection and consummation of a life that is truly sociable. What action soever of thine therefore that either immediately or afar off, hath not reference to the common good, that is an exorbitant and disorderly action; yea it is seditious; as one among the people who from such and such a consent and unity, should factiously divide and separate himself."

What Marcus meant (core philosophy)

Marcus asserts that humans exist within interconnected systems. Actions should contribute to harmony and cooperation rather than fragmentation. Self-centered behavior disrupts the natural order because it separates the individual from the collective. Virtue aligns personal conduct with mutual benefit. True strength enhances connection rather than undermining it.

Dating translation (what this means emotionally/socially)
Dating sometimes encourages adversarial thinking:
- power games
- emotional withholding
- strategic manipulation.

Marcus suggests that actions rooted in division ultimately destabilize connection. Healthy dating does not mean self-sacrifice, but it does mean operating from mutual respect and shared humanity.

Ask: Does this behavior increase clarity and connection? Or does it create confusion and distance? Sustainable relationships grow from actions that support shared growth, not from strategies designed to gain advantage.

Savage takeaway
If your strategy requires disconnection to feel powerful, it is already misaligned.

Quiet power mantra
"I choose actions that strengthen healthy connection."

XXII. MUCH OF WHAT DISTURBS YOU IS CHILDISH NOISE
"Children's anger, mere babels[69]; wretched souls bearing up dead bodies, that they may not have their fall so soon: even as it is in that common dirge song."

What Marcus meant (core philosophy)
Marcus reduces much human drama to immaturity. Anger, outrage, and emotional theatrics often resemble children arguing without perspective. People carry attachments long after they have lost vitality, trying to preserve what is already finished. Stoicism teaches emotional distance from noise. Not every expression of intensity deserves equal seriousness. Many conflicts arise not from deep philosophical difference but from unregulated emotion and unconscious behavior. Seeing this clearly removes the illusion of significance.

Dating translation (what this means emotionally/socially)
Dating environments amplify emotional displays:
- dramatic arguments
- reactive texts
- performative anger
- unresolved attachment to relationships that are already emotionally over.

Marcus invites a reframing: Not every emotional outburst reflects deep meaning. Sometimes it is simply immaturity expressing itself. Dating maturity means recognizing when someone is reacting from emotional childhood rather than grounded self-awareness. You do not need to match their intensity. Clarity comes from observing without immediately engaging.

---

[69] In English, babels is the plural form of babel, referring to a confused noise, a scene of noisy confusion, or a visionary, impractical scheme.

Savage takeaway
Not every conflict is deep. Some of it is just emotional noise.

Quiet power mantra
"I do not match chaos with participation."

XXIII. SEE THE CAUSE WITHOUT THE STORY
"Go to the quality of the cause from which the effect doth proceed. Behold it by itself bare and naked, separated from all that is material. Then consider the utmost bounds of time that that cause, thus and thus qualified, can subsist and abide."

What Marcus meant (core philosophy)
Marcus encourages analytical clarity. Instead of reacting to appearances or emotional packaging, examine the underlying cause directly. Strip away narrative, projection, and external decoration. Once the true cause is identified, consider its lifespan. Most causes are temporary and limited. Understanding root causes dissolves exaggerated emotional reactions. Stoicism values seeing things as they are, not as they feel.

Dating translation (what this means emotionally/socially)
In dating, people often react to surface-level behaviors instead of examining deeper patterns:
* a sudden withdrawal might come from fear or insecurity
* excessive intensity might come from loneliness rather than compatibility
* inconsistency might come from emotional unavailability.

Marcus teaches: Look beyond presentation. Identify the core pattern.
Then ask: Is this a temporary phase or a structural trait?

This distinction prevents wasted emotional investment in patterns unlikely to change.

Savage takeaway
Stop reacting to the performance. Identify the pattern.

Quiet power mantra
"I see causes clearly, not just effects."

XXIV. YOUR MIND OPERATING WELL IS ALREADY ENOUGH
"Infinite are the troubles and miseries, that thou hast already been put to, by reason of this only, because that for all happiness it did not suffice thee, or, that thou didst not account it sufficient happiness, that thy understanding did operate according to its natural constitution."

What Marcus meant (core philosophy)
Marcus identifies dissatisfaction as arising from undervaluing internal alignment. When people believe happiness requires external achievement or validation, they create endless dissatisfaction. Stoicism teaches that a mind functioning according to reason, clarity, and virtue is already sufficient for well-being. Seeking more is not inherently wrong, but believing that internal alignment is insufficient creates unnecessary suffering.

Dating translation (what this means emotionally/socially)
Dating often becomes a search for completion:
- someone to validate worth
- someone to fix loneliness
- someone to confirm identity.

Marcus flips this perspective. If your mind is aligned, discerning, and grounded, you are already operating from sufficiency. Desperation arises when internal clarity is dismissed as not enough. When you recognize internal alignment as fulfillment, dating shifts from seeking rescue to exploring connection.

Savage takeaway
You were never incomplete. You just kept outsourcing your sense of enoughness.

Quiet power mantra
"My clarity is already sufficient."

XXV. EXAMINE THEIR NATURE BEFORE CARING ABOUT THEIR OPINION

"When any shall either impeach thee with false accusations, or hatefully reproach thee, or shall use any such carriage towards thee, get thee presently to their minds and understandings, and look in them, and behold what manner of men they be. Thou shalt see, that there is no such occasion why it should trouble thee, what such as they are think of thee. Yet must thou love them still, for by nature they are thy friends. And the Gods themselves, in those things that they seek from them as matters of great moment, are well content, all manner of ways, as by dreams and oracles, to help them as well as others."

What Marcus meant (core philosophy)
Marcus advises examining the character of those who judge or criticize you. Once you understand their limitations, fears, or lack of clarity, their opinions lose emotional weight. This is not contempt but perspective. Stoicism encourages compassion without emotional submission. You may recognize someone's flaws while still maintaining goodwill toward them. Understanding dissolves unnecessary distress.

Dating translation (what this means emotionally/socially)
Dating exposes people to criticism, rejection, and projection:
- someone labeling you incorrectly
- an ex rewriting the narrative
- partners misunderstanding your intentions.

Marcus suggests pausing and asking:
- Who is this person?
- What level of awareness are they operating from?
- Would their perspective define truth?

Seeing their internal world clearly removes the need to internalize their judgment. Compassion can exist without agreement or self-abandonment.

Savage takeaway
Not every opinion deserves emotional access to you.

Quiet power mantra
"I see clearly who is speaking before I decide what matters."

XXVI. WHETHER FATE OR CHANCE, YOUR RESPONSE IS STILL YOURS

"Up and down, from one age to another, go the ordinary things of the world; being still the same. And either of everything in particular before it come to pass, the mind of the universe doth consider with itself and deliberate: and if so, then submit for shame unto the determination of such an excellent understanding: or once for all it did resolve upon all things in general; and since that whatsoever happens, happens by a necessary consequence, and all things indivisibly in a manner and inseparably hold one of another. In sum, either there is a God, and then all is well; or if all things go by chance and fortune, yet mayest thou use thine own providence in those things that concern thee properly; and then art thou well."

What Marcus meant (core philosophy)
Marcus offers two philosophical possibilities: Either the universe unfolds through intelligent order, or events arise through chance and necessity.

His conclusion is the same regardless: peace comes from focusing on what remains within your control.
- If existence is guided by divine reason, then trust the order.
- If existence unfolds randomly, then rely on your own reason.

In both scenarios, emotional stability comes from accepting what happens while directing effort toward internal governance. Stoicism removes the need to solve metaphysical certainty before living wisely.

Dating translation (what this means emotionally/socially)
Dating often triggers existential questions:
- Why did this happen?
- Was this meant to be?
- Is this fate or bad luck?

Marcus would say the answer matters less than your response. Whether a connection ends because of destiny, incompatibility, or random timing, your task remains the same:
- Act with integrity.
- Learn from the experience.
- Continue moving with intention.

Searching endlessly for cosmic meaning can become avoidance of personal agency. Dating maturity means recognizing that you can operate wisely regardless of whether events feel purposeful or accidental.

Savage takeaway
It doesn't matter whether it was fate or chaos. What matters is how you show up next.

Quiet power mantra
"I focus on my response, not on explaining the universe."

261

XXVII. TIME SWEEPS EVERYTHING AWAY

"Within a while the earth shall cover us all, and then she herself shall have her change. And then the course will be, from one period of eternity unto another, and so a perpetual eternity. Now can any man that shall consider with himself in his mind the several rollings or successions of so many changes and alterations, and the swiftness of all these rulings; can he otherwise but contemn in his heart and despise all worldly things? The cause of the universe is as it were a strong torrent, it carrieth all away."

What Marcus meant (core philosophy)

Marcus emphasizes impermanence. Everything passes:

- People
- Achievements
- Conflicts
- Reputations.

Time moves like a torrent, carrying away all forms. This perspective is not meant to create despair but freedom. When you recognize the temporary nature of external things, attachment loosens and priorities clarify. What remains meaningful is how you lived, not what you accumulated or controlled.

Dating translation (what this means emotionally/socially)

Dating drama often feels permanent:

- heartbreak feels endless
- rejection feels defining
- attraction feels eternal.

Marcus zooms out. Years from now, most moments that feel overwhelming today will fade into memory. The urgency you feel now is often created by proximity, not by true permanence. Understanding impermanence helps you:

- release obsession faster
- avoid overinvesting in fleeting dynamics
- value present connection without clinging.

Dating clarity comes when you stop treating temporary experiences as permanent identity markers.

Savage takeaway

Time humbles everything. Don't build your identity around moments that won't last.

Quiet power mantra

"This too moves with time."

XXVIII. TRUE PHILOSOPHY REQUIRES SIMPLICITY, NOT PERFORMANCE

"And these your professed politicians, the only true practical philosophers of the world, (as they think of themselves) so full of affected gravity, or such professed lovers of virtue and honesty, what wretches be they in very deed; how vile and contemptible in themselves? O man! what ado doest thou keep? Do what thy nature doth now require. Resolve upon it, if thou mayest: and take no thought, whether anybody shall know it or no. Yea, but sayest thou, I must not expect a Plato's commonwealth. If they profit though

never so little, I must be content; and think much even of that little progress. Doth then any of them forsake their former false opinions that I should think they profit? For without a change of opinions, alas! what is all that ostentation, but mere wretchedness of slavish minds, that groan privately, and yet would make a show of obedience to reason, and truth? Go too now and tell me of Alexander and Philippus, and Demetrius Phalereus. Whether they understood what the common nature requireth, and could rule themselves or no, they know best themselves. But if they kept a life, and swaggered; I (God be thanked) am not bound to imitate them. The effect of true philosophy is, unaffected simplicity and modesty. Persuade me not to ostentation and vainglory."

What Marcus meant (core philosophy)

Marcus criticizes performative wisdom. Many claim virtue while chasing status, recognition, or admiration. True philosophy does not require spectacle or approval. It expresses itself through quiet consistency and modest action. Progress does not require perfection. Even small shifts toward alignment matter. Stoicism rejects the need to appear wise. It values being aligned over being admired.

Dating translation (what this means emotionally/socially)

Dating culture often encourages performance:
- curated personas
- strategic emotional displays
- projecting confidence or mystery for effect.

Marcus invites radical simplicity. You do not need to perform enlightenment, emotional intelligence, or desirability. Authentic alignment creates more sustainable connection than calculated presentation. Also, you are not obligated to imitate relationship models that look impressive externally but lack internal integrity. Dating maturity means:
- choosing authenticity over image
- valuing genuine growth over dramatic transformation narratives
- letting consistency replace performance.

Savage takeaway

If your authenticity disappears when someone is watching, it was performance.

Quiet power mantra

"I choose simplicity over spectacle."

XXIX. SEE FROM ABOVE AND RELEASE THE NEED FOR SIGNIFICANCE

"From some high place as it were to look down, and to behold here flocks, and there sacrifices, without number; and all kind of navigation; some in a rough and stormy sea, and some in a calm: the general differences, or different estates of things, some, that are now first upon being; the several and mutual relations of those things that are together; and some other things that are at their last. Their lives also, who were long ago, and theirs who shall be hereafter, and the present estate and life of those many nations of barbarians that are now in the world, thou must likewise consider in thy mind. And how many there be, who never so much as heard of thy name, how many that will soon forget it; how many who but even now did commend thee, within a very little while perchance will speak ill of thee. So that neither fame, nor honour, nor anything else that this world doth afford, is worth the while. The sum then of all; whatsoever

doth happen unto thee, whereof God is the cause, to accept it contentedly: whatsoever thou doest, whereof thou thyself art the cause, to do it justly: which will be, if both in thy resolution and in thy action thou have no further end, than to do good unto others, as being that, which by thy natural constitution, as a man, thou art bound unto."

What Marcus meant (core philosophy)
Marcus introduces the "view from above."

By mentally stepping back and observing humanity across time and scale, personal concerns shrink into proportion. Fame, reputation, praise, and criticism become fleeting and insignificant against the vast flow of existence. This perspective dissolves ego attachment. Two principles remain:
* Accept what happens beyond your control.
* Act justly in what depends on you.
Meaning arises not from recognition but from alignment with nature and contribution to others.

Dating translation (what this means emotionally/socially)
Dating often magnifies small moments into identity-defining events:
* worrying about how you appear
* obsessing over reputation or status
* overvaluing approval or fearing criticism.
Marcus invites a zoom-out. Most people will not know your story. Those who do may forget or reinterpret it. Praise turns into criticism. Interest turns into indifference. When you release the need for lasting significance, dating becomes lighter. The goal shifts from being admired or remembered to simply showing up with integrity. Connection becomes less performative and more honest.

Savage takeaway
If you stopped trying to be impressive and focused on being aligned, most of your anxiety would disappear.

Quiet power mantra
"I act justly without needing recognition."

XXX. MANY PROBLEMS EXIST ONLY IN YOUR INTERPRETATION
"Many of those things that trouble and straiten thee, it is in thy power to cut off, as wholly depending from mere conceit and opinion; and then thou shalt have room enough."

What Marcus meant (core philosophy)
Marcus reminds us that much suffering is self-created through interpretation. External events may trigger discomfort, but mental framing amplifies or sustains distress. By examining and removing distorted assumptions, mental space opens. Stoicism teaches that clarity often comes not from adding solutions but from subtracting false beliefs. Freedom arises when unnecessary narratives are dropped.

Dating translation (what this means emotionally/socially)

Dating anxiety frequently comes from imagined scenarios:

- assuming rejection before confirmation
- overanalyzing communication
- projecting future failure onto present uncertainty.

Marcus would say: How much of your stress comes from reality, and how much from interpretation? When you remove imagined meanings, many problems dissolve:

- Fact: they haven't replied yet.
- Story: they are losing interest, something is wrong, I am not enough.

Dating maturity includes challenging internal narratives before reacting externally.

Savage takeaway

Half your stress is not real. It's a story you haven't questioned yet.

Quiet power mantra

"I release unnecessary interpretation."

XXXI. EVERYTHING PASSES QUICKLY; PERSPECTIVE RESTORES PEACE

"To comprehend the whole world together in thy mind, and the whole course of this present age to represent it unto thyself, and to fix thy thoughts upon the sudden change of every particular object. How short the time is from the generation of anything, unto the dissolution of the same; but how immense and infinite both that which was before the generation, and that which after the generation of it shall be. All things that thou seest, will soon be perished, and they that see their corruptions, will soon vanish away themselves. He that dieth a hundred years old, and he that dieth young, shall come all to one."

What Marcus meant (core philosophy)

Marcus emphasizes temporal humility. Everything arises briefly and disappears again within the vastness of time. Life spans, achievements, conflicts, and identities all compress into small moments when viewed from eternity. Recognizing this does not diminish life's value. It reduces unnecessary attachment to transient concerns. Acceptance of impermanence allows deeper presence.

Dating translation (what this means emotionally/socially)

Dating intensity often comes from treating present experiences as permanent truths. Marcus encourages perspective:

- this attraction is temporary
- this disappointment is temporary
- this phase of your life is temporary.

When you remember how quickly circumstances change, urgency softens and clarity increases. You begin to invest in experiences without clinging to outcomes. Dating becomes less about securing permanence and more about engaging authentically in the moment.

Savage takeaway
Nothing lasts long enough to justify losing yourself over it.

Quiet power mantra
"I hold lightly what time will carry away."

XXXII. LOOK INTO THE MINDS OF THOSE WHO JUDGE
"What are their minds and understandings; and what the things that they apply themselves unto: what do they love, and what do they hate for? Fancy to thyself the estate of their souls openly to be seen. When they think they hurt them shrewdly, whom they speak ill of; and when they think they do them a very good turn, whom they commend and extol: O how full are they then of conceit, and opinion!"

What Marcus meant (core philosophy)
Marcus urges you to examine the inner world of those whose words affect you. People often believe their praise or criticism carries weight, yet both are usually shaped by personal bias, insecurity, or misunderstanding. Their judgments reflect their own perceptions more than objective truth. When you imagine their minds clearly, the emotional power of their opinions weakens. Stoicism teaches that understanding the limitations of others dissolves unnecessary emotional entanglement.

Dating translation (what this means emotionally/socially)
Dating exposes you to constant evaluation:
- compliments that inflate ego
- criticism that wounds
- mixed feedback that confuses identity.

Marcus reminds you that both praise and blame are filtered through someone else's perspective. Someone may think they are deeply hurting you by rejecting you, or believe they are elevating you through validation. In reality, both reactions reveal more about their worldview than your inherent value. Dating maturity means receiving feedback without surrendering self-definition.

Savage takeaway
Praise and criticism often come from the same place: someone else's projection.

Quiet power mantra
"I see the speaker before I accept the message."

XXXIII. LOSS IS ONLY CHANGE WE RESIST
"Loss and corruption, is in very deed nothing else but change and alteration; and that is it, which the nature of the universe doth most delight in, by which, and according to which, whatsoever is done, is well done. For that was the estate of worldly things from the beginning, and so shall it ever be. Or wouldest thou rather say, that all things in the world have gone ill from the beginning for so many ages, and shall ever go ill? And then among so many deities, could no divine power be found all this while, that could rectify the things of the world? Or is the world, to incessant woes and miseries, for ever condemned?"

What Marcus meant (core philosophy)

Marcus reframes loss as transformation rather than destruction. Change is not evidence of failure or cosmic injustice. It is the fundamental process through which the universe operates. Resistance to change creates the illusion of loss as tragedy. Stoicism views alteration as natural and necessary. Without it, growth, renewal, and evolution would be impossible.

Dating translation (what this means emotionally/socially)

In dating, people often interpret endings as damage:

- the relationship failed
- time was wasted
- something was lost permanently.

Marcus would argue that change itself is not harmful. It becomes painful only when we expect permanence from something designed to evolve.

- A breakup is change.
- Emotional distance is change.
- Shifting attraction is change.

Seeing transformation as natural removes the narrative that something has gone "wrong." Dating maturity means allowing relationships to evolve without framing every shift as loss.

Savage takeaway

Nothing was stolen from you. It changed form.

Quiet power mantra

"I accept change as natural movement."

XXXIV. EVERYTHING WE WORSHIP IS JUST MATERIAL

"How base and putrid, every common matter is! Water, dust, and from the mixture of these bones, and all that loathsome stuff that our bodies do consist of: so subject to be infected, and corrupted. And again those other things that are so much prized and admired, as marble stones, what are they, but as it were the kernels of the earth? gold and silver, what are they, but as the more gross faeces of the earth? Thy most royal apparel, for matter, it is but as it were the hair of a silly sheep, and for colour, the very blood of a shell-fish; of this nature are all other things. Thy life itself, is some such thing too; a mere exhalation of blood: and it also, apt to be changed into some other common thing."

What Marcus meant (core philosophy)

Marcus strips away illusion by reducing admired objects to their basic physical components. Beauty, status symbols, and prized possessions lose their mystique when examined materially. This perspective prevents overattachment and vanity. Stoicism encourages detachment from external markers of value because they are transient and fundamentally ordinary. Meaning arises from how one lives, not from what one possesses or displays.

Dating translation (what this means emotionally/socially)

Dating culture often elevates superficial markers:

- status

- appearance
- lifestyle aesthetics
- perceived desirability.

Marcus invites radical realism. The person you idolize is still human. The image you chase is constructed. Attraction may feel magical, but beneath it are ordinary physical and psychological realities. This perspective reduces pedestal-building and helps you relate to others as equals rather than ideals. Dating maturity means appreciating attraction without becoming hypnotized by illusion.

Savage takeaway
The pedestal disappears when you see clearly.

Quiet power mantra
"I see reality beyond appearance."

XXXV. STOP COMPLAINING ABOUT WHAT IS NATURAL

"Will this querulousness, this murmuring, this complaining and dissembling never be at an end? What then is it, that troubleth thee? Doth any new thing happen unto thee? What doest thou so wonder at? At the cause, or the matter? Behold either by itself, is either of that weight and moment indeed? And besides these, there is not anything. But thy duty towards the Gods also, it is time thou shouldst acquit thyself of it with more goodness and simplicity."

What Marcus meant (core philosophy)
Marcus challenges habitual complaint. Most frustrations arise from expecting reality to behave differently than it naturally does. Nothing truly new is happening. Human patterns repeat endlessly.

Stoicism asks: is the situation genuinely extraordinary, or are you reacting as though it is? Complaining prolongs resistance. Acceptance restores simplicity.

Dating translation (what this means emotionally/socially)
Dating frustrations often feel uniquely unfair:
- ghosting
- mixed signals
- emotional unavailability
- mismatched expectations.

Marcus reminds you that these are not new phenomena. Humans have always struggled with connection, misunderstanding, and desire. Recognizing this reduces personal victimization. Dating maturity means shifting from "Why is this happening to me?" to "How do I respond wisely?"

Savage takeaway
You suffer less when you stop expecting humans to stop being human.

Quiet power mantra
"I meet reality without complaint."

XXXVI. TIME DOES NOT CHANGE THE NATURE OF THINGS
"It is all one to see these things for a hundred of years together or but for three years."

What Marcus meant (core philosophy)
Marcus emphasizes the repetitive nature of human experience.

Whether you observe life briefly or over a long span, the same patterns appear:
- desire
- conflict
- change
- growth
- decay.

Duration does not fundamentally alter reality. Human behavior and the nature of events remain consistent across time. Stoicism uses this perspective to reduce urgency and attachment. Seeing the recurring nature of events helps prevent overreacting to temporary moments.

Dating translation (what this means emotionally/socially)
In dating, people often believe their current situation is uniquely significant:
- "This is different from everything before."
- "This moment defines my future."

Marcus suggests stepping back. Relationship dynamics repeat across time:
- attraction cycles
- emotional highs and lows
- compatibility challenges.

Recognizing recurring patterns helps you avoid dramatizing present experiences. Dating maturity comes from recognizing patterns rather than getting lost in the illusion of novelty.

Savage takeaway
Your situation feels unique, but the pattern is ancient.

Quiet power mantra
"I see patterns clearly instead of dramatizing moments."

XXXVII. THEIR WRONGDOING BELONGS TO THEM
"If he have sinned, his is the harm, not mine. But perchance he hath not."

What Marcus meant (core philosophy)
Marcus highlights two essential principles:
- First, another person's wrongdoing harms their own character more than anyone else.
- Second, humility requires acknowledging that your interpretation might be incorrect.

Stoicism encourages emotional distance from others' actions while maintaining openness to alternative perspectives. This balance prevents both unnecessary resentment and premature judgment.

Dating translation (what this means emotionally/socially)

Dating often involves interpreting others' behavior quickly:

- assuming malicious intent
- labeling someone as toxic or harmful
- internalizing rejection as personal harm.

Marcus offers two stabilizing questions: If they acted poorly, that reflects their character, not your worth. And are you absolutely certain you understand their intent? Dating maturity means avoiding both extremes:

- overpersonalizing others' actions
- prematurely villainizing them.

Clarity requires space between observation and interpretation.

Savage takeaway

Their behavior reveals them, not you. And sometimes, you don't yet know the full story.

Quiet power mantra

"I release ownership of others' actions."

XXXVIII. WHETHER ORDER OR CHAOS, ACCEPT WHAT IS

"Either all things by the providence of reason happen unto every particular, as a part of one general body; and then it is against reason that a part should complain of anything that happens for the good of the whole; or if, according to Epicurus, atoms be the cause of all things and that life be nothing else but an accidentary confusion of things, and death nothing else, but a mere dispersion and so of all other things: what doest thou trouble thyself for?"

What Marcus meant (core philosophy)

Marcus returns to a recurring Stoic argument: Either the universe is guided by intelligent order, or it unfolds through random processes. In both cases, excessive distress is irrational.

- If existence is ordered, trust the larger system.
- If existence is random, worry accomplishes nothing.

Peace arises from accepting reality rather than resisting it.

Dating translation (what this means emotionally/socially)

Dating often generates endless questioning:

- Was this meant to happen?
- Why did this end?
- Is this fate or coincidence?

Marcus cuts through the loop. Regardless of whether events feel destined or accidental, your task remains the same:

- Respond with clarity.
- Act with integrity.
- Continue moving forward.

Obsessing over metaphysical explanations distracts from practical alignment.

Savage takeaway
Meaning is less important than how you choose to respond.

Quiet power mantra
"I accept reality without needing cosmic explanations."

XXXIX. THE RATIONAL MIND IS NOT DESTROYED BY CHANGE

"Sayest thou unto that rational part, Thou art dead; corruption hath taken hold on thee? Doth it then also void excrements? Doth it like either oxen, or sheep, graze or feed; that it also should be mortal, as well as the body?"

What Marcus meant (core philosophy)
Marcus distinguishes between the physical body and the rational mind. The body undergoes decay and biological processes, but the rational faculty represents a different dimension of human existence. He challenges fear of corruption by questioning whether the essential rational self is truly harmed by physical change. Stoicism emphasizes that identity rooted in reason remains stable even as external conditions shift.

Dating translation (what this means emotionally/socially)
In dating, people often equate emotional pain or rejection with personal damage:
- "This broke me."
- "I'm ruined after this."

Marcus would argue that external experiences do not destroy your rational core. Heartbreak affects emotion, but it does not erase your ability to think clearly, grow, or choose wisely moving forward. Dating maturity involves separating temporary emotional states from permanent identity. You are not diminished by experiences that challenge you.

Savage takeaway
Your core self isn't damaged just because your feelings are.

Quiet power mantra
"My rational self remains intact."

XL. PRAY FOR FREEDOM FROM ATTACHMENT, NOT FOR CONTROL

"Either the Gods can do nothing for us at all, or they can still and allay all the distractions and distempers of thy mind. If they can do nothing, why doest thou pray? If they can, why wouldst not thou rather pray, that they will grant unto thee, that thou mayst neither fear, nor lust after any of those worldly things which cause these distractions and distempers of it? Why not rather, that thou mayst not at either their absence or presence, be grieved and discontented: than either that thou mayst obtain them, or that thou mayst avoid them? For certainly it must needs be, that if the Gods can help us in anything, they may in this kind also. But thou wilt say perchance, 'In those things the Gods have given me my liberty: and it is in mine own power to do what I will.' But if thou mayst use this liberty, rather to set thy mind at true liberty, than wilfully with baseness and servility of mind to affect those things, which either to compass or to avoid is not in thy power, wert not thou better? And as for the Gods, who hath told thee,

that they may not help us up even in those things that they have put in our own power? whether it be so or no, thou shalt soon perceive, if thou wilt but try thyself and pray. One prayeth that he may compass his desire, to lie with such or such a one, pray thou that thou mayst not lust to lie with her. Another how he may be rid of such a one; pray thou that thou mayst so patiently bear with him, as that thou have no such need to be rid of him. Another, that he may not lose his child. Pray thou that thou mayst not fear to lose him. To this end and purpose, let all thy prayer be, and see what will be the event."

What Marcus meant (core philosophy)

Marcus shifts the focus of desire. Instead of asking for external outcomes, ask for internal freedom. Stoicism teaches that suffering arises from attachment to what is outside our control. Fear and craving create emotional turbulence. True liberation comes not from securing or avoiding external things but from loosening their grip on the mind. The wise person seeks mastery over reaction rather than mastery over circumstance. Freedom is internal independence.

Dating translation (what this means emotionally/socially)

In dating, most people wish for outcomes:

- "Let them choose me."
- "Let this work out."
- "Let this person change."
- "Let me avoid rejection."

Marcus would redirect these desires. Wish instead for:

- clarity instead of obsession
- emotional steadiness instead of anxiety
- freedom from needing validation.

The deepest power in dating is not securing the relationship but remaining internally stable whether it appears or disappears. When attachment loosens, connection becomes more authentic because it is no longer driven by fear or desperation.

Savage takeaway

Stop wishing for outcomes. Start wishing for freedom from needing them.

Quiet power mantra

"I release attachment to what I cannot control."

XLI. KEEP YOUR MIND STEADY EVEN WHEN THE BODY OR WORLD IS DISTURBED

'In my sickness' (saith Epicurus of himself:) 'my discourses were not concerning the nature of my disease, neither was that, to them that came to visit me, the subject of my talk; but in the consideration and contemplation of that, which was of especial weight and moment, was all my time bestowed and spent and among others in this very thing, how my mind, by a natural and unavoidable sympathy partaking in some sort with the present indisposition of my body, might nevertheless keep herself free from trouble, and in present possession of her own proper happiness. Neither did I leave the ordering of my body to the physicians altogether to do with me what they would, as though I expected any great matter from them, or as though I thought it a matter of such great consequence, by their means to recover my health: for my

present estate, methought, liked me very well, and gave me good content.' Whether therefore in sickness (if thou chance to sicken) or in what other kind of extremity soever, endeavour thou also to be in thy mind so affected, as he doth report of himself: not to depart from thy philosophy for anything that can befall thee, nor to give ear to the discourses of silly people, and mere naturalists.

What Marcus meant (core philosophy)

Marcus praises emotional sovereignty. Even when the body suffers or circumstances become difficult, the rational mind can remain grounded and content. External discomfort does not require internal disturbance. Stoicism encourages maintaining philosophical alignment regardless of situation. True stability lies in refusing to abandon clarity when challenged. Wisdom is consistency under pressure.

Dating translation (what this means emotionally/socially)

Dating emotional highs and lows often destabilize people:
- anxiety during uncertainty
- emotional pain after rejection
- excitement turning into loss of self-control.

Marcus reminds you that emotional experience does not require losing internal balance. You can feel deeply while remaining anchored. Dating maturity means:
- staying aligned with your values even when emotions surge
- not abandoning your standards because attraction feels intense
- maintaining self-possession during emotional storms.

Your emotional state may fluctuate, but your core clarity does not need to.

Savage takeaway

Strong feelings are not permission to abandon your principles.

Quiet power mantra

"My clarity remains steady through every emotional season."

XLII. GIVE FULL ATTENTION TO WHAT IS BEFORE YOU

"It is common to all trades and professions to mind and intend that only, which now they are about, and the instrument whereby they work."

What Marcus meant (core philosophy)

Marcus highlights disciplined presence. Every craft requires focused attention on the task at hand. Mastery comes from directing energy toward what is currently being done rather than scattering attention across past regrets or future anxieties. Stoicism teaches that clarity emerges when the mind stops wandering and commits fully to present action. Distraction weakens effectiveness. Presence strengthens it.

Dating translation (what this means emotionally/socially)

Dating anxiety often comes from mental time travel:
- replaying past relationships
- anticipating future outcomes
- overthinking where things are going instead of experiencing where they are.

Marcus suggests a simpler approach: Focus on what is happening now.
- Are you communicating honestly?
- Are you observing clearly?
- Are you responding thoughtfully?

Dating maturity means engaging fully in the present interaction rather than projecting narratives onto it. Connection grows through attention, not anticipation.

Savage takeaway
You lose clarity when you date the future instead of the person in front of you.

Quiet power mantra
"I give my full attention to what is present."

XLIII. EXPECT HUMAN NATURE AND RESPOND WITH VIRTUE

"When at any time thou art offended with any one's impudency, put presently this question to thyself: 'What? Is it then possible, that there should not be any impudent men in the world! Certainly it is not possible.' Desire not then that which is impossible. For this one, (thou must think) whosoever he be, is one of those impudent ones, that the world cannot be without. So of the subtile and crafty, so of the perfidious, so of every one that offendeth, must thou ever be ready to reason with thyself. For whilst in general thou dost thus reason with thyself, that the kind of them must needs be in the world, thou wilt be the better able to use meekness towards every particular. This also thou shalt find of very good use, upon every such occasion, presently to consider with thyself, what proper virtue nature hath furnished man with, against such a vice, or to encounter with a disposition vicious in this kind. As for example, against the unthankful, it hath given goodness and meekness, as an antidote, and so against another vicious in another kind some other peculiar faculty. And generally, is it not in thy power to instruct him better, that is in an error? For whosoever sinneth, doth in that decline from his purposed end, and is certainly deceived, And again, what art thou the worse for his sin? For thou shalt not find that any one of these, against whom thou art incensed, hath in very deed done anything whereby thy mind (the only true subject of thy hurt and evil) can be made worse than it was. And what a matter of either grief or wonder is this, if he that is unlearned, do the deeds of one that is unlearned? Should not thou rather blame thyself, who, when upon very good grounds of reason, thou mightst have thought it very probable, that such a thing would by such a one be committed, didst not only not foresee it, but moreover dost wonder at it, that such a thing should be. But then especially, when thou dost find fault with either an unthankful, or a false man, must thou reflect upon thyself. For without all question, thou thyself art much in fault, if either of one that were of such a disposition, thou didst expect that he should be true unto thee: or when unto any thou didst a good turn, thou didst not there bound thy thoughts, as one that had obtained his end; nor didst not think that from the action itself thou hadst received a full reward of the good that thou hadst done. For what wouldst thou have more? Unto him that is a man, thou hast done a good turn: doth not that suffice thee? What thy nature required, that hast thou done. Must thou be rewarded for it? As if either the eye for that it seeth, or the feet that they go, should require satisfaction. For as these being by nature appointed for such an use, can challenge no more, than that they may work according to their natural constitution: so man being born to do good unto others whensoever he doth a real good unto any by helping them out of error; or though but in middle things, as in matter of wealth, life, preferment, and the like, doth help to further their desires he doth that for which he was made, and therefore can require no more."

What Marcus meant (core philosophy)

Marcus teaches radical acceptance of human nature. Impudent, selfish, deceitful, or flawed people exist because humanity contains a range of character types. Expecting a world without difficult personalities creates unnecessary frustration. Wisdom lies in:

- anticipating imperfection
- responding with appropriate virtue
- avoiding shock at predictable behavior.

He also emphasizes that helping others is its own reward. Acting virtuously fulfills your nature regardless of how others respond. Expectation of external reward creates disappointment.

Dating translation (what this means emotionally/socially)

Dating frustration often comes from expecting people to behave ideally:

- expecting emotional maturity where there is none
- expecting honesty from someone who has shown inconsistency
- expecting gratitude for kindness.

Marcus offers a powerful shift: If someone repeatedly demonstrates a trait, believe it and adjust expectations. Instead of reacting with outrage each time, recognize that human variety includes immaturity, avoidance, and imperfection. Dating maturity means:

- seeing clearly who someone is
- adjusting your behavior accordingly
- offering kindness without attachment to outcome.

Also, when you act with integrity, that action itself is complete. You do not need external validation for behaving well.

Savage takeaway

You suffer less when you stop being surprised by predictable behavior.

Quiet power mantra

"I respond with virtue, not expectation."

THE TENTH BOOK
Stop Performing For Approval

I. TRUE CONTENTMENT IS INNER SUFFICIENCY

"O my soul, the time I trust will be, when thou shalt be good, simple, single, more open and visible, than that body by which it is enclosed. Thou wilt one day be sensible of their happiness, whose end is love, and their affections dead to all worldly things. Thou shalt one day be full, and in want of no external thing: not seeking pleasure from anything, either living or insensible, that this world can afford; neither wanting time for the continuation of thy pleasure, nor place and opportunity, nor the favour either of the weather or of men. When thou shalt have content in thy present estate, and all things present shall add to thy content: when thou shalt persuade thyself, that thou hast all things; all for thy good, and all by the providence of the Gods: and of things future also shalt be as confident, that all will do well, as tending to the maintenance and preservation in some sort, of his perfect welfare and happiness, who is perfection of life, of goodness, and beauty; who begets all things, and containeth all things in himself, and in himself doth recollect all things from all places that are dissolved, that of them he may beget others again like unto them. Such one day shall be thy disposition, that thou shalt be able, both in regard of the Gods, and in regard of men, so to fit and order thy conversation, as neither to complain of them at any time, for anything that they do; nor to do anything thyself, for which thou mayest justly be condemned."

What Marcus meant (core philosophy)

Marcus describes the evolution of the soul toward simplicity and sufficiency. True peace comes when the mind no longer depends on external circumstances for satisfaction. Contentment arises from alignment with nature and acceptance of what exists now. The Stoic ideal is internal fullness:

- not needing external validation
- not chasing pleasure for completion
- trusting that events unfold within a larger order.

Freedom emerges when desire quiets and presence becomes enough.

Dating translation (what this means emotionally/socially)

Dating often begins from lack:

- needing validation
- seeking emotional completion
- chasing someone to fill an internal gap.

Marcus describes a different starting point. Dating from internal sufficiency changes everything:

- you do not chase approval
- you do not fear being alone
- connection becomes exploration rather than survival.

When you feel internally whole, relationships become partnerships rather than rescue missions. Dating maturity means arriving as someone who already feels complete enough.

276

Savage takeaway
The moment you stop needing someone to complete you is the moment you become capable of real connection.

Quiet power mantra
"I am internally full before I reach outward."

II. FOLLOW YOUR NATURE IN LAYERS
"As one who is altogether governed by nature, let it be thy care to observe what it is that thy nature in general doth require. That done, if thou find not that thy nature, as thou art a living sensible creature, will be the worse for it, thou mayest proceed. Next then thou must examine, what thy nature as thou art a living sensible creature, doth require. And that, whatsoever it be, thou mayest admit of and do it, if thy nature as thou art a reasonable living creature, will not be the worse for it. Now whatsoever is reasonable, is also sociable, Keep thyself to these rules, and trouble not thyself about idle things."

What Marcus meant (core philosophy)
Marcus outlines a hierarchy of decision-making:
1. Act according to human nature.
2. Ensure actions do not harm your emotional or physical well-being.
3. Ensure actions align with reason and social harmony.

Reason acts as the final filter. Not everything that feels good is aligned with wisdom. Stoicism encourages layered evaluation rather than impulsive reaction.

Dating translation (what this means emotionally/socially)
Dating decisions often happen in reverse:
- emotional impulse first
- rational reflection later.

Marcus suggests a better process:
- Does this align with my nature as a human seeking connection?
- Does it support my well-being?
- Does it remain consistent with reason and integrity?

Attraction alone is not enough. Emotional desire must pass through rational clarity. Dating maturity means balancing instinct with discernment.

Savage takeaway
Just because it feels good doesn't mean it aligns with who you are becoming.

Quiet power mantra
"I choose what aligns with both feeling and reason."

III. YOU ARE STRONGER THAN YOU THINK
"Whatsoever doth happen unto thee, thou art naturally by thy natural constitution either able, or not able to bear. If thou beest able, be not offended, but bear it according to thy natural constitution, or as nature hath enabled thee. If thou beest not able, be not offended. For it will soon make an end of thee, and itself, (whatsoever it be) at the same time end with thee. But remember, that whatsoever by the strength of opinion, grounded upon a certain apprehension of both true profit and duty, thou canst conceive tolerable; that thou art able to bear that by thy natural constitution."

277

What Marcus meant (core philosophy)

Marcus argues that human beings possess natural resilience. If something happens, one of two things is true: you are capable of enduring it or it will end alongside your capacity. Much suffering comes from believing we cannot handle what we are actually equipped to survive. Stoicism emphasizes reframing perception. When the mind recognizes purpose or duty, tolerance expands.

Dating translation (what this means emotionally/socially)

Dating pain often feels unbearable:
- Rejection
- Uncertainty
- Emotional vulnerability.

Marcus reminds you: If you are experiencing it, you already possess the capacity to endure it. Your belief about your resilience shapes your actual resilience. When you view experiences as meaningful growth rather than catastrophic harm, your ability to hold them increases. Dating maturity includes trusting your emotional durability.

Savage takeaway

You are not fragile. You have survived every emotional experience so far.

Quiet power mantra

"I am capable of bearing what comes."

IV. CORRECT WITH KINDNESS, RELEASE WHAT YOU CANNOT CHANGE

"Him that offends, to teach with love and meekness, and to show him his error. But if thou canst not, then to blame thyself; or rather not thyself neither, if thy will and endeavours have not been wanting."

What Marcus meant (core philosophy)

Marcus proposes a clear ethical approach toward others' mistakes:
- first, guide with patience and gentleness
- second, accept when change is not possible.

Stoicism rejects harsh correction driven by ego. Instruction should come from goodwill, not superiority. However, Marcus also warns against unnecessary self-blame. If you have acted with sincerity and effort, you are not responsible for whether the other person learns. Wisdom includes knowing when influence ends.

Dating translation (what this means emotionally/socially)

Dating often creates the impulse to fix or reshape someone:
- explaining repeatedly
- hoping insight will change behavior
- believing love or clarity will transform them.

Marcus reframes this: Offer clarity once, with kindness. If they cannot receive it, release responsibility. Dating maturity means recognizing the difference between communication and control. You are responsible for honest expression, not for someone else's evolution.

Savage takeaway
Your job is to communicate clearly, not to convert someone into who you wish they were.

Quiet power mantra
"I offer truth gently and release the outcome."

V. NOTHING THAT HAPPENS IS RANDOM TO YOUR LIFE
"Whatsoever it be that happens unto thee, it is that which from all time was appointed unto thee. For by the same coherence of causes, by which thy substance from all eternity was appointed to be, was also whatsoever should happen unto it, destinated and appointed."

What Marcus meant (core philosophy)
Marcus expresses the Stoic idea of interconnected causality. Everything unfolds through a chain of events linked to prior causes. Your experiences are not isolated accidents but part of a larger unfolding. Stoicism encourages acceptance not as passivity but as alignment with reality. Resistance to what has already occurred creates suffering. Acceptance restores balance.

Dating translation (what this means emotionally/socially)
Dating experiences often feel unfair or confusing:
- meeting someone at the wrong time
- connections ending unexpectedly
- lessons arriving through painful dynamics.

Marcus invites you to see experiences as part of your development rather than interruptions to it. Whether viewed as destiny or cause-and-effect, every interaction shapes who you become. Dating maturity includes trusting that experiences contribute to growth even when their purpose is not immediately clear.

Savage takeaway
Stop asking why it happened. Start asking how it shaped you.

Quiet power mantra
"I accept what arrives as part of my unfolding."

VI. YOU ARE PART OF THE WHOLE, NOT SEPARATE FROM IT
"Either with Epicurus[70], we must fondly imagine the atoms to be the cause of all things, or we must needs grant a nature. Let this then be thy first ground, that thou art part of that universe, which is governed by nature. Then secondly, that to those parts that are of the same kind and nature as thou art, thou hast relation of kindred. For of these, if I shall always be mindful, first as I am a part, I shall never be displeased with anything, that falls to my particular share of the common chances of the world. For nothing that is behoveful unto the whole, can be truly hurtful to that which is part of it. For this being the common privilege of all natures, that they contain nothing in themselves that is hurtful unto them; it

---

[70] Epicurus (341–270 BC) was the founder of Epicureanism, a school often viewed as the "rival" to Stoicism. While Stoics prioritized virtue, Epicureans prioritized the absence of pain (*ataraxia*).

cannot be that the nature of the universe (whose privilege beyond other particular natures, is, that she cannot against her will by any higher external cause be constrained,) should beget anything and cherish it in her bosom that should tend to her own hurt and prejudice. As then I bear in mind that I am a part of such an universe, I shall not be displeased with anything that happens. And as I have relation of kindred to those parts that are of the same kind and nature that I am, so I shall be careful to do nothing that is prejudicial to the community, but in all my deliberations shall they that are of my kind ever be; and the common good, that, which all my intentions and resolutions shall drive unto, as that which is contrary unto it, I shall by all means endeavour to prevent and avoid. These things once so fixed and concluded, as thou wouldst think him a happy citizen, whose constant study and practice were for the good and benefit of his fellow citizens, and the carriage of the city such towards him, that he were well pleased with it; so must it needs be with thee, that thou shalt live a happy life."

What Marcus meant (core philosophy)
Marcus emphasizes belonging within a larger system. You are not separate from the universe or from other people. You are a part within a greater whole. Two insights follow:
- What benefits the whole cannot truly harm its parts.
- Ethical living involves contributing to collective harmony.

Stoicism encourages seeing oneself as a citizen of a shared reality rather than an isolated individual.

Dating translation (what this means emotionally/socially)
Dating often becomes hyper-individualistic:
- focusing only on personal gain
- treating relationships as transactions
- viewing others as competitors or obstacles.

Marcus encourages a relational mindset. Healthy connection arises when both individuals consider the shared space between them. Dating maturity means:
- acting in ways that support mutual well-being
- considering how choices affect the relational ecosystem
- valuing cooperation over domination.

When you approach relationships from shared humanity rather than self-centered strategy, connection becomes more stable and meaningful.

Savage takeaway
Relationships fail when you treat them as battles instead of shared systems.

Quiet power mantra
"I act as part of something larger than myself."

VII. CHANGE IS NOT LOSS, IT IS CONTINUATION
"All parts of the world, (all things I mean that are contained within the whole world), must of necessity at some time or other come to corruption. Alteration I should say, to speak truly and properly; but that I may be the better understood, I am content at this time to use that more common word. Now say I, if so be that this be both hurtful unto them, and yet unavoidable, would not, thinkest thou, the whole itself be in a sweet case, all the parts of it being subject to alteration, yea and by their making itself fitted for

corruption, as consisting of things different and contrary? And did nature then either of herself thus project and purpose the affliction and misery of her parts, and therefore of purpose so made them, not only that haply they might, but of necessity that they should fall into evil; or did not she know what she did, when she made them? For either of these two to say, is equally absurd. But to let pass nature in general, and to reason of things particular according to their own particular natures; how absurd and ridiculous is it, first to say that all parts of the whole are, by their proper natural constitution, subject to alteration; and then when any such thing doth happen, as when one doth fall sick and dieth, to take on and wonder as though some strange thing had happened? Though this besides might move not so grievously to take on when any such thing doth happen, that whatsoever is dissolved, it is dissolved into those things, whereof it was compounded. For every dissolution is either a mere dispersion, of the elements into those elements again whereof everything did consist, or a change, of that which is more solid into earth; and of that which is pure and subtile or spiritual, into air. So that by this means nothing is lost, but all resumed again into those rational generative seeds of the universe; and this universe, either after a certain period of time to lie consumed by fire, or by continual changes to be renewed, and so for ever to endure. Now that solid and spiritual that we speak of, thou must not conceive it to be that very same, which at first was, when thou wert born. For alas! all this that now thou art in either kind, either for matter of substance, or of life, hath but two or three days ago partly from meats eaten, and partly from air breathed in, received all its influx, being the same then in no other respect, than a running river, maintained by the perpetual influx and new supply of waters, is the same. That therefore which thou hast since received, not that which came from thy mother, is that which comes to change and corruption. But suppose that that for the general substance, and more solid part of it, should still cleave unto thee never so close, yet what is that to the proper qualities and affections of it, by which persons are distinguished, which certainly are quite different?"

What Marcus meant (core philosophy)

Marcus dismantles the fear of change by reframing it as natural transformation rather than destruction. Nothing truly disappears. Everything changes form, dissolving into its elements and re-entering the ongoing process of existence. The mistake humans make is expecting permanence from a system built on movement. He also emphasizes identity as fluid. The physical and experiential components of a person are constantly renewing, like a river fed by new waters. Stoicism teaches that resisting change creates unnecessary suffering because change is the fundamental structure of reality.

Dating translation (what this means emotionally/socially)

Dating often feels like loss when relationships end or evolve:

- "I lost them."
- "I lost what we had."
- "I lost who I was with them."

Marcus reframes this. Nothing is truly lost. It changes form:

- connection becomes memory
- lessons become growth
- identity evolves through experience.

Even your own self is continuously changing. The person you were when a relationship began is not the same person now. Dating maturity means accepting transformation without clinging to earlier versions of yourself or others. You are not meant to stay static.

Savage takeaway
You didn't lose it. It transformed, and so did you.

Quiet power mantra
"I move with change instead of mourning permanence."

VIII. BECOME WHO YOU CLAIM TO BE

"Now that thou hast taken these names upon thee of good, modest, true; of ἔμφρων[71], σύμφρων[72], ὑπέρφρων[73]; take heed lest at any times by doing anything that is contrary, thou be but improperly so called, and lose thy right to these appellations. Or if thou do, return unto them again with all possible speed. And remember, that the word ἔμφρων notes unto thee an intent and intelligent consideration of every object that presents itself unto thee, without distraction. And the word σύμφρων, a ready and contented acceptation of whatsoever by the appointment of the common nature, happens unto thee. And the word ὑπέρφρων, a super-extension, or a transcendent, and outreaching disposition of thy mind, whereby it passeth by all bodily pains and pleasures, honour and credit, death and whatsoever is of the same nature, as matters of absolute indifferency, and in no wise to be stood upon by a wise man. These then if inviolably thou shalt observe, and shalt not be ambitious to be so called by others, both thou thyself shalt become a new man, and thou shalt begin a new life. For to continue such as hitherto thou hast been, to undergo those distractions and distempers as thou must needs for such a life as hitherto thou hast lived, is the part of one that is very foolish, and is overfond of his life. Whom a man might compare to one of those half-eaten wretches, matched in the amphitheatre with wild beasts; who as full as they are all the body over with wounds and blood, desire for a great favour, that they may be reserved till the next day, then also, and in the same estate to be exposed to the same nails and teeth as before. Away therefore, ship thyself; and from the troubles and distractions of thy former life convey thyself as it were unto these few names; and if thou canst abide in them, or be constant in the practice and possession of them, continue there as glad and joyful as one that were translated unto some such place of bliss and happiness as that which by Hesiod and Plato is called the Islands of the Blessed, by others called the Elysian Fields. And whensoever thou findest thyself; that thou art in danger of a relapse, and that thou art not able to master and overcome those difficulties and temptations that present themselves in thy present station: get thee into any private corner, where thou mayst be better able. Or if that will not serve forsake even thy life rather. But so that it be not in passion but in a plain voluntary modest way: this being the only commendable action of thy whole life that thus thou art departed, or this having been the main work and business of thy whole life, that thou mightest thus depart. Now for the better remembrance of those names that we have spoken of, thou shalt find it a very good help, to remember the Gods as often as may be: and that, the thing which they require at our hands of as many of us, as are by nature reasonable creation is not that with fair words, and outward show of piety and devotion we should flatter them, but that we should become like unto them: and that as all other natural creatures, the fig tree for example; the dog the bee: both do, all of them, and apply themselves unto that which by their natural constitution, is proper unto them; so man likewise should do that, which by his nature, as he is a man, belongs unto him."

What Marcus meant (core philosophy)
Marcus focuses on identity as practice rather than label. If you claim virtues such as wisdom, clarity, and discipline, your actions must align with them. Otherwise, the title becomes empty. He defines three core qualities:

---

[71] In Greek, ἔμφρων (*émphrōn*) translates to "sensible," "prudent," or "in one's right mind."
[72] In Greek, σύμφρων (*sýmphrōn*) translates to "of one mind," "concurring," or "harmonious."
[73] In Greek, ὑπέρφρων (*hypérphrōn*) means "arrogant," "haughty," or "high-minded."

282

- ἔμφρων: thoughtful awareness and attentive perception.
- σύμφρων: willing acceptance of what happens according to nature.
- ὑπέρφρων: transcendence over external highs and lows.

The aim is not to be seen as virtuous but to embody virtue consistently. Transformation requires leaving old patterns behind. Clinging to familiar suffering is compared to willingly returning to harm.

Stoicism demands self-honesty: become what you claim to value.

Dating translation (what this means emotionally/socially)
Dating often involves identity statements:
- "I have strong boundaries."
- "I value honesty."
- "I want something healthy."

Marcus would ask: do your actions reflect these claims? Embodied alignment looks like:
- noticing behavior clearly instead of romanticizing it (ἔμφρων)
- accepting reality instead of resisting it (σύμφρων)
- not being controlled by attraction, validation, or fear (ὑπέρφρων).

Dating maturity means becoming the person you say you are, especially when it is inconvenient. Leaving old patterns may feel uncomfortable, but returning to them knowingly is self-betrayal.

Savage takeaway
You are not defined by what you say you value, but by what you consistently choose.

Quiet power mantra
"I live the values I claim."

IX. DO NOT LET YOUR MIND DRIFT INTO UNCONSCIOUS LIVING

"Toys and fooleries at home, wars abroad: sometimes terror, sometimes torpor, or stupid sloth: this is thy daily slavery. By little and little, if thou doest not better look to it, those sacred dogmata will be blotted out of thy mind. How many things be there, which when as a mere naturalist, thou hast barely considered of according to their nature, thou doest let pass without any further use? Whereas thou shouldst in all things so join action and contemplation, that thou mightest both at the same time attend all present occasions, to perform everything duly and carefully and yet so intend the contemplative part too, that no part of that delight and pleasure, which the contemplative knowledge of everything according to its true nature doth of itself afford, might be lost. Or, that the true and contemplative knowledge of everything according to its own nature, might of itself, (action being subject to many lets and impediments) afford unto thee sufficient pleasure and happiness. Not apparent indeed, but not concealed. And when shalt thou attain to the happiness of true simplicity, and unaffected gravity? When shalt thou rejoice in the certain knowledge of every particular object according to its true nature: as what the matter and substance of it is; what use it is for in the world: how long it can subsist: what things it doth consist of: who they be that are capable of it, and who they that can give it, and take it away?"

What Marcus meant (core philosophy)

Marcus warns about mental drift. Daily distractions, emotional swings, and unconscious habits slowly erode philosophical clarity if left unchecked. Wisdom requires joining two modes:

- action (engaging fully with life)
- contemplation (understanding the nature of things).

True simplicity comes from seeing reality clearly:

- what something actually is
- how long it lasts
- what purpose it serves.

Stoicism encourages disciplined awareness. Without it, the mind slips back into confusion and reactivity.

Dating translation (what this means emotionally/socially)

Dating becomes chaotic when you operate on autopilot:

- chasing excitement without reflection
- repeating patterns without learning
- reacting emotionally without understanding dynamics.

Marcus suggests integrating observation with participation. While dating:

- notice behavior patterns
- understand emotional triggers
- recognize the lifespan and nature of situations.

Clarity transforms experience. You stop being swept away by emotional drama and begin understanding what is actually happening. Dating maturity means being both participant and observer.

Savage takeaway

If you don't consciously examine your patterns, you unconsciously repeat them.

Quiet power mantra

"I act fully while seeing clearly."

X. MOST PEOPLE ARE JUST HUNTING SOMETHING

"As the spider, when it hath caught the fly that it hunted after, is not little proud, nor meanly conceited of herself: as he likewise that hath caught an hare, or hath taken a fish with his net: as another for the taking of a boar, and another of a bear: so may they be proud, and applaud themselves for their valiant acts against the Sarmatai, or northern nations lately defeated. For these also, these famous soldiers and warlike men, if thou dost look into their minds and opinions, what do they for the most part but hunt after prey?"

What Marcus meant (core philosophy)

Marcus reduces human ambition to pursuit behavior. Many achievements that appear grand or heroic are driven by the same instinctual chase:

- acquisition
- conquest
- status.

By recognizing this, he strips away illusion and encourages perspective. Much of what people celebrate is simply the satisfaction of desire. Stoicism teaches detachment from external applause and comparison.

Dating translation (what this means emotionally/socially)
In dating, people often pursue:
- attention
- validation
- ego boosts
- status through association.

What looks like romance may sometimes be pursuit for the sake of winning rather than genuine connection. Understanding this helps you:
- avoid mistaking chase energy for emotional depth
- recognize when someone values the conquest more than the relationship.

Dating maturity means distinguishing between attraction rooted in curiosity versus attraction rooted in ego-driven pursuit.

Savage takeaway
Not everyone chasing you wants you. Some just want the win.

Quiet power mantra
"I see the difference between connection and conquest."

XI. CONTEMPLATE CONSTANT CHANGE TO BUILD TRUE STRENGTH
"To find out, and set to thyself some certain way and method of contemplation, whereby thou mayest clearly discern and represent unto thyself, the mutual change of all things, the one into the other. Bear it in thy mind evermore, and see that thou be thoroughly well exercised in this particular. For there is not anything more effectual to beget true magnanimity."

What Marcus meant (core philosophy)
Marcus advises deliberate contemplation of transformation. Observing how everything changes into something else builds perspective and emotional resilience. Magnanimity, or greatness of soul, comes from understanding impermanence:
- beginnings become endings
- endings become beginnings.

Recognizing constant transformation prevents attachment to temporary states.

Dating translation (what this means emotionally/socially)
Dating often feels overwhelming because moments are treated as permanent:
- early excitement feels eternal
- conflict feels catastrophic
- endings feel final.

Marcus encourages remembering that all stages evolve. Understanding the fluid nature of relationships creates emotional steadiness:

- attraction evolves
- dynamics shift
- people grow or separate.

Dating maturity means holding experiences lightly without diminishing their meaning. You can fully engage while knowing everything moves.

Savage takeaway
Nothing stays the same long enough to justify panic.

Quiet power mantra
"I stay steady because I understand change."

XII. WALK STRAIGHT AND IGNORE THE NOISE

"He hath got loose from the bonds of his body, and perceiving that within a very little while he must of necessity bid the world farewell, and leave all these things behind him, he wholly applied himself, as to righteousness in all his actions, so to the common nature in all things that should happen unto him. And contenting himself with these two things, to do all things justly, and whatsoever God doth send to like well of it: what others shall either say or think of him, or shall do against him, he doth not so much as trouble his thoughts with it. To go on straight, whither right and reason directed him, and by so doing to follow God, was the only thing that he did mind, that, his only business and occupation."

What Marcus meant (core philosophy)
Marcus defines radical simplicity of purpose:
- act justly
- accept what happens.

Everything else is noise. When you recognize life's brevity, reputation, judgment, and external interference lose importance. The only true work is alignment with reason and virtue. Stoicism strips life down to essential priorities: Right action. Acceptance. Forward movement.

Dating translation (what this means emotionally/socially)
Dating becomes exhausting when attention shifts to:
- what others think of your choices
- how you appear
- whether you are winning or losing socially.

Marcus offers clarity. Focus on:
- behaving with integrity
- accepting outcomes without resistance.

When you stop managing perception and start walking straight according to your values, dating becomes dramatically simpler. Dating maturity means less performance and more alignment.

Savage takeaway
Your path gets clearer when you stop caring who is watching.

Quiet power mantra
"I walk straight regardless of opinion."

XIII. DROP SUSPICION AND MOVE WITH CLARITY

"What use is there of suspicion at all? or, why should thoughts of mistrust, and suspicion concerning that which is future, trouble thy mind at all? What now is to be done, if thou mayest search and inquiry into that, what needs thou care for more? And if thou art well able to perceive it alone, let no man divert thee from it. But if alone thou doest not so well perceive it, suspend thine action, and take advice from the best. And if there be anything else that doth hinder thee, go on with prudence and discretion, according to the present occasion and opportunity, still proposing that unto thyself, which thou doest conceive most right and just. For to hit that aright, and to speed in the prosecution of it, must needs be happiness, since it is that only which we can truly and properly be said to miss of, or miscarry in."

What Marcus meant (core philosophy)
Marcus discourages unnecessary suspicion and future-focused anxiety. Instead:
- investigate clearly what can be known now
- act based on reason
- seek guidance when clarity is lacking.

The focus is not perfect certainty but correct intention. Happiness lies in acting justly, not controlling outcomes.

Dating translation (what this means emotionally/socially)
Dating overthinking often sounds like:
- "What if they're lying?"
- "What if this goes wrong later?"
- "What if I misread everything?"

Marcus suggests replacing suspicion with process:
- Observe reality.
- Gather information.
- Act according to your best understanding.

If you lack clarity, pause rather than spiral. Dating maturity means choosing clarity over paranoia.

Savage takeaway
Suspicion is not intuition. Clear observation is.

Quiet power mantra
"I act on clarity, not imagined futures."

XIV. TRUE BALANCE IS REASON GUIDING EVERYTHING

"What is that that is slow, and yet quick? merry, and yet grave? He that in all things doth follow reason for his guide."

What Marcus meant (core philosophy)
Marcus describes the paradoxical nature of wisdom. A rational person moves:
- quickly when needed
- patiently when required
- with joy and seriousness simultaneously.

Reason creates flexibility rather than rigidity. Emotional extremes settle into balanced responsiveness. Stoicism is not coldness but integrated stability.

(no title)

Dating translation (what this means emotionally/socially)
Healthy dating energy often feels contradictory:
- emotionally open yet grounded
- excited yet calm
- interested yet unattached.

Reason allows you to adjust without losing center. Dating maturity means responding appropriately instead of reacting impulsively. You become adaptable without becoming unstable.

Savage takeaway
Balance isn't neutrality. It's intelligent responsiveness.

Quiet power mantra
"I let reason guide my pace and response."

XV. DO WHAT IS RIGHT WITHOUT SEEKING APPLAUSE
"In the morning as soon as thou art awaked, when thy judgment, before either thy affections, or external objects have wrought upon it, is yet most free and impartial: put this question to thyself, whether if that which is right and just be done, the doing of it by thyself, or by others when thou art not able thyself; be a thing material or no. For sure it is not. And as for these that keep such a life, and stand so much upon the praises, or dispraises of other men, hast thou forgotten what manner of men they be? that such and such upon their beds, and such at their board: what their ordinary actions are: what they pursue after, and what they fly from: what thefts and rapines they commit, if not with their hands and feet, yet with that more precious part of theirs, their minds: which (would it but admit of them) might enjoy faith, modesty, truth, justice, a good spirit."

What Marcus meant (core philosophy)
Marcus advises beginning each day with alignment to justice rather than ego. Right action matters regardless of:
- who performs it
- who witnesses it
- who praises or criticizes it.

He also dismantles the authority of public opinion by reminding us that those judging are flawed themselves. Stoicism removes dependence on validation.

Dating translation (what this means emotionally/socially)
Dating decisions often become influenced by external approval:
- friends' opinions
- social media perception
- fear of judgment.

Marcus suggests returning to one question: Is this action aligned with integrity? Not:
- Will people approve?
- Will I look successful?

Dating maturity means acting according to your values even when it contradicts external narratives.

Savage takeaway
The crowd judging your choices is rarely living with integrity themselves.

Quiet power mantra
"I do what is right, not what is applauded."

XVI. ACCEPT WHAT COMES AND GOES WITHOUT RESISTANCE
"Give what thou wilt, and take away what thou wilt, saith he that is well taught and truly modest, to Him that gives, and takes away. And it is not out of a stout and peremptory resolution, that he saith it, but in mere love, and humble submission."

What Marcus meant (core philosophy)
Marcus describes acceptance without bitterness. True strength is not rigid resistance but calm willingness to receive and release whatever life presents. This acceptance comes not from defeat but from trust in the natural order. Stoicism teaches that peace emerges when attachment softens. The wise person does not cling to gains or resent losses. Humility replaces control.

Dating translation (what this means emotionally/socially)
Dating becomes painful when you grip tightly:
- trying to force outcomes
- resisting endings
- clinging to expectations.

Marcus encourages a softer posture:
- Welcome what arrives.
- Release what leaves.

This does not mean passivity. It means refusing to fight reality after it has already revealed itself. Dating maturity means loving fully without attempting to possess permanently.

Savage takeaway
Peace begins when you stop arguing with reality.

Quiet power mantra
"I receive and release without resistance."

XVII. LIVE ACCORDING TO YOUR NATURE, EVEN IF OTHERS DISAPPROVE
"So live as indifferent to the world and all worldly objects, as one who liveth by himself alone upon some desert hill. For whether here, or there, if the whole world be but as one town, it matters not much for the place. Let them behold and see a man, that is a man indeed, living according to the true nature of man. If they cannot bear with me, let them kill me. For better were it to die, than so to live as they would have thee."

What Marcus meant (core philosophy)
Marcus advocates independence from external pressure. Your integrity should not depend on acceptance by others. Living according to reason and virtue

matters more than fitting into collective expectations. Stoicism values internal authority over social conformity. The worst fate is not rejection but abandoning oneself to satisfy external demands.

Dating translation (what this means emotionally/socially)
Dating often pressures people into:
- shrinking themselves to be liked
- tolerating misalignment to avoid loneliness
- adjusting values to maintain connection.

Marcus's advice is uncompromising: Be fully aligned with yourself. If someone cannot accept who you truly are, the solution is not self-erasure. Dating maturity means choosing authenticity over approval.

Savage takeaway
Better to lose the relationship than lose yourself inside it.

Quiet power mantra
"I remain true even when misunderstood."

XVIII. STOP DISCUSSING VIRTUE AND START EMBODYING IT
"Make it not any longer a matter of dispute or discourse, what are the signs and proprieties of a good man, but really and actually to be such."

What Marcus meant (core philosophy)
Marcus calls for action over theory. Endless analysis of what goodness looks like becomes avoidance if not followed by practice. Stoicism values lived philosophy. Virtue is demonstrated through behavior, not discussion. Clarity is proven through action.

Dating translation (what this means emotionally/socially)
In dating, people often talk about:
- wanting healthy relationships
- valuing communication
- seeking emotional maturity.

Marcus would ask: are you practicing these qualities? Dating maturity means:
- setting boundaries rather than discussing boundaries endlessly
- communicating directly rather than theorizing about honesty
- choosing aligned partners rather than debating alignment.

Integrity is revealed through choices.

Savage takeaway
Stop talking about standards. Start living them.

Quiet power mantra
"I embody what I claim to value."

XIX. SEE LIFE FROM A WIDER SCALE

"Ever to represent unto thyself; and to set before thee, both the general age and time of the world, and the whole substance of it. And how all things particular in respect of these are for their substance, as one of the least seeds that is; and for their duration, as the turning of the pestle in the mortar once about. Then to fix thy mind upon every particular object of the world, and to conceive it, (as it is indeed,) as already being in the state of dissolution, and of change; tending to some kind of either putrefaction or dispersion; or whatsoever else it is, that is the death as it were of everything in his own kind."

What Marcus meant (core philosophy)
Marcus encourages cosmic perspective. When viewed against the scale of time and existence, individual events become small and temporary. Understanding impermanence reduces attachment and fear. Stoicism teaches that perspective dissolves unnecessary emotional weight.

Dating translation (what this means emotionally/socially)
Dating experiences often feel overwhelming because they are viewed through a narrow lens. Marcus suggests widening the frame:
*   this moment is temporary
*   this person is part of a larger journey
*   this experience will change.

Perspective does not diminish meaning; it softens panic. Dating maturity includes holding intensity while remembering its impermanence.

Savage takeaway
What feels massive now is a brief moment in a much larger story.

Quiet power mantra
"I see my experiences from a wider horizon."

XX. STRIP AWAY STATUS AND SEE HUMANITY CLEARLY

"Consider them through all actions and occupations, of their lives: as when they eat, and when they sleep; when they are in the act of necessary exoneration, and when in the act of lust. Again, when they either are in their greatest exultation; and in the middle of all their pomp and glory; or being angry and displeased, in great state and majesty, as from an higher place, they chide and rebuke. How base and slavish, but a little while ago, they were fain to be, that they might come to this; and within a very little while what will be their estate, when death hath once seized upon them."

What Marcus meant (core philosophy)
Marcus dismantles illusions of superiority. Regardless of status, every person shares the same fundamental human realities:
*   biological needs
*   emotional impulses
*   mortality.

Seeing others clearly removes intimidation and envy. Stoicism encourages recognizing shared humanity beneath appearances.

Dating translation (what this means emotionally/socially)
Dating often places people on pedestals:
- idolizing someone's attractiveness or success
- feeling inferior or intimidated
- overvaluing status.

Marcus reminds you that everyone is fundamentally human. When you strip away projection, you see people more accurately. Dating maturity means meeting others as equals rather than elevating or diminishing them.

Savage takeaway
The person you're intimidated by still brushes their teeth and has bad days.

Quiet power mantra
"I see others clearly without pedestal or fear."

XXI. TRUST WHAT ARRIVES AS PART OF THE WHOLE
"That is best for every one, that the common nature of all doth send unto every one, and then is it best, when she doth send it."

What Marcus meant (core philosophy)
Marcus expresses radical acceptance of timing and circumstance. What happens is not random but part of a larger natural unfolding. The Stoic stance is not passive resignation but trust that events occur within an interconnected system. The right moment is when something happens, not when we wish it had happened. Peace comes from alignment with timing rather than resistance to it.

Dating translation (what this means emotionally/socially)
Dating frustration often centers on timing:
- "Why didn't this happen sooner?"
- "Why did this end now?"
- "Why did I meet them when I wasn't ready?"

Marcus reframes timing as part of the process rather than an obstacle. Instead of resisting:
- accept when connection begins
- accept when dynamics shift
- accept when endings arrive.

Dating maturity includes trusting that experiences unfold when they are meant to shape you, not when you feel most comfortable.

Savage takeaway
The right timing is the timing that actually happens.

Quiet power mantra
"I trust the timing of what arrives."

XXII. ALIGN YOUR DESIRE WITH THE WORLD'S MOVEMENT

"The earth, saith the poet, doth often long after the rain. So is the glorious sky often as desirous to fall upon the earth, which argues a mutual kind of love between them. And so (say I) doth the world bear a certain affection of love to whatsoever shall come to pass With thine affections shall mine concur, O world. The same (and no other) shall the object of my longing be which is of thine. Now that the world doth love it is true indeed so is it as commonly said, and acknowledged, when, according to the Greek phrase, imitated by the Latins, of things that used to be, we say commonly, that they love to be."

What Marcus meant (core philosophy)

Marcus speaks about harmony with reality. Rather than forcing personal desires against the flow of events, align your will with what unfolds naturally. The Stoic ideal is not suppressing desire but refining it so that what you want matches what is. Acceptance becomes participation rather than resistance.

Dating translation (what this means emotionally/socially)

Dating pain often arises when desire fights reality:
- wanting someone who is unavailable
- resisting clear incompatibility
- clinging to a version of the relationship that does not exist.

Marcus suggests a powerful shift: Want what is real.
- If someone shows interest, meet it.
- If someone withdraws, accept it.

Dating maturity means aligning desire with truth rather than fantasy.

Savage takeaway

Suffering begins when you want reality to be different from what it is.

Quiet power mantra

"I desire what is real."

XXIII. EVERY PATH LEADS TO PEACE IF YOU ACCEPT IT

"Either thou dost continue in this kind of life and that is it, which so long thou hast been used unto and therefore tolerable: or thou doest retire, or leave the world, and that of thine own accord, and then thou hast thy mind: or thy life is cut off; and then mayst thou rejoice that thou hast ended thy charge. One of these must needs be. Be therefore of good comfort."

What Marcus meant (core philosophy)

Marcus simplifies existential anxiety. No matter what happens, outcomes resolve into one of a few possibilities:
- continuing as you are
- choosing change
- life ending.

Each path contains its own resolution. Fear comes from imagining endless uncertainty, but reality always moves toward conclusion. Stoicism teaches comfort through clarity about life's finite options.

Dating translation (what this means emotionally/socially)

Dating often feels overwhelming because of imagined endless possibilities. Marcus reduces complexity:

- you stay
- you leave
- circumstances change on their own.

Understanding this reduces emotional paralysis. Dating maturity means recognizing that no situation traps you permanently. Every dynamic eventually resolves.

Savage takeaway

You are never as stuck as your mind tells you.

Quiet power mantra

"I move forward knowing every path resolves."

XXIV. SOLITUDE IS AN INNER STATE, NOT A LOCATION

"Let it always appear and be manifest unto thee that solitariness, and desert places, by many philosophers so much esteemed of and affected, are of themselves but thus and thus; and that all things are them to them that live in towns, and converse with others as they are the same nature everywhere to be seen and observed: to them that have retired themselves to the top of mountains, and to desert havens, or what other desert and inhabited places soever. For anywhere it thou wilt mayest thou quickly find and apply that to thyself; which Plato saith of his philosopher, in a place: as private and retired, saith he, as if he were shut up and enclosed about in some shepherd's lodge, on the top of a hill. There by thyself to put these questions to thyself or to enter in these considerations: What is my chief and principal part, which hath power over the rest? What is now the present estate of it, as I use it; and what is it, that I employ it about? Is it now void of reason or no? Is it free, and separated; or so affixed, so congealed and grown together as it were with the flesh, that it is swayed by the motions and inclinations of it?"

What Marcus meant (core philosophy)

Marcus rejects the idea that peace requires physical escape. True solitude is internal.

Whether surrounded by crowds or alone in isolation, the key question is: Is your mind free and governed by reason? Stoicism emphasizes inner autonomy. External environments matter less than internal clarity.

Dating translation (what this means emotionally/socially)

Many people believe:

- a relationship will create peace
- or being single will create peace.

Marcus suggests both assumptions are incomplete. Peace comes from internal independence. You can feel grounded while dating or single, social or alone. Dating maturity means maintaining internal space even while emotionally connected to another person.

Savage takeaway

Changing your relationship status doesn't fix a restless mind.

Quiet power mantra

"My peace travels with me wherever I am."

XXV. RESISTING REALITY IS RUNNING FROM THE LAW

"He that runs away from his master is a fugitive. But the law is every man's master. He therefore that forsakes the law, is a fugitive. So is he, whosoever he be, that is either sorry, angry, or afraid, or for anything that either hath been, is, or shall be by his appointment, who is the Lord and Governor of the universe. For he truly and properly is Nόμος[74], or the law, as the only νέμων[75], or distributor and dispenser of all things that happen unto any one in his lifetime—Whatsoever then is either sorry, angry, or afraid, is a fugitive."

What Marcus meant (core philosophy)

Marcus frames emotional resistance as fleeing from reality itself. The "law" is not a legal system but the governing order of existence. When we resist what has happened or fear what may come, we attempt to escape the natural structure of events. Stoicism does not deny emotion but warns against fighting inevitability. Acceptance is not weakness. It is alignment with reality.

Dating translation (what this means emotionally/socially)

Dating pain often comes from resisting what is already clear:
- being angry at someone's true character
- grieving longer because you reject the ending
- fearing outcomes you cannot control.

Marcus suggests that emotional struggle intensifies when you resist what is already unfolding. Dating maturity means recognizing reality early and aligning with it instead of fighting it. Acceptance reduces unnecessary suffering.

Savage takeaway

You suffer most when you argue with what is already true.

Quiet power mantra

"I align with reality instead of resisting it."

XXVI. TRUST THE UNSEEN PROCESSES

"From man is the seed, that once cast into the womb man hath no more to do with it. Another cause succeedeth, and undertakes the work, and in time brings a child (that wonderful effect from such a beginning!) to perfection. Again, man lets food down through his throat; and that once down, he hath no more to do with it. Another cause succeedeth and distributeth this food into the senses, and the affections: into life, and into strength; and doth with it those other many and marvellous things, that belong unto

---

[74] In Greek, Νόμος (*Nómos*) primarily translates to "Law" or "Custom," but its meaning stretches from legal statutes to the very "laws of nature."

[75] In Greek, νέμων (*némōn*) is the present participle of the verb νέμω (*némō*), which translates to "distributing," "alloting," or "dispensing."

man. These things therefore that are so secretly and invisibly wrought and brought to pass, thou must use to behold and contemplate; and not the things themselves only, but the power also by which they are effected; that thou mayst behold it, though not with the eyes of the body, yet as plainly and visibly as thou canst see and discern the outward efficient cause of the depression and elevation of anything."

What Marcus meant (core philosophy)

Marcus highlights invisible processes guiding life. Many essential transformations occur beyond conscious control:

- biological development
- internal healing
- unseen causal chains.

Stoicism teaches trust in the underlying processes of existence rather than obsession with control. Wisdom includes recognizing that not everything must be managed directly.

Dating translation (what this means emotionally/socially)

Dating often triggers control impulses:

- wanting instant clarity
- forcing emotional timelines
- trying to engineer outcomes.

Marcus reminds you that connection evolves through unseen processes:

- emotional bonding develops gradually
- compatibility reveals itself over time
- understanding grows organically.

Dating maturity includes allowing processes to unfold without constant interference.

Savage takeaway

Not everything meaningful happens because you force it.

Quiet power mantra

"I trust what is unfolding beyond my control."

XXVII. HISTORY REPEATS, ONLY THE PLAYERS CHANGE

"Ever to mind and consider with thyself; how all things that now are, have been heretofore much after the same sort, and after the same fashion that now they are: and so to think of those things which shall be hereafter also. Moreover, whole dramata, and uniform scenes, or scenes that comprehend the lives and actions of men of one calling and profession, as many as either in thine own experience thou hast known, or by reading of ancient histories; (as the whole court of Adrianus, the whole court of Antoninus Pius, the whole court of Philippus, that of Alexander, that of Cræsus): to set them all before thine eyes. For thou shalt find that they are all but after one sort and fashion: only that the actors were others."

What Marcus meant (core philosophy)

Marcus emphasizes recurring human patterns. Across history:

- ambitions repeat
- conflicts repeat
- emotional dynamics repeat.

The illusion of novelty disappears when viewed through a wider lens. Stoicism encourages recognizing patterns to reduce emotional reactivity.

Dating translation (what this means emotionally/socially)

Dating often feels unique and unprecedented:

- "This situation has never happened before."
- "No one has felt this way."

Marcus suggests recognizing recurring relational patterns:

- attachment styles
- power dynamics
- emotional cycles.

Understanding that human behavior repeats helps you avoid personalization and emotional overwhelm. Dating maturity means seeing patterns instead of dramatizing singular events.

Savage takeaway

The story feels new, but the pattern is ancient.

Quiet power mantra

"I recognize patterns instead of romanticizing chaos."

XXVIII. RESISTANCE IS OPTIONAL, ACCEPTANCE IS INEVITABLE

"As a pig that cries and flings when his throat is cut, fancy to thyself every one to be, that grieves for any worldly thing and takes on. Such a one is he also, who upon his bed alone, doth bewail the miseries of this our mortal life. And remember this, that unto reasonable creatures only it is granted that they may willingly and freely submit unto Providence: but absolutely to submit, is a necessity imposed upon all creatures equally."

What Marcus meant (core philosophy)

Marcus contrasts two forms of submission:

- unwilling resistance filled with suffering
- conscious acceptance grounded in understanding.

All beings eventually submit to reality. The difference is whether one does so willingly. Stoicism values voluntary alignment with what cannot be avoided. Freedom lies in choosing acceptance before force requires it.

Dating translation (what this means emotionally/socially)

In dating, people often prolong suffering by resisting inevitable truths:

- refusing to accept incompatibility
- holding onto relationships already ending
- replaying emotional pain instead of integrating it.

Marcus encourages choosing acceptance early. Dating maturity means surrendering to reality with awareness rather than being dragged toward it through repeated suffering.

Savage takeaway

You will accept reality eventually. Wisdom is accepting it sooner.

Quiet power mantra

"I choose acceptance before resistance becomes suffering."

XXIX. DO NOT GRIEVE OVER LOSING WHAT YOU WOULD HAVE LEFT ANYWAY

"Whatsoever it is that thou goest about, consider of it by thyself, and ask thyself, What? because I shall do this no more when I am dead, should therefore death seem grievous unto me?"

What Marcus meant (core philosophy)

Marcus challenges attachment by reframing loss through mortality. Everything we experience will eventually end. Death simply reveals the temporary nature that was always present.

The Stoic insight is this: If something's value depends on permanence, its value is already unstable. Grief often arises from the illusion that experiences should last indefinitely. Wisdom comes from appreciating without clinging.

Dating translation (what this means emotionally/socially)

In dating, endings feel catastrophic because people assume continuation is owed:
* "We were supposed to last."
* "I can't believe it ended."

Marcus invites a different question: If all relationships are temporary in the scale of life, why treat endings as betrayal instead of completion? Dating maturity means appreciating connection while accepting its impermanence. Endings do not erase meaning.

Savage takeaway

Everything ends eventually. The tragedy is believing it wasn't always temporary.

Quiet power mantra

"I appreciate without needing permanence."

"XXX. WHEN ANGER ARISES, LOOK FOR YOUR REFLECTION

"When thou art offended with any man's transgression, presently reflect upon thyself; and consider what thou thyself art guilty of in the same kind. As that thou also perchance dost think it a happiness either to be rich, or to live in pleasure, or to be praised and commended, and so of the rest in particular. For this if thou shalt call to mind, thou shalt soon forget thine anger; especially when at the same time this also shall concur in thy thoughts, that he was constrained by his error and ignorance so to do: for how can he choose as long as he is of that opinion? Do thou therefore if thou canst, take away that from him, that forceth him to do as he doth."

What Marcus meant (core philosophy)

Marcus reframes anger through self-awareness. When someone behaves poorly:
* remember shared human tendencies
* recognize that people act according to their beliefs and understanding.

Compassion arises from recognizing ignorance rather than assuming malice. Stoicism encourages humility: before judging others, examine similar patterns within yourself.

Dating translation (what this means emotionally/socially)
Dating triggers strong reactions:
- frustration with avoidance
- anger at dishonesty
- resentment toward emotional immaturity.

Marcus suggests, before reacting, ask: Have I ever acted from insecurity, desire, or misunderstanding? This does not excuse harmful behavior but reduces emotional escalation. Dating maturity means responding from clarity instead of reactive judgment.

Savage takeaway
The traits that trigger you often mirror something you recognize in yourself.

Quiet power mantra
"I respond with understanding instead of reaction."

XXXI. EVERYTHING VANISHES, INCLUDING WHAT SEEMS IMPORTANT NOW

"When thou seest Satyro, think of Socraticus and Eutyches, or Hymen, and when Euphrates, think of Eutychio, and Sylvanus, when Alciphron, of Tropaeophorus, when Xenophon, of Crito, or Severus. And when thou doest look upon thyself, fancy unto thyself some one or other of the Cæsars; and so for every one, some one or other that hath been for estate and profession answerable unto him. Then let this come to thy mind at the same time; and where now are they all? Nowhere or anywhere? For so shalt thou at all time be able to perceive how all worldly things are but as the smoke, that vanisheth away: or, indeed, mere nothing. Especially when thou shalt call to mind this also, that whatsoever is once changed, shall never be again as long as the world endureth. And thou then, how long shalt thou endure? And why doth it not suffice thee, if virtuously, and as becometh thee, thou mayest pass that portion of time, how little soever it be, that is allotted unto thee?"

What Marcus meant (core philosophy)
Marcus emphasizes impermanence through historical perspective. People who once seemed powerful or significant disappear into obscurity. Fame, status, and identity fade. Stoicism uses this perspective to reduce attachment to transient concerns. The only lasting value is living virtuously within the time allotted.

Dating translation (what this means emotionally/socially)
Dating often magnifies current experiences:
- obsessing over someone's opinion
- feeling defined by one relationship
- fearing rejection as permanent identity.

Marcus reminds you that all moments pass. The person who feels central to your world today may one day be a distant memory. Dating maturity includes prioritizing how you show up rather than clinging to outcomes.

Savage takeaway
The person you're losing sleep over may one day be barely a memory.

Quiet power mantra
"I focus on who I am, not who stays."

XXXII. TURN EVERY EXPERIENCE INTO STRENGTH

"What a subject, and what a course of life is it, that thou doest so much desire to be rid of. For all these things, what are they, but fit objects for an understanding, that beholdeth everything according to its true nature, to exercise itself upon? Be patient, therefore, until that (as a strong stomach that turns all things into his own nature; and as a great fire that turneth in flame and light, whatsoever thou doest cast into it) thou have made these things also familiar, and as it were natural unto thee."

What Marcus meant (core philosophy)

Marcus encourages transformation through perception. Difficult experiences are not obstacles but material for growth. Like fire turning fuel into flame, the rational mind transforms challenges into strength. Stoicism reframes adversity as training rather than punishment.

Dating translation (what this means emotionally/socially)

Dating struggles often feel like burdens to escape:
- emotional discomfort
- miscommunication
- heartbreak.

Marcus suggests seeing these as training grounds:
- refining discernment
- strengthening boundaries
- deepening emotional intelligence.

Dating maturity means integrating experiences rather than trying to avoid them entirely. Every dynamic teaches something about yourself and others.

Savage takeaway

The situation you want to escape is often the one shaping your strength.

Quiet power mantra

"I transform every experience into growth."

XXXIII. BE SO CLEAR IN CHARACTER THAT DOUBT CANNOT LIVE THERE

"Let it not be in any man's power, to say truly of thee, that thou art not truly simple, or sincere and open, or not good. Let him be deceived whosoever he be that shall have any such opinion of thee. For all this doth depend of thee. For who is it that should hinder thee from being either truly simple or good? Do thou only resolve rather not to live, than not to be such. For indeed neither doth it stand with reason that he should live that is not such. What then is it that may upon this present occasion according to best reason and discretion, either be said or done? For whatsoever it be, it is in thy power either to do it, or to say it, and therefore seek not any pretences, as though thou wert hindered. Thou wilt never cease groaning and complaining, until such time as that, what pleasure is unto the voluptuous, be unto thee, to do in everything that presents itself, whatsoever may be done conformably and agreeably to the proper constitution of man, or, to man as he is a man. For thou must account that pleasure, whatsoever it be, that thou mayest do according to thine own nature. And to do this, every place will fit thee. Unto the cylindrus, or roller, it is not granted to move everywhere according to its own proper motion, as neither

unto the water, nor unto the fire, nor unto any other thing, that either is merely natural, or natural and sensitive; but not rational for many things there be that can hinder their operations. But of the mind and understanding this is the proper privilege, that according to its own nature, and as it will itself, it can pass through every obstacle that it finds, and keep straight on forwards. Setting therefore before thine eyes this happiness and felicity of thy mind, whereby it is able to pass through all things, and is capable of all motions, whether as the fire, upwards; or as the stone downwards, or as the cylindrus through that which is sloping: content thyself with it, and seek not after any other thing. For all other kind of hindrances that are not hindrances of thy mind either they are proper to the body, or merely proceed from the opinion, reason not making that resistance that it should, but basely, and cowardly suffering itself to be foiled; and of themselves can neither wound, nor do any hurt at all. Else must he of necessity, whosoever he be that meets with any of them, become worse than he was before. For so is it in all other subjects, that that is thought hurtful unto them, whereby they are made worse. But here contrariwise, man (if he make that good use of them that he should) is rather the better and the more praiseworthy for any of those kind of hindrances, than otherwise. But generally remember that nothing can hurt a natural citizen, that is not hurtful unto the city itself, nor anything hurt the city, that is not hurtful unto the law itself. But none of these casualties, or external hindrances, do hurt the law itself; or, are contrary to that course of justice and equity, by which public societies are maintained: neither therefore do they hurt either city or citizen."

What Marcus meant (core philosophy)

Marcus is talking about radical internal integrity. Not perfection. Not reputation management. Alignment.

He is saying: Live in such a way that if someone calls you fake, dishonest, or small, they are simply wrong. Not because you defended yourself. Because your character is consistent.

And here is the core Stoic truth: No external force prevents you from being sincere, honest, or good. That choice belongs entirely to you. You are only blocked by your own hesitation.

Marcus pushes even harder: If living requires abandoning your integrity, then the problem is not life itself, but the way you are living it. Real pleasure comes from acting in alignment with your nature as a rational, ethical human. Not from approval. Not from comfort. From congruence.

Dating translation (what this means emotionally/socially)

This is one of the most powerful dating principles in the entire book. Most dating pain comes from self-abandonment:
* pretending to be cooler than you are
* hiding needs
* tolerating behavior that violates your values
* shrinking to avoid rejection.

Marcus says: Stop trying to win outcomes. Start becoming internally undeniable.

Dating maturity means:
* You speak clearly.
* You act honestly.
* You remain open without becoming performative.

If someone misunderstands you, that is their perception. Your responsibility is alignment, not universal agreement.

And here's the savage truth: You stop complaining about dating when authenticity itself becomes the reward.

Savage takeaway
Integrity removes drama because you stop negotiating against yourself.

Quiet power mantra
"I am clear, sincere, and aligned regardless of outcome."

The deeper Stoic mechanics (this is the genius part)
Marcus compares the rational mind to something unstoppable.
- Fire can be smothered.
- Water can be blocked.
- A rolling object can be stopped.

But the mind, when aligned with reason, moves through obstacles without being damaged by them. External problems are not true obstacles. Only internal surrender is. Most dating obstacles are:
- fear of rejection
- fear of loss
- fear of being misunderstood.

These are not external barriers. They are interpretations.

And Marcus is ruthless here: Nothing external harms your character unless you allow it to corrupt your mind.

Dating translation (advanced level)
Someone ghosts you.
Does that damage your integrity? No.

Someone rejects you.
Does that make you less sincere? No.

Someone misunderstands you.
Does that change your alignment? No.

The only real loss happens when you abandon who you are to avoid discomfort.

Savage takeaway (level two)
Dating becomes peaceful when your identity stops depending on results.

Quiet power mantra
"My character moves forward even when circumstances resist."

XXXIV. ALL THINGS ARE LEAVES

"As he that is bitten by a mad dog, is afraid of everything almost that he seeth: so unto him, whom the dogmata have once bitten, or in whom true knowledge hath made an impression, everything almost that he sees or reads be it never so short or ordinary, doth afford a good memento; to put him out of all grief and fear, as that of the poet, 'The winds blow upon the trees, and their leaves fall upon the ground. Then do the trees begin to bud again, and by the spring-time they put forth new branches. So is the generation of men; some come into the world, and others go out of it.' Of these leaves then thy children are. And they also that applaud thee so gravely, or, that applaud thy speeches, with that their usual acclamation, ἀξιοπίστως[76], O wisely spoken I and speak well of thee, as on the other side, they that stick not to curse thee, they that privately and secretly dispraise and deride thee, they also are but leaves. And they also that shall follow, in whose memories the names of men famous after death, is preserved, they are but leaves neither. For even so is it of all these worldly things. Their spring comes, and they are put forth. Then blows the wind, and they go down. And then in lieu of them grow others out of the wood or common matter of all things, like unto them. But, to endure but for a while, is common unto all. Why then shouldest thou so earnestly either seek after these things, or fly from them, as though they should endure for ever? Yet a little while, and thine eyes will be closed up, and for him that carries thee to thy grave shall another mourn within a while after."

What Marcus meant (core philosophy)

Marcus is confronting our attachment to recognition, judgment, and legacy. He reminds us that everyone is temporary. Praise, criticism, memory, fame, even the people who carry your story forward are transient like leaves falling from a tree. True knowledge changes perception. Once you understand impermanence, everyday moments become reminders that nothing external holds lasting power over you. Stoicism teaches emotional freedom through recognizing that all social validation and rejection are fleeting cycles rather than permanent truths.

Dating translation (what this means emotionally/socially)

Dating becomes painful when we treat temporary reactions as permanent verdicts:

- someone's approval feels like proof of worth
- rejection feels like a lifelong label
- ghosting feels like a final judgment.

Marcus reframes this:

- people enter and exit your life like seasons
- admiration and criticism are equally temporary
- the person praising you today and the one dismissing you tomorrow are both passing through.

Dating maturity means:

- not overvaluing applause
- not overfearing rejection
- recognizing that most dynamics are brief chapters, not eternal stories.

When you stop chasing permanence from temporary people, you regain emotional sovereignty.

---

[76] In Greek, ἀξιοπίστως (axiopístōs) is an adverb that translates to "credibly," "reliably," or "trustworthily."

Savage takeaway
The people you're trying to impress and the ones who misunderstood you are both just passing leaves.

Quiet power mantra
"I release attachment to praise and fear, knowing all things pass."

XXXV. BE READY FOR ALL THAT COMES

"A good eye must be good to see whatsoever is to be seen, and not green things only. For that is proper to sore eyes. So must a good ear, and a good smell be ready for whatsoever is either to be heard, or smelt: and a good stomach as indifferent to all kinds of food, as a millstone is, to whatsoever she was made for to grind. As ready therefore must a sound understanding be for whatsoever shall happen. But he that saith, O that my children might live! and, O that all men might commend me for whatsoever I do! is an eye that seeks after green things; or as teeth, after that which is tender."

What Marcus meant (core philosophy)
Marcus is teaching emotional neutrality and resilience. A healthy eye does not demand only pleasant sights, and a strong mind does not demand only pleasant experiences. Wisdom means being prepared to encounter reality as it is, not only the parts we prefer. When we insist on outcomes that feel good or safe, we weaken our perception and become reactive rather than grounded. Stoicism encourages cultivating an understanding that is steady and ready for whatever arises.

Dating translation (what this means emotionally/socially)
In dating, many people unconsciously seek only "green things":
- constant validation
- easy chemistry
- reassurance without discomfort.

Marcus reframes this:
- real connection includes awkwardness, uncertainty, and growth
- not every moment will feel flattering or smooth
- maturity comes from engaging with reality, not chasing idealized emotional comfort.

Dating strength means:
- hearing feedback without collapse
- experiencing disappointment without losing direction
- allowing relationships to unfold instead of forcing only pleasant outcomes.

Savage takeaway
If you only want the easy parts, you're not building strength. You're building fragility.

Quiet power mantra
"I meet reality fully, not selectively."

XXXVI. EVEN THE GOOD ARE NOT MOURNED BY ALL

"There is not any man that is so happy in his death, but that some of those that are by him when he dies, will be ready to rejoice at his supposed calamity. Is it one that was virtuous and wise indeed? will there not some one or other be found, who thus will say to himself; "Well now at last shall I be at rest from this pedagogue. He did not indeed otherwise trouble us much: but I know well enough that in his heart, he did much condemn us." Thus will they speak of the virtuous. But as for us, alas how many things be there, for which there be many that glad would be to be rid of us. This therefore if thou shalt think of whensoever thou diest, thou shalt die the more willingly, when thou shalt think with thyself; I am now to depart from that world, wherein those that have been my nearest friends and acquaintances, they whom I have so much suffered for, so often prayed for, and for whom I have taken such care, even they would have me die, hoping that after my death they shall live happier, than they did before. What then should any man desire to continue here any longer? Nevertheless, whensoever thou diest, thou must not be less kind and loving unto them for it; but as before, see them, continue to be their friend, to wish them well, and meekly, and gently to carry thyself towards them, but yet so that on the other side, it make thee not the more unwilling to die. But as it fareth with them that die an easy quick death, whose soul is soon separated from their bodies, so must thy separation from them be. To these had nature joined and annexed me: now she parts us; I am ready to depart, as from friends and kinsmen, but yet without either reluctancy or compulsion. For this also is according to Nature."

What Marcus meant (core philosophy)

Marcus is confronting the illusion that universal approval or lasting gratitude exists. Even the virtuous are misunderstood, judged, or quietly resented by others. Some people will feel relief when someone leaves, not because that person was wrong, but because human relationships are complex and self-centered by nature. Stoicism teaches acceptance of this reality without bitterness. Kindness should not depend on being fully appreciated. True peace comes from acting with integrity regardless of how others ultimately perceive you.

Dating translation (what this means emotionally/socially)

In relationships and dating, we often believe:
- if we are loving enough, people will value us forever
- sacrifice guarantees loyalty
- emotional investment ensures mutual attachment.

Marcus reframes this:
- people may benefit from you yet still feel burdened by you
- someone you loved deeply may feel relief when things end
- others' reactions reflect their inner world, not your worth.

Dating maturity means:
- loving without expecting permanent validation
- understanding that endings are not always mutual emotionally
- releasing the need to be universally cherished.

You can care deeply while accepting that not everyone experiences your presence the same way.

Savage takeaway

Even the best people are not loved by everyone. Stop trying to be the exception.

Quiet power mantra

"I act with kindness without needing lasting approval."

305

XXXVII. EXAMINE THE END BEHIND EVERY ACTION

"Use thyself; as often, as thou seest any man do anything, presently (if it be possible) to say unto thyself, What is this man's end in this his action? But begin this course with thyself first of all, and diligently examine thyself concerning whatsoever thou doest."

What Marcus meant (core philosophy)
Marcus teaches intentional awareness. Every action is driven by an underlying motive or aim. Wisdom comes from learning to recognize the "end" or purpose behind behavior, both in others and especially within yourself. Stoicism emphasizes self-examination before judgment. Understanding motives reveals truth more clearly than reacting to surface behavior alone.

Dating translation (what this means emotionally/socially)
In dating, people often focus on actions without asking why:
- Why did they text now?
- Why did they pull away?
- Why did I respond that way?

Marcus suggests:
- look for the intention behind behavior
- question your own motives before analyzing theirs
- understand emotional patterns by identifying desired outcomes.

Dating maturity means:
- recognizing when someone seeks validation, control, connection, or avoidance
- asking yourself what you truly want from a situation
- aligning actions with conscious intention rather than emotional impulse.

Savage takeaway
Behavior without examining motive is just guesswork. Start with yourself.

Quiet power mantra
"I understand the intention behind my actions."

XXXVIII. THE TRUE DRIVER IS WITHIN

"Remember, that that which sets a man at work, and hath power over the affections to draw them either one way, or the other way, is not any external thing properly, but that which is hidden within every man's dogmata, and opinions: That, that is rhetoric; that is life; that (to speak true) is man himself. As for thy body, which as a vessel, or a case, compasseth thee about, and the many and curious instruments that it hath annexed unto it, let them not trouble thy thoughts. For of themselves they are but as a carpenter's axe, but that they are born with us, and naturally sticking unto us. But otherwise, without the inward cause that hath power to move them, and to restrain them, those parts are of themselves of no more use unto us, than the shuttle is of itself to the weaver, or the pen to the writer, or the whip to the coachman."

What Marcus meant (core philosophy)
Marcus emphasizes that inner beliefs and judgments, not external circumstances, drive emotions and actions. The body and external tools are merely instruments.

What truly shapes life is the internal framework of thoughts, values, and interpretations. Stoicism teaches that control lies within perception and belief, not in outer conditions.

Dating translation (what this means emotionally/socially)

In dating, it often feels like others "make" us feel certain ways:

- they hurt me
- they made me insecure
- they caused my anxiety.

Marcus reframes this:

- internal interpretations create emotional responses
- beliefs about love, rejection, or worth influence reactions more than events themselves
- changing perspective shifts emotional experience.

Dating maturity means:

- recognizing personal narratives that shape reactions
- choosing interpretations consciously
- understanding that emotional power comes from internal beliefs, not external triggers alone.

Savage takeaway

It's not what happens. It's what your mind decides it means.

Quiet power mantra

"My inner beliefs shape my emotional world."

THE ELEVENTH BOOK
Quiet Power Is Loud Enough

I. THE NATURE AND POWER OF A REASONABLE SOUL

"The natural properties, and privileges of a reasonable soul are: That she seeth herself; that she can order, and compose herself: that she makes herself as she will herself: that she reaps her own fruits whatsoever, whereas plants, trees, unreasonable creatures, what fruit soever they bear, they bear them unto others, and not to themselves. Again; whensoever, and wheresoever, sooner or later, her life doth end, she hath her own end nevertheless. For it is not with her, as with dancers and players, who if they be interrupted in any part of their action, the whole action must needs be imperfect: but she in what part of time or action soever she be surprised, can make that which she hath in her hand whatsoever it be, complete and full, so that she may depart with that comfort, "I have lived; neither want I anything of that which properly did belong unto me." Again, she compasseth the whole world, and penetrateth into the vanity, and mere outside of it, and stretcheth herself unto the infiniteness of eternity; and considers withal, and sees clearly this, that neither they that shall follow us, shall see any new thing that we have not seen, nor they that went before anything more than we. As proper is it, and natural to the soul of man to love her neighbour, to be true and modest; and to regard nothing so much as herself: whereby it appears, that sound reason and justice comes all to one, and therefore that justice is the chief thing that reasonable creatures ought to propose unto themselves as their end."

What Marcus meant (core philosophy)

Marcus describes the autonomy and self-governance of the rational soul. Unlike external things, the soul has the power to shape itself, reflect on itself, and complete its own purpose regardless of circumstance. Life does not need perfect conditions or a flawless ending to be whole. At any moment, a person can make their life complete through conscious intention. Stoicism teaches that meaning comes from internal alignment with reason, justice, and integrity rather than external achievements or uninterrupted narratives.

Dating translation (what this means emotionally/socially)

In dating, many people feel incomplete when relationships end or when timelines do not unfold perfectly:
- believing the story is unfinished without closure
- feeling interrupted or "cut off" before fulfillment
- measuring worth by external outcomes.

Marcus reframes this:
- you carry your own completeness
- no relationship defines whether your story is whole
- even unexpected endings can still be complete chapters.

Dating maturity means:
- defining fulfillment internally, not through relationship status
- recognizing that you always retain agency over meaning
- valuing integrity and authenticity over external validation.

308

Savage takeaway

Your life is not unfinished because someone left. You complete your own story.

Quiet power mantra

"I am self-complete, regardless of external endings."

II. DIVIDE THINGS TO SEE THEM CLEARLY

"A pleasant song or dance; the Pancratiast's exercise, sports that thou art wont to be much taken with, thou shalt easily contemn; if the harmonious voice thou shalt divide into so many particular sounds whereof it doth consist, and of every one in particular shall ask thyself; whether this or that sound is it, that doth so conquer thee. For thou wilt be ashamed of it. And so for shame, if accordingly thou shalt consider it, every particular motion and posture by itself: and so for the wrestler's exercise too. Generally then, whatsoever it be, besides virtue, and those things that proceed from virtue that thou art subject to be much affected with, remember presently thus to divide it, and by this kind of division, in each particular to attain unto the contempt of the whole. This thou must transfer and apply to thy whole life also."

What Marcus meant (core philosophy)

Marcus teaches a method of detachment through analysis. By breaking something appealing into its basic parts, its emotional hold weakens. Many things seem powerful only because we experience them as a unified illusion. When examined piece by piece, they lose their overwhelming influence. Stoicism encourages rational examination to prevent external pleasures or distractions from dominating the mind.

Dating translation (what this means emotionally/socially)

In dating, attraction or obsession often comes from idealized narratives:
- projecting fantasy onto chemistry
- romanticizing charisma or status
- confusing emotional intensity with compatibility.

Marcus suggests:
- break attraction into components
- examine behaviors instead of the fantasy
- separate appearance, words, and actions.

Dating maturity means:
- seeing clearly instead of idealizing
- understanding that infatuation often dissolves under honest observation
- valuing virtue over emotional spectacle.

Savage takeaway

What overwhelms you usually survives because you refuse to look at it closely.

Quiet power mantra

"I see clearly beyond illusion."

III. BE READY WITHOUT DRAMA

'That soul which is ever ready, even now presently (if need be) from the body, whether by way of extinction, or dispersion, or continuation in another place and estate to be separated, how blessed and happy is it! But this readiness of it, it must proceed, not from an obstinate and peremptory resolution of

309

the mind, violently and passionately set upon opposition, as Christians are wont; but from a peculiar judgment; with discretion and gravity, so that others may be persuaded also and drawn to the like example, but without any noise and passionate exclamations."

What Marcus meant (core philosophy)

Marcus describes calm readiness for change or ending. True strength is not dramatic defiance but quiet acceptance grounded in understanding. Stoicism values inner steadiness rather than emotional intensity. Preparedness comes from clarity, not rebellion or theatrical resistance.

Dating translation (what this means emotionally/socially)

In relationships, readiness often looks like:
- knowing when to leave without chaos
- accepting endings without needing dramatic closure
- standing firm without emotional theatrics.

Dating maturity means:
- emotional independence
- calm detachment when necessary
- letting go from strength rather than reaction.

Savage takeaway

The strongest exit is quiet certainty, not loud resistance.

Quiet power mantra

"I release with calm strength."

IV. GOODNESS IS ITS OWN REWARD

"Have I done anything charitably? then am I benefited by it. See that this upon all occasions may present itself unto thy mind, and never cease to think of it. What is thy profession? to be good. And how should this be well brought to pass, but by certain theorems and doctrines; some concerning the nature of the universe, and some concerning the proper and particular constitution of man?"

What Marcus meant (core philosophy)

Marcus emphasizes internal reward. Acts of kindness benefit the doer regardless of external response. Virtue is not transactional. The goal of life is to be good according to reason and understanding, guided by principles about both the universe and human nature.

Dating translation (what this means emotionally/socially)

In dating, people often give with expectation:
- kindness hoping for reciprocation
- emotional labor expecting loyalty
- generosity seeking validation.

Marcus reframes this:
- goodness is complete the moment you act with integrity
- someone's reaction does not define the value of your behavior
- kindness strengthens you regardless of outcome.

Dating maturity means:
- giving without scorekeeping
- recognizing that integrity is self-rewarding
- choosing character over approval.

Savage takeaway
If you were kind, you already won. Their response is irrelevant.

Quiet power mantra
"My integrity is its own reward."

V. LIFE AS THEATER AND THE LESSON OF TRAGEDY

"Tragedies were at first brought in and instituted, to put men in mind of worldly chances and casualties: that these things in the ordinary course of nature did so happen: that men that were much pleased and delighted by such accidents upon this stage, would not by the same things in a greater stage be grieved and afflicted: for here you see what is the end of all such things; and that even they that cry out so mournfully to Cithaeron, must bear them for all their cries and exclamations, as well as others. And in very truth many good things are spoken by these poets; as that (for example) is an excellent passage: "But if so be that I and my two children be neglected by the Gods, they have some reason even for that," &c. And again, "It will but little avail thee to storm and rage against the things themselves," &c. Again, "To reap one's life, as a ripe ear of corn;" and whatsoever else is to be found in them, that is of the same kind. After the tragedy, the ancient comedy was brought in, which had the liberty to inveigh against personal vices; being therefore through this her freedom and liberty of speech of very good use and effect, to restrain men from pride and arrogancy. To which end it was, that Diogenes took also the same liberty. After these, what were either the Middle, or New Comedy admitted for, but merely (or for the most part at least) for the delight and pleasure of curious and excellent imitation? "It will steal away; look to it," &c. Why, no man denies, but that these also have some good things whereof that may be one: but the whole drift and foundation of that kind of dramatical poetry, what is it else, but as we have said?"

What Marcus meant (core philosophy)
Marcus uses theater as a metaphor for life. Tragedies were meant to prepare people emotionally by showing that suffering, loss, and unexpected events are part of nature's design. By witnessing hardship in stories, people learn to accept reality without excessive resistance. Comedy, especially satire, served to humble pride and expose human flaws. Stoicism teaches that life unfolds like a drama with predictable cycles, and wisdom lies in observing without becoming overwhelmed.

Dating translation (what this means emotionally/socially)
Dating often feels intensely personal, but Marcus suggests viewing experiences like scenes in a play:
- heartbreak is not unique to you alone
- emotional highs and lows follow familiar patterns
- even dramatic endings are part of the human script.

Reframing relationships as chapters rather than catastrophes helps:
- reduce emotional over-identification
- recognize recurring dynamics
- maintain perspective during chaos.

Dating maturity means:
- understanding that emotional drama is part of human storytelling
- learning from patterns rather than resisting them
- keeping self-awareness even during intense moments.

Savage takeaway
You are not the only one in the tragedy. You are just playing your scene.

Quiet power mantra
"I observe my story without losing myself in it."

VI. YOUR CURRENT PATH IS SUFFICIENT
"How clearly doth it appear unto thee, that no other course of thy life could fit a true philosopher's practice better, than this very course, that thou art now already in?"

What Marcus meant (core philosophy)
Marcus reminds himself that the present circumstances of life are not obstacles to philosophy but the exact environment needed to practice it. Stoicism rejects the idea that wisdom requires ideal conditions. Whatever situation you find yourself in is the appropriate training ground for growth, discipline, and understanding.

Dating translation (what this means emotionally/socially)
In dating and relationships, people often think:
- "I will grow once I meet the right person"
- "My healing will begin after this phase ends"
- "If circumstances were different, I would be stronger."

Marcus reframes this:
- your current experiences are already shaping your wisdom
- difficult dynamics are practice for emotional clarity
- growth happens within reality, not outside it.

Dating maturity means:
- seeing present challenges as training, not delay
- recognizing that every interaction refines self-knowledge
- trusting that you are already in the right place for growth.

Savage takeaway
You don't need a different life to grow. This one is the training.

Quiet power mantra
"This moment is my practice."

VII. SEPARATION FROM OTHERS IS SEPARATION FROM THE WHOLE
"A branch cut off from the continuity of that which was next unto it, must needs be cut off from the whole tree: so a man that is divided from another man, is divided from the whole society. A branch is cut off by another, but he that hates and is averse, cuts himself off from his neighbour, and knows not that at

the same time he divides himself from the whole body, or corporation. But herein is the gift and mercy of God, the Author of this society, in that, once cut off we may grow together and become part of the whole again. But if this happen often the misery is that the further a man is run in this division, the harder he is to be reunited and restored again: and however the branch which, once cut off afterwards was graffed in, gardeners can tell you is not like that which sprouted together at first, and still continued in the unity of the body."

What Marcus meant (core philosophy)

Marcus compares humanity to branches of one tree. Separation from others through hatred or resentment is not just distance from individuals but from the greater whole of humanity. Division harms the one who separates as much as anyone else. Stoicism values connection, reconciliation, and social harmony. While reconnection is possible, repeated withdrawal hardens the divide and makes unity more difficult to restore.

Dating translation (what this means emotionally/socially)

In dating and relationships, emotional withdrawal can become self-protection:

- shutting down after betrayal
- avoiding connection to prevent pain
- hardening into isolation.

Marcus suggests:

- resentment disconnects you from more than just one person
- emotional walls isolate you from broader connection
- reconciliation or openness keeps you aligned with your nature.

Dating maturity means:

- protecting boundaries without abandoning connection
- recognizing when detachment becomes emotional exile
- allowing yourself to reconnect even after being hurt.

Savage takeaway

When you close yourself off from others, you don't just reject them. You shrink your own world.

Quiet power mantra

"I remain open to connection without losing myself."

VIII. HOLD YOUR VALUES AND YOUR KINDNESS

"To grow together like fellow branches in matter of good correspondence and affection; but not in matter of opinions. They that shall oppose thee in thy right courses, as it is not in their power to divert thee from thy good action, so neither let it be to divert thee from thy good affection towards them. But be it thy care to keep thyself constant in both; both in a right judgment and action, and in true meekness towards them, that either shall do their endeavour to hinder thee, or at least will be displeased with thee for what thou hast done. For to fail in either is equally base."

What Marcus meant (core philosophy)

Marcus teaches dual integrity: maintain correct judgment and action while preserving goodwill toward others. Agreement is not required for connection. Stoicism encourages firmness in values without hostility. True strength is the ability to stand firm without losing compassion.

313

Dating translation (what this means emotionally/socially)
In relationships, disagreement often leads to:
- abandoning personal truth to maintain harmony
- or becoming cold and defensive to protect identity.

Marcus reframes this:
- you can disagree without losing kindness
- boundaries do not require bitterness
- respect does not require agreement.

Dating maturity means:
- holding your standards calmly
- refusing to compromise integrity for approval
- maintaining emotional warmth even when others oppose you.

Savage takeaway
Stand firm without becoming hard.

Quiet power mantra
"I hold my truth with kindness."

IX. NATURE ALWAYS WORKS TOWARD THE BETTER

"It is not possible that any nature should be inferior unto art, since that all arts imitate nature. If this be so; that the most perfect and general nature of all natures should in her operation come short of the skill of arts, is most improbable. Now common is it to all arts, to make that which is worse for the better's sake. Much more then doth the common nature do the same. Hence is the first ground of justice. From justice all other virtues have their existence. For justice cannot be preserved, if either we settle our minds and affections upon worldly things; or be apt to be deceived, or rash, and inconstant."

What Marcus meant (core philosophy)
Marcus argues that nature operates with inherent wisdom. Just as art refines raw material toward improvement, nature guides events toward greater balance and justice. Stoicism teaches trust in the larger order of existence. Justice emerges from aligning with reason and resisting distraction, impulsivity, or attachment to superficial concerns.

Dating translation (what this means emotionally/socially)
In dating, painful experiences often feel pointless or unfair:
- rejection feels random
- incompatibility feels like failure
- timing feels cruel.

Marcus reframes this:
- experiences refine emotional clarity
- challenges redirect toward better alignment
- growth emerges from difficulty.

Dating maturity means:
- trusting that experiences shape discernment
- prioritizing integrity over short-term pleasure
- allowing lessons to strengthen judgment.

Savage takeaway
Even what feels like loss is often refinement.

Quiet power mantra
"I trust growth through experience."

X. THINGS DO NOT CHASE YOU, YOU CHASE THEM

"The things themselves (which either to get or to avoid thou art put to so much trouble) come not unto thee themselves; but thou in a manner goest unto them. Let then thine own judgment and opinion concerning those things be at rest; and as for the things themselves, they stand still and quiet, without any noise or stir at all; and so shall all pursuing and flying cease."

What Marcus meant (core philosophy)
Marcus reminds us that external things are neutral. Desire and fear come from our judgments, not from the objects themselves. We project urgency, meaning, and emotional weight onto things that are otherwise still and indifferent. Stoicism teaches that by calming our judgments, we end unnecessary striving and avoidance.

Dating translation (what this means emotionally/socially)
In dating, emotional chaos often comes from internal interpretation:
- chasing validation
- fearing rejection
- assigning urgency to outcomes.

Marcus reframes this:
- the person or situation is not chasing you emotionally
- your thoughts create the pursuit or avoidance
- calm judgment reduces emotional turbulence.

Dating maturity means:
- recognizing when anxiety is self-created
- stepping back from urgency narratives
- allowing situations to exist without forcing emotional reaction.

Savage takeaway
It's not chasing you. Your thoughts are running toward it.

Quiet power mantra
"I calm my judgment and find peace."

XI. THE SOUL AS A PERFECT SPHERE

"Then is the soul as Empedocles[77] doth liken it, like unto a sphere or globe, when she is all of one form and figure: when she neither greedily stretcheth out herself unto anything, nor basely contracts herself, or lies flat and dejected; but shineth all with light, whereby she does see and behold the true nature, both that of the universe, and her own in particular."

---

[77] Empedocles was the pre-Socratic philosopher who first proposed that the world is composed of four elements: Earth, Air, Fire, and Water.

What Marcus meant (core philosophy)

Marcus describes the ideal state of the soul as balanced and whole. It neither reaches desperately outward nor collapses inwardly in despair. A rational soul remains centered, illuminated by understanding. Stoicism values equilibrium: freedom from both craving and emotional collapse.

Dating translation (what this means emotionally/socially)

In relationships, people often oscillate between extremes:
- overreaching for connection or approval
- withdrawing into insecurity or hopelessness.

Marcus suggests:
- emotional wholeness comes from internal stability
- self-worth should not expand or shrink based on external response
- clarity arises when the mind remains balanced.

Dating maturity means:
- showing interest without desperation
- accepting loss without self-erasure
- remaining internally grounded regardless of external dynamics.

Savage takeaway

Desperation stretches you. Rejection collapses you. Strength keeps you whole.

Quiet power mantra

"I remain centered and whole."

XII. LET OTHERS CHOOSE THEIR OPINIONS

"Will any contemn me? let him look to that, upon what grounds he does it: my care shall be that I may never be found either doing or speaking anything that doth truly deserve contempt. Will any hate me? let him look to that. I for my part will be kind and loving unto all, and even unto him that hates me, whom-soever he be, will I be ready to show his error, not by way of exprobation[78] or ostentation of my patience, but ingenuously and meekly: such as was that famous Phocion, if so be that he did not dissemble. For it is inwardly that these things must be: that the Gods who look inwardly, and not upon the outward appearance, may behold a man truly free from all indignation and grief. For what hurt can it be unto thee whatsoever any man else doth, as long as thou mayest do that which is proper and suitable to thine own nature? Wilt not thou (a man wholly appointed to be both what, and as the common good shall require) accept of that which is now seasonable to the nature of the universe?"

What Marcus meant (core philosophy)

Marcus emphasizes internal sovereignty. Others' judgments belong to them. Your responsibility is to maintain integrity and kindness regardless of external reactions. Stoicism teaches that emotional freedom comes from focusing on one's own actions rather than controlling others' opinions.

---

[78] In English, exprobation (often spelled exprobration or historically exprobation) is an archaic term for reproach, censure, or upbraiding.

Dating translation (what this means emotionally/socially)

In dating, rejection or criticism often feels personal:

- worrying about being misunderstood
- trying to control how others perceive you
- feeling wounded by someone's dislike.

Marcus reframes this:

- others' opinions reflect their perspective, not your essence
- your role is to act with integrity
- kindness does not require approval.

Dating maturity means:

- letting go of reputation management
- responding with dignity instead of defensiveness
- remaining aligned with your values regardless of others' reactions.

Savage takeaway

Their opinion is their responsibility. Your character is yours.

Quiet power mantra

"I remain kind without needing approval."

XIII. THE PARADOX OF SEEKING APPROVAL

"They contemn one another, and yet they seek to please one another: and whilst they seek to surpass one another in worldly pomp and greatness, they most debase and prostitute themselves in their better part one to another."

What Marcus meant (core philosophy)

Marcus exposes the contradiction of human social behavior. People simultaneously judge others while craving their approval. The pursuit of status often leads individuals to compromise their deeper values. Stoicism teaches detachment from external validation to preserve inner integrity.

Dating translation (what this means emotionally/socially)

Modern dating often mirrors this paradox:

- people criticize dating culture yet seek validation within it
- competing for attention while feeling disconnected
- sacrificing authenticity to appear desirable.

Marcus suggests:

- approval-seeking erodes self-respect
- comparison creates insecurity
- authenticity requires stepping outside performative competition.

Dating maturity means:

- valuing alignment over status
- choosing authenticity over performance
- refusing to trade integrity for attention.

Savage takeaway

Chasing approval often means abandoning yourself.

Quiet power mantra

"I choose authenticity over approval."

XIV. TRUE SIMPLICITY DOES NOT ANNOUNCE ITSELF

"How rotten and insincere is he, that saith, "I am resolved to carry myself hereafter towards you with all ingenuity and simplicity." O man, what doest thou mean! what needs this profession of thine? the thing itself will show it. It ought to be written upon thy forehead. No sooner thy voice is heard, than thy countenance must be able to show what is in thy mind: even as he that is loved knows presently by the looks of his sweetheart what is in her mind. Such must he be for all the world, that is truly simple and good, as he whose arm-holes are offensive, that whosoever stands by, as soon as ever he comes near him, may as it were smell him whether he will or no. But the affectation of simplicity is nowise laudable. There is nothing more shameful than perfidious friendship. Above all things, that must be avoided. However true goodness, simplicity, and kindness cannot so be hidden, but that as we have already said in the very eyes and countenance they will show themselves."

What Marcus meant (core philosophy)

Marcus warns against performative virtue. Genuine goodness does not need declarations or announcements. Authentic character reveals itself naturally through behavior, expression, and presence. Pretending to be simple or sincere is itself a form of insincerity. Stoicism values alignment between inner character and outward action, where integrity becomes self-evident rather than proclaimed.

Dating translation (what this means emotionally/socially)

In dating, people often signal virtue instead of embodying it:
* saying "I'm honest" instead of being honest
* declaring emotional maturity instead of demonstrating it
* presenting curated authenticity rather than living it.

Marcus suggests:
* real character is felt, not advertised
* sincerity shows through consistency
* true kindness does not require explanation.

Dating maturity means:
* watching actions over words
* letting your own integrity speak without performance
* recognizing that genuine connection comes from authenticity, not branding.

Savage takeaway

If someone has to announce their sincerity, question it.

Quiet power mantra

"My authenticity speaks for itself."

XV. HAPPINESS COMES FROM INNER GOVERNANCE

"To live happily is an inward power of the soul, when she is affected with indifferency, towards those things that are by their nature indifferent. To be thus affected she must consider all worldly objects both divided and whole: remembering withal that no object can of itself beget any opinion in us, neither can come to us, but stands without still and quiet; but that we ourselves beget, and as it were print in ourselves opinions concerning them. Now it is in our power, not to print them; and if they creep in and

lurk in some corner, it is in our power to wipe them off. Remembering moreover, that this care and circumspection of thine, is to continue but for a while, and then thy life will be at an end. And what should hinder, but that thou mayest do well with all these things? For if they be according to nature, rejoice in them, and let them be pleasing and acceptable unto thee. But if they be against nature, seek thou that which is according to thine own nature, and whether it be for thy credit or no, use all possible speed for the attainment of it: for no man ought to be blamed, for seeking his own good and happiness."

What Marcus meant (core philosophy)

Marcus teaches that happiness arises from internal judgment rather than external conditions. Objects and events themselves carry no emotional power; the mind assigns meaning. Stoicism encourages neutrality toward things that are inherently indifferent and emphasizes the ability to revise or erase harmful interpretations. True well-being comes from aligning with one's nature and pursuing what is genuinely good, independent of reputation or external approval.

Dating translation (what this means emotionally/socially)

In dating, emotional suffering often comes from interpretations:

- assuming rejection means personal failure
- attaching identity to relationship outcomes
- assigning meaning to neutral events.

Marcus reframes this:

- events do not create emotions; interpretations do
- you can change the story you tell yourself
- happiness grows from internal clarity rather than external validation.

Dating maturity means:

- recognizing thoughts as choices
- releasing narratives that cause unnecessary suffering
- pursuing what aligns with your true nature, regardless of social perception.

Savage takeaway

Your thoughts, not the situation, create the emotional weight.

Quiet power mantra

"I choose interpretations that support my peace."

XVI. SEE THINGS IN THEIR TRUE CONTEXT

"Of everything thou must consider from whence it came, of what things it doth consist, and into what it will be changed: what will be the nature of it, or what it will be like unto when it is changed; and that it can suffer no hurt by this change. And as for other men's either foolishness or wickedness, that it may not trouble and grieve thee; first generally thus; What reference have I unto these? and that we are all born for one another's good: then more particularly after another consideration; as a ram is first in a flock of sheep, and a bull in a herd of cattle, so am I born to rule over them. Begin yet higher, even from this: if atoms be not the beginning of all things, than which to believe nothing can be more absurd, then must we needs grant that there is a nature, that doth govern the universe. If such a nature, then are all worse things made for the better's sake; and all better for one another's sake. Secondly, what manner of men they be, at board, and upon their beds, and so forth. But above all things, how they are forced by their opinions that they hold, to do what they do; and even those things that they do, with what pride and self-conceit they do them. Thirdly, that if they do these things rightly, thou hast no reason to be grieved. But if

319

not rightly, it must needs be that they do them against their wills, and through mere ignorance. For as, according to Plato's opinion, no soul doth willingly err, so by consequent neither doth it anything otherwise than it ought, but against her will. Therefore are they grieved, whensoever they hear themselves charged, either of injustice, or unconscionableness, or covetousness, or in general, of any injurious kind of dealing towards their neighbours. Fourthly, that thou thyself doest transgress in many things, and art even such another as they are. And though perchance thou doest forbear the very act of some sins, yet hast thou in thyself an habitual disposition to them, but that either through fear, or vainglory, or some such other ambitious foolish respect, thou art restrained. Fifthly, that whether they have sinned or no, thou doest not understand perfectly. For many things are done by way of discreet policy; and generally a man must know many things first, before he be able truly and judiciously to judge of another man's action. Sixthly, that whensoever thou doest take on grievously, or makest great woe, little doest thou remember then that a man's life is but for a moment of time, and that within a while we shall all be in our graves. Seventhly, that it is not the sins and transgressions themselves that trouble us properly; for they have their existence in their minds and understandings only, that commit them; but our own opinions concerning those sins. Remove then, and be content to part with that conceit of thine, that it is a grievous thing, and thou hast removed thine anger. But how should I remove it? How? reasoning with thyself that it is not shameful. For if that which is shameful, be not the only true evil that is, thou also wilt be driven whilest thou doest follow the common instinct of nature, to avoid that which is evil, to commit many unjust things, and to become a thief, and anything, that will make to the attainment of thy intended worldly ends. Eighthly, how many things may and do oftentimes follow upon such fits of anger and grief; far more grievous in themselves, than those very things which we are so grieved or angry for. Ninthly, that meekness is a thing unconquerable, if it be true and natural, and not affected or hypocritical. For how shall even the most fierce and malicious that thou shalt conceive, be able to hold on against thee, if thou shalt still continue meek and loving unto him; and that even at that time, when he is about to do thee wrong, thou shalt be well disposed, and in good temper, with all meekness to teach him, and to instruct him better? As for example; My son, we were not born for this, to hurt and annoy one another; it will be thy hurt not mine, my son: and so to show him forcibly and fully, that it is so in very deed: and that neither bees do it one to another, nor any other creatures that are naturally sociable. But this thou must do, not scoffingly, not by way of exprobation, but tenderly without any harshness of words. Neither must thou do it by way of exercise, or ostentation, that they that are by and hear thee, may admire thee: but so always that nobody be privy to it, but himself alone: yea, though there be more present at the same time. These nine particular heads, as so many gifts from the Muses, see that thou remember well: and begin one day, whilest thou art yet alive, to be a man indeed. But on the other side thou must take heed, as much to flatter them, as to be angry with them: for both are equally uncharitable, and equally hurtful. And in thy passions, take it presently to thy consideration, that to be angry is not the part of a man, but that to be meek and gentle, as it savours of more humanity, so of more manhood. That in this, there is strength and nerves, or vigour and fortitude: whereof anger and indignation is altogether void. For the nearer everything is unto unpassionateness, the nearer it is unto power. And as grief doth proceed from weakness, so doth anger. For both, both he that is angry and that grieveth, have received a wound, and cowardly have as it were yielded themselves unto their affections. If thou wilt have a tenth also, receive this tenth gift from Hercules the guide and leader of the Muses: that is a mad man's part, to look that there should be no wicked men in the world, because it is impossible. Now for a man to brook well enough, that there should be wicked men in the world, but not to endure that any should transgress against himself, is against all equity, and indeed tyrannical."

What Marcus meant (core philosophy)

Marcus presents a comprehensive framework for dealing with difficulty, especially with other people. Everything should be viewed through its origin, composition, and inevitable transformation. Human behavior is driven by beliefs, ignorance, or limitation rather than pure malice. Stoicism encourages humility, recognizing that we share the same flaws as those we judge. Anger arises from personal interpretation, not from the actions themselves. True strength lies in calm understanding, perspective on life's brevity, and unwavering gentleness. Meekness is not weakness but invincible stability.

Dating translation (what this means emotionally/socially)
In dating and relationships, emotional pain often comes from:
- assuming others act with intentional harm
- reacting with anger or resentment
- forgetting shared human imperfection.

Marcus reframes this through several lenses:
- people act according to their beliefs and limitations
- you are not immune to the same flaws
- misjudgment is often ignorance rather than cruelty
- life is short, making prolonged anger irrational.

Dating maturity means:
- choosing understanding over reactive anger
- recognizing that others' behavior reflects their internal framework
- maintaining composure and kindness even when wronged.

Strength in relationships is not dominance or retaliation but emotional steadiness.

Savage takeaway
Calm understanding is power. Anger is surrender.

Quiet power mantra
"I respond with clarity, patience, and strength."

XVII. WATCH AND CORRECT THE MOVEMENTS OF YOUR MIND

"Four several dispositions or inclinations there be of the mind and understanding, which to be aware of, thou must carefully observe: and whensoever thou doest discover them, thou must rectify them, saying to thyself concerning every one of them, This imagination is not necessary; this is uncharitable: this thou shalt speak as another man's slave, or instrument; than which nothing can be more senseless and absurd: for the fourth, thou shalt sharply check and upbraid thyself; for that thou doest suffer that more divine part in thee, to become subject and obnoxious to that more ignoble part of thy body, and the gross lusts and concupiscences thereof."

What Marcus meant (core philosophy)
Marcus describes active mental discipline. The mind generates impulses and interpretations that must be examined and corrected. He outlines four internal distortions: unnecessary thoughts, unkind judgments, surrendering autonomy to external influence, and allowing higher reason to be ruled by lower impulses. Stoicism emphasizes constant self-awareness and correction to maintain alignment with reason and virtue.

321

Dating translation (what this means emotionally/socially)

In dating, the mind often creates suffering through unchecked patterns:

- overthinking scenarios that are not necessary
- interpreting others harshly or defensively
- acting from emotional dependence rather than autonomy
- letting desire or insecurity override wisdom.

Marcus suggests:

- question thoughts before believing them
- recognize when reactions are driven by ego or fear
- keep your higher self in command.

Dating maturity means:

- interrupting reactive narratives
- refusing to abandon self-respect for emotional comfort
- maintaining clarity even in emotionally charged situations.

Savage takeaway

Not every thought deserves authority. Challenge it.

Quiet power mantra

"My higher mind leads my reactions."

XVIII. REMAIN IN ALIGNMENT WITH YOUR NATURE

"What portion soever, either of air or fire there be in thee, although by nature it tend upwards, submitting nevertheless to the ordinance of the universe, it abides here below in this mixed body. So whatsoever is in thee, either earthy, or humid, although by nature it tend downwards, yet is it against its nature both raised upwards, and standing, or consistent. So obedient are even the elements themselves to the universe, abiding patiently wheresoever (though against their nature) they are placed, until the sound as it were of their retreat, and separation. Is it not a grievous thing then, that thy reasonable part only should be disobedient, and should not endure to keep its place: yea though it be nothing enjoined that is contrary unto it, but that only which is according to its nature? For we cannot say of it when it is disobedient, as we say of the fire, or air, that it tends upwards towards its proper element, for then goes it the quite contrary way. For the motion of the mind to any injustice, or incontinency, or to sorrow, or to fear, is nothing else but a separation from nature. Also when the mind is grieved for anything that is happened by the divine providence, then doth it likewise forsake its own place. For it was ordained unto holiness and godliness, which specially consist in an humble submission to God and His providence in all things; as well as unto justice: these also being part of those duties, which as naturally sociable, we are bound unto; and without which we cannot happily converse one with another: yea and the very ground and fountain indeed of all just actions."

What Marcus meant (core philosophy)

Marcus compares human reason to natural elements that obey universal order. Even elements act in accordance with the greater whole, while humans often resist their own nature through injustice, fear, or emotional disturbance. Stoicism teaches that harmony comes from aligning with reason, justice, and acceptance of universal order. Emotional turmoil often signals separation from one's true nature.

Dating translation (what this means emotionally/socially)
In relationships, misalignment often appears as:
- acting against your values to keep someone
- reacting from fear instead of integrity
- resisting reality instead of accepting it.

Marcus reframes this:
- emotional chaos often comes from leaving your true nature
- alignment with values restores stability
- acceptance of what is brings peace faster than resistance.

Dating maturity means:
- choosing integrity over impulse
- accepting outcomes without self-betrayal
- grounding decisions in personal truth rather than emotional turbulence.

Savage takeaway
Every time you abandon your nature, you create your own suffering.

Quiet power mantra
"I remain aligned with my true nature."

XIX. ONE TRUE END CREATES INNER CONSISTENCY
"He that hath not one and the self-same general end always as long as he liveth, cannot possibly be one and the self-same man always. But this will not suffice except thou add also what ought to be this general end. For as the general conceit and apprehension of all those things which upon no certain ground are by the greater part of men deemed good, cannot be uniform and agreeable, but that only which is limited and restrained by some certain proprieties and conditions, as of community: that nothing be conceived good, which is not commonly and publicly good: so must the end also that we propose unto ourselves, be common and sociable. For he that doth direct all his own private motions and purposes to that end, all his actions will be agreeable and uniform; and by that means will be still the same man."

What Marcus meant (core philosophy)
Marcus argues that identity requires a stable guiding purpose. Without a consistent overarching aim, a person becomes fragmented and inconsistent. However, this purpose must not be purely self-serving. True alignment comes from orienting life toward the common good. Stoicism teaches that personal stability emerges when actions consistently serve reason, virtue, and collective harmony.

Dating translation (what this means emotionally/socially)
In dating, inconsistency often comes from unclear internal direction:
- shifting standards depending on attraction
- abandoning values for temporary emotion
- changing identity to match partners.

Marcus suggests:
- define a core purpose or standard for how you show up
- align decisions with long-term values, not momentary feelings
- relationships should fit your guiding principles, not redefine them.

Dating maturity means:
- knowing who you are across situations
- maintaining integrity regardless of romantic pressure
- choosing partners aligned with your deeper values.

Savage takeaway

If your purpose keeps changing, so will your identity.

Quiet power mantra

"My actions align with my true purpose."

XX. THE COUNTRY MOUSE AND THE CITY MOUSE

"Remember the fable of the country mouse and the city mouse, and the great fright and terror that this was put into."

What Marcus meant (core philosophy)

Marcus references a simple moral tale to highlight the illusion of glamour versus genuine peace. The country mouse lives simply but safely, while the city mouse enjoys luxury mixed with anxiety. Stoicism values tranquility over external prestige. Comfort without peace is not true happiness.

Dating translation (what this means emotionally/socially)

In relationships, "city mouse" dynamics often appear as:
- exciting but unstable connections
- high-status or dramatic relationships that create anxiety
- chasing intensity instead of calm compatibility.

Marcus suggests:
- peace matters more than spectacle
- emotional safety outweighs external appeal
- simplicity often leads to greater contentment.

Dating maturity means:
- recognizing when excitement masks instability
- choosing calm over chaos
- valuing security without boredom.

Savage takeaway

Luxury without peace is just decorated stress.

Quiet power mantra

"I choose peace over illusion."

XXI. COMMON OPINIONS ARE CHILDHOOD FEARS

"Socrates was wont to call the common conceits and opinions of men, the common bugbears of the world: the proper terror of silly children."

What Marcus meant (core philosophy)

Marcus echoes Socrates in dismissing collective fears shaped by social conditioning. Many societal expectations and anxieties are irrational constructs. Stoicism encourages independent judgment instead of submission to popular opinion.

Dating translation (what this means emotionally/socially)

Modern dating is filled with social "bugbears":

- timelines for marriage or milestones
- status comparisons
- fear of being single or "behind."

Marcus suggests:

- many pressures are socially invented fears
- freedom comes from questioning cultural narratives
- authenticity replaces performative conformity.

Dating maturity means:

- rejecting arbitrary timelines
- defining success personally
- refusing to live according to collective anxiety.

Savage takeaway

Most dating fears are inherited myths, not reality.

Quiet power mantra

"I release socially invented fears."

XXII. QUIET HUMILITY OVER STATUS

"The Lacedæmonians at their public spectacles were wont to appoint seats and forms for their strangers in the shadow, they themselves were content to sit anywhere."

What Marcus meant (core philosophy)

Marcus highlights Spartan humility. True strength does not require recognition or preferential treatment. Stoicism values modesty, service, and self-possession over displays of status.

Dating translation (what this means emotionally/socially)

In relationships, ego often appears as:

- needing to feel chosen publicly
- seeking status through association
- demanding validation through position.

Marcus suggests:

- confidence does not require superiority
- humility creates genuine connection
- self-worth is internal, not hierarchical.

Dating maturity means:

- showing respect without seeking dominance
- valuing mutual equality
- letting actions reflect strength rather than demanding acknowledgment.

Savage takeaway

Real confidence doesn't need the best seat in the room.

Quiet power mantra

"My worth is quiet and steady."

XXIII. GRATITUDE AND THE FEAR OF UNRETURNED GOODNESS

"What Socrates answered unto Perdiccas[79], why he did not come unto him, Lest of all deaths I should die the worst kind of death, said he: that is, not able to requite the good that hath been done unto me."

What Marcus meant (core philosophy)

Marcus recalls Socrates emphasizing the weight of gratitude and reciprocity. The greatest loss is not physical death but failing to honor or return genuine goodness received from others. Stoicism values integrity in relationships, where acknowledgment and repayment of kindness reflect moral responsibility.

Dating translation (what this means emotionally/socially)

In relationships, imbalance often appears as:
*   receiving emotional investment without reciprocation
*   taking kindness for granted
*   avoiding situations where genuine reciprocity is required.

Marcus suggests:
*   recognize and honor genuine effort or love
*   avoid dynamics where gratitude cannot exist
*   reciprocity strengthens dignity on both sides.

Dating maturity means:
*   valuing mutual effort
*   acknowledging emotional generosity
*   choosing relationships where appreciation flows both ways.

Savage takeaway

The worst loss isn't rejection. It's failing to honor real kindness.

Quiet power mantra

"I give and receive with gratitude and integrity."

XXIV. KEEP EXAMPLES OF THE WORTHY IN YOUR MIND

"In the ancient mystical letters of the Ephesians, there was an item, that a man should always have in his mind some one or other of the ancient worthies."

What Marcus meant (core philosophy)

Marcus highlights the importance of role models. Keeping examples of virtuous individuals in mind provides guidance, inspiration, and moral calibration. Stoicism encourages learning through observation and imitation of excellence.

Dating translation (what this means emotionally/socially)

In dating, role models shape expectations:
*   observing healthy relationship dynamics
*   modeling emotional maturity and respect
*   choosing ideals that reflect growth rather than dysfunction.

---

[79] Perdiccas is mentioned by Marcus Aurelius as a symbol of the futility of ambition and the fleeting nature of power.

Dating maturity means:
- asking what a wise or grounded person would do in your situation
- learning from examples instead of repeating unconscious patterns
- setting standards based on admired qualities.

Savage takeaway
If you don't choose your models, culture chooses them for you.

Quiet power mantra
"I follow examples that elevate me."

XXV. LOOK TO THE SKY FOR ORDER AND SIMPLICITY

"The Pythagoreans were wont betimes in the morning the first thing they did, to look up unto the heavens, to put themselves in mind of them who constantly and invariably did perform their task: as also to put themselves in mind of orderliness, or good order, and of purity, and of naked simplicity. For no star or planet hath any cover before it."

What Marcus meant (core philosophy)
Marcus references the Pythagorean practice of observing the heavens as a reminder of consistency, clarity, and natural order. Stoicism values alignment with universal order, encouraging individuals to emulate the steadiness and simplicity seen in nature.

Dating translation (what this means emotionally/socially)
In relationships, chaos often comes from inconsistency:
- unpredictable communication
- unclear intentions
- emotional volatility.

Marcus suggests:
- consistency is a sign of alignment
- simplicity and transparency create trust
- steady behavior reflects inner order.

Dating maturity means:
- valuing reliability over excitement alone
- showing up consistently
- seeking clarity instead of complexity.

Savage takeaway
Consistency is more attractive than intensity.

Quiet power mantra
"I move with clarity and steady purpose."

XXVI. TRUE DIGNITY DOES NOT DEPEND ON APPEARANCE

"How Socrates looked, when he was fain to gird himself with a skin, Xanthippe his wife having taken away his clothes, and carried them abroad with her, and what he said to his fellows and friends, who were ashamed; and out of respect to him, did retire themselves when they saw him thus decked."

What Marcus meant (core philosophy)
Marcus recalls Socrates maintaining composure and dignity despite outward embarrassment or discomfort. Stoicism teaches that external appearances cannot diminish inner worth. True character remains intact regardless of circumstance.

Dating translation (what this means emotionally/socially)
In dating, vulnerability or awkward moments can feel humiliating:
- feeling exposed after rejection
- worrying about how others perceive you
- equating embarrassment with loss of value.

Marcus suggests:
- dignity comes from inner stability, not external image
- discomfort does not define worth
- self-respect remains even in imperfect situations.

Dating maturity means:
- embracing vulnerability without shame
- refusing to let embarrassment dictate identity
- holding confidence independent of circumstances.

Savage takeaway
Embarrassment only matters if you decide it does.

Quiet power mantra
"My dignity is internal."

XXVII. LIFE REQUIRES LEARNING
"In matter of writing or reading thou must needs be taught before thou can do either: much more in matter of life. "For thou art born a mere slave, to thy senses and brutish affections;" destitute without teaching of all true knowledge and sound reason."

What Marcus meant (core philosophy)
Marcus emphasizes that wisdom is learned, not innate. Just as skills require instruction, living well requires deliberate training of the mind. Without discipline and learning, humans default to impulse and emotion rather than reason.

Dating translation (what this means emotionally/socially)
In relationships, many struggles come from lack of emotional education:
- repeating unhealthy patterns
- reacting from instinct rather than awareness
- confusing intensity with compatibility.

Marcus suggests:
- emotional intelligence must be developed consciously
- self-awareness is a skill built over time
- growth comes from learning, not instinct alone.

Dating maturity means:
- reflecting on patterns instead of repeating them
- learning communication and boundaries intentionally
- treating relationships as areas of growth and practice.

Savage takeaway
Love isn't just felt. It's learned.

Quiet power mantra
"I grow wiser through practice and learning."

XXVIII. EVEN VIRTUE WILL BE CRITICIZED
"My heart smiled within me." "They will accuse even virtue herself; with heinous and opprobrious words."

What Marcus meant (core philosophy)
Marcus reminds himself that criticism is inevitable, even for those acting virtuously. No action, no matter how good, escapes judgment or misunderstanding. Stoicism teaches internal validation rather than dependence on external approval. True contentment comes from knowing one's intentions are aligned with virtue, regardless of public opinion.

Dating translation (what this means emotionally/socially)
In relationships and dating:
- doing the right thing may still attract criticism
- setting boundaries may be framed as selfishness
- honesty may be misinterpreted as harshness.

Marcus suggests:
- expect misunderstanding without losing integrity
- remain internally aligned even when judged
- do not abandon values to avoid criticism.

Dating maturity means:
- accepting that you cannot control perception
- choosing authenticity over approval
- trusting inner clarity over external noise.

Savage takeaway
If you live honestly, someone will still misunderstand you. Continue anyway.

Quiet power mantra
"I stay true even when misunderstood."

XXIX. LONGING FOR WHAT IS NOT PRESENT
"As they that long after figs in winter when they cannot be had; so are they that long after children, before they be granted them."

What Marcus meant (core philosophy)
Marcus speaks about desire misaligned with timing. Wanting something outside its natural season creates unnecessary suffering. Stoicism teaches acceptance of natural rhythms and patience with unfolding events.

Dating translation (what this means emotionally/socially)
In dating and life:
- longing for commitment before readiness
- forcing timelines that do not align naturally
- comparing life stages with others.

Marcus suggests:
- desire becomes suffering when it ignores reality
- patience aligns you with natural progression
- fulfillment often requires timing beyond personal control.

Dating maturity means:
- allowing relationships to evolve naturally
- recognizing when urgency is self-created
- trusting that some things cannot be forced.

Savage takeaway
Wanting figs in winter doesn't make them grow faster.

Quiet power mantra
"I respect timing and natural unfolding."

XXX. ACCEPT CHANGE AS NATURAL
"As often as a father kisseth his child, he should say secretly with himself," (said Epictetus,) "tomorrow perchance shall he die." But these words be ominous. No words ominous (said he) that signify anything that is natural: in very truth and deed not more ominous than this, "to cut down grapes when they are ripe." Green grapes, ripe grapes, dried grapes, or raisins: so many changes and mutations of one thing, not into that which was not absolutely, but rather so many several changes and mutations, not into that which hath no being at all, but into that which is not yet in being.

What Marcus meant (core philosophy)
Marcus emphasizes acceptance of impermanence. Change, loss, and transformation are natural processes, not tragedies imposed by fate. Recognizing transience deepens appreciation without clinging. Stoicism encourages loving fully while understanding that all things evolve and transform.

Dating translation (what this means emotionally/socially)
In relationships:
- fearing loss can prevent genuine presence
- attachment grows painful when permanence is expected
- endings are transformations rather than annihilations.

Marcus suggests:
- appreciate moments fully without assuming permanence
- accept that relationships evolve or end naturally
- transformation is continuation, not disappearance.

Dating maturity means:
- loving without clinging
- accepting change without bitterness
- seeing endings as transitions rather than failures.

Savage takeaway

Nothing truly disappears. It only changes form.

Quiet power mantra

"I embrace change as part of life's rhythm."

XXXI. PROTECT YOUR FREE WILL AND MASTER ASSENT

"Of the free will there is no thief or robber," out of Epictetus; whose is this also: that we should find a certain art and method of assenting; and that we should always observe with great care and heed the inclinations of our minds, that they may always be with their due restraint and reservation, always charitable, and according to the true worth of every present object. And as for earnest longing, that we should altogether avoid it: and to use averseness in those things only, that wholly depend of our own wills. It is not about ordinary petty matters, believe it, that all our strife and contention is, but whether, with the vulgar, we should be mad, or by the help of philosophy wise and sober, said he.

What Marcus meant (core philosophy)

Marcus draws from Epictetus to emphasize that free will is inviolable. External forces cannot steal the inner power to choose how we respond. The discipline lies in "assent" which is the act of agreeing with or believing our thoughts and impressions. Stoicism teaches careful awareness before accepting emotional reactions as truth. True struggle is not against circumstances but between irrational impulse and philosophical clarity.

Dating translation (what this means emotionally/socially)

In relationships, emotional chaos often begins with unchecked mental assent:
- believing assumptions without evidence
- attaching meaning too quickly
- reacting from urgency or longing.

Marcus suggests:
- pause before accepting emotional narratives
- examine whether a thought deserves agreement
- avoid intense craving that removes emotional balance.

Dating maturity means:
- recognizing that emotional reactions are choices, not inevitabilities
- maintaining agency over interpretation
- reserving emotional energy for what truly aligns with your values.

Savage takeaway

No one steals your peace. You hand it over when you agree with the wrong thoughts.

Quiet power mantra

"I choose my thoughts with intention."

XXXII. STOP COMPETING FOR WHAT YOU ALREADY POSSESS

Socrates said, "What will you have? the souls of reasonable, or unreasonable creatures? Of reasonable. But what? Of those whose reason is sound and perfect? or of those whose reason is vitiated and corrupted? Of those whose reason is sound and perfect. Why then labour ye not for such? Because we have them already. What then do ye so strive and contend between you?"

What Marcus meant (core philosophy)
Marcus recalls Socrates questioning unnecessary conflict. Humans often fight and compete despite already possessing what truly matters: rational capacity and shared humanity. Stoicism highlights the absurdity of rivalry driven by ego when fundamental equality exists.

Dating translation (what this means emotionally/socially)
In dating, unnecessary competition appears as:
- comparing yourself to others for validation
- competing for attention or status
- seeing relationships as battles rather than connections.

Marcus suggests:
- stop measuring worth through comparison
- recognize shared human value
- seek partnership instead of rivalry.

Dating maturity means:
- stepping out of competitive dynamics
- valuing mutual respect over "winning"
- understanding that connection grows from cooperation, not comparison.

Savage takeaway
You don't need to compete for worth you already possess.

Quiet power mantra
"I release comparison and stand in my inherent value."

THE TWELFTH BOOK
Leave Clean
(Legacy Over Drama)

I. LIVE FULLY NOW BY ALIGNING WITH NATURE

"Whatsoever thou doest hereafter aspire unto, thou mayest even now enjoy and possess, if thou doest not envy thyself thine own happiness. And that will be, if thou shalt forget all that is past, and for the future, refer thyself wholly to the Divine Providence, and shalt bend and apply all thy present thoughts and intentions to holiness and righteousness. To holiness, in accepting willingly whatsoever is sent by the Divine Providence, as being that which the nature of the universe hath appointed unto thee, which also hath appointed thee for that, whatsoever it be. To righteousness, in speaking the truth freely, and without ambiguity; and in doing all things justly and discreetly. Now in this good course, let not other men's either wickedness, or opinion, or voice hinder thee: no, nor the sense of this thy pampered mass of flesh: for let that which suffers, look to itself. If therefore whensoever the time of thy departing shall come, thou shalt readily leave all things, and shalt respect thy mind only, and that divine part of thine, and this shall be thine only fear, not that some time or other thou shalt cease to live, but thou shalt never begin to live according to nature: then shalt thou be a man indeed, worthy of that world, from which thou hadst thy beginning; then shalt thou cease to be a stranger in thy country, and to wonder at those things that happen daily, as things strange and unexpected, and anxiously to depend of divers things that are not in thy power."

What Marcus meant (core philosophy)

Marcus teaches that fulfillment is available in the present moment, not in some future achievement. Happiness is self-denied when we cling to the past or worry about the future. Alignment with nature comes through acceptance of what happens, commitment to truth and justice, and independence from external opinion or bodily discomfort. Stoicism encourages living in accordance with reason and virtue now, rather than postponing life until circumstances feel ideal.

Dating translation (what this means emotionally/socially)

In relationships and dating, people often delay happiness:
* waiting for the "right" partner to feel complete
* holding onto past hurt instead of being present
* allowing others' opinions to shape choices.

Marcus suggests:
* fulfillment begins with inner alignment, not relationship status
* accept experiences as part of your path without resistance
* act with honesty and integrity regardless of external response.

Dating maturity means:
* living fully in the present rather than projecting happiness into the future
* releasing attachment to past narratives
* choosing authenticity over approval.

Savage takeaway
You don't need a different future to start living fully now.

Quiet power mantra
"I live aligned with truth and presence today."

II. FREE THE MIND FROM WHAT IS NOT TRULY YOURS

"God beholds our minds and understandings, bare and naked from these material vessels, and outsides, and all earthly dross. For with His simple and pure understanding, He pierceth into our inmost and purest parts, which from His, as it were by a water pipe and channel, first flowed and issued. This if thou also shalt use to do, thou shalt rid thyself of that manifold luggage, wherewith thou art round about encumbered. For he that does regard neither his body, nor his clothing, nor his dwelling, nor any such external furniture, must needs gain unto himself great rest and ease. Three things there be in all, which thou doest consist of; thy body, thy life, and thy mind. Of these the two former, are so far forth thine, as that thou art bound to take care for them. But the third alone is that which is properly thine. If then thou shalt separate from thyself, that is from thy mind, whatsoever other men either do or say, or whatsoever thou thyself hast heretofore either done or said; and all troublesome thoughts concerning the future, and whatsoever, (as either belonging to thy body or life:) is without the jurisdiction of thine own will, and whatsoever in the ordinary course of human chances and accidents doth happen unto thee; so that thy mind (keeping herself loose and free from all outward coincidental entanglements; always in a readiness to depart:) shall live by herself, and to herself, doing that which is just, accepting whatsoever doth happen, and speaking the truth always; if, I say, thou shalt separate from thy mind, whatsoever by sympathy might adhere unto it, and all time both past and future, and shalt make thyself in all points and respects, like unto Empedocles his allegorical sphere, "all round and circular," &c., and shalt think of no longer life than that which is now present: then shalt thou be truly able to pass the remainder of thy days without troubles and distractions; nobly and generously disposed, and in good favour and correspondency, with that spirit which is within thee."

What Marcus meant (core philosophy)
Marcus teaches radical mental clarity through separation of what truly belongs to you from what does not. The body and external circumstances require care but are not the essence of self. The mind alone is fully yours. Freedom arises when you detach your inner state from past regrets, future anxieties, others' actions, and uncontrollable events. Stoicism encourages focusing solely on what is within your control: just action, truthful speech, and acceptance of reality.

Dating translation (what this means emotionally/socially)
In relationships, mental burden often comes from entanglements that are not truly yours:
- replaying past conversations
- worrying about others' opinions
- projecting future fears
- attaching identity to external circumstances.

Marcus suggests:
- separate your mind from external noise
- focus on present integrity rather than past or future stories
- maintain inner independence regardless of relationship outcomes.

334

Dating maturity means:
- refusing to carry emotional baggage that does not belong to you
- accepting what happens without internal chaos
- prioritizing inner alignment over external validation.

Savage takeaway
Most of what weighs you down isn't yours. Drop it.

Quiet power mantra
"My mind is free, present, and aligned."

III. WHY DO WE VALUE OTHERS' OPINIONS MORE THAN OUR OWN?

"I have often wondered how it should come to pass, that every man loving himself best, should more regard other men's opinions concerning himself than his own. For if any God or grave master standing by, should command any of us to think nothing by himself but what he should presently speak out; no man were able to endure it, though but for one day. Thus do we fear more what our neighbours will think of us, than what we ourselves."

What Marcus meant (core philosophy)
Marcus questions the contradiction of human behavior. We claim to value ourselves most, yet allow external judgment to outweigh our own inner evaluation. Stoicism teaches that self-respect should come from internal alignment with reason and virtue, not from public approval. The fear of others' opinions reveals dependence on external validation rather than genuine self-governance.

Dating translation (what this means emotionally/socially)
In relationships, this shows up as:
- shaping behavior to be perceived favorably
- staying in situations to avoid judgment
- worrying about appearances more than inner truth.

Marcus suggests:
- trust your internal compass over social pressure
- recognize how much energy is spent managing perception
- prioritize authentic self-respect over external approval.

Dating maturity means:
- choosing what feels aligned rather than what looks acceptable
- valuing your own judgment above collective opinion
- refusing to perform for validation.

Savage takeaway
You say you love yourself, but whose voice actually decides your choices?

Quiet power mantra
"My inner judgment matters more than external opinion."

IV. TRUST THE ORDER OF WHAT IS BEYOND YOUR CONTROL

"How come it to pass that the Gods having ordered all other things so well and so lovingly, should be overseen in this one only thing, that whereas there hath been some very good men that have made many covenants as it were with God and by many holy actions and outward services contracted a kind of familiarity with Him; that these men when once they are dead, should never be restored to life, but be extinct for ever. But this thou mayest be sure of, that this (if it be so indeed) would never have been so ordered by the Gods, had it been fit otherwise. For certainly it was possible, had it been more just so and had it been according to nature, the nature of the universe would easily have borne it. But now because it is not so, be therefore confident that it was not fit it should be so… For were not the Gods both just and good in the highest degree, thou durst not thus reason with them. Now if just and good, it could not be that in the creation of the world, they should either unjustly or unreasonably oversee anything."

What Marcus meant (core philosophy)

Marcus wrestles with existential questions about justice and mortality. His conclusion is rooted in Stoic trust in universal order. If something occurs in reality, it must belong within the natural structure of the whole. Stoicism encourages acceptance of what cannot be fully understood, trusting that the larger system operates beyond individual perspective.

Dating translation (what this means emotionally/socially)

In relationships, people often struggle with:
- why good people experience heartbreak
- why effort does not always lead to lasting connection
- why fairness does not always appear in outcomes.

Marcus reframes this:
- not everything that happens will feel just from a personal viewpoint
- lack of understanding does not equal lack of meaning
- acceptance brings peace faster than endless questioning.

Dating maturity means:
- releasing the need to fully understand every ending
- trusting that experiences serve growth even when unclear
- letting go of narratives about what "should" have happened.

Savage takeaway

Not everything needs explanation to be accepted.

Quiet power mantra

"I trust the unfolding beyond my understanding."

V. TRAIN YOURSELF EVEN IN WHAT SEEMS IMPOSSIBLE

"Use thyself even unto those things that thou doest at first despair of. For the left hand we see, which for the most part lieth idle because not used; yet doth it hold the bridle with more strength than the right, because it hath been used unto it."

What Marcus meant (core philosophy)

Marcus highlights the power of deliberate practice. Abilities grow through repeated use, even when initially weak or unfamiliar. The example of the left hand becoming strong through necessity shows that skill and resilience are cultivated through effort rather than inherent talent. Stoicism encourages training the mind through disciplined action until virtue becomes natural.

Dating translation (what this means emotionally/socially)
In relationships, growth often requires developing unfamiliar skills:
- setting boundaries when you are used to overgiving
- communicating honestly instead of avoiding conflict
- choosing self-respect over old emotional habits.

Marcus suggests:
- discomfort signals growth, not failure
- emotional strengths develop through repetition
- what feels unnatural today can become second nature.

Dating maturity means:
- practicing healthier patterns even when awkward
- trusting that consistency builds emotional strength
- embracing growth rather than retreating into familiarity.

Savage takeaway
What feels hard now is just a skill you haven't trained yet.

Quiet power mantra
"I strengthen through practice."

VI. MEDITATE ON REALITY AND PREPARE THE MIND
"Let these be the objects of thy ordinary meditation: to consider, what manner of men both for soul and body we ought to be, whensoever death shall surprise us: the shortness of this our mortal life: the immense vastness of the time that hath been before, and will be after us: the frailty of every worldly material object: all these things to consider, and behold clearly in themselves, all disguisement of external outside being removed and taken away. Again, to consider the efficient causes of all things: the proper ends and references of all actions: what pain is in itself; what pleasure, what death: what fame or honour, how every man is the true and proper ground of his own rest and tranquillity, and that no man can truly be hindered by any other: that all is but conceit and opinion. As for the use of thy dogmata, thou must carry thyself in the practice of them, rather like unto a pancratiastes[80], or one that at the same time both fights and wrestles with hands and feet, than a gladiator. For this, if he lose his sword that he fights with, he is gone: whereas the other hath still his hand free, which he may easily turn and manage at his will."

What Marcus meant (core philosophy)
Marcus outlines a mental discipline grounded in clarity and preparation. Regular contemplation of mortality, impermanence, and the true nature of things strips away illusion. Peace arises from understanding that external events do not control inner stability. Stoicism teaches adaptability: philosophy should function like a versatile fighter who can respond to any circumstance without reliance on external tools.

---

[80] In English, pancratiastes (from the Greek *pankratiastēs*) refers to a competitor in the pancratium, the ancient Greek combat sport that combined wrestling and boxing.

Dating translation (what this means emotionally/socially)
In relationships, emotional resilience comes from:
- understanding impermanence without fear
- recognizing that validation, fame, or status are temporary
- knowing that inner stability does not depend on another person.

Marcus suggests:
- cultivate adaptability instead of rigid expectations
- develop internal tools rather than relying on external reassurance
- recognize that emotional peace comes from your own mindset.

Dating maturity means:
- handling unexpected changes with flexibility
- grounding identity internally rather than relationally
- practicing emotional self-sufficiency.

Savage takeaway
If your stability depends on one external thing, you're fighting with one weapon.

Quiet power mantra
"I remain adaptable and internally steady."

VII. SEE THINGS BY THEIR TRUE STRUCTURE
"All worldly things thou must behold and consider, dividing them into matter, form, and reference, or their proper end."

What Marcus meant (core philosophy)
Marcus advises analytical clarity. Everything should be understood through three lenses: its material substance, its shape or structure, and its purpose or end. Stoicism teaches that breaking experiences into their essential components reduces illusion and emotional exaggeration. Clear perception leads to rational response.

Dating translation (what this means emotionally/socially)
In relationships, emotional confusion often comes from seeing situations as overwhelming wholes rather than examining them clearly:
- separating attraction from compatibility
- distinguishing intention from outcome
- understanding whether a dynamic serves growth or distraction.

Marcus suggests:
- analyze rather than react
- understand the purpose behind experiences
- see situations for what they are, not what emotion paints them to be.

Dating maturity means:
- evaluating relationships based on substance and direction
- recognizing when something lacks alignment with your deeper goals
- choosing clarity over romanticized interpretation.

Savage takeaway

When you break things down clearly, illusions lose power.

Quiet power mantra

"I see things as they truly are."

VIII. TRUE HAPPINESS COMES FROM ALIGNMENT

"How happy is man in this his power that hath been granted unto him: that he needs not do anything but what God shall approve, and that he may embrace contentedly, whatsoever God doth send unto him?"

What Marcus meant (core philosophy)

Marcus emphasizes the freedom found in alignment with divine order or natural law. Happiness arises when actions align with virtue and acceptance replaces resistance. Stoicism teaches that peace comes from living according to higher principles rather than personal desire alone.

Dating translation (what this means emotionally/socially)

In relationships, struggle often comes from resisting reality:

- trying to control outcomes
- forcing incompatible connections
- rejecting what unfolds naturally.

Marcus suggests:

- act with integrity regardless of outcome
- accept experiences as part of your path
- contentment grows from alignment rather than control.

Dating maturity means:

- embracing what happens without internal war
- trusting that authenticity leads to better outcomes
- releasing attachment to forced narratives.

Savage takeaway

Peace begins when you stop fighting what is.

Quiet power mantra

"I act with integrity and accept what comes."

IX. ACCUSE NO ONE

"Whatsoever doth happen in the ordinary course and consequence of natural events, neither the Gods, (for it is not possible, that they either wittingly or unwittingly should do anything amiss) nor men, (for it is through ignorance, and therefore against their wills that they do anything amiss) must be accused. None then must be accused."

What Marcus meant (core philosophy)

Marcus advocates radical acceptance. Events arise through natural processes, and human mistakes often come from ignorance rather than intentional harm. Stoicism encourages releasing blame to reduce unnecessary suffering and maintain emotional equilibrium.

Dating translation (what this means emotionally/socially)
In relationships:

- blame prolongs emotional attachment to pain
- assuming malicious intent intensifies resentment
- understanding limitation fosters compassion.

Marcus suggests:

- many people act from lack of awareness rather than cruelty
- releasing blame frees emotional energy
- acceptance reduces internal turmoil.

Dating maturity means:

- acknowledging hurt without cultivating bitterness
- understanding human imperfection
- moving forward without needing villains.

Savage takeaway
Blame keeps you tied to what already ended.

Quiet power mantra
"I release blame and choose peace."

X. DO NOT BE SURPRISED BY WHAT IS NATURAL

"How ridiculous and strange is he, that wonders at anything that happens in this life in the ordinary course of nature!"

What Marcus meant (core philosophy)
Marcus reminds himself that many events feel shocking only because we forget their inevitability. Change, conflict, loss, and imperfection are natural parts of existence. Stoicism encourages expecting reality rather than being disturbed by it.

Dating translation (what this means emotionally/socially)
In relationships, people are often surprised by:

- misunderstandings
- incompatibility
- emotional change.

Marcus suggests:

- recognize that these are natural aspects of human connection
- expectation of perfection creates unnecessary suffering
- resilience comes from anticipating reality rather than resisting it.

Dating maturity means:

- normalizing challenges instead of dramatizing them
- accepting human complexity
- staying steady when predictable difficulties arise.

Savage takeaway
Life is less shocking when you stop expecting perfection.

Quiet power mantra
"I accept reality without surprise."

XI. WHATEVER THE NATURE OF THE UNIVERSE, YOUR MIND REMAINS FREE

"Either fate, (and that either an absolute necessity, and unavoidable decree; or a placable and flexible Providence) or all is a mere casual confusion, void of all order and government. If an absolute and unavoidable necessity, why doest thou resist? If a placable and exorable Providence, make thyself worthy of the divine help and assistance. If all be a mere confusion without any moderator, or governor, then hast thou reason to congratulate thyself; that in such a general flood of confusion thou thyself hast obtained a reasonable faculty, whereby thou mayest govern thine own life and actions. But if thou beest carried away with the flood, it must be thy body perchance, or thy life, or some other thing that belongs unto them that is carried away: thy mind and understanding cannot. Or should it be so, that the light of a candle indeed is still bright and lightsome until it be put out: and should truth, and righteousness, and temperance cease to shine in thee whilest thou thyself hast any being?"

What Marcus meant (core philosophy)

Marcus examines every possible structure of reality and concludes that inner freedom remains constant regardless. If life is determined by fate, resistance is pointless. If guided by providence, alignment with virtue invites support. If chaotic, the gift of reason becomes even more valuable as a personal compass. Stoicism teaches that external uncertainty does not threaten inner virtue. Truth, justice, and self-control remain within personal control until life itself ends.

Dating translation (what this means emotionally/socially)

In relationships, uncertainty often creates anxiety:
- wondering whether outcomes are destiny or coincidence
- feeling powerless when things change unexpectedly
- fearing loss of control.

Marcus suggests:
- regardless of circumstances, your inner character remains yours
- external outcomes do not extinguish personal integrity
- emotional stability comes from self-governance, not predictability.

Dating maturity means:
- staying aligned with values regardless of outcome
- maintaining self-respect even when relationships shift
- recognizing that internal strength persists despite external chaos.

Savage takeaway

No matter what happens outside you, your character remains yours to keep.

Quiet power mantra

"My inner light remains steady."

XII. BEFORE JUDGING, QUESTION YOUR ASSUMPTIONS

"At the conceit and apprehension that such and such a one hath sinned, thus reason with thyself; What do I know whether this be a sin indeed, as it seems to be? But if it be, what do I know but that he himself hath already condemned himself for it? And that is all one as if a man should scratch and tear his own face, an object of compassion rather than of anger. Again, that he that would not have a vicious man to sin, is like unto him that would not have moisture in the fig, nor children to welp nor a horse to neigh, nor anything else that in the course of nature is necessary. For what shall he do that hath such an habit? If thou therefore beest powerful and eloquent, remedy it if thou canst."

What Marcus meant (core philosophy)

Marcus promotes humility in judgment. We often assume wrongdoing without full understanding. Even when someone errs, they may already suffer internally from their actions. Stoicism encourages compassion rather than anger, recognizing that human behavior arises from habit and ignorance. If correction is possible, it should be offered constructively rather than through condemnation.

Dating translation (what this means emotionally/socially)

In relationships, quick judgment often fuels conflict:
- assuming malicious intent without full context
- reacting with anger instead of curiosity
- expecting others to behave outside their nature.

Marcus suggests:
- question your interpretation before reacting
- recognize that many people struggle internally with their own actions
- approach correction with calm clarity rather than emotional attack.

Dating maturity means:
- replacing immediate judgment with understanding
- recognizing patterns without personalizing everything
- offering clarity where possible, releasing anger where not.

Savage takeaway

Not every offense deserves anger. Sometimes it deserves understanding.

Quiet power mantra

"I respond with clarity instead of assumption."

XIII. LET TRUTH AND FITTINGNESS GUIDE YOU

"If it be not fitting, do it not. If it be not true, speak it not. Ever maintain thine own purpose and resolution free from all compulsion and necessity."

What Marcus meant (core philosophy)

Marcus reduces ethical living to two essential filters: truth and appropriateness. Actions and words should be governed by alignment with reality and reason rather than pressure or impulse. Stoicism values autonomy of purpose, where decisions arise from conscious choice rather than external coercion or internal compulsion.

Dating translation (what this means emotionally/socially)

In relationships:
- saying things to please rather than to be honest creates misalignment
- acting from pressure or fear weakens integrity
- abandoning inner clarity leads to confusion.

Marcus suggests:
- speak truthfully without unnecessary embellishment
- avoid actions that feel internally misaligned
- maintain independence from emotional pressure.

Dating maturity means:

- choosing authenticity over convenience
- setting boundaries rooted in truth
- acting from conscious intention rather than reaction.

Savage takeaway

If it's not true or aligned, it's not yours to carry.

Quiet power mantra

"I act and speak from truth."

XIV. SEE EVERYTHING BY ITS TRUE NATURE

"Of everything that presents itself unto thee, to consider what the true nature of it is, and to unfold it, as it were, by dividing it into that which is formal: that which is material: the true use or end of it, and the just time that it is appointed to last."

What Marcus meant (core philosophy)

Marcus reinforces analytical clarity. Understanding arises from examining structure, substance, purpose, and duration. Stoicism teaches that emotional disturbance often comes from misunderstanding the nature or lifespan of things.

Dating translation (what this means emotionally/socially)

In relationships:

- distinguishing chemistry from compatibility
- recognizing whether a connection serves growth or distraction
- understanding that some relationships are temporary by nature.

Marcus suggests:

- evaluate relationships realistically
- understand purpose and timing rather than forcing permanence
- clarity reduces unnecessary attachment.

Dating maturity means:

- recognizing when a connection has fulfilled its purpose
- releasing expectations that conflict with reality
- seeing dynamics as they are, not as imagined.

Savage takeaway

Everything has a purpose and a lifespan. Know both.

Quiet power mantra

"I understand the true nature of what appears."

XV. REMEMBER THE HIGHER PART WITHIN YOU

"It is high time for thee, to understand that there is somewhat in thee, better and more divine than either thy passions, or thy sensual appetites and affections. What is now the object of my mind, is it fear, or suspicion, or lust, or any such thing? To do nothing rashly without some certain end; let that be thy first care. The next, to have no other end than the common good. For, alas! yet a little while, and thou art no more: no more will any, either of those things that now thou seest, or of those men that now are living, be any more. For all things are by nature appointed soon to be changed, turned, and corrupted, that other things might succeed in their room."

343

What Marcus meant (core philosophy)

Marcus calls attention to the higher rational self that exists beyond impulse and desire. Stoicism emphasizes living according to reason and shared good rather than reactive emotion. Awareness of mortality sharpens focus on meaningful action and reduces attachment to fleeting concerns.

Dating translation (what this means emotionally/socially)

In relationships:
- intense emotions can overshadow long-term alignment
- reacting from fear or desire leads to regret
- remembering impermanence restores perspective.

Marcus suggests:
- pause and examine what drives your actions
- choose decisions aligned with deeper values
- prioritize growth and mutual good over momentary emotional highs.

Dating maturity means:
- letting wisdom lead over impulse
- making choices that respect both yourself and others
- remembering that temporary feelings should not dictate lasting decisions.

Savage takeaway

You are more than your impulses. Act like it.

Quiet power mantra

"My higher self leads my choices."

XVI. REMOVE OPINION AND FIND CALM

"Remember that all is but opinion, and all opinion depends of the mind. Take thine opinion away, and then as a ship that hath stricken in within the arms and mouth of the harbour, a present calm; all things safe and steady: a bay, not capable of any storms and tempests: as the poet hath it."

What Marcus meant (core philosophy)

Marcus teaches that emotional turbulence originates in interpretation rather than events themselves. By removing or reframing opinions, the mind returns to calm stability. Stoicism frames peace as a state created internally through disciplined perception.

Dating translation (what this means emotionally/socially)

In relationships:
- narratives about rejection or meaning create emotional storms
- assumptions amplify distress
- changing perspective transforms emotional experience.

Marcus suggests:
- question the story you attach to events
- recognize that interpretation shapes emotion
- remove unnecessary judgments to regain calm.

344

Dating maturity means:
- pausing before assigning meaning
- recognizing how thoughts shape feelings
- cultivating inner steadiness regardless of external change.

Savage takeaway
The storm isn't the event. It's the story you tell about it.

Quiet power mantra
"I release interpretation and return to calm."

XVII. NOTHING ENDS IN EVIL SIMPLY BECAUSE IT ENDS
"No operation whatsoever it be, ceasing for a while, can be truly said to suffer any evil, because it is at an end. Neither can he that is the author of that operation; for this very respect, because his operation is at an end, be said to suffer any evil. Likewise then, neither can the whole body of all our actions (which is our life) if in time it cease, be said to suffer any evil for this very reason, because it is at an end; nor he truly be said to have been ill affected, that did put a period to this series of actions. Now this time or certain period, depends of the determination of nature: sometimes of particular nature, as when a man dieth old; but of nature in general, however; the parts whereof thus changing one after another, the whole world still continues fresh and new. Now that is ever best and most seasonable, which is for the good of the whole. Thus it appears that death of itself can neither be hurtful to any in particular, because it is not a shameful thing (for neither is it a thing that depends of our own will, nor of itself contrary to the common good) and generally, as it is both expedient and seasonable to the whole, that in that respect it must needs be good. It is that also, which is brought unto us by the order and appointment of the Divine Providence; so that he whose will and mind in these things runs along with the Divine ordinance, and by this concurrence of his will and mind with the Divine Providence, is led and driven along, as it were by God Himself; may truly be termed and esteemed the θεοφόρητος[81], or divinely led and inspired."

What Marcus meant (core philosophy)
Marcus reframes endings as natural transitions rather than harms. Nothing becomes evil simply because it concludes. Death and completion are part of the universal cycle that keeps existence renewed. Stoicism encourages alignment with the broader order of nature, recognizing that what benefits the whole is inherently appropriate, even when personally difficult.

Dating translation (what this means emotionally/socially)
In relationships:
- endings are often interpreted as failures or losses
- people assume something went "wrong" simply because it ended
- closure is resisted because permanence is expected.

Marcus suggests:
- completion is not harm
- some connections fulfill their purpose and naturally conclude
- meaning exists in the experience, not only in longevity.

---

[81] In Greek, θεοφόρητος (*theophórētos*) translates to "God-inspired," "divinely possessed," or "carried by God."

Dating maturity means:
- seeing endings as transitions rather than tragedies
- recognizing growth even when relationships end
- aligning emotionally with natural change instead of resisting it.

Savage takeaway

An ending isn't a failure. It's a completed chapter.

Quiet power mantra

"I honor endings as natural completion."

XVIII. KEEP THREE TRUTHS ALWAYS READY

"These three things thou must have always in a readiness: first concerning thine own actions, whether thou doest nothing either idly, or otherwise, than justice and equity do require: and concerning those things that happen unto thee externally, that either they happen unto thee by chance, or by providence; of which two to accuse either, is equally against reason. Secondly, what like unto our bodies are whilest yet rude and imperfect, until they be animated: and from their animation, until their expiration: of what things they are compounded, and into what things they shall be dissolved. Thirdly, how vain all things will appear unto thee when, from on high as it were, looking down thou shalt contemplate all things upon earth, and the wonderful mutability, that they are subject unto: considering withal, the infinite both greatness and variety of things aerial and things celestial that are round about it. And that as often as thou shalt behold them, thou shalt still see the same: as the same things, so the same shortness of continuance of all those things. And, behold, these be the things that we are so proud and puffed up for."

What Marcus meant (core philosophy)

Marcus presents three grounding meditations:
1. Act with justice and intention.
2. Accept external events without blame, whether random or divinely ordered.
3. Gain perspective by viewing life from a broader cosmic scale, recognizing impermanence.

Stoicism teaches humility through perspective and inner stability through ethical action.

Dating translation (what this means emotionally/socially)

In relationships:
- focus on acting with integrity rather than controlling outcomes
- stop blaming fate or people endlessly for what happens
- remember that many emotional dramas shrink when viewed from a larger perspective.

Marcus suggests:
- ask whether your actions align with fairness and purpose
- accept that some outcomes lie beyond control
- zoom out when emotions feel overwhelming.

Dating maturity means:
- acting intentionally rather than reactively
- releasing excessive importance placed on temporary situations
- remembering that today's emotional storms become small over time.

Savage takeaway
Most drama fades when you zoom out far enough.

Quiet power mantra
"I act justly and keep perspective."

XIX. REMOVE OPINION AND YOU REMOVE DISTRESS

"Cast away from thee opinion, and thou art safe. And what is it that hinders thee from casting of it away? When thou art grieved at anything, hast thou forgotten that all things happen according to the nature of the universe; and that him only it concerns, who is in fault; and moreover, that what is now done, is that which from ever hath been done in the world, and will ever be done, and is now done everywhere: how nearly all men are allied one to another by a kindred not of blood, nor of seed, but of the same mind. Thou hast also forgotten that every man's mind partakes of the Deity, and issueth from thence; and that no man can properly call anything his own, no not his son, nor his body, nor his life; for that they all proceed from that One who is the giver of all things: that all things are but opinion; that no man lives properly, but that very instant of time which is now present. And therefore that no man whosoever he dieth can properly be said to lose any more, than an instant of time."

What Marcus meant (core philosophy)
Marcus returns to a core Stoic principle: suffering arises primarily from interpretation, not events themselves. By removing judgment or opinion, emotional disturbance dissolves. He also emphasizes interconnectedness, impermanence, and the present moment as the only true possession. Stoicism teaches that perspective transforms pain into acceptance.

Dating translation (what this means emotionally/socially)
In relationships:
- distress often comes from the story attached to events
- assumptions about meaning amplify emotional reactions
- attachment to permanence creates fear of loss.

Marcus suggests:
- question the narrative behind emotional pain
- remember that human behavior follows patterns that have always existed
- recognize that the present moment is the only true reality.

Dating maturity means:
- separating fact from interpretation
- reducing emotional suffering by releasing unnecessary meaning
- grounding yourself in the present rather than imagined futures.

Savage takeaway
You're rarely upset by the event. You're upset by your interpretation.

Quiet power mantra
"I release opinion and return to presence."

XX. EVERYTHING THAT ONCE FELT IMPORTANT FADES

"Let thy thoughts ever run upon them, who once for some one thing or other, were moved with extraordinary indignation; who were once in the highest pitch of either honour, or calamity; or mutual hatred and enmity; or of any other fortune or condition whatsoever. Then consider what's now become of all those things. All is turned to smoke; all to ashes, and a mere fable; and perchance not so much as a fable. As also whatsoever is of this nature… and how vile every object of such earnest and vehement prosecution is; and how much more agreeable to true philosophy it is, for a man to carry himself in every matter that offers itself; justly, and moderately, as one that followeth the Gods with all simplicity. For, for a man to be proud and high conceited, that he is not proud and high conceited, is of all kind of pride and presumption, the most intolerable."

What Marcus meant (core philosophy)

Marcus reflects on impermanence and perspective. Events that once felt monumental eventually fade into insignificance. Stoicism teaches humility through awareness of time's passage and encourages moderation, simplicity, and sincerity instead of emotional extremity or ego-driven pursuits.

Dating translation (what this means emotionally/socially)

In relationships:
- intense emotional highs and lows often feel permanent but are temporary
- conflicts that seem overwhelming now will likely fade into memory
- ego can disguise itself as virtue or moral superiority.

Marcus suggests:
- zoom out and view current emotions through the lens of time
- avoid over-investing in temporary drama
- act simply, justly, and without emotional theatrics.

Dating maturity means:
- recognizing that today's obsession may be tomorrow's footnote
- releasing pride disguised as righteousness
- choosing calm integrity over emotional escalation.

Savage takeaway

Most things you're stressing about will one day be barely a memory.

Quiet power mantra

"I choose simplicity, humility, and perspective."

XXI. KNOW THE DIVINE THROUGH EXPERIENCE AND REASON

"To them that ask thee, Where hast thou seen the Gods, or how knowest thou certainly that there be Gods, that thou art so devout in their worship? I answer first of all, that even to the very eye, they are in some manner visible and apparent. Secondly, neither have I ever seen mine own soul, and yet I respect and honour it. So then for the Gods, by the daily experience that I have of their power and providence towards myself and others, I know certainly that they are, and therefore worship them."

What Marcus meant (core philosophy)
Marcus argues that belief in higher order comes not only from sight but from experience and rational inference. Just as we respect the unseen soul through its effects, we recognize divine order through the patterns of life and providence. Stoicism embraces reverence for the rational structure of the universe rather than blind faith.

Dating translation (what this means emotionally/socially)
In relationships:
- not everything meaningful is visible or easily proven
- trust often grows through lived experience rather than external validation
- deeper understanding comes from observing patterns rather than demanding certainty.

Marcus suggests:
- respect internal intuition alongside external evidence
- recognize unseen forces shaping emotional growth
- trust what reveals itself through consistent experience.

Dating maturity means:
- valuing internal knowing alongside observable behavior
- recognizing that emotional wisdom grows from experience
- trusting patterns rather than chasing constant proof.

Savage takeaway
You don't need to see something physically to recognize its truth.

Quiet power mantra
"I trust wisdom revealed through experience."

XXII. HAPPINESS IS CLARITY AND RIGHT ACTION
"Herein doth consist happiness of life, for a man to know thoroughly the true nature of everything; what is the matter, and what is the form of it: with all his heart and soul, ever to do that which is just, and to speak the truth. What then remaineth but to enjoy thy life in a course and coherence of good actions, one upon another immediately succeeding, and never interrupted, though for never so little a while?"

What Marcus meant (core philosophy)
Marcus defines happiness as clarity combined with ethical action. Understanding reality and living truthfully creates a seamless flow of meaningful activity. Stoicism emphasizes consistency: virtue practiced moment by moment builds a coherent and fulfilling life.

Dating translation (what this means emotionally/socially)
In relationships:
- happiness comes from alignment between understanding and behavior
- clarity about reality prevents emotional confusion
- consistent integrity builds stable connection.

Marcus suggests:
- seek clear understanding rather than idealized fantasy
- act justly even in emotionally complex situations
- build relationships through consistent right action.

Dating maturity means:
- aligning behavior with values
- communicating honestly and directly
- creating continuity through integrity.

Savage takeaway
Happiness isn't found. It's built through repeated aligned actions.

Quiet power mantra
"I live through clear understanding and right action."

XXIII. ALL MINDS SHARE A COMMON CONNECTION

"There is but one light of the sun, though it be intercepted by walls and mountains, and other thousand objects. There is but one common substance of the whole world, though it be concluded and restrained into several different bodies, in number infinite. There is but one common soul, though divided into innumerable particular essences and natures. So is there but one common intellectual soul, though it seem to be divided. And as for all other parts of those generals which we have mentioned, as either sensitive souls or subjects, these of themselves (as naturally irrational) have no common mutual reference one unto another, though many of them contain a mind, or reasonable faculty in them, whereby they are ruled and governed. But of every reasonable mind, this the particular nature, that it hath reference to whatsoever is of her own kind, and desireth to be united: neither can this common affection, or mutual unity and correspondency, be here intercepted or divided, or confined to particulars as those other common things are."

What Marcus meant (core philosophy)
Marcus describes the unity underlying apparent separation. Just as sunlight remains singular despite obstacles, reason and consciousness share a common source. Stoicism emphasizes human interconnectedness and the natural inclination toward unity among rational beings.

Dating translation (what this means emotionally/socially)
In relationships:
- connection arises from shared humanity rather than surface differences
- people naturally seek unity and understanding
- isolation often results from forgetting this common bond.

Marcus suggests:
- approach others with awareness of shared nature
- seek understanding rather than division
- recognize that true connection transcends superficial barriers.

Dating maturity means:
- seeing others as fundamentally similar rather than adversarial
- cultivating empathy through shared humanity
- recognizing that connection is a natural instinct, not a rare miracle.

Savage takeaway
Beneath differences, we're built from the same light.

Quiet power mantra
"I move toward unity and understanding."

XXIV. EXAMINE WHAT YOU TRULY DESIRE

"What doest thou desire? To live long. What? To enjoy the operations of a sensitive soul; or of the appetitive faculty? or wouldst thou grow, and then decrease again? Wouldst thou long be able to talk, to think and reason with thyself? Which of all these seems unto thee a worthy object of thy desire? Now if of all these thou doest find that they be but little worth in themselves, proceed on unto the last, which is, in all things to follow God and reason. But for a man to grieve that by death he shall be deprived of any of these things, is both against God and reason."

What Marcus meant (core philosophy)
Marcus challenges us to question our attachments. Many desires, longevity, sensation, expression, or growth, appear meaningful but are ultimately transient and limited. Stoicism teaches that true worth lies not in temporary experiences but in living according to reason and higher principles. Fear of losing fleeting pleasures contradicts rational understanding of life's nature.

Dating translation (what this means emotionally/socially)
In relationships:
- people often chase emotional highs without questioning their deeper value
- fear of losing connection may come from attachment to temporary feelings
- long-term fulfillment requires alignment with deeper values rather than momentary desire.

Marcus suggests:
- ask what truly matters beneath emotional cravings
- distinguish between fleeting excitement and meaningful alignment
- prioritize integrity and purpose over temporary gratification.

Dating maturity means:
- choosing depth over intensity alone
- recognizing that not every desire leads to lasting fulfillment
- grounding decisions in values rather than impulses.

Savage takeaway
Not everything you want is actually worth wanting.

Quiet power mantra
"I choose what aligns with my higher nature."

XXV. SEE LIFE FROM THE SCALE OF TIME

"What a small portion of vast and infinite eternity it is, that is allowed unto every one of us, and how soon it vanisheth into the general age of the world: of the common substance, and of the common soul also what a small portion is allotted unto us: and in what a little clod of the whole earth (as it were) it is that

351

thou doest crawl. After thou shalt rightly have considered these things with thyself; fancy not anything else in the world any more to be of any weight and moment but this, to do that only which thine own nature doth require; and to conform thyself to that which the common nature doth afford."

What Marcus meant (core philosophy)

Marcus emphasizes perspective through cosmic scale. Individual life occupies only a brief moment within vast eternity. Recognizing this reduces attachment to trivial concerns and redirects focus toward living according to one's nature and contributing to the whole. Stoicism encourages humility and clarity through awareness of life's brevity.

Dating translation (what this means emotionally/socially)

In relationships:
- many conflicts feel overwhelming but are small in the grand scale
- worrying about status, perception, or minor disappointments distracts from deeper purpose
- clarity comes when viewed from a broader perspective.

Marcus suggests:
- focus on living authentically rather than chasing approval
- prioritize meaningful connection over trivial drama
- remember that time is limited and precious.

Dating maturity means:
- investing energy where it truly matters
- releasing attachment to small emotional battles
- aligning actions with long-term growth and purpose.

Savage takeaway

When you zoom out far enough, only what aligns with your nature truly matters.

Quiet power mantra

"I live according to my true nature."

XXVI. RETURN ALWAYS TO THE STATE OF YOUR MIND

"What is the present estate of my understanding? For herein lieth all indeed. As for all other things, they are without the compass of mine own will: and if without the compass of my will, then are they as dead things unto me, and as it were mere smoke."

What Marcus meant (core philosophy)

Marcus brings everything back to a single focal point: the condition of the mind. External circumstances exist outside personal control and therefore should not dominate emotional experience. Stoicism teaches that inner understanding determines peace or disturbance. What lies outside the will is ultimately insubstantial compared to the governance of one's own perception.

Dating translation (what this means emotionally/socially)

In relationships:
- over-focusing on others' actions creates emotional instability
- trying to control external outcomes leads to frustration
- inner clarity matters more than external validation.

Marcus suggests:
- continually check the state of your own mind
- release attachment to what lies beyond your control
- recognize that many external concerns fade when internal alignment is restored.

Dating maturity means:
- prioritizing emotional self-governance
- refusing to let others' behavior define your peace
- grounding yourself internally before reacting outwardly.

Savage takeaway
If it's outside your control, it's smoke. Focus on your mind.

Quiet power mantra
"My peace begins with my own understanding."

XXVII. DEATH IS A NATURAL DISMISSAL, NOT A TRAGEDY
"To stir up a man to the contempt of death this among other things, is of good power and efficacy, that even they who esteemed pleasure to be happiness, and pain misery, did nevertheless many of them contemn death as much as any. And can death be terrible to him, to whom that only seems good, which in the ordinary course of nature is seasonable? to him, to whom, whether his actions be many or few, so they be all good, is all one; and who whether he behold the things of the world being always the same either for many years, or for few years only, is altogether indifferent? O man! as a citizen thou hast lived, and conversed in this great city the world. Whether just for so many years, or no, what is it unto thee? Thou hast lived (thou mayest be sure) as long as the laws and orders of the city required; which may be the common comfort of all. Why then should it be grievous unto thee, if (not a tyrant, nor an unjust judge, but) the same nature that brought thee in, doth now send thee out of the world? As if the praetor should fairly dismiss him from the stage, whom he had taken in to act a while. Oh, but the play is not yet at an end, there are but three acts yet acted of it? Thou hast well said: for in matter of life, three acts is the whole play. Now to set a certain time to every man's acting, belongs unto him only, who as first he was of thy composition, so is now the cause of thy dissolution. As for thyself; thou hast to do with neither. Go thy ways then well pleased and contented: for so is He that dismisseth thee."

What Marcus meant (core philosophy)
Marcus reframes death as a natural conclusion rather than a loss. Life is like a role played on a stage; the timing of departure belongs to nature, not to personal control. Stoicism teaches acceptance of life's duration and encourages living well rather than clinging to length. Peace comes from recognizing that completion does not diminish the value of existence.

Dating translation (what this means emotionally/socially)
Applied emotionally:
- fear of endings often comes from attachment to duration rather than meaning
- a relationship's worth is not measured by how long it lasts but by how well it was lived
- acceptance of natural closure reduces suffering.

353

Marcus suggests:
- view endings as part of life's structure rather than personal injustice
- appreciate experiences without demanding permanence
- exit chapters with dignity and peace.

Dating maturity means:
- valuing depth over longevity alone
- leaving when the role has ended without resentment
- understanding that closure belongs to the natural flow of life.

Savage takeaway
The value of the play isn't how long it runs. It's how well you performed your part.

Quiet power mantra
"I accept beginnings and endings with grace."

THE CLASSICS UNLOCKED COLLECTION

The **Classics Unlocked Collection** reframes timeless works of philosophy, literature, and strategy through the lens of modern relationships and human behavior. Each volume preserves the original classic text while revealing the hidden psychological insights that still shape how we think, love, and connect today. By bridging ancient wisdom with contemporary dating realities, this series invites readers to rediscover familiar masterpieces as living guides for emotional clarity, self-command, and power in modern relationships.

THE ART OF WAR & DATING

The Art of War & Dating unlocks Sun Tzu's legendary strategies and translates them into the battlefield of modern romance. Through sharp insights and practical reframing, this book explores timing, boundaries, emotional positioning, and strategic awareness in relationships. It is not about manipulation. It is about understanding dynamics, protecting your energy, and learning when to advance, when to wait, and when to walk away with strength.

MEDITATIONS & DATING

Meditations & Dating draws from the private reflections of Roman emperor Marcus Aurelius to offer a grounded, powerful approach to modern relationships. Blending Stoic philosophy with contemporary dating challenges, this book explores emotional discipline, detachment without bitterness, and the quiet confidence that comes from mastering yourself instead of trying to control others. Calm, honest, and deeply human, it is a guide for anyone seeking clarity and peace within the chaos of modern connection.

FROM THE DATING UNEXPERT

I didn't write these books to tell women what to do. I wrote them because I watched too many brilliant women blame themselves for systems that were never built for them to win.

Every book I've written exists for a different moment in a woman's life not to fix her, but to remind her who she already is when she's not apologizing, bargaining, or shrinking to survive.

If this book helped you see more clearly, the others are here to meet you wherever you are next.

THE BREAKUP BAND-AID
(The one that started it all)
This was written for the woman in acute emotional pain. The one who can't sleep, can't eat, can't stop replaying the ending. It doesn't rush healing or romanticize strength. It simply holds you steady while the bleeding slows and reminds you that heartbreak is not a personal failure, it's a human one. This book exists to keep you company in the dark so you don't confuse pain with truth.

THE DATING SURVIVAL BIBLE
This is the field guide. The pattern decoder. The moment you stop asking *"What's wrong with me?"* and start asking *"What keeps repeating and why?"* It's designed to take women out of emotional free-fall and into clarity, discernment, and self-trust. Not rules. Not games. Just reality, clearly labeled.

THE RED FLAG TRANSLATOR
This book exists for the moment your intuition starts whispering but you don't yet trust it. It puts language to what you feel but can't quite articulate: the subtle tells, the phrases that sound harmless but aren't, the behaviors that always lead to the same ending. It's not about suspicion. It's about fluency.

1001 DATING IDEAS
Not every book needs to be heavy. This one is about joy, curiosity, creativity, and remembering that dating doesn't have to feel like a job interview or a trauma reenactment. It's here to reintroduce play, intention, and choice back into connection without abandoning your standards.

BECOMING HER
This book is not about dating at all. It's about identity. It's for the woman who is done centering her life around being chosen and ready to return to herself: her voice, her intuition, her power, her inner coherence. This is the book women read when they stop asking for permission and start living from alignment.

THE ULTIMATE WOMAN'S GUIDE TO LETTING GO

This one is for the season after survival when the noise fades and something quieter, deeper, and more honest begins to emerge. It doesn't force closure. It doesn't rush forgiveness. It teaches release without erasure and helps women put down what they were never meant to carry.

A SINGLE GIRL'S GUIDE SERIES

(Including IVF, sex, and the bucket list)

These books exist to normalize the full, complex, joyful reality of modern womanhood. Desire. Choice. Biology. Humor. Autonomy. They are reminders that there is no single timeline, no single script, and no single way to build a meaningful life. You get to choose and you don't owe anyone an explanation.

AND IF YOU LEARN BEST BY PLAYING...

I've also created games, worksheets, prompts, and tools designed to help you integrate this work into real life not just understand it intellectually. These are for women building businesses, rebuilding confidence, redefining love, or simply learning how to trust themselves again.

You'll find all of that at **yourdatingunexpert.etsy.com**

FINAL WORD

You don't need all of these books.
You don't need to read them in order.
You don't need to become someone else.
You just need the right words at the right moment.

Take what helps. Leave what doesn't. And trust that the version of you this work is pointing toward has been there all along waiting patiently for you to stop abandoning her.

With love,
Your Dating UnExpert